Spenserian allegory and Elizabethan biblical exegesis

The Manchester Spenser

The Manchester Spenser is a monograph and text series devoted to historical and textual approaches to Edmund Spenser – to his life, times, places, works and contemporaries.

A growing body of work in Spenser and Renaissance studies, fresh with confidence and curiosity and based on solid historical research, is being written in response to a general sense that our ability to interpret texts is becoming limited without the excavation of further knowledge. So the importance of research in nearby disciplines is quickly being recognised, and interest renewed: history, archaeology, religious or theological history, book history, translation, lexicography, commentary and glossary – these require treatment for and by students of Spenser.

The Manchester Spenser, to feed, foster and build on these refreshed attitudes, aims to publish reference tools, critical, historical, biographical and archaeological monographs on or related to Spenser, from several disciplines, and to publish editions of primary sources and classroom texts of a more wide-ranging scope.

The Manchester Spenser consists of work with stamina, high standards of scholarship and research, adroit handling of evidence, rigour of argument, exposition and documentation.

The series will encourage and assist research into, and develop the readership of, one of the richest and most complex writers of the early modern period.

General Editor J. B. Lethbridge
Associate General Editor Joshua Reid
Editorial Board Helen Cooper, Thomas Herron, Carol V. Kaske, James C. Nohrnberg & Brian Vickers

Also available

Literary Ralegh and visual Ralegh Christopher M. Armitage (ed.)
A concordance to the rhymes of The Faerie Queene Richard Danson Brown & J. B. Lethbridge
A supplement of the Faery Queene: By Ralph Knevet Christopher Burlinson & Andrew Zurcher (eds)
Pastoral poetry of the English Renaissance: An anthology Sukanta Chaudhuri (ed.)
Monsters and the poetic imagination in Edmund Spenser's 'The Faerie Queene': 'Most ugly shapes and horrible aspects' Maik Goth
Celebrating Mutabilitie: Essays on Edmund Spenser's Mutabilitie Cantos Jane Grogan (ed.)
Castles and colonists: An archaeology of Elizabethan Ireland Eric Klingelhofer
Shakespeare and Spenser: Attractive opposites J. B. Lethbridge (ed.)
A Fig for Fortune: By Anthony Copley Susannah Monta Brietz
Spenser and Virgil: The pastoral poems Syrithe Pugh
Renaissance erotic romance: Philhellene Protestantism, Renaissance translation and English literary politics Victor Skretkowicz
God's only daughter: Spenser's Una as the invisible Church Kathryn Walls

Spenserian allegory and Elizabethan biblical exegesis

A context for *The Faerie Queene*

MARGARET CHRISTIAN

Manchester University Press

Copyright © Margaret Christian 2016

The right of Margaret Christian to be identified as the author of this work has been asserted by her in accordance with the Copyright, Designs and Patents Act 1988.

Published by Manchester University Press
Altrincham Street, Manchester M1 7JA, UK
www.manchesteruniversitypress.co.uk

British Library Cataloguing-in-Publication Data is available

ISBN 978 0 7190 8384 6 *hardback*
ISBN 978 1 5261 3950 4 *paperback*

First published by Manchester University Press in hardback 2016

This edition first published 2019

The publisher has no responsibility for the persistence or accuracy of URLs for any external or third-party internet websites referred to in this book, and does not guarantee that any content on such websites is, or will remain, accurate or appropriate.

Typeset by Out of House Publishing, Stroud

*dedicated to the memory of
Ruth Evangeline Olsen*

Contents

Introduction: a context for *The Faerie Queene*   1

Part I   Backgrounds: allegorical reading in Spenser's England

1. Traditional scriptural interpretation and sixteenth-century allegoresis: old and new   11
2. Allegorical reading in occasional Elizabethan liturgies   35
3. Allegorical reading in sermon references to history and current events   64

Part II   The preachers' Bible and Spenser's *Faerie Queene*: alternate allegories

4. "The ground of Storie": genealogy in biblical exegesis and the Legend of Temperance   85
5. "Waues of weary wretchednesse": Florimell and the sea   104
6. Saracens, Assyrians, and Spaniards: allegories of the Armada   129
7. "a goodly amiable name for mildness": Mercilla and other Elizabethan types   157
8. Court and courtesy: sermon contexts for Spenser's Book VI   178
9. "Now lettest thou thy servant depart": scriptural tradition and the close of *The Faerie Queene*   208

Conclusion   223

Works cited   226
Index   247

Introduction: a context for *The Faerie Queen*

Spenser characterized *The Faerie Queene* as "*an historicall fiction*" created to "*fashion a gentleman or noble person in virtuous and gentle discipline.*" He explained his work to his friend Walter Raleigh as an alternative to "*good discipline deliuered plainly in way of precepts, or sermoned at large*" – an alternative, that is, to religious rhetoric like liturgies, homilies, and sermons.[1] Spenser admitted that his method of "*clowdily enwrap*[ing]" his teaching "*in Allegorical deuises*" "*will seeme displeasaunt*" to some. At the remove of four centuries, however, it is more likely that explicitly religious rhetoric, rather than Spenser's historical fiction, will seem displeasant, or at least unfamiliar. *Spenserian Allegory and Elizabethan Biblical Exegesis* introduces the reader to this once-ubiquitous religious rhetoric and its approach to the Bible. In showing something of how Spenser and his contemporaries read and listened to the Bible, the book will also demonstrate how sermons, homilies, and liturgies trained original readers to understand Spenser's allegorical method and thus can illuminate many of the episodes and characters of the poem.

Spenserians have always produced biographical, textual, prosodic, and other historically based works. In the past decades, many studies that emphasize deconstructive, gender, and psychoanalytic approaches have also appeared. Valuable and insightful as they are, such studies employ categories that were not part of the mental equipment available to original readers of *The Faerie Queene* and cannot bring us closer to the original readers' experience. The New Historicism and Cultural Materialism

---

1 "A Letter of the Authors expounding his *whole intention in the course of this worke*," in *Spenser: The Faerie Queene*, 2nd edn by A. C. Hamilton for Longman Annotated English Poets (Harlow and London: Pearson Education, 2001), 714–18. Although the *Oxford English Dictionary* uses this sentence to illustrate the fourth sense of the verb "sermon" ("To speak, utter, declare"), I hear Spenser playing as well with the more common meaning "To preach (*of* a thing)."

redirected readers to the importance of understanding the context in which works of art have been produced, but some works using this approach have been criticized for reckless generalization – extrapolating whole climates of thought from small morsels of contemporary gossip or single anecdotes – and for reading every text and historical situation for its analysis of power relations, ignoring other motivations for the production of art and the practice of religion.

Among the historical studies produced in the second half of the twentieth century are a handful that drew attention to annotations in early printed copies of *The Faerie Queene*. Recent articles have expanded this line of inquiry, providing biographical details of the first annotator and identifying the source of many annotations.[2] The implicit premise was that belated readers could learn from those closer to Spenser in time, especially if the early readers had known the author.[3] (Their findings: though early readers varied in their degree of literary sensitivity and religious preoccupation, all appeared to consider the moral allegory as key to understanding the poem. Further, many early readers enjoyed identifying contemporary or recent situations like Spanish occupation of the Low Countries and figures like Elizabeth and Leicester as models for the events and characters of the poem.) Similar in the value it places on temporal proximity, *Spenserian Allegory and Elizabethan Biblical Exegesis* looks at *The Faerie Queene* in its cultural context, privileging Elizabethans' own analysis of their preoccupations and motivations.

In a sense, this approach represents a return to basics. In Spenser's time, religious works (including sermons and homilies) represented the largest

2 One recent study is Anne Lake Prescott's "Two Copies of the 1596 *Faerie Queene*: Annotations and an Unpublished Poem on Spenser," *Spenser Studies* 23 (2008), 261–73. Bart Van Es lists the twentieth-century studies and provides biography in "The Life of John Dixon, *The Faerie Queene*'s First Annotator," *Notes & Queries* 48.3 (2001), 259–61; Austen Saunders, in "New Light on a Puzzling Annotation to Spenser's *Faerie Queen*," *Notes & Queries* 57.3 (2010), 356–7, traces several of Dixon's annotations to the marginal notes on Revelation in the Geneva Bible.

3 Walter Oakeshott, for instance, claimed in "Carew Ralegh's Copy of Spenser," *The Library* n.s. 26 (1971), 1–21, that Sir Walter himself may have made some of its annotations (13), and James A. Riddell and Stanley Stewart claim that Ben Jonson himself delivered to Raleigh "the paper ... of the Allegories of his Fayrie Queen," which identified the Puritans as "the Blating beast" and "the Q of Scots" as "the false Duessa" (*Jonson's Spenser: Evidence and Historical Criticism* [Pittsburgh, 1995], 23). John Manning asserted the most ambitious expectation for this line of inquiry: that "modern readings of the poem's historical allegory will have to be radically revised in the light of the contemporary identifications of the characters" ("Notes and Marginalia in Bishop Percy's Copy of Spenser's *Works* [1611]," *Notes & Queries* 31 [1984], 225–7).

Introduction: a context for The Faerie Queene

category of the book trade as well as its most reliable sellers.[4] But surprisingly few Spenserians are familiar with them or their relevance to the poet. I haven't read all such works by any means, and the quotations in this book represent only a sampling of the most relevant printed Elizabethan religious rhetoric that I happen to have read.

My entry point into this literature thirty years ago was A. F. Herr's *The Elizabethan Sermon: A Survey and Bibliography*,[5] which lists printed texts. Millar MacLure's *Register of Sermons Preached at Paul's Cross, 1534–1642*[6] includes titles of printed and manuscript sermons (and notations of sermons known to have been preached at England's premier outdoor pulpit but otherwise lost) in its chronological listing. More recently, Peter McCullough and his collaborators have provided lists of sermons, introductory essays, and analyses from a range of literary and historical starting points.[7] The easiest way to access these documents now is via the database Early English Books Online, which makes available the University of Michigan's microfilmed images of each page of the original books, as well as the keyed and searchable full text of some 33,000 titles. One can search for documents by author, title, or other key word, as well as bibliographic number, and search the full text of available titles for key words of interest. (I have silently expanded abbreviations when quoting from these early printed works.)

Spenser called *The Faerie Queene*'s method, or "*deuises*," "*Allegoricall*." That is, he was writing an allegory, a narrative which he encoded with metaphorical meanings and expected to be read accordingly. A related idea is allegoresis, interpreting a text written with straightforward literal intent as if it were an allegory. The Bible was the most important

---

4 "Religion dominated the retail book trade, composing more than two-fifths of that trade." Alan B. Farmer and Zachary Lesser, "What is Print Popularity? A Map of the Elizabethan Book Trade," in *The Elizabethan Top Ten: Defining Print Popularity in Early Modern England*, ed. Andy Kesson and Emma Smith, Material Readings in Early Modern Culture (Burlington, VT: Ashgate, 2013), 30. Manuscript sermons are also relevant in establishing cultural context, but my study focuses almost exclusively on printed sermons.
5 Philadelphia, 1940.
6 Centre for Renaissance and Reformation Studies, Victoria College, University of Toronto, 1958, revised and expanded by Peter Pauls and Jackson Campbell Boswell for Dovehouse Editions in 1989.
7 *Sermons at Court: Politics and Religion in Elizabeth and Jacobean Preaching* (Cambridge, 1998), *The English Sermon Revised: Religion, Literature and History 1600–1750*, co-edited with Lori Anne Ferrell (Manchester University Press, 2000), and *The Oxford Handbook of the Early Modern Sermon*, co-edited with Hugh Adlington and Emma Rhatigan (Oxford University Press, 2011).

text subject to this kind of reading, although the extent to which it was properly read as allegorical was hotly debated in the sixteenth century. Accordingly, my book begins with "Traditional Scriptural Interpretation and Sixteenth-Century Allegoresis," a chapter of definitions and examples that illustrate the theory and practice of biblical allegoresis in Western Christianity up through the sixteenth century.

How might one justify reading the Bible as if it encoded non-literal meanings? Providentialism, the belief that God is in control of everything that happens – in fact, that he is the author of the unfolding history of the world – is key to the allegorical and typological readings common in religious rhetoric directed to the laity. Although Tacitean and other more skeptical modes of history were in competition with popular providentialism in Renaissance England,[8] in pulpit discourse, God was usually understood to be responsible for all events, those of secular as well as biblical history.[9] Oneself and one's contemporaries no less than biblical figures were characters in God's story.

The traditional Christian approach to biblical exegesis was already well established when Nicholas of Lyra applied the label "four-fold method" to the range of readings (the four are the literal, allegorical, moral or tropological, and anagogical). Notwithstanding his scornful dismissal of Nicholas's formula and of allegorical reading, William Tyndale's theory and practice had much in common with the tradition. The chapter closes with examples of glosses from the Geneva Bible, which demonstrate the popularity and general acceptance (and by extension, the transparency) of allegorical reading. Allegoresis was so deeply ingrained as a habit of mind during the sixteenth century that such readings needed no theoretical apology or even explanation.

Besides biblical commentary, an important point of access to the Bible was the liturgy. The second chapter reviews several "occasional" liturgies: prayers and scripture readings distributed by Elizabeth Tudor's Church of England (or by individual bishops or freelancing clergymen) to respond to specific occasions. These scripts for religious services cite selected Bible stories as parallels for (and by extension, allegories of) Elizabethan emergencies like plague, Muslim invasions in Europe, the St.

---

8 See, for instance, Michelle Zerba's recent *Doubt and Skepticism in Antiquity and the Renaissance* (Cambridge, MA: Cambridge University Press, 2012).
9 But see, e.g., Diane Willen, "The Case of Thomas Gataker: Confronting Superstition in Seventeenth-Century England," *Sixteenth Century Journal* 43 (2012), 727–49. Gataker considered "irrational ... providentialism" to be superstitious.

Bartholomew's Massacre, the expected Spanish invasion, or threats to the Queen (whether illness or plots). Other liturgies petition God for success in various military expeditions, which they view as parallel to Old Testament military campaigns. Two separate liturgies, one official and the other issued by an individual, offer readings and prayers for November 17, Accession Day. This chapter demonstrates how the liturgists treated Elizabethan current events as comparable, even interchangeable, with events recounted in the Bible, with important implications for a reading of *The Faerie Queene*: its original readers (indeed, all Elizabethan churchgoers) had abundant training in the mental gymnastics required by its "darke conceit."

God being the author of Elizabethan current events as well as biblical history, Chapter 3, "Allegorical Reading in Sermon References to History and Current Events," demonstrates how printed Elizabethan sermons and homilies use biblical terms and parallels, not just to discuss or refer to well-known historical events, anecdotes, and persons, but also those contemporary with the speaker and his audience. Preachers looked to history, both biblical and secular, to reveal universal moral principles and God's eternal purposes. This chapter gives particular attention to William Barlow's sermon at Paul's Cross, London's premier pulpit, after the execution of Essex and Thomas Holland's 1599 Queen's Day sermon in St. Paul's Cathedral, demonstrating how these and other examples assume sermon-goers to be adepts in allegoresis.

These initial chapters on biblical interpretation, liturgy, and sermons seek to demonstrate how intertwined, in the Elizabethan religious consciousness, biblical characters and events were with individuals' everyday lives and with national and international events. Religious rhetoric constantly drew the attention of listeners to allegorical and typological connections between the Bible and the rest of life, preparing them not only to find spiritual meaning in England's unfolding history and their own experience, but also (if they were so inclined) to read *The Faerie Queene*. The following six chapters show how a consciousness of this intertwining brings valuable insights to selected episodes and themes of *The Faerie Queene*. Chapter 4, "'The ground of Storie': Genealogy in Biblical Exegesis and the Legend of Temperance," examines sixteenth-century ways of constructing and interpreting genealogies. Contemporary analysis of the discrepancies between the lists of Christ's forebears in the gospels of Matthew and Luke, and sermon references (especially by Richard Curteys and Edwin Sandys) to Elizabeth's family tree, demonstrate how genealogies might be fashioned to praise Elizabeth. Awareness of the cultural resources Spenser used in creating (and his first readers used in making sense of) these lists of ancestors relieves us of the burden of distilling a consistent moral and political message from passages like the chronicle histories that Arthur, Guyon, and Britomart encounter.

Besides offering training in reading both allegories and genealogies, Elizabethan sermons are a rich depository of images also used in *The Faerie Queene*. The fifth chapter, "'Waues of weary wretchednesse': Florimell and the Sea," examines sermon uses of the image of the sea and the ship to demonstrate that the ocean, for Elizabethans, represented the spiritual dangers of the world, the flesh, and the devil. Sermons by Richard Madox, Robert Wilkinson, and others, as well as Geneva Bible illustrations and glosses, provide parallels for the various settings of Florimell's adventures and a key to their moral meaning. The sea setting sharpens the point of this episode's references to divine intervention, and the sermons show how locating these episodes near, on, and under the sea is perfect, in terms of contemporary culture, for Spenser's dramatization of the incompleteness of the single life and the impulse that propels men and women toward their destiny of married love.

The sixth chapter, "Saracens, Assyrians, and Spaniards: Allegories of the Armada," sets the Souldan episode, an allegory of the defeat of the Spanish Armada, in dialogue with sermons that use Bible stories to develop the same message. Thomas Drant, preaching in 1584, Meredith Hanmer (1586), and William Gravet (1587) demonstrate how preachers drew a comparison between Islam and Roman Catholicism, just as Spenser would, while sermons celebrating the defeat itself (by John Prime, Thomas White, and Stephen Gosson) show how Spenser and the preachers drew on the same biblical themes and even motifs: horses, chariot, and hardware, all agents of God's judgment.

The threat Mary Stuart posed to Elizabeth was *"sermoned at large"* as well as represented in *The Faerie Queene*. Accordingly, the seventh chapter, "'a goodly amiable name for mildness': Mercilla and Other Elizabethan Types," places Spenser's allegory in the context of sermons preached to Elizabeth about the Northern Rebellion and Mary Stuart: Edwin Sandys's and Thomas Drant's in 1570, Tobias Matthew's in 1572, John Whitgift's in 1574, and Peter Wentworth's and Richard Fletcher's in 1587. Public sermons by Edward Harris and William Gravet in 1587, the year of Mary Stuart's execution, and Thomas White's in 1589, all show biblical typology shading into nationalism in ways that have much in common with Spenser's allegory.

"Court and Courtesy: Sermon Contexts for Spenser's Book VI," the eighth chapter, steps back from the topical and typological to focus more broadly on cultural attitudes toward court and the ideas of courtesy reflected in sermons and biblical exegesis. Contemporary English translations of continental preachers John Calvin, Ludwig Lavater, and Rudolf Gwalther, as well as sermons by John King, Henry Smith, William Burton, James Pilkington, John More, and many others, demonstrate that courtesy was a Christian virtue originating in the character of God and that Spenser's ideal courtier had important biblical role models in Joseph, Moses, David, and Nehemiah.

What message does an aging queen need to hear? Preachers have often tried to focus their hearers' minds on their own inevitable deaths, and Elizabeth's preachers were no exception. Chapter 9, " 'Now lettest thou thy servant depart': Scriptural Tradition and the Close of *The Faerie Queene*," considers the *Cantos of Mutabilitie*, in particular the two stanzas of the "unperfite" eighth canto, in the context of court sermons by Thomas Drant (1570), Richard Curteys (1575), the anonymous "L. S." (1593), and Anthony Rudd (1596), all sermons that urge the Queen to consider her death. In the context of court sermons in the *memento mori* tradition, the "unperfite" eighth canto emerges as a *nunc dimittis* in Elizabeth's voice, meant to be understood as the Queen's response to Mutabilitie's challenge and Nature's vindication of Cynthia: the prototypical Faerie Queene's imagined farewell to life as a Christian and as England's queen.

Parts of chapters 4, 5, and 9 appeared earlier as articles in other publications. I wish to thank the editors of *Spenser Studies* and *Christianity and Literature* for their endorsement and their publishers for permission to adapt them for use here. The National Endowment for the Humanities offered support during two summer seminars that helped me learn more about the religious culture of the sixteenth century. The Pennsylvania State University and my campus, Penn State Lehigh Valley, especially directors of academic affairs Eugene Slaski and subsequently Kenneth Thigpen, have supported me with travel funds and released time from teaching. Librarians at the Folger Shakespeare Library, the Huntington Library, the British Library, and the Bodleian Library put old books in my hands before they were available digitally.

With this book, I follow a trail blazed by Carol Kaske, Richard Mallette, John N. King, Debora Shuger, Harold Weatherby, Kenneth Borris, Darryl Gless, Anthea Hume, Naseeb Shaheen, Sean Kane, and David Norbrook, among others. Michael J. B. Allen, Seth Weiner, Hans J. Hillerbrand, and, again, John N. King are among those who have offered generous encouragement as early readers of this work, seminar leaders, and collaborators. More recently, Peter McCullough, John N. King, and especially J. B. Lethbridge have read particularly carefully, offering wholesome cautions. I am very grateful for all I've learned over many years from these and other scholars, teachers, mentors, and colleagues. It will be only too obvious that I should have learned much more.

I am grateful for Ed Christian's enthusiasm for this project from its beginning and for Mary, Paul, and Peter Christian's forbearance during its slow progress through their growing-up years. I am very thankful to my husband Rob Ernst and mother Pat Foster for their steady confidence and gentle prodding through the final months of revision. I have been inspired throughout by the memory of my grandmother and dedicatee, learned lady Ruth Evangeline Olsen. Her doting, exacting love, her generosity to me and my children, and her faith in the transformative power of education have made impossible things seem possible.

I have kept faith with Spenser in using original spelling in quotations from primary sources but silently expanded typical Elizabethan abbreviations ("y^e" becomes "the," for example, and ~ becomes "n" or "m," as indicated by context). Likewise, where "vv" substitutes for "w" in the original (presumably because the type drawer was running short of "w"), I have availed myself of digital inexhaustibility.

Part I
Backgrounds: allegorical reading in Spenser's England

1

Traditional scriptural interpretation and sixteenth-century allegoresis: old and new

This chapter offers a brief orientation to allegorical and typological reading within the Christian tradition. In allegorical reading, or allegoresis, the writer finds a figurative or hidden message in a biblical text previously presumed to be literal. In typology, a literal person or object functioned as a precursor or anticipatory example of someone or something to come. Typology and allegorical reading were "traditional" both in the sense that they were already well established in the first century of the Common Era and thus practiced by New Testament authors, and in the sense that many scriptural passages developed "traditional" (that is to say, standard or fixed) readings very early. This chapter uses the parable of the sower (itself an allegory) and the brief narrative of the rivalry between Mary and Martha (presented in the scriptures as literal but nevertheless subject to allegoresis) to sample what the Fathers say about their approach to scripture's non-literal sense, which they call "a similitude," or "spiritual" and "mystical." Finally, it registers William Tyndale's and the 1560 Geneva Bible commentators' theoretical dismissal but practical adoption of these strategies of allegoresis.

Many critics and literary historians provide useful introductions to the classical and biblical exegetical traditions that we know as allegory and typology.[1] Several emphasize the discontinuity between allegory and typology, which depends on the historicity of its terms and developed as a description of the way in which the Old Testament is related to the

---

1 Besides Erich Auerbach's "Figura" in *Scenes from the Drama of European Literature* (Minneapolis, MN: University of Minnesota Press, 1984), see A. C. Charity's *Events and Their Afterlife: The Dialectics of Christian Typology in the Bible and Dante* (Cambridge: Cambridge University Press, 1966), Barbara Lewalski's *Protestant Poetics and the Seventeenth-Century Religious Lyric* (Princeton, NJ: Princeton University Press, 1979), and Carol V. Kaske's article "Bible" in the *Spenser Encyclopedia*, ed. A. C. Hamilton (Toronto: University of Toronto Press, 1990), pp. 87–90.

New. In the present work, the distinction is less interesting to me than the tendency of both to allow a writer to speak of one thing or person while meaning another, so particularly when discussing persons, I will use terms relating to typology and allegory more or less interchangeably.

Biblical models for allegorical exegesis

"In the beginning was the Word." Then came interpretation, personal application, and explanation. Thus the later sections of the Hebrew Bible, the Prophets and Writings, refer to historical events, persons, and places that feature in the Pentateuch: Joshua, David, and Ezra in their turn are types of Moses; the return from the Exile is a type of the Exodus; Jerusalem is a type of Eden.[2]

New Testament writers developed allegorical reading and practiced typology even more explicitly, as they quoted and interpreted the Hebrew scriptures in letters that would become part of the Christian Bible.[3] In Galatians, for instance, Paul interprets the Genesis story of the sons of Abraham's two wives, the free Sarah and the servant Hagar, "by an allegorie." "By an allegorie," glosses the Bishops' Bible of 1568, "that is another thyng is meant." In this case, Paul contrasts the Christian church (which he sees figured by Sarah's son) and the synagogue (figured by Hagar's son). The implication: those in the second group will not be reckoned as God's children.

Paul's Hagar/Sarah comparison might more strictly be called a typology rather than allegory, given that both Hagar and Sarah are treated both as literal persons as well as anticipatory examples of the Christian and the Jew. Similarly, in John 1, John the Baptist, catching sight of Jesus, exclaims, "Beholde that Lambe of God, which taketh away the sinne of the world." The designation "Lambe of God," referring to Genesis 22, where Abraham, not ready to reveal God's test to Isaac, says, "God will prouide him a lambe for a burnt offering,"[4] identifies Jesus as the "antitype" to

---

2 See especially Michael Fishbane, *Biblical Interpretation in Ancient Israel* (Oxford: Clarendon, 1985), 350–79; Northrop Frye, *The Great Code: The Bible and Literature* (New York, NY: Harcourt, 1982); and Jon Whitman's "Introduction" and chapters 4 and 5 of *Interpretation and Allegory: Antiquity to the Modern Period*, ed. Jon Whitman (Brill: Leiden, 2000).

3 See Auerbach's "Figura," Leonhard Goppelt, *Typos: The Typological Interpretation of the Old Testament in the New* (1939), trans. Donald H. Madvig, foreword by E. Earle Ellis (Grand Rapids, MI: Eerdmans, 1982), and Jon Whitman's chapter 6 of *Interpretation and Allegory*.

4 *The Geneva Bible: A Facsimile of the 1560 Edition* (Madison, WI: University of Wisconsin Press, 1969).

whom the sacrificial animals of the Old Testament pointed forward as "types." (In other phraseology, the sacrificial animals were "shadows" of the "true" Lamb of God.)

A further New Testament example of typology occurs in 1 Corinthians 10. Paul reviews Israel's experience in the wilderness: they were led by the pillar of cloud, passed through the Red Sea (a type of baptism), ate the manna and drank the water God provided (types of the communion bread and wine), and then fell into idolatry and sexual immorality. But the people of the Exodus are to be read as types as well as historical persons with their own reality (here in the Bishops' Bible[5]): "All these thinges happened vnto them for ensamples: but they are written to put vs in remembraunce, whom the endes of the worlde are come vpon." The book of Exodus bears a hidden message for Paul's audience; what happened to its characters happened for the sake of Paul's readers.

Turnabout is fair play: in subsequent generations, readers of the New Testament practiced allegoresis, developing a limited number of accepted readings and moral applications, which became standard, sometimes within only a generation or two.[6] To get a sample of the range of interpretations and then the rapid establishment of a few oft-repeated ones as dominant, Matthew 13:3–23, the parable of the sower, can serve as a representative example.

Traditional interpretations of the parable of the sower

One recalls that the seed fell variously on the path, among stones and thorns, and also on good ground, with consequences for its productivity. Jesus had told his disciples that the seed was "the word of the kingdom" planted in hearers' hearts. Clement of Rome (late first century), however, did not see this Matthean guideline as ruling out his interpretation of the

---

5 Available from the Chadwyck-Healey database The Bible in English, http://www.galileo.usg.edu/express?link=zlbe.

6 For the hermeneutical practice of the church Fathers, among them Origen, Cyril of Jerusalem, Hippolytus, Tertullian, Ambrose, Hilary, John Chrysostom, pseudo-Barnabas, Justin, Gregory of Nyssa, Clement, and Basil, see Jean Danielou, *From Shadows to Reality: Studies in the Biblical Typology of the Fathers* (1959), trans. Dom Wulstan Hibberd (London: Burns & Oates, 1960), and Henri de Lubac, *Medieval Exegesis: The Four Senses of Scripture* (1959), trans. E. M. Macierowski (Grand Rapids, MI: Eerdmans, 2000), and Karlfried Froehlich, *Biblical Interpretation from the Church Fathers to the Reformation* (Burlington, VT: Ashgate, 2010). See also Kenneth Burke, *The Rhetoric of Religion: Studies in Logology* (Berkeley, CA: University of California Press, 1961).

seed as the physical body, with the parable as an allegory of the resurrection. This passage is from Clement 24:

> Let us consider, beloved, how the Lord continually proves to us that there shall be a future resurrection, of which He has rendered the Lord Jesus Christ the first-fruits by raising Him from the dead. Let us contemplate, beloved, the resurrection which is at all times taking place ... Let us behold the fruits [of the earth], how the sowing of grain takes place. The sower goes forth, and casts it into the ground; and the seed being thus scattered, though dry and naked when it fell upon the earth, is gradually dissolved. Then out of its dissolution the mighty power of the providence of the Lord raises it up again, and from one seed many arise and bring forth fruit.[7]

The image of the "death" of a kernel of wheat when it falls to the ground, enabling it to then produce many seeds, is from John 12:24 and remains current in religious discourse. But Clement's appropriation of the parable of the sower in this context did not become standard. It illustrates the tendency of exegetes to adapt biblical language from apparently unrelated passages to embellish their style or buttress their teaching.

Origen did something analogous when, in explaining the parable consistently with the original Matthean gloss, he made a graceful allusion to the crown of thorns Jesus wore at his crucifixion:

> There are those who still have thorns with which they crown and dishonour Jesus, those, namely, who are choked by the cares, and riches, and pleasures of life, and though they have received the word of God, do not bring it to perfection.[8]

By linking two passages, Origen refers the allegorical thorns of the parable to details of the historical story of the crucifixion.

Clement of Alexandria (late second to early third centuries) thought of the seed as God's word in the sense of God's personified wisdom or truth, the Logos. He explains that philosophy, "whatever has been well said by ... [the Stoic, or the Platonic, or the Epicurean, or the Aristotelian] sects, which teach righteousness along with a science pervaded by piety,"

---

7 Clement of Rome, *The First Epistle of Clement to the Corinthians*, trans. Alexander Roberts, James Donaldson, in *The Ante-Nicene Fathers* 1 (Grand Rapids, MI: Eerdmans, 1953), 11–12.
8 Origen, *Commentary on the Gospel of John*, Book I, chapter 12. "The Gospel Contains the Ill Deeds Also Which Were Done to Jesus," trans. Allan Menzies, in *The Ante-Nicene Fathers* 10 (Grand Rapids, MI: Eerdmans, 1951), 304.

Scriptural interpretation and 16th-century allegoresis

> [came] down from God to men ... For the husbandman of the soil which is among men is one; He who from the beginning, from the foundation of the world, sowed nutritious seeds; He who in each age rained down the Lord, the Word.

The variability in the growth and harvest is due to the "differences" in "times and places."[9] Similarly, Clement's contemporary Tertullian seems in passing to take the seed as humankind rather than God's word when he refers to God as "the founder of the universe, the Governor of the whole world, the Fashioner of humanity, the Sower of universal nations."[10]

Few interpreters followed up on Clement's and Tertullian's universalism, however. Resonating better with later writers was Clement's idea that the parable supported a teaching that there would be "Degrees of Glory in Heaven":

> there are various abodes, according to the worth of those who have believed ... These chosen abodes, which are three, are indicated by the numbers in the Gospel – the thirty, the sixty, the hundred. And the perfect inheritance belongs to those who attain to "a perfect man," according to the image of the Lord.[11]

The best place in heaven is reserved for the most perfect – virgins, who yield hundredfold fruit.

Athanasius of Alexandria (early to mid-fourth century) also interprets the degree of reward in heaven as relating to the degree of virtue on earth:

> Not with virgins alone is such a field adorned; nor with monks alone but also with honourable matrimony and the chastity of each one ... Nor is mercy confined to the perfect, but it is sent down also among those who occupy the middle and the third ranks, so that He might rescue all men generally to salvation. To this intent He hath prepared many mansions with the Father, so that although the dwelling-place is various in proportion to the advance in moral attainment, yet all of us are within the wall.[12]

---

9 Clement of Alexandria, *The Stromata, or Miscellanies*, Book I, chapter VII, ed. A. Cleveland Cox, in *The Ante-Nicene Fathers* 2 (Grand Rapids, MI: Eerdmans, 1951), 308.
10 Tertullian, *An Answer to the Jews*, trans. Sydney Thelwall, in *The Ante-Nicene Fathers* 3 (Grand Rapids, MI: Eerdmans, 1951), 152.
11 Clement of Alexandria, *The Stromata, or Miscellanies*, Book VI, chapter XIV, ed. A. Cleveland Cox, in *The Ante-Nicene Fathers* 2 (Grand Rapids, MI: Eerdmans, 1951), 506.
12 Athanasius of Alexandria, "Letter X. Easter, 338," trans. John Cardinal Newman, ed. Archibald Robertson, in *The Nicene and Post-Nicene Fathers*, ser. 2, vol. 4 (Grand Rapids, MI: Eerdmans, 1953), 529.

The focus is on the varying degrees of "moral attainment" that those "within the wall" have reached.

Jerome (late fourth to early fifth centuries) is also interested in the distinctions that can be made among those "rescue[d] ... to salvation." According to the headnote, Jerome refuted "The fourth proposition of Jovinianus, that all who are saved will have equal reward" with a general appeal to the parable's "various yields of thirty, sixty, and a hundred fold": "we read that the good ground brought forth fruit, some a hundred fold, some sixty fold, and some thirty fold; and, on the other hand, that the bad ground admitted of three degrees of sterility: but Jovinianus makes only two classes, the good soil and the bad."[13]

Chrysostom followed Athanasius in stressing that the parable demonstrates God's "mercy" in accepting Christians' efforts at virtue that fall short of the full hundred:

> And yet if both the land be good, and the Sower one, and the seed the same, wherefore did one bear a hundred, one sixty, one thirty? Here again the difference is from the nature of the ground, for even where the ground is good, great even therein is the difference. Seest thou, that not the husbandman is to be blamed, nor the seed, but the land that receives it? not for its nature, but for its disposition. And herein too, great is His mercy to man, that He doth not require one measure of virtue, but while He receives the first, and casts not out the second, He gives also a place to the third.[14]

Chrysostom falls into line with Athanasius and most intervening commentators, thus demonstrating that, despite the arbitrariness ascribed by the reformers to medieval practitioners of biblical interpretation, independent acts of allegoresis did not usually result in novel conclusions.

By the twelfth century, when the *Glossa Ordinaria* or Ordinary Gloss on the Bible was compiled, Athanasius's reading had become standard: the sower's variable returns of thirty, sixty, or one hundred were associated with the varying levels of "advance[ment] in moral attainment" manifested by marriage, widowhood, and virginity. Throughout the medieval period, the reference to thirty is "ad nuptias," to sixty "ad viduas," and to one hundred "ad virginitatem."[15]

---

13 Jerome, *Against Jovinianus*, Book II, trans. and intro. W. H. Fremantle, in *The Nicene and Post-Nicene Fathers*, ser. 2, vol. 6 (Grand Rapids, MI: Eerdmans, 1954), 387 (headnote), 403.
14 John Chrysostom, *Homilies on Matthew*, Homily XLIV, trans. George Prevost, in *The Nicene and Post-Nicene Fathers*, ser. 1, vol. 10 (Grand Rapids, MI: Eerdmans, 1989), 275.
15 *Mattheus XIII, Biblia latina cum glossa ordinaria: a facsimile reprint of the editio princeps. Adolph Rusch of Strassburg 1480/81*, vol. 4 (Brepols: Turnhout, 1992).

So stable was the tradition that John Fisher offered exactly this to the auditors of his Paul's Cross sermon in 1525:

> The lowest degree of this spiritualnes is in the state of matrimony: ... if this sacrament truely be kepte/ there the encrease of frute is thyrtyfolde.
>
> The myddell degree is in the state of wydowheed ... Here the encrease of frute is thre skore folde.
>
> The thyrd is in the state of virginite ...: and this encrease is an hundred folde so moche.[16]

Thus the "degrees of virtue" interpretation of the parable was still being preached in England almost fourteen centuries after it was first recorded.

The most enduring themes found in this passage, arising earlier and continuing beyond the vogue of the virginity/widowhood/matrimony application, were moral applications to the preacher and his hearers. Justin Martyr (early to mid-second century) uses Jesus's image of seed as verbally-transmitted truth to explain why he prolongs his dialogue with Trypho even while suspecting him of not participating in good faith: "I speak all things simply and candidly, as my Lord said: 'A sower went forth to sow the seed; and some fell by the wayside; and some among thorns, and some on stony ground, and some on good ground.' I must speak, then, in the hope of finding good ground somewhere."[17]

Origen (early third century) found a similar theme, alluding to the sower parable as mandating the spread of true religion by proclamation only. In *Contra Celsus*, he notes that:

> the Christ, the Reformer of the whole world, ... did not need to employ against men whips, and chains, and tortures, as was the case under the former economy. For when the sower went forth to sow, the doctrine [as opposed to coercion] sufficed to sow the word everywhere.[18]

Here again, the emphasis is on the sower's role in spreading religious teaching verbally.

---

16 John Fisher, *A sermon had at Paulis by the commandment of the most reuerend father in god my lorde legate* (London, 1526), sig. G. STC (2nd edn) 10892. Available from the database Early English Books Online.

17 Justin Martyr, *Dialogue with Trypho*, CXXV, ed. Alexander Roberts and James Donaldson, rev. A. Cleveland Coxe, in *The Ante-Nicene Fathers* 1 (Grand Rapids, MI: Eerdmans), 262.

18 Origen, *Contra Celsus* [Against Celsus], Book IV, chapter 9, trans. Frederick Crombie, in *The Ante-Nicene Fathers* 4 (Grand Rapids, MI: Eerdmans, 1951), 500.

More than two centuries after Justin, Chrysostom makes a related point about the sower and the obligation of the preacher (in this case, the apostle Paul) to be optimistic and tireless:

> "I am become all things to all men," not expecting, however, to save all, but that I may save though it be but a few. And so great care and service have I undergone, as one naturally would who was about saving all, far however from hoping to gain all: which was truly magnanimous and a proof of burning zeal. Since likewise the sower sowed every where, and saved not all the seed, notwithstanding he did his part.[19]

Augustine repeats the thought: "For what fear did it cause him, that 'some seed fell on the way side, and some on rocky places, and some among thorns'? If he had been afraid of these unmanageable grounds, he would never have got to the good ground."[20] And indeed, well into the early modern period preachers and commentators, most familiarly perhaps Hugh Latimer in his Sermon of the Plow,[21] follow the Fathers in deriving from this parable the moral duty of the clergy to preach, many citing not only the original parable, but the Fathers as well.

If the various kinds of ground represent various classes of hearers, those hearers may have a duty as well as the preacher. Gregory of Nazianzen (mid- to late fourth century) develops this angle, using the parable to rebuke in advance those of his audience who will not accept his teaching:

> For either we shall have spoken in the ears of them that will hear, and our words will bear some fruit, namely an advantage to you (since the Sower soweth the Word upon every kind of mind; and the good and fertile bears fruit), or else you will depart despising this discourse of ours as you have despised others, and having drawn from it further material for gainsaying and railing at us, upon which to feast yourselves yet more.[22]

---

19 John Chrysostom, *Homilies on I Corinthians*, Homily XXII, trans. H. K. Cornish and John Medley, in *The Nicene and Post-Nicene Fathers*, ser. 1, vol. 12 (Grand Rapids, MI: Eerdmans), 128–9.
20 Augustine, Sermon LI [CI Ben.], in *Sermons on Selected Lessons of the New Testament*, trans. R. G. MacMullen, in *The Nicene and Post-Nicene Fathers*, ser. 1, vol. 6 (Grand Rapids, MI: Eerdmans, rpt. 1991), 423.
21 Hugh Latimer, "A notable sermon ... preached in the Shroudes at Poules church ... on the xviii. day of January. Anno. 1548," in *27 sermons preached by ... Maister Hugh Latimer* (London, 1562), STC (2nd edn) 15276. Available from the database Early English Books Online.
22 Gregory Nazianzen, "Oration XXVII, The First Theological Oration: A Preliminary Discourse against the Eunomians," trans. Charles Gordon Browne and James Edward Swallow, in *The Nicene and Post-Nicene Fathers*, ser. 2, vol. 7 (Grand Rapids, MI: Eerdmans, 1955), 285.

Augustine also emphasizes the moral responsibility of the hearers:

> this only concerns us, that we be not "the way side," nor "the rock," nor "the thorns," but "the good ground." Be our heart well-prepared ... Let it not be "the way side," where the enemy as a bird may take away the seed trodden down by the passers by. Let it not be "the rock," where the shallow soil makes it spring up immediately, so that it cannot bear the sun. Let it not be the "thorns," the lusts of this world, the anxieties of an ill-ordered life ... Let the thorns be rooted up, the field prepared, the seeds put in.[23]

More than a thousand years later, Erasmus strikes the same note in his paraphrase on the parable:

> [Jesus] setteth fourth a parable, signyfying that many on euery side come runnyng to the preachyng of the gospell, and yet fruite springeth not in them all: whiche chaunceth not by the faulte of the teacher, but by the faulte of the hearers. Nor lyke fruite springeth not in all the hearers, but accordyng as euery manne bryngeth a mynde voyde from worldlye cares and desyres ... By thys parable Iesus taught vs, with what studye and desyre the heauenlye doctryne ought to be receyued, yf we desyre that fruit should spring of it.[24]

One might imagine that the freedom of allegorical reading allows a reader to get any and every meaning from a given passage. But the parable of the sower tended to yield not a luxuriant fantasia of imaginative interpretations, but a few distinct themes.

Traditional interpretations of Jesus's visit to Martha and Mary

The parable of the sower was allegorical from the start, with the definitive interpretation supplied in the text – perhaps a check on interpretive ingenuity. Thus one might expect more variability in interpretation when an allegorical significance of a passage is not provided by the biblical text. But one straightforward bit of narrative, Luke 10:38–42's anecdote of Jesus's entertainment at Martha and Mary's home, though well known and frequently subjected to allegoresis, gave rise to a similarly limited range of themes. Origen was the first to assert that "Mary is the symbol of the contemplative life, Martha of the active,"[25] and even this statement

---

23 Augustine, Sermon LI [CI Ben.], 423.
24 Desiderius Erasmus, *The first tome or volume of the Paraphrase of Erasmus vpon the Newe Testamente* (London, 1548), STC (2nd edn) 2854.5, sig. K3^v, K5. Available from the database Early English Books Online.
25 Origen, *Ioan.*, fragment 80, quoted by Kim Paffenroth, "Allegorizations of the Active and Contemplative Lives in Philo, Origen, Augustine, and Gregory," 1999, The Ecole Initiative. Available online http://ecole.evansville.edu/articles/allegory.html.

of what became the established interpretation of the story is a glancing reference rather than a developed analysis, suggesting that the idea was uncontroversial from the start.

Ambrose, in the late fourth century, restated the complementarity of the two sisters, with Martha (recalled with details from the John 11 story of Lazarus's resurrection) now representing the works of "mourning and confession of sins." In assuring his audience that sincere repentance (metaphorically, death) will meet with forgiveness (metaphorically, resurrection), he writes, "Christ will come to your grave, and if He finds there weeping for you Martha the woman of good service, and Mary who carefully heard the Word of God, like holy Church which has chosen the best part, He will be moved with compassion"[26] and forgive the hearer's sins. The mourning sisters allegorize the attitude recommended to the auditors.

Ambrose's younger contemporary Augustine formulated the relative merits of the two sisters' preoccupations in terms of the present and the afterlife:

> Ye see then ... that in these two women the two lives are figured, the life present, and the life to come, the life of labour, and the life of quiet, the life of sorrow, and the life of blessedness, the life temporal, and the life eternal.[27]

Thus, without denying their historical status as individual women, biblical exegetes very early came to a standard allegorical shorthand, using Mary and Martha as figures or types signifying abstract qualities.

The familiar character sketch is explicitly stated as symbolic in Gregory the Great's *Morals on the Book of Job*:

> For what is set forth by Mary, who sitting down gave ear to the words of our Lord, saving the life of contemplation? and what by Martha, so busied with outward services, saving the life of action? Now Martha's concern is not reproved, but that of Mary is even commended. For the merits of the active life are great, but of the contemplative, far better. Whence Mary's part is said to be "never taken away from her," in that the works of the

---

26 Ambrose, *Two Books Concerning Repentance*, Book 2, chapter 7, trans. H. De Romestin, in *The Nicene and Post-Nicene Fathers*, ser. 2, vol. 10 (Grand Rapids, MI: Eerdmans, 1955), 352.
27 Augustine, Sermon LIV [CIV Ben.], in *Sermons on Selected Lessons of the New Testament*, trans. R. G. MacMullen, in *The Nicene and Post-Nicene Fathers*, ser. 1, vol. 6 (Grand Rapids, MI: Eerdmans, rpt. 1991), 423.

active life pass away together with the body, while the joys of the contemplative life are made more lively at the end.[28]

A spiritual lesson is "set forth by Mary" or "by Martha" through the mere mention of their names.

Notwithstanding the preference commentators express for contemplation (following Jesus's value judgment, of course), "the best part" could not always be preferred in practice. In a letter written shortly after becoming Bishop of Rome, Gregory links Mary and Martha to the older pair of allegorical sisters Rachel and Leah:

> I have loved the beauty of the contemplative life as a Rachel, barren, but keen of sight and fair, who, though in her quietude she is less fertile, yet sees the light more keenly. But, by what judgment I know not, Leah has been coupled with me in the night, to wit, the active life; fruitful, but tender-eyed; seeing less, but bringing forth more. I have longed to sit at the feet of the Lord with Mary, to take in the words of His mouth; and lo, I am compelled to serve with Martha in external affairs, to be careful and troubled about many things.[29]

In this piece of allegoresis, Leah is "the active life" and Rachel "the contemplative life," while Gregory is Jacob, "coupled [with Leah] in the night" "by what judgment I know not," when he "loved the beauty of … Rachel." Sitting "at the feet of the Lord with Mary" may be more heavenly, but the church's affairs in this world demand service. Gregory's ease in assuming that his reader will not only assign the right qualities to Mary and Martha, but also appreciate the relevance of Jacob's marriage to Leah, demonstrate the commonplace nature of his allegoresis.

The standard interpretation is given further authority by the Glossa Ordinaria, which emphasizes "duae vitae innocentes." "Per martham operibus actuosa devotio· qua proximo in charitate sociamur. Per mariam religiosa menti intentio in dei verbo· qua in dei amore suspiramus."[30] Centuries later, Erasmus calls the Mary/Martha episode "this Parable" (as if it were primarily a symbolic story) as well as one of the "plaine exaumples

---

28 Gregory the Great, *Morals on the Book of Job*, Book VI, ¶61, trans. John Henry Parker (London, 1844), 361.
29 Gregory the Great, *Register of the Epistles of Saint Gregory the Great*, Book I, The Month of September, Indiction IX, Being the First Year of His Ordination, Epistle V, trans. James Barmby, in *The Nicene and Post-Nicene Fathers*, ser. 2, vol. 12 (Grand Rapids, MI: Eerdmans, 1989), 75b.
30 Lucas X, *Biblia latina cum glossa ordinaria: a facsimile reprint of the editio princeps Adolph Rusch of Strassburg 1480/81*, vol. 4 (Brepols: Turnhout, 1992).

of experience" that teach – teach listeners, that is, less at this date to exalt the contemplative life than to cherish cooperation and mutual respect between average working-day Christians and evangelical scholar-preachers ["being long in learning the thing that thei may afterward teache"]:

> suche as do altogether geue hede vnto those thinges whiche do most nerest concerne and touche the life euerlastyng, although they seme as holidayemenne, to repose theymselfes from all corporall businesse: yet they dooe more good then the others, because they doe the thyng most chiefly requisite to be doen. Nor the one must grutche not against the other, forasmuche as euery one of them accordyng to his gyft which he hath receiued of god, serueth me in my membres.[31]

Though their historical actuality is never denied, Martha and Mary appear, into the sixteenth century and beyond, primarily as allegorical figures – in a word, they are types.

Statements about and categories of biblical exegesis

Allegorical reading developed as a biblical hermeneutic before the time of Christ and is on display in the New Testament as a way of reading the Hebrew Bible. That is, whether or not a particular biblical passage was originally written as an allegory, New Testament writers and the church Fathers took passages of scripture and created allegorical interpretations of them – the process known as allegoresis. This process, theorized during and thus associated with the Christian Middle Ages, developed much earlier, as we have seen. What did the Fathers say about the methods that yielded allegorical and typological readings such as those sampled earlier in this chapter?

Some argued that it was not justifiable to go beyond Jesus's own explicit interpretation. Tertullian, the contemporary of Clement of Alexandria, sees "[the parable] of the sower, (which He [Jesus] interprets)"[32] as the quintessential example of a parable that needed no further explanation. Chrysostom explicitly warned against over-interpretation: "as I am always saying, the parables must not be explained throughout word for word, since many absurdities will follow."[33] In a well-known passage, Augustine warned against reading the parables too curiously:

---

31 Erasmus, *The first tome or volume of the Paraphrase of Erasmus*, sig. Q4, Q5.
32 Tertullian, *On the Resurrection of the Flesh*, trans. Peter Holmes, in *The Ante-Nicene Fathers* 3 (Grand Rapids, MI: Eerdmans, 1951), 568.
33 John Chrysostom, *Homilies on Matthew*, Homily XLVII, trans. George Prevost, in *The Nicene and Post-Nicene Fathers*, ser. 1, vol. 10 (Grand Rapids, MI: Eerdmans, 1989), 285.

Now ye know that those three places mentioned yesterday where the seed did not grow, "the way side," "the stony ground," and "the thorny places," are the same as these "tares" [of the following parable]. They received only a different name under a different similitude ... [I]n parables and similitudes one thing may be called by many names; therefore there is nothing inconsistent in my telling you that that "way side," that "stony ground," those "thorny places," are bad Christians, and that they too are the "tares." Is not Christ called "the Lamb"? Is not Christ "the Lion" too? ... [B]esides this it may happen that under a figure, things very different from one another may be called by one and the same name. For what is so different as Christ and the devil? yet both Christ and the devil are called "a lion." Christ is called "a lion:" "The Lion hath prevailed of the tribe of Judah;" and the devil is called a lion: "Know ye not that your adversary the Devil walketh about as a roaring lion, seeking whom he may devour?" Both the one and the other then is a lion; the one a lion by reason of His strength; the other for his savageness; the one a lion for His "prevailing;" the other for his injuring. The devil again is a serpent, "that old serpent;" are we commanded then to imitate the devil, when our Shepherd told us, "Be ye wise as serpents, and simple as doves"?[34]

The reader of biblical symbolic language should not be disturbed by the lack of internal consistency or the multiplication of images for one literal referent. Augustine's caution applies to *The Faerie Queene*: "in parables and similitudes one thing may be called by many names; therefore there is nothing inconsistent" in Spenser sometimes making one point and sometimes another – a prime example being Carol Kaske's insight that several of its key images appear *in bono* and *in malo*.[35] Spenser scholars will also remember Gordon Teskey's contention that, compared with Spenser, "There is no poet for whom the techniques of close reading are more unsuitable if relied on exclusively, or more likely to mislead if mechanically applied."[36] Certainly Spenser's original readers, confronted week after week at church with examples of the polyvalence of biblical images, were primed to adopt a flexible attitude in reading *The Faerie Queene's* allegory.

Less cautious than Augustine about free-form interpretation but happy to theorize, Origen "put forward a tripartite schema of biblical

---

34 Augustine, Sermon XXIII [LXXIII Ben.], *Sermons on Selected Lessons of the New Testament*, trans. R. G. MacMullen, in *The Nicene and Post-Nicene Fathers*, ser. 1, vol. 6 (Grand Rapids, MI: Eerdmans, rpt. 1991), 334.
35 *Spenser and Biblical Poetics* (Ithaca: Cornell University Press), 1999.
36 Gordon Teskey, "Thinking Moments in *The Faerie Queene*," *Spenser Studies: A Renaissance Poetry Annual* 22 (2007), 103–25; the quote is from 111.

interpretation: physical (historical), moral, and spiritual (allegorical or anagogical), corresponding to his tripartite division of humans into body, soul, and spirit."[37] He insisted (for instance, in a chapter title) that "Scripture Contains Many Contradictions, and Many Statements Which are Not Literally True, But Must Be Read Spiritually and Mystically," citing as examples the contradictory but symbolically meaningful place-names in the various gospels.[38]

Centuries later, Gregory the Great expressed a similar outlook on scripture in describing what he called "the mystical mode" of biblical interpretation:

> Saving the historical verity, I proposed to myself to make out the sayings of blessed Job and of his friends by the mystical mode of interpretation: for … Holy Writ takes care to hold out in promise the Redeemer of the world in all its statements … And hence blessed Job is in the Latin tongue rendered "grieving," that both by his name and by his wounds the Passion of our Redeemer might be signified.

Gregory did not deny that the story of Job was literally true ("Saving the historical verity"), but he, like other commentators, felt free to take a non-allegorical passage of scripture and make an allegory out of it: "And [Job's] wife strives to persuade [Job] to curse, in that all the carnal minds within the pale of Holy Church prove abettors of the cunning Tempter. For she, who prompts him to cursing, represents the life of the carnal sort."[39] Thus, according to Gregory, the story of Job should be read as the "Letter of the Authors" stipulates *The Faerie Queene* should be read: one must keep in mind that the Faerie Queene is "*the most excellent and glorious person of our soueraine the Queene*" and England, "*her kingdome*," is the poem's "*Faery land*," just as the book of Job prefigures Jesus's story and provides parallels (and thus moral guidance) to Christians.

Symbolic modes of biblical interpretation developed ahead of formal theory for many centuries, but eventually the scholastic penchant for categories would provide labels for points that could be isolated along the

---

37 R. Gerald Hobbs, "BIBLE: Biblical Hermeneutics and Exegesis," *The Oxford Encyclopedia of the Reformation*, 4 vols. (Oxford: Oxford University Press, 1996), 1.152–71.
38 Origen, *Commentary on the Gospel of John*, Book 10, chapter 4, trans. Allan Menzies, in *The Ante-Nicene Fathers*, 10 (Grand Rapids, MI: Eerdmans, 1951), 383. Origen has a different set of difficulties in mind than Cranmer's narratee in the first homily, "A Fruitefull Exhortacion to the Readyng of Holye Scripture."
39 Gregory the Great, *Morals on the Book of Job*, Book VI, ¶1, trans. John Henry Parker (London, 1844), 312–13.

spectrum of legitimate scriptural interpretation found in the writings of Clement of Alexandria, Augustine, Gregory, and the others. Nicholas of Lyra (1270–1349) summarized that range when, in the preface to one of his celebrated commentaries, he quoted the well-known mnemonic couplet:

> Littera gesta docet, quid credas allegoria,
> Moralis quid agas, quo tendas anagogia.[40]

("The letter teaches the events, the allegory what you should believe, the moral [sense] what you should do, the anagogy where you are headed.") Though the comments cited in this chapter predate Nicholas, each can be slotted into one or more of his categories.

All commentators "sav[ed] the historical verity," as Gregory put it – believed, first, in "the letter," that the Bible reported actual events. Beyond this, commentators followed the New Testament writers in believing that the incidents of the Old Testament prefigured events in the life of Jesus. This is "allegoria" or typology, "what you should believe." As Gregory wrote of the book of Job, "Holy Writ [specifically the Old Testament] takes care to hold out in promise the Redeemer of the world in all its statements." Thus Matthew, in reporting that the infant Jesus's parents took him first to Egypt and then out of Egypt to Nazareth (Matthew 2:14–15), quotes Hosea 11:1's reference to the Exodus ("When Israel was young, I loued him, and called my sonne out of the lande of Egypt"[41]), as we saw Gregory relate the meaning of Job's name to Jesus's suffering in the crucifixion.

Besides teaching the historical events and the promise of the Redeemer, "All scripture is ... profitable ... to reproue, to correction, to instruction which is in ryghteousnesse" (2 Timothy 3:16).[42] Through tropology, the commentators found in scripture moral guidance. Thus Justin Martyr learned from the parable that, as a good sower, he "must speak" regardless of how unpromising the listener seemed, and Gregory of Nazianzen, Augustine, and Erasmus variously challenge and encourage sermon-goers to be "good soil," or receptive listeners. Other examples

---

40 "de commendatione sacrae Scripturae in generali [General Commendation of Scripture]," *Patrologia Latina* 113:28c; "*In moralitates Bibliorum*" 33c. Available from the Patrilogia Latina Database.
41 *The. holie. Bible conteynyng the olde Testament and the newe* [Bishops' Bible] (London, 1568), CLXXXII (sig. Z6), STC (2nd edn) 2099. Available from the database Early English Books Online.
42 Ibid., CXXVI (sig. Q6).

of tropological reading are the readings of the Mary/Martha story that impress on the listeners their duty to express love both by doing works of charity and by contemplating Christ – and to discern the right time for each. Clement of Rome's resurrection-oriented reading of the parable of the sower and Clement of Alexandria's and Jerome's finding that the references to thirty, sixty, and hundred pertain to rewards in heaven are examples of anagogy, the eschatological sense of scripture, as are Augustine's and Gregory's assertions that Martha figured this life and Mary the life to come.

Sixteenth-century English exegetical theory and practice: Tyndale

Even a haphazard overview of the Fathers' interpretive practice and review of the medieval definitions makes it clear that, whatever reform-minded English champions of vernacular translation and the literal sense might say in disparagement of the non-literal "senses of scripture," both the Fathers they laid claim to and their own practice show ample evidence of continuity with interpretive tradition. Political theorist and Bible translator William Tyndale, whose statements on and practice of biblical exegesis continued to influence English religious rhetoric long past his death in 1536, may be taken as representative.

In *The Obedience of a Christen Man*,[43] the book that developed a rationale for Henry to repudiate the authority of the Pope, Tyndale appears to repudiate the interpretive tradition he inherited. Citing the familiar formulation, he notes that traditional medieval commentators "devide the scripture into iiii. senses/ the literall/ tropologicall/ allegoricall & anagogical," but explains that this does a tremendous disservice to the text:

> The literall sence is become nothinge at all. For the pope hath taken it cleane awaye and hath made it his possession. He hath partly locked it vp with the false & counterfayted leyes of his tradicions ceremonies & fayned lyes And partly dryueth men from it with violence of swerde ... The tropologicall sence [pointedly spelled "chopologicall" farther down the page] perteyneth to good maners (saie they) and teacheth what we ought to doo. The allegory is appropriate to fayth/ & the anagogical to hope and thinges aboue.[44]

Tyndale goes on to say that, since the tropological sense "is but an allegorie of maners and [the] anagogical an allegory of hope," "this worde

---

43 "The iiii. senses of the scripture," in *The Obedience of a Christen Man* (Antwerp), 1528; facsimile edn (Norwood, NJ: Walter J. Johnson, Inc., 1977), fols. 129–50ᵛ.
44 Ibid., fols. 129–9ᵛ.

allegorie comprehendeth them both and is ynough."⁴⁵ The problem with referring to an allegorical sense, according to Tyndale, is "the scripture hath but one sence which is the literall sence."⁴⁶ The idea that allegorical reading is more "spiritual" was mistaken: "God is a sprite and all his wordes are spirituall. His literall sence is spirituall and all his wordes are spirituall."⁴⁷

Tyndale grants that scripture makes use of allegories and other figures of speech, but these are not further "senses" of any text: "that which the proverbe/ similitude/ redell [riddle] or allegory signifieth is ever the literall sence which thou must seke out diligently."⁴⁸ (One notes that Tyndale uses the word "allegory" more loosely than we might today, encompassing "similitude" and "example" as well as "extended metaphor.") In interpreting the figurative passages, Tyndale insists that "we ... [find] out the litterall sence of the scripture by the processe of the texte or by a lyke texte of another place."⁴⁹ That is, the context surrounding the figurative passage (or the treatment of similar themes elsewhere in scripture) must govern the interpretation of the Bible's allegories.

Tyndale's main aversion, of course, is to allegorical readings of passages of the Bible whose literal sense is on the surface and perfectly clear. Since he is so hard on the practitioners of traditional interpretation, whom he says "feign false descant and juggling allegories, to stablish their kingdom withal,"⁵⁰ it comes as a bit of a surprise to find Tyndale himself practicing allegoresis on perfectly straightforward biblical passages. One such reading, on Peter striking off Malchus's ear and Jesus restoring it, features the law, as Peter's sword, wounding the sinner. (The gospel, as Christ, transforms and heals him.)⁵¹ Another, on Noah's drunken nakedness,

---

45 Ibid., fol. 129ᵛ. Medieval commentators agreed, subsuming allegory, tropology, and anagogy under "the sense of faith" or "the spiritual sense" (as opposed to "the literal sense").
46 Ibid., fol. 129ᵛ.
47 Ibid., fol. 134ᵛ.
48 Ibid., fol. 130.
49 Ibid., fol. 131. Compare the strategy Tyndale recommends in "The Prologue to the Epistle of the Hebrews," in *Tyndale's New Testament*, ed. and intro. David Daniell (New Haven, CT: Yale University Press, 1989) for understanding passages in Hebrews that his readers might find difficult: "no scripture is of private interpretation: but must be expounded according to the general articles of our faith and agreeable to other open and evident texts, and confirmed or compared to like sentences" (346).
50 "The Prologue to the Prophet Jonas," in *Tyndale's Old Testament: Being the Pentateuch of 1530, Joshua to 2 Chronicles of 1537, and Jonah*, ed. and intro. David Daniell (New Haven, CT: Yale University Press, 1992), 629.
51 "The iiii. senses of the scripture," fols. 131–1ᵛ.

positions the gospel as Noah's "privey members" because it is "wherewith we are begot," and the Pope as "our weked ham" [wicked Ham] who made a mockery of God's word.[52]

Is Tyndale inconsistent in offering such readings of scripture? He claims not, since such "allegories are not sence of the scripture: but fre thinges besides the scripture and all together in the libertie of the spirite."[53] Allegorical readings can be "apte & honsome,"[54] as he claims his Noah/Ham example is, but, as he says of his spin on Peter and Malchus, "This allegory proveth no thinge neither can doo. For it is not the scripture."[55] Arguing doctrine requires the warrant of scripture understood literally, while expressing a scriptural doctrine aptly and handsomely can be done through allegoresis.

Thus, Tyndale would have appreciated Gregory's allusion to Rachel and Leah above as an apt and handsome way to express regret, assuming he could have sympathized with the occasion (Gregory finding himself obliged to become pope): "For a similitude or an example doeth prynte a thinge moch deper in the wittes of a man then doeth a playne speakynge and leaveth behynde hym as it were a stynge to pricke him forwarde and to awake him with all."[56] Gregory did not claim he had discovered the "sense" of the Jacob story; he merely used allegoresis to make his misgivings more rhetorically impressive. "[T]here is not a better, vehementer or mightier thing to make a man understand withal than an allegory. For allegories make a man quick witted and print wisdom in him and maketh it to abide, where bare words go but in at the one ear and out at the other," says Tyndale,[57] much as Spenser explained to Raleigh that he "*conceiued*" that his earnest purpose of "*fashion[ing] a gentleman or noble person in vertuous and gentle discipline shoulde be most plausible and pleasing, being coloured with an historicall fiction*."[58] The reformist champion of biblical translation and literal reading approved of and practiced allegoresis on appropriate occasions as a rhetorical device – an insight that

---

52 Ibid., fols. 136–6ᵛ.
53 Ibid., fol. 131.
54 Ibid.
55 Ibid., fol. 132.
56 Ibid.
57 "A prologe in to the thirde boke of Moses, called Leviticus," in *Tyndale's Old Testament*, 145–6.
58 Edmund Spenser, "A Letter of the Authors expounding his *whole intention in the course of this worke*," in *Spenser: The Faerie Queene*, 2nd edn by A. C. Hamilton for Longman Annotated English Poets (Harlow and London: Pearson Education, 2001), 714–18.

puts imaginative literature like *The Faerie Queene* in closer proximity to contemporary religious rhetoric than many twenty-first-century readers might have been aware.

Since allegorical reading is not the key to understanding scripture, Tyndale provides an alternate paradigm, most succinctly in his "The Prologue to the Prophet Jonas":

> The scripture containeth three things in it: first the law to condemn all flesh: secondarily, the gospel, that is to say, promises of mercy for all that repent ... and submit themselves to be scholars to learn to keep the law and to learn to believe the mercy that is promised them: and thirdly, the stories and lives of those scholars, both what chances fortuned them, and also by what means their schoolmaster taught them and made them perfect, and how he tried the true from the false.[59]

Any allegories that one constructs using biblical "stories and lives" should chime with one of the other two things one finds in scripture: should, that is, condemn sin (in the individual or the institution – Tyndale's favorite target is the traditional church and its personnel) or offer hope through the gospel.

Tyndale finds fault with allegoresis, then, not in principle, because (for instance) a passage of Holy Writ must not serve any purpose or teach any lesson other than its own literal message in its own context. He objects to fanciful readings only when they "ly" or "juggle," or when interpreters "read [the stories] as things no more pertaining unto them[selves], than a tale of Robin Hood."[60] Thus he saw no inconsistency between his insistence on the literal interpretation of scripture and those marginal glosses in his own translations that treat Bible characters and their stories as allegories for contemporary characters and situations, much as Spenser's "*historicall fiction*" created allegories for some of the same individuals and issues.

For instance, in Numbers 14, the Israelites, fearful because of the report of the spies, refuse to enter the Promised Land and are about to stone Moses. God declares his intention of destroying the people, and Moses tries to dissuade him. The text reads, "And Moses said unto the Lord: then the Egyptians shall hear it, for thou broughtest this people with thy might from among them." Tyndale's gloss notes a discrepancy between Moses's behavior and that of the Bishop of Rome: "The pope would not so have

---

59 "The Prologue to the Prophet Jonas," in *Tyndale's Old Testament*, 628.
60 Ibid., 629.

prayed if they had been about to stone him."⁶¹ In its understated irony, this allegorical shorthand comparing the Pope to Moses would presumably print mistrust of the Pope's leadership deeper in the reader's heart than a simple assertion of his lack of forgiveness and self-sacrifice – just as seventeenth-century readers found Spenser's Geryoneo to be a rhetorically impressive stand-in for the Pope.⁶² Tyndale is not claiming that this particular passage proves something about the Pope (that he has no jurisdiction in England and is not motivated by the spirit of Christ), though he argued those very points elsewhere from "open texts." But he found this characterization of the Pope as the anti-Moses consistent with the literal sense of scripture and thus used it as "a stynge to pricke [the reader] forwarde and to awake him."⁶³ Tyndale's snide marginal jab operates in the same way as Spenser's allegorical portraits of the traditional church's personnel.

Sixteenth-century English exegetical theory and practice: 1560 Geneva Bible annotations

Tyndale's notions of legitimate interpretations of scripture, as well as his penchant for allegoresis for rhetorical purposes, guided those of later translators and commentators. Those who prepared the 1560 edition of the Geneva Bible inherited the earlier scholar's emphasis on the literal sense as well as his paradigm of scriptural interpretation, and supplied their influential glosses accordingly:

> And considering how hard a thing it is to vnderstand the holy Scriptures, ... we haue also indeauored ... to gather brief annotations vpon all the hard places, aswel for the vnderstanding of suche wordes as are obscure, and for the declaration of the text, as for the application of the same as may moste apperteine to Gods glorie and the edification of his Churche.⁶⁴

Thus, some glosses are devoted to expounding the "hard places," among them figurative expressions within the text, making "true and simple" (spiritual and literal, Tyndale might say) what is "obscure" through its use of figurative language.

---

61 *Tyndale's Old Testament*, 220.
62 See John Manning, "Notes and Marginalia in Bishop Percy's Copy of Spenser's *Works* (1611)," *Notes & Queries* 31 (1984), 225–7. The reference to Geryoneo is on 226.
63 "The iiii. senses of the scripture," fol. 131.
64 "TO OVR BELOVED IN THE LORD THE BRETHREN OF England, Scotland, Ireland, &c," in *The Geneva Bible: A Facsimile of the 1560 edition*, sig. ***4.

The most notable and thoroughgoing example of allegorical reading in the Geneva glosses is their treatment of the Song of Songs. For instance, the first verse, "Let him kisse me with the kisses of his mouth," is glossed "This is spoken in the persone of the Church, or of the faithful soule, inflamed with the desire of Christ, whome she loueth." The fourth verse, "I am blacke, ô daughters of Ierusalem, but comelie," is glossed "The church confesseth her spots & sinne, but hathe confidence in that fauour of Christ." Sixteenth-century biblical exegesis represents much more continuity than change, as such passages make clear. After all, the allegorical interpretation of Song of Songs had been long established in Christian scriptural tradition (as its precursor was in Judaism as early as the first century of the Common Era), allowing the Genevan scholars to regard their commentary as making the figurative literal, and hence spiritually useful for the reader. This traditional interpretation also accustomed Spenser's original audience to allegorical reading.

Many glosses that strike the reader as offering an allegorical reading, rather than making literal an otherwise confusing biblical metaphor, mainly serve the purpose of applying the spiritual sense – that is, the condemnation of sin and the promise of God's mercy in the gospel – to the reader or to contemporary situations and institutions. The Geneva glosses often combine tropology with allegory or typology in this way. When the Bible stories are morally applied (that is, treated as allegories of contemporary persons and situations), the nation of Israel and the city of Jerusalem becomes the church. In commenting on Psalm 102:14, "thy seruants delite in the stones [of Jerusalem]," the gloss reads, "The more that the Church is in miserie, and desolation, the more oght the faithful to loue and pitie it." Prophets become "ministers," as in this gloss on the commissioning of the prophet Jeremiah in Jeremiah 1:10 ("I set thee ouer the nations"): "He sheweth, what is the authoritie of Gods true ministers, which by his worde haue power to beat downe whatsoeuer lifteth it self vp against God."

The most extended example is an illustration (accompanying the text of Exodus 14; see Figure 1) of the Israelites on the edge of the Red Sea. The engraving, also featured on the title page, pictures the literal sense, while the caption allegorizes and applies the lesson.

The text reads:

> In this figure foure chief points are to be considered. first that the Church of God is euer subiect in this worlde to the Crosse & to be afflicted after one sort or other. The second, that the ministers of God following their vocation shalbe euil spoken of, and murmured against, euen of them that pretend the

In this figure foure chief points are to be considered. first that the Church of God is euer subiect in this worlde to the Crosse & to be afflicted after one sort or other. The second, that the ministers of God following their vocation shalbe euil spoken of, and murmured against, euen of them that pretend the same cause and religion that thei do. The third, that God delivereth not his Church incontinently out of dangers, but to exercise their faith and pacience continueth their troubles, yea and often tymes augmeteth them as the Israelites were now in lesse hope of their liues then when thei were in Egypt. The fourth point is, that when the dangers are moste great, then Gods helpe is moste ready to succour: for the Israelites had on ether side the, huge rockes & mountaines, before them the Sea, behinde them moste cruel enemies, so that there was no way left to escape to mans iudgement.

Fig. 1. Illustration of Exodus 14 with a caption providing allegorical commentary. Geneva Bible (1560), fol. 30ᵛ. Reproduced by permission of the Huntington Library (call no. 55362).

same cause and religion that thei do. The third, that God delivereth not his Church incontinently out of dangers, but to exercise their faith and pacience continueth their troubles, yea and often tymes augmenteth them as the Israelites were now in lesse hope of their liues then when thei were in Egypt. The fourth point is, that when the dangers are moste great, then Gods helpe is moste ready to succour: for the Israelites had on ether side them, huge rockes & mountaines, before them the Sea, behinde them moste cruel enemies, so that there was no way left to escape to mans iudgement.

"The church of God" and "the ministers of God" indicate reflexive allegorical/typological interpretations of biblical Israel and the prophets. The tropological application (that Christians must demonstrate faith and patience) is less explicit but present.

The Geneva glosses sometimes treat historical episodes as if they are allegories of epochs in the spiritual life, rather as Spenser makes his allegory of St. George and the reformation in England in Book I serve also as an allegory of individual spiritual growth. The Geneva translation of Isaiah 11:1 reads, "there shal come a rod forthe of the stocke of Ishai [Jesse]." The gloss explains, "Because the captiuitie of Babylon was a figure of the spiritual captiuitie vnder sinne, he sheweth that our true deliuerance must come by Christ for as Dauid came out of Ishai a man without dignitie." The gloss then closes with a quintessentially medieval and utterly Spenserian analogy of the physical to the spiritual: "so Christ shulde come of a poore carpenters house as out of a dead stocke."

Conclusion

It is probably easier in the twenty-first century than it was in the sixteenth to see continuities between patristic example, the medieval categories, and Tyndale's and the Geneva commentators' biblical interpretive practice. Those continuities spring from a shared commitment to pointing all of human history, including an individual believer's life history, to Christ, and applying scripture's meaning to the life of the church.[65]

The patristic tradition of interpreting both literally and mystically or spiritually, as continued in Tyndale's principles and the Geneva Bible's glosses, can help twenty-first century readers make sense of some sixteenth-century English uses of the Bible that might otherwise seem peculiar. These uses (discussed in the next chapter) include the wholesale appropriation of scripture for officially distributed special prayers and liturgical services of the time – verses rewritten with plural pronouns (or feminine singular, if Elizabeth was being commemorated) and assembled into new "psalm collages"[66] in blithe disregard for their original form and, one might think, their integrity as sacred texts. The interpretive tradition can enable latter-day readers to appreciate the propriety of the typological applications of scripture that were standard in English sermons of the period: Old Testament stories were "about" the defeat of the Armada, or the success of the Reformation, or the urgency of providing funding for scholars at the universities. The exegetical tradition can even elucidate a project like Spenser's in *The Faerie Queene*: the words Spenser chooses to describe the way his poem relates to Elizabeth and her kingdom ("type," "shadow," "image," "figure") are those used by the church Fathers to describe the way the events and persons recounted in the Hebrew Bible

---

65 See David Lyle Jeffrey's review article "Houses of the Interpreter: Spiritual Exegesis and the Retrieval of Authority," *Books and Culture* 8.3 (May/June 2002), particularly 31.
66 I borrow this apt phrase from Susan Felch, for instance in her essay "'Halff a Scrypture Woman': Heteroglossia and Female Authorial Agency in Prayers by Lady Elizabeth Tyrwhit, Anne Lock, and Anne Wheathill," in *English Women, Religion, and Textual Production, 1500–1625*, ed. Micheline White (Burlington, VT: Ashgate, 2011).

are related to the person and life of Christ and those of his followers.[67] For Spenser's original readers, hearing "*good discipline sermoned at large, as they use,*" or even reading the Bible on one's own, always meant being invited to put oneself in the biblical text and to learn that the story was, paradoxically, both historically true and about oneself.[68] A "continued allegorie, or darke conceite" was a more familiar, less dauntingly arcane way to receive wholesome teaching than we, at a remove of four centuries, might be aware.

---

67 For instance, in the "Letter of the Authors" and the Proems to Books I, II, and III.
68 The Genevan commentator notes that later biblical writers read themselves backward into the earlier stories. While the text of Psalm 44:5 reads, "Through thee haue we thrust back our aduersaries: by thy Name haue we troaden downe them that rose vp against vs," the note explains that the thrusting back was done by earlier generations: "Because thei & their forefathers made bothe one Church thei applie it to them selues, which before thei did attribute to their fathers."

2

Allegorical reading in occasional Elizabethan liturgies

An occasional liturgy is a service of prayers and Bible readings responding to a specific occasion – a local or national emergency like an earthquake, epidemic, or threatened invasion, or a national celebration like the anniversary of Queen Elizabeth's accession to the throne. In order to appreciate how occasional liturgies relate to *The Faerie Queene*, it will be helpful to recall the biblical structure of the liturgy that Spenser's original readers regularly heard in church and were encouraged to use in household prayers.

The English church conformed to Christian tradition in reciting the Psalter each month. Along with the Psalms recited during Morning Prayer and Evening Prayer, one Old Testament and one New Testament "lesson" were also read, with the idea that, in the course of a year, daily worshippers would hear the Old Testament ("except certain books and Chapters, which be least edifying and might best be spared and therefore be left unread"[1]), selections from the deuterocanonical books, and the complete New Testament (three times). Holy Communion, a separate service following Morning Prayer on Sundays and holy days, also had scripture readings – an "epistle" (usually from the New Testament – one of the epistles, Acts, or Revelation – but occasionally from Isaiah or another Old Testament prophet) and a "gospel" (from Matthew, Mark, Luke, or John).

The liturgy's Bible readings and its overarching structure, the Christian year, made for a story-based worship service. The story of Jesus's life, of course, received the most emphasis: not only did the congregation recite its basic outlines in the Creed and memorialize the Passion in the communion service, but the New Testament lesson rehearsed the gospels and Acts three times each year during Morning Prayer, and each

---

1 *The Book of Common Prayer 1559: The Elizabethan Prayer Book*, ed. John E. Booty (Charlottesville, VA: University Press of Virginia for the Folger Shakespeare Library, 1976), 25.

Holy Communion throughout the year had its proper gospel reading. Occasional liturgies, then, reveal how Elizabethans perceived biblical story to reflect current events and related concerns, rather as *The Faerie Queene*'s allegorical fiction embodies ethical and national concerns.

The Church of England distributed many such liturgies during Elizabeth's reign, prescribing "psalms," prayers, and scripture readings it deemed appropriate for the given occasion. Bishops and freelancing clergymen occasionally did the same. These religious services mined the Bible as a source of commentaries on and allegories of Elizabethan emergencies.[2] This chapter will first look more or less chronologically at several of the liturgies that were distributed in response to crises, and then turn to Queen's Day liturgies. These services essentially trained Elizabethans to think about their national life by means of Bible stories. By the 1590s, this training provided Spenser with readers primed for enjoying *The Faerie Queene* as a moralizing roman à clef, an alternate way of thinking about their national life.

Praying through the plague

One of the earliest Elizabethan occasional liturgies is from 1563 and responds to "*this tyme of mortalitie, and other afflictions, wherwith the Realme at this present is visited*" – an epidemic of bubonic plague considered the worst in London's history.[3] This liturgy developed a theological explanation for this epidemic that would be applied to many subsequent crises as well: God had graciously appointed Henry to free the English people from the yoke of Roman tyranny and bring them the Bible in English. Under Edward, God benefited them with vernacular worship services and Protestant explanations of the sacraments. The English embraced Edward's reforms with insufficient enthusiasm, and merited punishment: hence Mary Tudor's reconciliation with Rome and burning of Protestants. Now, in the 1560s, God's mercy in placing Elizabeth on the

---

2 Alexandra Walsham, *Providence in Early Modern England* (Oxford: Oxford University Press, 1999) devotes a chapter section, "Prayers Fit for the Time," to these liturgies, demonstrating how they reinforced popular providentialism, the understanding that public and private events reveal God's will and work, and linking them with the "corporate acts of contrition" of medieval and Catholic communities (149).

3 More than 20,000 died, some quarter or third of the city's population. *A Fourme to be vsed in Common prayer twyse a weke, and also an order of publique fast, to be vsed euery Wednesday in the weeke* (London, 1563), sig. A1. STC (2nd edn) 16506. Available from the database Early English Books Online.

throne and Protestant ministers in pulpits was not sufficiently appreciated. "[H]ath he not nowe at the laste, after almoste .xx. yeres [i.e., since Edward's accession] pacience and forbearyng of vs, sent vs the pestilence …?"[4]

The 1563 liturgy's preface (by Edmund Grindal, Bishop of London, later to be celebrated in *The Shepheardes Calender*), notes that "particular punishments, afflictions, and perils" had moved David, Jehosaphat, Hezekiah, Judith, Esther, and Daniel to confession, fasting, and prayer. The orders Grindal made for the London parishes and which Elizabeth directed to be followed throughout the country were "to excite and stirre vp all godly people … to pray earnestly and hartely to God, to turne away his deserued wrath from vs,"[5] just as if the 1563 plague were biblical and Elizabethans were contemporaries of biblical figures.

Grindal ordered that parishioners (the sick explicitly exempted) be encouraged to attend Morning Prayer on Wednesdays and Fridays as well as Sundays and holy days, a direction that would be duplicated in subsequent occasional liturgies. The form also specified chapters of the Bible that should substitute for the usual rotation of biblical lessons. Ten Old Testament lessons, one per service, were prescribed: 2 Samuel 24 (called 2 Kings in the Great Bible; David's numbering of Israel and God's sending a plague as punishment), Leviticus 26 and Deuteronomy 28 (both lists of covenant blessings for obedience and, in much more detail, curses consequent to unfaithfulness), Jeremiah 18 and 22 (the parable of the potter, with God claiming his right to unmake his vessel Judah if he chooses; and the prophet's challenge to King Zedekiah to rule justly), 2 Chronicles 34 (called 2 Paralipomenon in the Great Bible; Josiah's renewal of Judah's covenant with God), Isaiah 1 (a denunciation of unfaithful Judah), Ezekiel 18 and 19 (an assertion that God holds each individual personally accountable for sin, a call for national repentance, and a lament for Judah's kings), Joel 2 (an apocalyptic description of "the Day of the Lord" followed by a call to repentance and promises of restoration), Nehemiah 9 (called 2 Esdras in the Great Bible; the returned exiles making communal confession for Israel's sins), and Jonah 2 and 3 (the prophet's prayer and release from the fish's belly, and Nineveh's repentance and God's relenting). By their inclusion in the plague liturgies, incidents in the history of Israel and Nineveh are presented as allegories of the situation in England in 1563; the lesson biblical writers drew (and the liturgy stipulates) explicates the meaning of unfolding events in the worshippers' lives.

4 Ibid., sig. D3^v.
5 Ibid., sig. A2.

The New Testament lessons, less narrative-based, similarly emphasized repentance: Matthew 3 (Jesus's baptism and John the Baptist's rebuke of religious leaders), Matthew 6 and 7 (assurances and admonitions from the Sermon on the Mount), Matthew 24 and 25 (the apocalyptic signs of Jesus's coming and the end of the age, and the parables of the ten virgins, the talents, and the sheep and the goats), Luke 13 (parables of the growth of Jesus's kingdom and the final judgment as well as the sole account of a supernatural healing among the readings), Acts 2:22–47 (Peter's call to repentance on Pentecost), Romans 2 (God's condemnation of all humanity), Revelation 2 (the messages of commendation, reproof, and encouragement for the first four of the seven churches: Ephesus, Smyrna, Pergamos, and Thiatyra), and several chapters challenging Christians not to continue to sin but to lead upright and obedient lives: Romans 6, 12, and 13, Galatians 5, Ephesians 4 and 5, and 1 Timothy 2.

According to Grindal's directive, the service on Wednesday morning should include a fifteen-minute period of silence for private prayer, the litany, communion ("so oft as a just number of communicants shall be thereto disposed"), and a sermon – or, in the absence of an authorized preacher, one of seven listed homilies (each was divided into two or three parts to prevent the service from being too long). The first listed, "An Homyly, concernyng the Justice of God, in punyshyng of impenitent synners, and of his mercies towardes all such as in theyr afflictions vnfaynedly turne vnto hym," by Alexander Nowell, Dean of St. Paul's, was "Newly nowe set forth for that purpose."[6] The others were from the 1549 Book of Homilies ("of the declynyng from God" and "agaynst the feare of death") and its 1563 counterpart ("of Fastyng," "of Prayer," "of Almes deeds," and "of repentaunce").[7]

The new "Justice of God" homily applies the curses of Leviticus 26 and Deuteronomy 28 to the present auditors:

> Seing we haue so long despysed his iustice, requiryng our innocencie, he can not but visite with his iustice, punyshyng our iniquitie, and that, he doth more iustly execute vpon vs, then he dyd vppon his people of any tyme before vs.[8]

Biblical examples of God's mercy also apply to the sixteenth-century hearers:

6 Ibid., sigs. D1, A3ᵛ.
7 Ibid., sigs. A3ᵛ–A4.
8 Ibid., sig. D3ᵛ.

> There is yet no cause for all this why we should dispayre or distrust: but rather that we shoulde turne from our synnes, and return to our mercifull father ...
>
> For the declaration wherof, it shalbe shewed out of the Scriptures: ... And here the testimonie of Job, a man both sore punished and most fauoured of God, hath a worthy place.[9]

Testimony from David, Hezekiah, Jonah, Hagar and Ishmael, and the thief on the cross followed Job's; the world of the Bible embraced and included sixteenth-century England no less than the ancient Near East.[10] Plague-beset Londoners, with their physical symptoms as evidence of divine judgment, were figured in the sufferings of Job, whose boils indicated his apparent divine abandonment. Redcrosse's chastisement in the House of Holinesse is morally significant in a similar way, promoting the same "vertuous and gentle discipline" as Grindal, its delivery enwrapped in an allegory featuring a fictional St. George rather than biblical heroes.

The liturgy places the sixteenth-century worshipper firmly in the biblical milieu:

> ... in dede the hole wrytynges of the prophetes, & vniversally of all the Scriptures, be nothyng els but lyke callynges to true obedience, and to repentaunce ... by lyke promises & threatnynges ... And to prosecute this matter ... Dyd not the Lorde at the laste bryng vpon them all those euyls which he had threatened, namely, famyne, warre, and pestilence ...?[11]
>
> Nowe to come to our tymes ... hath not God lykewyse begonne this order of proceadyng with vs ...? hath he not sent amongest vs his Prophetes and preachers ...? And hath he not, I pray you, prosecuted the same his proceadings ... by sendyng vs ... warres, famines, exyles, horryble fyers? And hath he not nowe at the laste ... sent vs the pestilence, which of all sicknesses we moste feare and abhorre ...?[12]

Obedience leads to blessing and prosperity; disobedience brings God's curse no less in sixteenth-century England than in Old Testament times. The wars with France, which culminated in the loss of Calais, crop failures, and subsequent food shortages, and the religious repression of Mary's time were all "lyke callynges to true obedience, and to repentaunce," making the 1547–63 generation contemporary with the wicked Ninevites whom God threatened to destroy, and then, upon their

---

9 Ibid., sigs. D4^v–E1.
10 Ibid., sigs. E4^v–F1^v.
11 Ibid., sig. D2^v.
12 Ibid., sigs. D3–D3^v.

repentance, mercifully spared. The liturgy's exploration of English history in terms of Bible stories is analogous to *The Faerie Queene*'s way of touching on some of the same moments of religious and dynastic change through its "historicall fiction."

The 1563 plague liturgy stipulated that on Fridays there was to be no sermon, but that on Wednesdays, Fridays, and Sundays throughout the time of the plague, the litany, a special psalm, and "one of the prayers newly appointed" follow the scriptural part of the service. This "psalm," like others distributed in subsequent occasional liturgies, was actually a collation of verses from separate scripture passages chosen for their relevance to the current situation – in this case, references to "sickness," "plague," and weakness as well as their petitions for God's forgiveness and compassion and their promises of future faithfulness. The collation uses the first person plural in place of the first person singular of some of the biblical originals, inviting all England's participation in the expression of suffering and repentance originally attributed David, Jonah, Job, Daniel, or Israel collectively, and now specifically claimed as their own.

A companion publication surviving in Grindal's *Remains*, *A Forme of Meditation, very meete to be daylye used of house holders in their houses, in this daungerous and contagious time* was "Set forth accordyng to the order in the Quenes majesties Injunction" and thus may also be considered an official publication.[13] This household meditation also sets the 1563 epidemic in a biblical context:

> Did not we, through our wicked lives, wretchedly leese [lose] the Ark of thy holy word and the true ministration of thy sacraments, not many years ago, which the popish Philistines took from us? And now, when thou, through thy plagues laid upon them, hast miraculously sent it us again; see how bold we be, with the Bethsamites, unreverently to receive it.[14]

This allegory retells the events of the previous decade as a version of 1 Samuel 4–6. The contents of the Ark of the Covenant included the tables of the Ten Commandments, which stand in for "thy holy word," or the English Bible, removed from English churches in Mary's time. Aaron's rod, which budded to indicate his divine ordination, also preserved within the Ark, represents "the true ministration" – in this context, a

---

13 *Remains of Edmund Grindal, D.D.*, ed. for the Parker Society by William Nicholson (Cambridge, 1843), Appendix V, 477–84. Nicholson quotes Grindal's letter to Cecil in August 1563: "There was committed also to the print a short Meditation, to be used in private houses, which I suppose is abroad" (478).
14 Ibid., 480.

priesthood and rituals authorized within the English church rather than by the Pope. The sample of manna within the Ark signifies "thy sacraments," perhaps understood in this context according to the memorialist words of the 1559 prayer book. The Ark, or reformed English religion, was captured by "the popish Philistines." In the biblical story, people in five different Philistine cities where it was lodged as a trophy then suffered plagues, and the Ark was then returned on a cart pulled by unguided newly-calved cows. The absence of human intervention would allegorically correspond, perhaps, to the deaths by natural causes of Mary and Cardinal Pole on the same day and to the contemporary political situation in "popish" France, Spain, and the empire, which prevented foreign interference in the English succession and religious settlement.

The Ark crossed into Israel's territory at Beth-shemesh, where (according to the Great Bible reading) God "plaged the men ... because they had sene the arcke of the Lord."[15] (Later translations, including the Geneva and Bishops' Bible, would clarify the boldness and irreverence by making this "looked into" or "loked in" the Ark.) Given the offering of "fyue golden arsses and fyue golden mice" placed inside the Ark, scholars have long speculated that the judgment affecting both the Philistines and Bethshemites was also bubonic plague. Thus, the Bible story was made to allegorize the 1563 London plague, just as Spenser would create allegorical equivalents for moments of England's national and religious life. Grindal's expectation, that his hearers would easily decode and apply the individual details of the biblical story to England ("Did not we wretchedly leese the Ark?"), suggests that such services trained them well to decode and apply the details of Spenser's fiction.

When the plague returned to London in 1593, the prayers and composite psalm together with the fasting directions of the 1563 liturgy were reissued.[16] The range of readings had narrowed. The recommended Old Testament lessons were 2 Samuel 24 (a 1563 lesson: David's numbering of Israel and God's sending a plague as punishment) and 2 Kings 24 (the final conquest of Jerusalem and exile of its inhabitants, a variation that might stem from a misreading of the 1563 service's listing of 2 Samuel 24 as "The .2. Kinges. Cap .24."); the New Testament lesson choices were

---

15 1 Samuel 6, *The Byble in Englyshe* (1539), STC 2068. Available from the database Early English Books Online.

16 *Certaine praiers collected out of a fourme of godly meditations, set foorth by her Maiesties authoritie in the great mortalitie, in the fift yeere of her Highnesse raigne* (1593), STC (2nd edn) 16524.

Matthew 6 and 24 (both options in 1563). Once again, Londoners were led to see themselves and their leaders in biblical characters' tribulations and divine rescue – just as (by 1590) Spenser's readers were invited to read themselves and their leaders in his historical fictions.

Liturgies for military crises: Turkish invasions

The siege of Malta from May to September of 1565, an episode in the long contest between the Ottoman Empire and Spain for control of the Mediterranean, terrified European Christians: if the "greate Armie and navie of Turkes, Infidelles, and sworne enemies of christian religion ... should preuaile againste the Ile of *Malta*, it is vncertaine what further peril might folowe to the rest of Christendome." The appropriate response, for English Christians, would be to follow "the examples of Moses, Josaphat, Ezechias, and other godlie men": to pray.[17]

The listed options for Old Testament lessons recount more or less decisive divine interventions in Israel's military history: Exodus 14 and 15 (the crossing of the Red Sea), Exodus 17 (the battle with Amalek), Judges 7 (Gideon's defeat of the Midianites with 300 men), 1 Samuel 23 (David's escape from Saul's pursuit), 2 Kings 7 (the lifting of the Aramean siege of Samaria in Jehoram's time), 2 Kings 19 (the angelic slaughter of Sennacherib's soldiers in the siege of Jerusalem during Hezekiah's reign), or 2 Chronicles 20 (the divine ambush against the Ammonites and Moabites in Jehosaphat's time). Just as Sansjoy, Sansloy, Sansfoy, and the Souldan create allegorical figures to represent a Turkish and, by extension, a Spanish Roman Catholic threat, so these liturgies allegorically present the Turkish threat as Egyptian, Midianite, Amelekite, Aramean, and Assyrian.

Notwithstanding the Knights of St. John's successful defense of Malta (celebrated with an officially distributed prayer of thanksgiving later in 1565[18]), much of Europe remained in Ottoman hands, and in 1566 the English church distributed another form of prayer seeking *"the preseruation*

17 *A forme to be vsed in Common praier euery Wednesdaie and Fridaie ... to excite all godlie people to praie vnto God for the deliuerie of those Christians, that are now inuaded by the Turke*, STC (2nd edn) 16508.3, sig. A1ᵛ. Available from the database Early English Books Online. The form quoted here was distributed within the diocese of Norwich. Clay edited a version whose title page designated it for "the cittie and dioces of Sarum," which is STC (2nd edn) 16508.7. The London version is STC (2nd edn) 16508.

18 *A short forme of thankesgeuing to God for the delyuerie of the Isle of Malta from the inuasion and long siege therof by the great armie of the Turkes both by sea and lande, and for sundry other victories lately obteined by the Christians against the saide Turkes* (London, 1565), STC (2nd edn) 16509.

of those Christians and their countreys, that are nowe inuaded by the Turke in Hungary or elsewher." The threat to England was stated more plainly than in 1565:

> ... if the Infidels, who haue already a great part of that most goodly and strong kyngdome in theyr possession, shoulde preuayle wholly against the same (whiche God forbyd) all the rest of Christendom should lye as it were naked and open to the incursions and inuasions of the sayde sauage and moste cruell enemyes the Turkes, to the moste dreadfull daunger of whole Christendome ...[19]

The 1566 liturgy has different composite psalms, but the list of first lesson readings is repeated from the 1565 service with two additional choices: Joshua 10, Israel's victory in the battle where the sun stood still, with the execution of the five kings; and Acts 12, which opens with Herod's execution of James, continues with Peter's escape from prison, and closes with Herod dying in agony after accepting idolatrous flattery. These passages, featuring the humiliation and death of enemy kings, were perhaps chosen to recall Suleiman the Great's death at the battle of Szigetvar. No explicit equivalence is made, but once again the biblical stories function as examples and similitudes analogous to those in Book V of *The Faerie Queene*, allegories of what God can still do for his people in the sixteenth century.

A prayer during severe weather

The winter of 1571 was unusually cold across Europe. John Parkhurst as Bishop of Norwich distributed a special prayer "*to be sayd in the end of the mornyng prayer daily ... during the tyme of this hard and sharp wether of frost and snow.*"[20] The prayer quotes "thy seruaunt Moses" speaking for God to the English:

> Yf ye will not obey me/ but [walk]e on stubbornely againste me/ I will ponish you yet [seven] times more according to your synnes/ I will breake [the pr]yde of your pour [power] and I will make your Heauen as [yro]n & youre Earth as brasse/[21]

---

19 *A fourme to be vsed in common prayer, euery Sunday, Wednesday, and Fryday, through the whole realme* (London, 1566), STC (2nd edn) 16510. Available from the database Early English Books Online.
20 STC (2nd edn) 16510.5. Available from the database Early English Books Online.
21 A tight binding obscures the first few letters along the left margin of the left column of the three-column broadside.

The divine threat most relevant to Elizabethans, however, "I will smyte you with fa[mine] & with sicknes/ with heate & with cold," is not from Deuteronomy. The prayer's speaker, performing Moses's function, can make free with his name, and threats original to the Sinai desert reach fulfillment in Europe's Little Ice Age.

The prayer continues in recalling God's further threats: "I will destroy [the la]boure of your handes/ the fruytes of ye Earth/ your [heife]rs & cattell."[22] After a confession of sin and unworthiness (in this case, no specific instances of religious or other unfaithfulness are alleged), the reader calls God's attention to the local situation:

> Loke done O Lorde from heauen/ with thy pitefull eyes/ behold our lamentable estate/ the deepe snow hath ouerwhelmed the Earth/ the nipping frost hath consumed the fruytes therof/ thou that bringest forthe herbes and grasse for the vse of man & beast/ behold all is consumed and spent almost/ thou that preseruest man & beast/ make som prouision for both/ the cattell do groue [sic, for "grone"] & make pitiouse complaint/ the heards do low/ the flockes do bleet/ the byrdes do crie to the for succour and relefe. Lorde if th[e]y sterue/ our bodily foode doth perish/ for thou hast gyuen them vnto vs for meat: they haue not sinned but we haue transgressed/ they nede not to repent/ but we which haue offended/

The peroration is also quite moving:

> We are heare O Lorde before thy Maiestie falling to the ground/ confessinge our sinnes with sorowfull hartes and sobing sighes in fasting/ weping/ and turning wholely vnto thee/ cranyng [sic, for "crauyng"] Perdon for all oure misdeeds/ promising amendment and reforming of our synfull life/ according to thy holy worde/ beseeching thee most hartely ... to take awaye (if it be thy fatherly will and most for thy glory and our commoditie) this hard & sharpe wether/ melt this snow/ miligate [sic, for "mitigate"] this frost/ make bare the face of the Earth/ bring forth fruytes and grasse for the use of man & beast/ gyue seasonable wether/ preserue the kindes/ of beast and foule/ which thou hast made for the seruice of man

The Bible with its Mediterranean setting does not record a situation parallel to Norwich's during the winter of 1571. Nevertheless, given the providentialist and typological outlook current at the time (the same outlook that would make Spenser's allegorical method comprehensible to his first readers), it was entirely routine that the bishop ventriloquize God's

---

22 "Heifers" is more speculative than the other bracketed readings, but it fits the context, occurs elsewhere in the Geneva translation Parkhurst appears to depend on, and ends in the right letters.

servant Moses, making him speak to and on behalf of his parishioners, expressing sixteenth-century English concerns through a text three millennia old.

Liturgy after the Massacre of St. Bartholomew's Day

Unlike the very explicit prayers against the Turks, which detail their occasion and name the enemy as "Turkes, Infidels, and miscreants" or "Turkes, Infidels, and other enemies of the Gospell" and "that wicked monster and damned soule Mahumet,"[23] the October 1572 publication *A fourme of common prayer*, responding to the religious violence that began in Paris on August 24, discreetly refers to "this daungerous and perillous tymes [sic] of the troubles in Christendome."[24] A similar reticence is observed in the prayers: as churchgoers prayed for deliverance from enemies and for their enemies' conversion, individual judgment (or unpublished pastoral direction) determined whether the enemies referred to were French Catholics, the Guises, the Pope himself, or Catholics in general, including English Catholics.

Like other occasional liturgies, the 1572 form lists which chapters of the Bible were to be substituted for lessons dictated by the calendar. Many of the listed readings, overlapping with those in the 1563 plague liturgy, call listeners to repentance (Matthew 3, Luke 15, Acts 9, and Romans 2) or admonish them about Christian moral behavior (Matthew 5, 6, and 7; Romans 12; and Ephesians 5). Others suggest that those authorizing the liturgy interpreted the massacre apocalyptically: Matthew 24 and Luke 21 focus on the signs of the end, including persecution of Christ's followers; Luke 17 responds to the question of when the end will come; and Matthew 25 and 1 Thessalonians 5 emphasize the need to be ready for the end. Other readings (not recommended in previous forms of prayer) refer to Jesus's anticipation of his death and the persecution his followers will experience (Matthew 10 and 16, Luke 18, Romans 12, and 1 Thessalonians 2). Some urge obedience to rulers (Romans 13 and 1 Timothy 2), perhaps as a reminder to English Catholics that God upheld the authority of their queen.

---

23 E.g., in the 1566 order, sigs. B4^v to C1^v.

24 *A fourme of common prayer to be vsed, and so commaunded by auctoritie of the Queenes Maiestie, and necessarie for the present tyme and state 1572*, sig. A2, STC (2nd edn) 16511. Available from the database Early English Books Online.

Uniquely among services of which I am aware, the 1572 form does not include any Old Testament stories of Israel in crisis among its lessons. This is not because England is the only country that can be allegorically compared to Israel: the liturgies responding to the Turkish threat indicate that English worshippers were invited to think of European Christians (French Protestants among them) as Israelites under Philistine, Assyrian, or Egyptian attack. Perhaps the allegoresis of "Hebraic patriotism" fit the conditions of sectarian civil violence less comfortably.[25]

Liturgies for acts of God: the London earthquake

Late in the afternoon of Easter Wednesday, April 6, 1580, an earthquake struck the Dover Straits. Perhaps between 5.3 and 5.9 on the Richter scale, it triggered a devastating tsunami which engulfed Calais and damaged buildings far inland in both France and England; in London, chimneys collapsed and two children were killed by stones falling from the roof of Christchurch, near Newgate (a contemporary note records that "they were hearing a sermon," as many did during Easter week).[26] Bishop John Aylmer distributed an *Order of prayer ... to auert and turne Gods wrath from vs* for use in his London diocese.[27] This service prescribes Joel 1, Joel 2, or Isaiah 58 (chapters denouncing sin, calling for repentance and "true fasting," and threatening "the day of the Lord" in apocalyptic terms) as Old Testament lessons and Psalms 30, 46, and 91 (all assurances of God's protection in physical danger, including references to earthquake in Psalm 46). The "Homily of repentance, or a part thereof" was to be read "if there be no sermon." The service was to close with the singing of Psalm 46 (musical notation and a versified version were included).

Aylmer's publication shows a pastoral sensitivity to his parishioners' trauma in appending "A prayer to be vsed of all housholders, with their whole familie, euery Euening before they go to bed." (One imagines Aylmer concerned that children might be reluctant to go to sleep.) The prayer is addressed to God on "the throne of thy mercie seate" and refers to the earthquake as

---

25 Graeme Murdock, "The Importance of Being Josiah: An Image of Calvinist Identity," *Sixteenth Century Studies* 29.4 (Winter 1998), 1043–59
26 William Keatinge Clay, ed., *Liturgical Services of the Reign of Queen Elizabeth*, Parker Society (London, 1840), 567, refers to "Dr. Williams's ms."
27 *The order of prayer vpon Wednesdayes and Frydayes, to auert and turne Gods wrath from vs, threatned by the late terrible earthquake* (London, 1580), STC (2nd edn) 16512. Available from the database Early English Books Online.

Allegorical reading in occasional Elizabethan liturgies 47

thy shaking, and mouing of the earth, which is thy footestoole … which wee most shamefully haue polluted and defiled with our most wicked, sinfull, and rebellious liues, notwithstanding thy continuall crying and calling vpon vs by thy seruauntes, the Prophetes and preachers.[28]

Given God's mercy, however, even the earthquake could result in good:

Turne this Earthquake, O Lorde, to the benefite of thine elect, as thou didst when thou shookest the prison, loosedst the locks, fetters, and chaines of thy seruauntes, Paul and Silas, and broughtest them out of prison, and conuerted their keeper.

The apostles Paul and Silas are types of Elizabethans. Aylmer's allegoresis turns the biblical story from Acts into a challenge: sixteenth-century Elizabethans are honored to relive the biblical earthquake and participate in similarly providential results.

Later in the month, the London service was reprinted "*to be vsed in all parish churches and housholdes throughout the realme*," by order of the Privy Council.[29] This national version was enlarged by "A prayer for the estate of Christes Church," which asks that God grant Elizabeth "a swift foote to hunt out the bulles of Basan" familiar from Psalm 22 (associated in contemporary religious discourse with the Church of Rome, particularly with the Pope's edicts, or "bulls") – further evidence of the utterly routine use of biblical images and stories to discuss events current in England.

The enlarged reissue also included Arthur Golding's "Report of the Earthquake" and homily "A godlie Admonition for the time present," which had earlier been published separately as "*A discourse vpon the earthquake*."[30] In his homily, which would seem to be included in the national liturgy as a handy alternative to the prescribed "Homily of repentance," Golding warned that the Easter earthquake, so terrifying while only taking two lives, was merely a precursor to a threatened future, much more devastating judgment:

---

28 Ibid., sigs. C4ᵛ–D1ᵛ.
29 *The order of prayer, and other exercises, vpon Wednesdays and Frydayes, to auert and turne Gods wrath from vs, threatned by the late terrible earthquake* (London, 1580), STC (2nd edn) 16513. Available from the database Early English Books Online.
30 *A discourse vpon the earthquake that hapned throughe this realme of Englande, and other places of Christendom, the first of Aprill. 1580. betwene the houres of fiue and six in the euening*, STC (2nd edn) 11987. Available from the database Early English Books Online.

Many and wonderfull wayes hathe God in all ages moste mercifullye called all men to the knowledge of themselues, and to the amendement of their Religion and conuersation, before he haue laid his heauy hand in wrathful displeasure vpon them.

For example, "He warned the old world a hundred yeare and more, before he brought the floud vpon the Earth." The recent earthquake was a chastisement, just as "He chastised the Children of Israel diuerse wayes, ere he destroyed them in the wildernesse."[31] The "God is English/the English are Israelites" trope was so familiar as to be instantly assimilable.[32]

"I feare me," the script prompts the reader of the "godlie Admonition" to say, "that if the Prophet Esay were here aliue, hee woulde tell vs as hee sometime tolde the Jewes, that from the crowne of oure head to the sole of our foote, there is no whole or sounde part in oure body, but that all is full of sores, blains, and botches."[33] God is dealing with the English as he dealt with Israel and Judah, and the London situation in 1580 is correctly interpreted (according to the authorities) by comparison to familiar Bible stories. Churchgoers were receiving training in hearing one set of stories while thinking about their country – training they might apply, ten years farther on, to a reading of *The Faerie Queene*.

Liturgies for military crises: the anticipated Spanish invasion

Allegoresis of biblical stories and discovery of their contemporary significance continued to be a keynote of occasional liturgies throughout the 1580s. In 1586, with the conflict with Catholic Spain becoming more acute, Archbishop John Whitgift of Canterbury distributed *An order for publike Prayers to be vsed on Wednesdayes and Fridayes*. The preface strikes the usual note in regretting insufficient enthusiasm for the reformed religion, "the elect & chosen vine of his gospel."[34] It summons the province of Canterbury to prayer in conventionally biblical terms:

---

31 *The order of prayer, and other exercises*, sig. C2.
32 "God is English" is a printed marginal note (sig. P8ᵛ) in John Aylmer's *An harborowe for faithfull and trewe subiectes* (London, 1559), STC (2nd edn) 1005. Available from the database Early English Books Online.
33 Ibid., sig. F2ᵛ.
34 *An order for publike Prayers to be vsed on Wednesdayes and Frydayes in euery parish church within the Province of Canterburie, conuenient for this present time set forth by authoritie* (London, 1586), STC (2nd edn) 4587, sig. A2. Available from the database Early English Books Online.

charge the watchmen of the Lords citie, diligently & carefully to sounde the Trumpet in Sion, to gather the people together, to teach them in sackcloth & ashes to repent, to will them inwardly to rent their hearts and not outwardly their garments onely ... saying, Spare thy people (O Lord) and giue not thine heritage & beloued vineyard into reproch, that the wicked seed of Antichrist rule ouer it.[35]

Thus, even the preface is an extended metaphor: the clergy ("the watchmen") of the established church ("the Lords citie") should preach ("sounde the Trumpet") "diligently & carefully" in the church building or other conventional preaching place, or in perhaps in London ("in Sion"). (They are "ordered and straightly charged" in more literal terms in the preface as well.)

The biblical chapters with lessons "conuenient for this present time" were several chapters of Isaiah: 5 (the "song of the vineyard" rebuking Israel for its unfaithfulness), 58 and 59 (condemnation of Israel's sin and call for a "true fast"), and 65 (Israel's desolation and God's creation of a "new heaven and new earth"); Ezekiel 17 (a parable interpreting Babylon's conquest of Judah as God's judgment, promising eventual return); Zechariah 7 (neglect of repentance and failure to amend led to Judah's exile); Joel 1 or 2 (which denounce sin and threaten "the day of the Lord" in apocalyptic terms); Jonah 3 (the Ninevites repent and God spares them); Luke 16 (the parables of the unfaithful steward and of the rich man and Lazarus, both exhorting to charity); Luke 21 or Matthew 25 (the signs of the end and related parables); and 1 John 3 (Christian love, the hatred of the world, and the necessity for obedience).

Biblical analogies to current challenges continue in the language of the actual prayers. The "Dearth and Famine" prayer prescribed for the service (along with that for "Time of War") recalls the lifting of the siege of Samaria during the time of Elisha: God "suddenly turn[ed] in Samaria great scarcity and dearth into plenty and cheapness, and extreme famine into abundance of victual." The biblical scenario is envisioned as playing out in the present: God is besought to similarly "increase the fruits of the earth by thy heavenly benediction."[36]

During this period of national anxiety over the anticipated conflict with Spain, one strategy was to forestall invasion by engaging Philip's forces abroad, first in the Low Countries and then in Cadiz. Leicester's campaign in the Low Countries was part of this policy, but *A most necessary and godly prayer, for the preseruation of the right honourable the*

---

35 Ibid., sigs. A2ʳ–A3.
36 *The Book of Common Prayer*, 75.

Earle of Leicester,[37] printed shortly after he embarked, was not an official publication; its Victorian editor, William Keatinge Clay, surmised that it was "set forth, probably, by the Puritans."[38] The prayer reminds God that "thou hast made *Englande* a chosen shaft, and put him in thy quiver" to be wielded against "all the enemies of thy trueth."[39] God is besought that Elizabeth's

> noble wise Counseller, the honorable Earle of Leicester, her highnes Lieuetenant in those Countries ... [will enjoy] so good and honorable victories, as *Iosua* had against the fyue Kinges ... fyght for him sweete Sauiour, as thou dyddest for *Abraham*, when he ouercame the four mighty Kings ... and grant that as *Iosua* ouercame *Amalech* that sought to hinder the children of *Israell*, by the prayer of *Moses*, that our noble Counceller, valient Souldier, and faithful seruaunt to her Maiestie, may preuaile and vanquishe thy enemies ...[40]

Leicester becomes a type of Joshua, Abraham, and again Joshua successively, and worshippers using the liturgy are aligned with Moses, in this case Queen Elizabeth, praying for Joshua's success. (The comparisons between Moses, Josiah, David, et al., on the one hand, and Elizabeth on the other, was established in English religious rhetoric a generation earlier with comparisons of Henry and later Edward to biblical figures.)[41] The discovery via allegoresis of the Elizabethan champion within the biblical story anticipates and helps to explain Spenser's first and second generation of readers' discovery of Leicester in *The Faerie Queene*.[42]

Of course these biblical heroes did not enjoy their success by virtue of sophisticated equipment, any more than Spenser's Arthur did:

> We confess, O heavenly Father, all power to come from thy seat: neither the Trumpets of Rams' horns wherewith *Jerico* fell, nor *Samson's* jaw bone,

---

37 (London, 1585), STC (2nd edn) 7289. Available from the database Early English Books Online.
38 Clay, *Liturgical Services*, 467.
39 *A most necessary and godly prayer*, sig. A2ᵛ.
40 Ibid., sig. A3.
41 Students of the period owe John N. King's *Tudor Royal Iconography: Literature and Art in an Age of Religious Crisis* (Princeton, NJ: Princeton University Press, 1989) a debt for drawing attention to and analyzing this characteristic phenomenon.
42 For instance in copies discussed by Anon., "MS Notes to Spenser's *Faerie Queene*," *Notes & Queries* 4 (1957), 509–15; Alastair Fowler, "Oxford and London Marginalia to *The Faerie Queene*," *Notes & Queries* 8 (1961), 416–19; and Graham Hough, "First Commentary on *The Faerie Queene*: Annotations in Lord Bessborough's Copy of the First Edition of *The Faerie Queene*," *TLS* (April 9, 1964), 294.

Allegorical reading in occasional Elizabethan liturgies 51

nor *David's* stone, nor the Pitchers of *Gedion* have power or strength to prevail without thee.[43]

God is asked to send the "holy Angell" of Psalm 34:7 to "pitch his Tent amongst them, and euer mightily defende them."[44]

The prayer for Leicester was adapted in 1587 for an official service responding to the continuing Spanish threat and offering thanks for Drake's victory in the harbor of Cadiz.[45] The comparisons with Abraham and Joshua and the pitching of divine tents appear in this shorter version of the prayer, which closes with a request (appropriating Psalm 33:12) "that we, thy little and despised flock, may say with good King David ... *blessed are the folk that [the Lord Jehovah] hath chosen to be his inheritance*."[46] England is Israel; biblical language is the rightful English idiom. Fluency in biblical language as a medium for discussing English history and current events would prepare readers to accept Faery Land as England and Spenser's allegorical fiction as another medium for such discussion.

Typically for the last decades of Elizabeth's reign, the service recycles elements of previous liturgies. The directions for the service lists "the Homilies of repentance, fasting, and alms-deeds, lately published" as those that should be read "when there are no sermons" – a reference to the official 1586 liturgy discussed above. Likewise the prayers "heretofore published upon the like occasions" are recommended for use. The list of alternate lessons available for allegorical application to the Spanish threat is very close to those prescribed for the 1566 prayers against the Turks: Exodus 14, Exodus 17:8 and following, Joshua 10, Judges 7, 1 Samuel 17 (a new entry: David's victory against Goliath), 2 Kings 7, 2 Kings 19, 2 Chronicles 20, and Acts 12. The only passages missing from the 1566 list are Exodus 15 (the poetic retelling of the Red Sea crossing, already narrated as prose in the prescribed chapter 14) and 1 Samuel 23 (the less sensational of two stories of David's escape from Saul). The emphasis on repentance and dependence on God is thus complemented

---

43 *A most necessary and godly prayer*, sig. A3ᵛ; as the copy available in the database Early English Books Online is illegible at this point, I quote from Clay, *Liturgical Services*, 606n.
44 Ibid., sig. A3ᵛ.
45 *A prayer and thanksgiuing fit for this present: and to be vsed in the time of common prayer* (London, 1587), STC (2nd edn) 16518. Available from the database Early English Books Online, but the available copy (from the Folger) is incomplete. I quote from Clay, *Liturgical Services*, 604–7.
46 Clay, *Liturgical Services*, 607.

by encouragement to hope for a military victory allegorically equivalent to the destruction of Pharaoh's army in the Red Sea, Gideon's victory over the Midianites, or the divine lifting of Sennacherib's siege of Jerusalem. Missing are any readings encouraging an apocalyptic mindset, such as some on the 1563 list, or steadfastness under persecution, such as those prescribed in 1572. Through a typological reading of this selection of passages, England is invited to picture itself before the fact as an unexpectedly triumphant Israel, rather as Spenser develops a triumphant historical fiction in Book V, which notoriously fails to match up with actual events involving a literal Spain and Netherlands (or a literal England and Ireland). Certainly the 1586 selection of readings anticipated the vindication of 1588 much more successfully than various episodes of Book V reflect recent events, but there was no way to know the outcome of the anticipated conflict with Spain when the list of Bible readings was compiled. Allegoresis, a skill honed in church services using the occasional liturgies, could reflect wishful thinking, which the literal event might or might not have justified.

In 1588, still anticipating a Spanish invasion, the official church once again distributed special prayers and readings. The resulting publication recycles elements from previous occasional liturgies (including a version of the preface from the 1563 plague liturgy, which observes that God "doth after a sort threaten vs with wars and inuasion"[47] rather than "visite vs at this present with the plague and other greuous diseases"[48]). Similarly, the Plague preface refers to "the time of these present afflictions," while the 1588 version refers to "the time of these imminent dangers." Whether microbial or military, God's visitation or threat is a reason in both prefaces "to pray earnestly and hartily to God, to turne away his deserued wrath from vs."[49] The service incorporates all nine prayers in the liturgy distributed after the St. Bartholomew's Day Massacre and adds two others. (Of the eleven prayers, three express repentance and request forgiveness, while eight request deliverance or preservation.) In addition to the Plague preface and the Massacre prayers, the 1588 "invasion eve" service lists the same readings as the previous year's, minus only Acts 12. These overlaps between the liturgies highlight how naturally, in the flexible sixteenth-century mind, the same biblical story can apply in different circumstances – different not only in the sense that a biblical event

---

47 *A fourme of prayer, necessary for the present time and state* (London, 1588), STC (2nd edn) 16519, sig. A2ᵛ.
48 STC (2nd edn) 16506, sig. A2.
49 Both forms on the sigs. noted above; the spelling is that of STC 16519.

differs from an Elizabethan one, but also as one set of Elizabethan circumstances differs from another. The Bible story can, in different official publications, allegorically encode different events. The flexibility of allegoresis, whether in biblical exegesis or in imaginative literature, is analogous to (and may to a certain extent account for) the ease that individual early readers of *The Faerie Queene* seem to have felt in identifying a major character with more than one contemporary person, or conversely discovering the same contemporary person in more than one character.[50]

Liturgies for plots

In 1585, after Dr. Parry confessed his plot on Elizabeth's life, Thomas Cooper, Bishop of Winchester, authorized *An order of praier and thankes-giving, for the preseruation of the Queenes Maiesties life and salfetie*.[51] Whereas many prefaces seem to envision that their directions would remain in effect for the foreseeable future, or until conditions changed, Cooper modestly suggests a one-time news-based sermon and prayer:

> First, where anie Preacher is, the next Sunday after the receauing of this order, he shall make a Sermon of the authoritie and Maiestie of Princes, according to the worde of God, and how streight dutie of obedience is required of all good and Christian subiects, and what a greeuous and heynous thing it is both before God and man traiterouslie to seeke their destruction ... In the ende of which Sermon, he shall set forth and declare the briefe notes of the confession of the wicked purpose conceaued of late by Doctor Parry, to haue murdered the Queenes Maiestie ... Last of all he shall saie the praier here prescribed ... After the praier, there shall be songe or said the xxi. Psalme, or some other Psalme to the like effect [i.e., that the king credits God with the victory he has experienced].[52]

The prayer itself explicitly compares England's experience to that of David's realm: "assuredlie if thou haddest not bene now on our side (as

---

50 Walter Oakeshott, in "Carew Ralegh's Copy of Spenser," *The Library*, n.s. 26 (1971), 1–21, notes that Lady Raleigh identified Timias, Marinell, and Calidore as Sir Walter. Andrew Fleck, "Early Modern Marginalia in Spenser's *Faerie Queene* at the Folger," *Notes & Queries* 55.2 (2008), 165–70 finds that the reader Brook Bridges saw both the Duke of Alva and Philip of Spain in Geryoneo, just as the seventeenth-century annotator discussed in the anonymous "MS Notes to Spenser's *Faerie Queene*" "has no difficulty in giving Arthur and Artegal a quite different significance [at Duessa's trial] from that which they bear in other parts of the allegory" (512).
51 (London, 1585), STC (2nd edn) 16516.
52 Ibid., sig. A1ᵛ.

the Prophet Dauid saith) the whole fluds and waues of wickednes had ouerwhelmed vs, and we had been sunk into the bottomeles pit of infinite and vnspeakable miseries." In an eminently typical bit of allegoresis, David's experiences of plot and danger are made to speak for Elizabeth's, further priming Spenser's readers to see her in Mercilla and Una, other royal maidens under threat.

A different prayer for the same occasion, authorized but unpublished, makes another familiar biblical comparison. Elizabeth's accession delivered "us thy people, that were as Captives to Babylon, out of bondage and thraldom."[53] The discovery of Parry's plot was so remarkable that, "all wonderful circumstances considered, we may compare it with any Example of thy most wonderful kindness shewed to any Kings or Nations of old time, testified to us in thy Holy Scriptures."[54] The examples, no doubt familiar from earlier occasional liturgies' prescribed "lessons," are left in this instance to the individual worshipper's recollection.

When the Babington Plot was uncovered in 1586, Archbishop Whitgift of Canterbury promulgated a special order of worship, *An order of prayer and thankesgiuing, for the preseruation of her Maiestie and the realme, from the traiterous and bloodie practises of the Pope, and his adherents*.[55] The preface exclaims that:

> *Moses* and *Miriam*, and the whole hoste of Israel had neuer greater cause to sing vnto the Lorde for the ouerthrowe of *Pharao* and his armie: nor *Debora* and *Barac* for the victorie of *Sisera*:[56] nor *Iudith*, and the Citizens of *Bethulia* for the end of *Holofernes* and the flight of his hoste, then we haue for the wonderfull preseruation of the life of our most gracious *Queene*, and thereby for our owne safetie.[57]

The prayer which follows decorously refers to "the strange discouering, and the maner of apprehending of the malefactors, being many"[58] – allusions to the details of secret ciphers, messages hidden in hollowed-out stoppers of beer barrels, and other skullduggery. Four composite psalms assemble verses of praise and thanksgiving, in particular those that celebrate national rescue and implore God's protection. The alternate first

---

53 "A Prayer of Thanksgiving for the deliverance of her majesty from the murderous intention of D. Parry," in Clay, *Liturgical Services*, 587–90 (I quote 587).
54 Ibid., 588.
55 (London, 1586), STC (2nd edn) 16517.
56 Sic, perhaps for "the victory over Sisera."
57 *An order of prayer and thankesgiuing*, sig. A2ᵛ.
58 Ibid., sig. A4ᵛ.

lesson passages ("when [the Minister] shall see occasion") are Exodus 15 (the poetic version of the crossing of the Red Sea), Judges 5 (the song of Deborah), and one of several chapters recounting Haman's conspiracy and the Jews' deliverance: Esther 6, 7, 8, or 9.[59] Whether Esther's, Deborah's, or Moses's, Elizabethans could, via the service's allegoresis, see themselves in the nation delivered.

Queen's Day liturgies

Official liturgies and prayers for specific occasions continued to be published through the last fifteen years of Elizabeth's reign, with biblical epithets used to refer to enemies abroad and plotters at home, the tendency toward reprinting of old prayers for new crises becoming more marked. The 1588 form is the last I am aware of that prescribes a list of chapters as substitute lessons to provide biblical analogies for the crisis at hand. The foregoing examples illustrate the purpose and method with which the English church sought to give its people a sense of contemporaneity with ancient Israel – how in every occasion the Bible was used as an allegory of current events.

The church calendar was the normal cycle into which these occasional liturgies intruded according to need. The Christian year, with its landmarks of Advent, Christmas, Epiphany, Lent, Easter, and Pentecost, was further punctuated by holy days honoring biblical saints who had their story read during Holy Communion. St. Stephen's day, for instance, was commemorated with an "epistle" about his martyrdom from Acts 7, while the "gospel" for St. Thomas's day was from John 20, where Jesus offers the doubting disciple sensory evidence of His resurrection.

Elizabeth eventually joined the company of Sts. Stephen, Thomas, and the rest in having her own yearly commemoration during Morning Prayer – an anniversary that thus had religious overtones in the minds of Spenser's first readers. About 1569 or 1570, according to the preface to Thomas Holland's 1599 Queen's Day sermon (published in 1601), the anniversary of Elizabeth's accession to the throne on November 17, 1558, began to be celebrated as a holy day. The observance was never legislated,

> but hath bin meere voluntarily continued by the religious and dutifull subiects of this Realme in their thankefulnesse to God, and in their perfit

---

59 Ibid., sig. B4ᵛ.

zeale, tendring her Maiesties preservation in desiring the continuance therof to Gods glory, & the good of the church and common wealth of England.[60]

Some critics noted that displacing Bishop Hugh of Lincoln and giving the Queen his holy day verged on the idolatrous; it effectively beatified her. Holland's published response to their critique demonstrates that the challenge was taken seriously.[61] Eventually the day's festivities, or "celebrities publike," as he called them, included bell-ringing, bonfires, and triumphal processions.[62] But all of these "exercises and disports" were secondary from a priest's point of view, for whom the observances of "November's sacred seventeenth day" properly began with Morning Prayer.

The Accession Day order of service varied from the usual Morning Prayer in the same way other Holy Day liturgies did: by substituting different readings and prayers. In 1576, quite early in the history of Accession Day celebrations, the church authorized a liturgy for the occasion, *A form of Prayer, with thanks giving, to be used every year, the 17. of November, being the day of the Queen's Majesty's entry to her reign*,[63] marking the official inclusion of Elizabeth's accession in the English church year.

The official commemorative service is prefaced by 1 Timothy 2:1-3, the scriptural warrant for the Accession Day service: "I exhort you therefore, that first of all, prayers, supplications, intercessions, and giuing of thankes be made for all men: for Princes, and for all that are in authoritie ..."[64] The service proper opens like the standard Morning Prayer, substituting the "special Psalmes" 21, 85, and 124 for Psalms 86, 87, and 88, which would otherwise have been read in the morning on the 17th of the month. The lessons that would normally be assigned to November 17 (Ecclesiasticus

---

60 Thomas Holland, Ρανηγυρίς *D. Elizabethae, Dei gratia Angliae, Franciae, & Hiberniae Reginae. A sermon preached at Pauls in London the 17. of November Ann. Dom. 1599. the one and fortieth yeare of her Maiesties raigne, and augmented in those places wherein, for the shortness of the time, it could not there be delivered* ... (Oxford, 1601), STC 13597, sig. N4. Available from the database Early English Books Online.

61 Ibid., sigs. L4–O1.

62 Ibid., sig. P2.

63 *A fourme of prayer, with thankes geuyng, to be vsed euery yeere, the .17. of Nouember, beyng the day of the Queenes Maiesties entrie to her raigne* (London, 1576), STC (2nd edn) 16479. According to the Victorian editor, Henry Keatinge Clay, it was reissued in a more convenient format ("You shall vnderstand, that euery thing in this booke is placed in order, as it shall be vsed, without turning to and fro") in 1578 (Clay, *Liturgical Services*, 548), but this version is unavailable from the database Early English Books Online.

64 *A fourme of prayer*, sig. A1.

36 and John 9) were likewise replaced by designated passages in honor of the day. The first lesson offered a choice of three readings, each a composite of selections from multiple chapters recounting highlights from the stories of Jehosaphat (from 2 Chronicles), Hezekiah (from 2 Kings), and Josiah (also from 2 Kings). As usual, the substitute lessons were chosen to offer an interpretation of the current situation in England and for their implicit parallels to Queen Elizabeth's reign.

The second lesson, Romans 13, begins in the Bishops' Bible with the injunction, "Let euery soule be subiect vnto the hyer powers: For there is no power but of god. The powers that be, are ordeyned of God." After this reminder that Elizabeth ruled by divine right, the officiant and congregation prayed antiphonally for the Queen's continued health and safety and proceeded to "the Collect for the Queene, ... as it is in the Letanie."[65] Next follows a psalm, actually a collation of verses from eleven biblical psalms dwelling on themes of troubles past: enemies and exile, God's deliverance, and thanksgiving. The effect is, as usual, to place Elizabethans within the biblical text, presenting, for instance, the impression that the exile referred to in Psalm 107 was of the English in Geneva rather than Judeans in Babylon. Like other composite psalms, this collage uses the first person plural in place of the first person singular of some of the originals, inviting worshippers to identify with the biblical expressions of suffering and rescue.

There is no explicit direction that communion was to be part of the Accession Day service, but after another prayer for the Queen, Bible readings proper to the communion service (the epistle and the gospel) are incorporated: "For the Epistle of the day, reade i Pet. ii. beginning at ... *Dearely beloued, I beseche you.* &c. to ... *Feare God, honour the kyng.*" The Gospel ("reade Math. xxii.") offers further biblical endorsement for civic duties, recounting the conversation between Jesus and the Pharisees about the lawfulness of paying tribute to Caesar. After these exercises, the worshippers were to sing "The.xxi. Psalme in Metre" and hear a sermon, then sing another metrical psalm, the hundredth.[66]

---

65 Ibid., sig. A8.
66 Ibid., sig. B1v. The 1578 reissue that Clay saw offers, instead of the direction about the last two psalms, a metrical "thanksgiving, to be sung as the 81. Psalm," which appeals to God for various graces for Elizabeth ("A noble ancient Nurse, O Lord,/ in England let her reign:/ Her grace among us do afford,/ for ever to remain" [Clay, *Liturgical Services*, 558–60]); an anthem for use at Evening Prayer; and "A song of rejoicing for the prosperous Reign of our most gracious Sovereign Lady Queen Elizabeth."

Just as Thomas and Stephen and the other saints were commemorated on their days by a reading of their stories, the Old Testament lessons effectively recounted Elizabeth's story on her festival day. The readings present the monarch's reign in the light of two themes: her zeal in suppressing idol worship and promoting true religion, and England's dependence on God for national security. The stories of Hezekiah, Jehosaphat, and Josiah offer allegories of Elizabeth's service to God and His favor and care. Jehosaphat "sought the Lorde God of his father," "put downe yet more of the high places," and "sent Leuites ... [who] taught in Juda, and had the booke of the lawe of God with them, and went about ... and taught the people"[67] – a coded way of celebrating Elizabeth's reissue of her brother's prayer book, suppression of upapproved rituals, and sponsorship of the English Bible and a reformed clergy. Similarly, Hezekiah as her allegorical stand-in "brake the images," "claue to the Lorde," and "kept his commaundementes which the Lorde commaunded Moses."[68] Josiah likewise "brake downe the aulters of Baalim," saw "the decayed places of the temple repayred," and mourned that "our fathers haue not hearkned to the wordes of this booke."[69] Since the Bible itself included no literal accounts of Elizabeth, allegoresis created them.

In each case, God rewarded religious faithfulness by defending the nation: "when Jehosaphat ... was in great danger to be slaine, he cried vnto the Lord, and the Lord helped him, and chased his enimies away from him"; on another occasion, Jehosaphat's "enimies fel out amongst themselues, and slue one another."[70] Likewise, after Hezekiah appealed to the Lord the Assyrian commander broke off his siege of Jerusalem; during a later siege, "the angel of the Lorde went out, and smote in the hoast of the Assyrians, an hundred foure-score and fiue thousande."[71] Josiah received God's promise that Judah would enjoy peace during his time ("thyne eyes shall not see all the euyl which I wyll bryng vpon this place"); the reading does not include his death in battle with Pharaoh Neco.[72]

Thus, in the absence of any scriptures about Elizabeth, biblical liturgies celebrated her religious reforms and England's enjoyment of domestic and international peace through Hebraic patriotism in an allegorical

---

67 *A fourme of prayer*, sig. A2ᵛ.
68 Ibid., sig. A3ᵛ.
69 Ibid., sigs. A6, A6ᵛ.
70 Ibid., sigs. A2ᵛ, A3.
71 Ibid., sig. A5.
72 Ibid., sig. A7.

mode and on a heroic scale. On November 17, Josiah or Hezekiah or Jehosaphat "was" Elizabeth; their image-breaking and sending forth of Levites shadowed her religious reforms, whether already achieved or anticipated; their military success celebrated England's security and expressed pious hope for continued peace.[73] And though the comparisons to godly kings flatter Elizabeth, preachers amply demonstrated that such allegoresis also offered the opportunity to counsel the Queen on her duty – for instance, to uphold true religion by maintaining and promoting a godly and learned clergy as Supreme Governor of England's church.

So were the frolics of November 17 routinely preceded by the service? Edmund Bunny, in an alternate service privately published in 1585, suggested in his dedication to Archbishop Whitgift that "order shoulde be taken for the continuance of the exercise begunne in your Graces Predecessors time." His alternate liturgy would fill a void: the English had, he considered, "litle ... endeuoured our selues to bee thankefull" to God for Elizabeth's "godly and blessed raigne," and have been "negligent suters vnto him ... for the continuance of it."[74] His *Certaine prayers and other godly exercises, for the seuenteenth of November: Wherein we solemnize the blessed reigne of our gracious Soveraigne Lady Elizabeth* was published, like the authorized form, by the Queen's printer Christopher

---

73 See Chapter 6, below, for an Accession Day sermon that compares the Assyrian army's fate with the destruction of the Spanish invasion fleet in 1588.

74 *Certaine prayers and other godly exercises, for the seuenteenth of Nouember: Wherein we solemnize the blessed reigne of our gracious Soueraigne Lady Elizabeth* (London, 1585), STC (2nd edn) 4089, sig. A2. Available from the database Early English Books Online. Disinherited by his disappointed father when he declined to study law, Bunny became one of Grindal's protegés and an itinerant preacher, holding prebendaries in York, London, and Carlisle to support his work as a traveling evangelist. Bunny's service raises questions: if the authorized Accession Day service was indeed neglected, as he claims in his prefatory letter, how does that reflect on the use of other officially promulgated liturgies? When the Privy Council or a bishop so directed, did parishioners actually hear the special psalms, prayers, and chapters deemed relevant to a national crisis? It is important to note that the 1576 liturgy had official sponsorship and was "set forth by authoritie" in a reformatted version in 1578 and again in 1580, suggesting it enjoyed not only government support but also some level of demand. Also, the only two printings of Bunny's *Prayers* were both made the same year, the difference being in the A gathering, where one version, STC (rev. edn) 4089, is dedicated to Archbishop Whitgift of Canterbury and the other, STC (rev. edn) 4089.5, to Archbishop Sandys of York. It seems likely that Bunny was the one who felt most acutely the English church's need for his Accession Day service, and that the more and more frequent resort to occasional services during the last two decades of Elizabeth's reign suggests that the government believed them to be useful.

Barker. It follows to some extent the order and content of the official service, but substitutes prayers with clearer references to the occasion and provides commentary at many points. After the quote from 1 Timothy prefacing both his and the authorized form, Bunny notes that

> the Apostle, requiring thus much on the behalfe of those Magistrates, that then were hinderers of the glory of Christ; he requireth the same more iustly of vs, to whom God hath giuen so godly a Princes, and with her such a maner of gouernment, as directly tendeth to the aduauncement of the Gospell of Christ.[75]

For the General Confession "as in the book of Common prayer" stipulated in the official Accession Day liturgy, Bunny substitutes a "generall Confession" of unworthiness and ingratitude for God's mercy in giving England "so gracious a Princes, and with her so blessed a gouernement ... such as our fathers at no time haue seene."[76]

In lieu of the psalms prescribed in the official service (95, 21, 85, and 124), Bunny substitutes two composite psalms repackaging scripture to create new biblical poetry about English experience, thus inserting Elizabeth and her subjects into the sacred text. He explains that the composite psalms are

> to call to remembrance, in what case the Church of God with vs was, immediately before the reign of our gracious Soueraigne: so to finde out, howe good cause we haue in that respect to be thankefull to the maiestie of God for her. And the miserie that here is described, we found not onely in the cause of religion, but also in the ciuil estate likewise: from both of which it hath pleased God by her to deliver vs.[77]

First-person marginal glosses elucidate the psalm's treatment of recent English history: "Our miserie. In ciuill accompt. In Religion. Our miserie in generall further amplified. Our deliuerance."[78] The second psalm similarly

> set[s] forth vnto vs, how egerly yet the enemies of the Gospel are bent against our Superiors, and vs, for the Gospels sake; that so, whereas notwithstanding it hath pleased God euer to defend vs, we may therein perceiue, howe much we are bound to God for the same, and (if we respect a secondarie cause) to the prudent, and godly gouernement of our gratious Soueraigne. Wherein, first appealing to their owne conscience for their

---

75 Ibid., sig. B1ᵛ.
76 Ibid., sigs. B1ᵛ–B2.
77 Ibid., sigs. B2–2ᵛ.
78 Ibid., sigs. B2ᵛ–B3ᵛ.

naughtie dealings, afterward is described both how busily they endeuour our vtter destruction, and how litle (by the goodnes of God) they preuaile therein.[79]

Thus Bunny joins the authors of previous occasional liturgies in ignoring any humanist concerns about the original psalms' compositional and thematic integrity: on November 17, the Bible was about England's history, its narratives so many vehicles for the tenor of Elizabethan celebration.

After a Gloria Patri "for giuing vnto vs so gracious a Princesse, and for preseruing her in so good estate,"[80] came the lessons: "Certaine portions of Scripture taken out of the olde Testament: the one of Dauid, the other of Salomon. Which declare vnto vs, how carefull good Princes are on the behalfe of the glory of God, and, how well God doth like on them for the same." Bunny did not leave the discovery that Queen Elizabeth is typologically shadowed or allegorically enwrapped in these scriptures to the unscripted comment of the minister or the imagination of the individual worshipper:

> Which thing the more that we finde in our gracious Soueraigne, the more are we bound to God on that behalfe, and the better assurance may we conceiue of the protection and fauour of God towards her and al her people, against the open forces and secret practices of all her enemies.[81]

The first passage recounts how David, when his intention to build a temple was declined, saw that the Lord "did graciously accept of [my] willing minde" and "prepared with all my might ... gold, ... siluer, ... brasse, ... iron, ... and tymber."[82] A psalm of thanksgiving (again collated by Bunny) intervenes between the first and second lessons.

David's and Solomon's "great zeale ... towardes the house of the Lord"[83] found its counterpart in "the gouernement that nowe is established" and its care to repair "the ruines of [God's] Temple" – that is, the English church. Elizabeth's attention to the health of the church was good for the country: "howe speciall assurance, any State that followeth the same, may conceiue of the vndoubted protection of God."[84]

After the second lesson, the congregation proceeded to another composite psalm "of the excellencie of the Kingdome of Christ, desiring to

79 Ibid., sig. B4.
80 Ibid., sig. C1ᵛ.
81 Ibid., sig. C1ᵛ.
82 Ibid., sig. C2ᵛ.
83 Ibid., sig. C3
84 Ibid., sig. D2.

haue the same enlarged."[85] It is clear that Bunny envisioned the Accession Day service as including Holy Communion from his provision of "A Proper Preface" corresponding to those provided in the prayer book for the seasons of Christmas, Easter, Ascension, and Whitsunday:

> Especially at this present, not only, for that it hath pleased thee of thine infinite goodnes, long ago to do away our mourning weede and to clothe vs with ioy & gladnes, in giuing vnto vs so gracious a Princes ... but also, for that against many strange and mischieuous practises, most vniustly intended against her, at home & abroade, thou hast euer since preserued her in wonderful maner, and dayly yet doest, to the singular comfort of vs her subiects. Therefore with Angels, etc.[86]

There follows a Ramian "Table, declaring in what sort we may fruitfully solemnize the blessed reigne of our gracious Soueraigne." Bunny notes that it "may be some helpe to some of the Ministerie, with lesse labour of theirs to note vnto the people, whereunto to gather their consideration for this present" – i.e., to generate material relevant for a Queen's Day sermon – with topics ranging from "very good blessings" of the Queen's "outwarde" person and her "more inwarde, or speciall graces," to the behavior that should emanate from a thankful people ("Both in holines of life, generally: And in diligent following of our speciall functions besides, euery one as he is called"), to the means "to endeuour the continuance" of her reign (prayer, financial, and military support).[87] In its anatomy of the Queen's praiseworthy attributes and its program for the improvement of individual members of the audience, the table is closely related to Spenser's "Letter" to Raleigh explaining his plan for *The Faerie Queene*. "An Antheme" of three six-line stanzas rounds out the publication.

The relevance of Elizabeth's accession and its anniversary to *The Faerie Queene* could hardly be stronger. Sixteenth-century annotator John Dixon "interprets the marriage of Una and Redcrosse as the marriage of the true (English) church to Christ, an event which to him took place on the accession of Queen Elizabeth."[88] Furthermore, Roy Strong has identified Accession Day as a possible prototype for Gloriana's annual feast,[89] and one aspect of that feast was the religious commemoration. *The Faerie*

---

85 Ibid., sigs. D4–4ᵛ.
86 Ibid., sig. E2ᵛ.
87 The table is folded and glued into the book between sigs. E2 and E3.
88 Hough, "First Commentary on *The Faerie Queene*," 294.
89 Roy Strong, "The Popular Celebration of the Accession Day of Queen Elizabeth I," *Journal of the Warburg and Courtauld Institutes* 21 (1958), 86–103 (86).

Queene shares a design with Accession Day liturgies: it is a collection of stories to honor and celebrate and admonish the Queen; a collection of stories in which she is supposed to see herself and others are supposed to see her. Bunny's bid for patronage can be useful to us, then, in its unusual explicitness in pointing out the parallels between biblical kings and Elizabeth. Other occasional services, including the official Accession Day liturgy, leave such parallels implicit, taking allegoresis for granted as the normal way of using the Bible. By belaboring these links, Bunny confirms our sense of how Hebraic patriotism worked – as allegoresis, a strategy of biblical interpretation, whether on Accession Day or in any other Elizabethan context, which read (for instance) "England" for "Israel," "Elizabeth" for the exemplary king or queen under discussion, and "the church of England" for "the Temple."

Conclusion

Learned Spenserians have shown us that allegory is a rhetorically sophisticated and philosophically problematic mode, and that Spenser's use of that mode is oversimplified at our peril. This study complements such work, contending that *The Faerie Queene*'s original readers were conditioned in their interpretation of its "darke conceit" by one particular strand of biblical interpretation that was common at the time: allegoresis, the discovery of hidden messages about contemporary personages, events, and concerns in biblical texts. This tendency, as demonstrated in the current chapter, is quite evident in the official church's occasional liturgies and most striking in liturgies for Accession Day services.

The November 17 liturgies' celebration of Elizabeth via a series of stories of biblical kings is analogous to *The Faerie Queene*'s "shadowing" Elizabeth via a range of characters and their adventures. In *The Faerie Queene*, too, spiritual reform and military victory are indispensable themes in the celebration and admonition of Elizabeth.

Hebraic patriotism, then, represents a form of allegoresis culturally current in Spenser's day. In the next chapter about sermons, I will present more evidence that this use of scripture was wildly popular and the texts featuring such allegoresis invited straightforward interpretation, though the resulting sermons' tone ranges from admonition to celebration. These sermons provide parallels with Spenser's project and have been overlooked as an important analogue.

3

Allegorical reading in sermon references to history and current events

The writers of Accession Day liturgies, as we saw in the previous chapter, discovered in stories of Josiah, Hezekiah, and David allegorical versions of the achievements and adventures of their own Queen Elizabeth. In doing so, they followed traditions of biblical interpretation traceable back to the writers of the New Testament. The traditional view of history – not the only one current at the time, but the one allowing Bible stories to signify sixteenth-century events – was articulated by Augustine, Jerome, and Orosius. It emphasized, in Patrides's words, "the linear nature of history, beginning with Adam, with its 'central datum' in Jesus, and with its 'uni-dimensional movement in time' leading to the end" – that is, to the Last Judgment.[1] This view of history insists that temporal events have meaning because they reflect God's intention. C. S. Lewis writes,

> The Hebrews saw their whole past as a revelation of the purposes of Jahweh. Christianity, going on from there, makes world-history in its entirety a single, transcendentally significant story with a well-defined plot pivoted on the Creation, Fall, Redemption, and Judgment.[2]

"World-history in its entirety" includes not only such biblical events as the Creation, the Fall, and Redemption, but classical and modern history, and contemporary events, even local happenings of no interest to historians or outsiders. History moves in only one direction (in contrast to the cyclical view of the Platonists), but within the linear progression of the one story are echoes and repetitions of key plot points, resemblances between individual events that reward typological analysis.

---

1 C. A. Patrides, *The Grand Design of God: The Literary Form of the Christian View of History* (London: Routledge, 1972), 17.
2 *The Discarded Image: An Introduction to Medieval and Renaissance Literature* (Cambridge: Cambridge University Press, 1964), 174.

Thus, according to this traditional view, all of history should be read in the context of the Bible, as part of the same God-authored story. "God is the authour of historie," says Peter Martyr.[3] According to Charity,

> To God's acts, or at least to his fulfilling act, whether promised or past, Christianity claims, all events are related and related historically. They have the same ultimate causes as it, and they all share together with it in the one order of contingent cause and effect, in the same history of act and response.[4]

The study of history thus became a search for spiritual meaning: "by studying the past we can learn not only historical but also metahistorical or transcendental truth."[5] If God is the author of events, then those events will be expressive and mutually resonant, as are elements in any other purposefully created work of art. A providentialist view provides biblical scholars with the basis for recognizing these mutual resonances, which appear as patterns and repetitions – types and antitypes – and deepen and focus the meaning of the whole. Barbara Lewalski explains that typological interpretation "takes the Bible not as a multi-level allegory, but as a complex literary work whose full literal meaning is revealed only by careful attention to its poetic texture and to its pervasive symbolic mode – typology."[6]

As demonstrated in the preceding chapter, the authors of occasional liturgies for the English church embraced typology as a form of allegory inhering in the events recounted in the biblical text: Elizabeth "was" David, Hezekiah, and Josiah. For biblical scholars of their providentialist outlook, "Typological exegesis is ... not a disclosure of the *sensus plenior* [fuller sense] of the text ... It is rather a disclosure of the plenitude

---

3 Peter Martyr Vermigli, *The common places of the most famous and renowmed diuine Doctor Peter Martyr diuided into foure principall parts: with a large addition of manie theologicall and necessarie discourses, some neuer extant before*. Translated and partlie gathered by Anthonie Marten (London, 1583), vol. I, p. 49, STC (2nd edn) 24669, available from the database Early English Books Online. Vermigli's Latin *Loci communes D. Petri Martyris Vermilii, Florentini* was published in London the same year (STC [2nd edn] 24668), also available from the database Early English Books Online. Marten's translation of the Virmigli compilation comes as close to a normative summary of the learned Elizabethan theological consensus as we have.
4 A. C. Charity, *Events and Their Afterlife: The Dialectics of Christian Typology in the Bible and Dante* (Cambridge: Cambridge University Press, 1966), 5.
5 Ibid., 174–5.
6 Barbara Lewalski, *Protestant Poetics and the Seventeenth-Century Religious Lyric* (Princeton, NJ: Princeton University Press, 1979), 117.

and mysterious workings of divine activity in history."[7] Here is Thomas Holland, Paul's Cross preacher on Accession Day 1599,[8] explaining typology to his congregation:

> this figure or type is mystically vnderstood of the whole text of the old testament, secretly woven in by the spirit of God, as the threed is, which the shittle carieth in the silkemans web, by which the partes of the whole are combined togither ... The figure I mention oft ... giueth life and inlighteneth the history, as the arteries giue life to the blood in the vaines ... And this is the salt, that seasoneth the old testament, without which oftentimes there is no more taste in the story of it, then in the white of an egge. The testimony of Christ is the spirit of prophecy.[9]

Holland paraphrases Augustine:

> not onely the tongue of those men, but the life also was propheticall ... Wherfore concerning them whose heartes were instructed in the wisedome of God, the prophecy of Christ, and of the church which was to come is to be scanned not only in their sayings, but in their doings also.[10]

Elizabethan divines embraced the traditional hermeneutic of typology based on the providentialist view of history. The occasional liturgies did not expound the biblical text so much as reveal the richness of the "single, transcendently significant story" in extending beyond the canon of the Old and New Testaments. For the Bible is not unique in this texture and mode. To one who holds this providentialist view of history, all history – current events and the details of one's personal life no less than well-known Bible stories – shares the same author and is thus subject to the same interpretation.

Lewalski does not see this; thus, when she discovers Protestant extensions of typology, she sounds surprised: "remarkably enough, Protestant exegetes assimilate the lives and experiences of contemporary Christians to the typological paradigm of recapitulations and fulfillments throughout history" – the "correlative typology" that puts the English "on much

---

7 Michael Fishbane, *Biblical Interpretation in Ancient Israel* (Oxford: Clarendon, 1985), 352.
8 Πανηγυρίς *D. Elizabethae Dei gratiâ Angliae Reginae a sermon preached in Pauls Church at London the 17 of November in the yeare of our Lord 1599, the 42 yeare of the most flourishing reigne of Queene Elizabeth* (London, 1601), STC (2nd edn) 13597. Available from the database Early English Books Online.
9 Ibid., sig. B1ᵛ.
10 Ibid., sig. B2.

the same spiritual plane" as Israel, "saved by faith and waiting in hope."[11] Thomas Luxon sees the implications of this historical paradigm, and is correct in his observation that, for those who subscribe to it, "life in this world is allegory."[12]

Lewalski finds it remarkable that ordinary people with their small concerns assimilated themselves to this pattern of providential history; Luxon seems a trifle contemptuous of a person who is content to "identify … one's self and one's own experience as figural, rather than fully real."[13] Other students of the period seem not to quite fathom that their sixteenth- and seventeenth-century counterparts actually held this providentialist view of history, and this failure leaves them unable to appreciate either typology or allegory in traditional terms. Hence Gordon Teskey speaks of all allegory as arbitrary and metaphorical, with a void between material and form, "the flesh and the letter," the events and the providential pattern that he would see as being arbitrarily, violently, imposed on them.[14] Perhaps because he does not share the widespread (though not universal) early modern conviction that all events proceeded from the hand of God and expressed his will, Teskey assumes that the "unrestrained totalization … we have observed in the fundamental image of allegory [is that of] Man enclosing the cosmos" rather than God as author.[15] Conversely, giving sensitive attention to this traditional way of treating history, both biblical and secular, ancient as well as recent, helps us understand Spenser's method when he represents historical figures in his fiction.

Though they believed God was author of "the single, transcendently significant story" and did not think of themselves as "enclosing the cosmos," many Elizabethan preachers accepted the role of expositor, seeking to show how various historical events, whether ancient or contemporary, momentous or minor, distant or local, fit into the "transcendently significant story" and to apply their "metahistorical or transcendental truth" to their congregations. Of course this notion of history was not universal

11 Lewalski, *Protestant Poetics*, 131, 126.
12 Thomas H. Luxon, *Literal Figures: Puritan Allegory and the Reformation Crisis in Representation* (Chicago and London: University of Chicago Press, 1995), 29.
13 Ibid., 43.
14 Gordon Teskey, "Allegory, Materialism, Violence," in *The Production of English Renaissance Culture*, ed. David Lee Miller, Sharon O'Dair, and Harold Weber (Ithaca, NJ: Cornell, 1994), 293–318 (315).
15 Gordon Teskey, *Allegory and Violence* (Ithaca, NJ: Cornell, 1996), 187. It is ironic but telling that Teskey finds that "Notable among [Spenser's] weaknesses is his lack of an imaginative grasp of the problem of history" (174).

in Elizabethan times – witness, for example, Philip Sidney's objection that history is too "captived to the truth of a foolish world" to furnish reliable moral instruction. But even if in this life one sees "the cruel Severus live prosperously,"[16] traditionalists would retort that when his history is seen in the context of the Last Judgment, it is less likely to move a student to emulate his cruelty.

Secular history in sermons

Writers of sixteenth-century guides to sermon preparation part company with Sidney; they assume that history, properly contextualized, teaches morality, and that preachers will use it. The reservations Niels Hemmingsen has about the use of certain "historical" material in moral instruction are quite different from Sidney's:

> the papistes, & especially the monkes ... haue laide before vs I know not what counterfaite petie sainctes, & haue fained them to haue liued al their life long so blameles, that they neuer offended, no not in the least thing. Such a fained description of persons, maketh rather to disperation then to the edifieng of the conscience, wrastling with the greatnes of sinne, & of the wrath of God. Therfore let vs take vnto vs true examples, and let vs leaue fayned examples for the Poetes, whiche are not to be handled of them whiche are called by saint Paule the Stewardes of the misteries of God. The sacred scripture and the true historie doth minister examples sufficiently.[17]

Hemmingsen's quarrel with the use of saints' lives as moral instruction was that the saints pictured there are unbelievably good; the model offered by such "fayned examples" is therefore ineffective for teaching. His concern about "the papistes" recalls Tyndale's in the "Prologue to Jonas":

> And one of the chiefest and fleshliest study they have, is to magnify the saints above measure and above the truth and with their poetry to make them greater then ever God made them. And if they find any infirmity or sin ascribed unto the saints, that they excuse with all diligence, diminishing the glory of the mercy of God and robbing wretched sinners of all their comfort.[18]

---

16 Philip Sidney, *A Defence of Poetry*, ed. Jan Van Dorsten, in *Miscellaneous Prose of Sir Philip Sidney* (Oxford: Clarendon, 1973), 90.
17 Niels Hemmingsen, *The Preacher, or methode of preaching* (London, 1574), sigs. D4–D4^v, STC (2nd edn) 13065. Available from the database Early English Books Online.
18 William Tyndale, "The Prologue to the Prophet Jonas," in *Tyndale's Old Testament: Being the Pentateuch of 1530, Joshua to 2 Chronicles of 1537, and Jonah*, ed. David Daniell (New Haven, CT: Yale, 1992), 629.

In contrast to Sidney, who values the poet because "he will show you in Tantalus, Atreus, and such like, nothing that is not to be shunned; in Cyrus, Aeneas, Ulysses, each thing to be followed,"[19] Hemmingsen and Tyndale consider consistency with human experience and Bible teaching more forceful spiritually than a flawless example.

Andreas Hyperius of Marburg, author of another handbook for preachers, agrees that the veracity and the consistency of historical examples with the doctrine of scripture are important conditions for their use:

> But in all Sermons ... this Caution is in any wise to bee marked and taken heede off, namelye that nothinge bee brought in or aleadged, but that whiche is certaine, substanciall, sounde, taken out of the holy Scriptures ... or out of the chiefe & moste allowable Historyographers, and by all meanes agreeinge with the doctrine expresly contayned in the volume of the Sacred Bible.[20]

In the event, many Elizabethan preachers showed much more interest in a purportedly historical incident's moral meaning than its factuality – a preoccupation they may have shared with (or even transmitted to) the readers of Spenser's allegory. For instance, John Dixon, who made his annotations in the 1590 *Faerie Queene* in 1597, "makes muddles about the surface narrative. Again and again he dives right through the story to the moral purpose underneath. It may be that in this he was not untypical of the readers of Spenser's day."[21] Certainly preachers regularly invited the poet and his readers to locate spiritual meanings in morsels of secular history.

From a preacher's point of view, even without any typological reference, history was essentially a compendium of exempla in which people do or say things for the sake of moral instruction. "All these things happened vnto them for ensamples," according to Paul as rendered by the Bishops' Bible translation of 1 Corinthians 10,[22] and what was true of the Israelites under Moses was just as true of figures of secular history. Classical history offered Anthony Rudd an illustration of ancient

---

19 Sidney, *A Defence of Poetry*, 88.
20 *The Practise of preaching, otherwise called the Pathway to the Pulpet*, trans. John Ludham (London, 1577), fol. 15, STC (2nd edn) 11758.5. Available from the database Early English Books Online.
21 Graham Hough, "First Commentary on *The Faerie Queene*: Annotations in Lord Bessborough's Copy of the First Edition of *The Faerie Queene*," *TLS* (April 9, 1964), 294.
22 Available from the Chadwyck-Healey database The Bible in English.

heroes who "numbered their days" in an exemplary way. According to his sermon's citation of Plutarch, the Spartans, in their solemn assembly, "were accustomed to decline themselues through three tenses of the Indicatiue moode." The "first Chorus ... of old men" would say, "*We were* once renowmed in the wars." The "lustie gallants, brauing it," would assert, "*We are* such men, make triall if you dare." The "boyes with great signe of militarie towardnes" would add, "*We shall be* one day farre more strong and valiant." This example from classical history illustrates a spiritual ideal also recorded in Rudd's text, Psalm 90:12, "Teach vs so to number our dayes, that we may applie our hearts vnto wisedome." Rudd reminds the Queen and her subjects that "it is meet for euery man to fall a numbring his yeares, that he may exactly know what place of seruice is assigned vnto him for the defence of the Realme."[23] Rudd did not claim that the Spartans were consciously putting the psalmist's words into practice, but he and his auditors considered Spartan culture part of the "single, transcendentally significant story" of salvation, and their traditions thus carried spiritual significance – or he at least considered their behavior a meaningful illustration of the psalm's admonition. In a world history authored by God, patterns will appear, and non-biblical material may help the preacher make his point.

The same principle led Spenser's friend and patron, Bishop John Young of Rochester, to allude to Alexander in his court sermon on ambition. He characterized ambition as

> a worme that dyeth not, a fire that goeth not out, it is immortall, unquencheable, as unsatiable as the graue, or as hell, it neuer sayeth [n]oe, it never hath inough, haue it neuer so muche. I reade of one who was so immoderate in this behalfe, that hee would not sticke to saye, that if he had made a conquest of all the earth, of the whole world, it woulde not satisfie him, and that he would bee right hartely sory that there were no more worlds to conquere.[24]

Young ignored Alexander's literary reputation as an ideal ruler and prince, using him as a counterexample to the Christian virtue of humility.

---

23 Anthony Rudd, *A sermon preached at Richmond before Queene Elizabeth of famous memorie, vpon the 28. of March, 1596* (London, 1603), 32, 1, 33, STC (2nd edn) 21432. Available from the database Early English Books Online.

24 John Young, *A sermon preached before the Queenes Maiestie, the second of March. An. 1575* (London, [1576]), sig. A8, STC (2nd edn) 26110. Available from the database Early English Books Online.

The same providentialist conviction that, as part of one God-authored story, classical history illustrates spiritual truth allowed Stephen Gosson, in proclaiming the sovereignty of God, to recall that

> *Pompey* was wont to say, that with one stampe of his foote hee could haue all *Italy* in armes. God may say that with one stampe of his foote hee can ouerthrow all *Italy*, and all the worlde beside when it is in armes.²⁵

Pompey's boast is typically remembered as irony: during his final contest with Caesar, senators taunted with him with its hollowness. But Pompey's humiliation was not Gosson's point. The fall of the Roman republic did not interest him; his concern was the spiritual truth he could memorably illustrate for his auditors.

Such illustrative anecdotes were perhaps even more effective when they referred to figures in English history, and thus took strength from the appeal to patriotic pride. In a court sermon in 1587, after listing several biblical kings whose godliness was rewarded by national prosperity, Peter Wentworth climaxed his catalog with a reference to British history:

> I wil onlye recite the wise exhortation, that S. Gregorie geueth Aldiberga, Queene of England in the behalfe of her husband, King Aldibertus … Gregorye … counselleth that godly & deuout Q. (being forward in the Gospell) that her husband Aldibertus king of England, in hope of his owne heauenly saluation, do winne also his subiects vnto Christianity.²⁶

The reference to the godly and devout Aldiberga is, strictly speaking, superfluous; a preacher could just exhort Queen Elizabeth on the basis of scripture to work for the spread of the gospel among her subjects. But Wentworth was confident that British history is fully as inspiring and instructive, its example as authoritative, as is the Bible.

A spiritually instructive passage of history could even be humorous, as is this tidbit selected by Bishop Curteys from the time of the Wars of the Roses for a 1573 court sermon. The preacher was condemning time-servers:

> They will leaue truthe, iustice, and equitie, and play the Englishe Coliar, who first met King Henry the sixte souldiers, and was beaten of them,

---

25 Stephen Gosson, *The trumpet of warre A sermon preached at Paules Crosse the seuenth of Maie 1598* (London, 1598), sig. D3ᵛ, STC (2nd edn) 12099. Available from the database Early English Books Online.
26 Peter Wentworth, *A sermon faithfullie and trulie published according as it was preached at the courte, at Greenewiche, the Twesday in Easter weeke* (London, 1587), sigs. B5–6, STC (2nd edn) 25346. Available from the database Early English Books Online.

for that he sayde he serued king Edward the fourth: Nexte he met king Edwarde the fourthes souldiers, and was beaten of them, for that he sayde he serued king Henry the sixt: Afterwarde he met a thirde bande of men, to whome he answered he serued the Diuell, who when they bad him be gone in the diuels name, so he answered he would: for quoth he, I haue bin beaten of king Henries men, and king Edwards men, for answering that I serued the one, and then the other, and now I haue sayd I serue the Diuell, I go without hurte, he is the beste master I met with this morning.[27]

Another humorous anecdote from the opposite end of the social scale concerned the limitations of human monarchs. One imagines Richard Madox chose this story for its special resonance with his congregation of mariners:

> It is written of *Edgar*, a King of the English *Saxons*, that walking on the stronde for his recreation at an ebbe, so soone as the floodde beganne, and he lothe to leaue walking, hee setteth downe his foote by the water syde, and thus began to speake: I charge thee thou Sea, to staye thy selfe, and you byllowes, that ye recoyle backe, touche not my foote, least I be angrie, and so thou perishe (for the displeasure of the King is death to the Subiect.) I am thy Soueraigne, and Lorde of thy Streames, and vnder mee thou holdest thy water channell. What? Dyd the Sea, thinke you tremble at his voice, or was the floodde quailed to heare him speake? no hardelie. For had hee not saued himselfe by flight, the salte foome would haue washed his tynsell Gowne. Which when the King had well espied, turning to his Bishops and Nobles that stoode by, hee charged them all straightlie, not to flatter him thenceforth, with any loftie tytle of power or puissance, because there was in him no might at all.[28]

Madox followed this anecdote with a reference to the famous story about Cyrus: when a favorite horse drowned in a tributary of the Tigris, he swore that he would break the river's power.

Such *dicta* and *acta* attributed to historical figures were not meant to illuminate the course of secular history directly and were often unconnected to crucial events in the lives of nations. Nevertheless, Edgar's insight, Cyrus's unreasonable impatience, Alexander's ambition,

---

27 Richard Curteys, *A sermon preached before the Queenes Maiestie, by the reuerende Father in God the Bishop of Chichester, at Grenewiche, the 14. day of Marche. 1573* (London, 1573), sigs. C7ᵛ–8. STC (2nd edn) 6135. Available from the database Early English Books Online.

28 Richard Madox. *A learned and a godly sermon, to be read of all men, but especially for all marryners, captaynes and passengers, which trauell the seas* (London, 1581), B8ᵛ–C1, STC (2nd edn) 17180. Available from the database Early English Books Online.

Pompey's claims of authority, and the collier's lack of commitment were not embellishments introduced to relieve a sermon's weighty moralizing, but encouragement to read the deeper meaning of history. Even minor details preserved spiritual meaning.

The Bible and recent English history

The use of history as example implies that it required careful interpretation. Even controversial and confusing events were assumed to reveal God's will and illustrate his purposes, provided they were understood correctly. When a particular spiritual interpretation of recent events required authoritative support, biblical analogies were helpful in establishing that meaning. One controversial figure, Anne Boleyn, was interpreted in flattering terms by John Aylmer, who was to become Bishop of London under the new Queen Elizabeth. Aylmer teaches that, like the biblical Queen Esther's, Anne Boleyn's personal attractions were a positive force in English history:

> Was not Quene Anne the mother of this blessed woman, the chief, first, and only cause of banyshing the beast of Rome, with all his beggerly baggage? was there euer in Englande a greater feate wrought by any man: then this was by a woman? I take not from kyng Henry the due praise of broching it, nor from that lambe of God king Edward, the finishing and perfighting of that was begon, though I giue hir, hir due commendacion. I know that that blessid martir of God Thomas Cranmer Byshop of Canterbury, did much trauaile in it, and furthered it: but if God had not gyuen Quene Anne fauour in the sight of the kynge, as he gaue to Hester in the sight of Nabucadnezar [sic, for Ahasuerus]: Haman and his company, The Cardinall, Wynchester, More, Rochest. and other wold sone haue trised vp Mardocheus with al the rest that leaned to that side. Wherfore though many deserued muche praise for the helping forwarde of it: yet the croppe and roote was the Quene, wiche God had endewed with wisdome that she coulde, and gyuen hir the minde that she would do it.[29]

Aylmer wrote in the first year of Elizabeth's reign, but scriptural comparisons as assertions of spiritual meanings for persons and issues were to be routine for generations to come. Thus Curteys, preaching in 1573,

---

29 John Aylmer, *An harborowe for faithfull and trewe subiectes agaynst the late blowne blaste, concerninge the gouernme[n]t of wemen. wherin be confuted all such reasons as a straunger of late made in that behalfe, with a briefe exhortation to obedience* (London, 1559), sig. B4ᵛ, STC (2nd edn) 1005. Available from the database Early English Books Online.

reminded his auditors of the "thornes and troubles" England had experienced under Catholic Mary Tudor and Archbishop Pole, comparing them to the notoriously murderous Queen of Israel "Athalia and hir bloudye Priest Matham."[30] In other sermons, Mary was compared with Saul, persecuting the anointed and godly David (Elizabeth). Thus biblical figures and stories functioned in sermons as they did in the liturgies discussed in the preceding chapter: as encoded versions of the Queen, her people, and other figures in current events, providing further evidence of the flexibly allegorical habit of mind churchgoing promoted for Spenser's first generation of readers.

The meaning of a historical fragment within the overall story – in the context of the Fall, Redemption, and Judgment – had to be more or less fixed before a preacher could employ it as a useful example; otherwise it would confuse rather than clarify. To recall the example of Wat Tyler, for instance, would not clarify the idea of overreaching, rebellion, or disobedience for a congregation that regarded him as a democratic hero, but Tyler's moral valence was clear enough to a courtly audience that he could lend negative weight to the idea of ambition, as in this passage of the sermon by Bishop Young of Rochester quoted earlier:

> It is commonly and truely sayde, that Jacke would be a gentleman, & no doubt so he would, and a noble man too, and a Prince if it might be. The historie of Jacke Cade, alias Jacke Strawe, Wate tyler, Bob carter, Tom miller, that rable and route of rascals, proues this mater sufficiently.[31]

For an Elizabethan audience, the moral message, once established, could inhere in the historical reference. In officially sanctioned religious texts, at least, the Peasants' Revolt evoked such a negative response that participants' names could be brought to bear against the evils of ambition or, as we will see, the attempted "innovation" of Essex.

Since kings ruled by the will of God, the example of an unsuccessful rebellion of any magnitude held, at least in Elizabethan sermons, negative moral value. The failure of such revolts was thus a moral and spiritual, as well as a political, victory credited to God's intervention. In his Queen's Day sermon of 1587, Edward Harris stressed that God judges those who resist the king, and cited biblical examples: Absalom revolt against David and Korah, Dathan, and Abiram's revolt against Moses. National history was just as instructive on the subject of rebellion:

---

30 Curteys, *A sermon preached before the Queenes Maiestie*, sig. B6.
31 Young, *A sermon preached before the Queenes Maiestie*, sigs. B1–1^v.

Allegorical reading in sermon references to history

Adde hereunto the examples of late traitors in this our owne Countrie, as *Sommeruile, Throgmorton, Babington,* & their complices, which like dunghill cockes entending to pearch vppon the head of this realme to the destruction thereof, were iustly constrained to crowe their last vppon the gallowes.[32]

John Somerville, an unstable young Catholic who boasted at an inn of his plan to shoot Queen Elizabeth with his pistol, had been imprisoned in Newgate (and found strangled within two hours) in December 1583. Francis Throckmorton, at work organizing a fifth column in anticipation of an invasion to free Mary Stuart, had been executed for treason in July 1584. Anthony Babington, whose plot finally provided Walsingham with evidence requiring Elizabeth to act against Mary, had been executed in September 1586. The government's view of these men and their activities is here presented as authoritative as the biblical tradition.[33]

Just as the audience understood the biblical revolts to be evil, they were supposed to accept that divine power overthrew the contemporary workings of moral and spiritual wickedness. God's intervention on Elizabeth's behalf was not only a religious interpretation of events but political propaganda, and a blessing was promised to those who rightly honored and served her. As Harris prayed, "The like (O Lord) we beseech thee bring vpon all the enemies of Elizabeth thine anointed, but let peace be vpon the Israel of God, and vpon all that vnfainedly seeke her true honour in the right feare of the Almightie."[34] Here we see national history paralleling the biblical history of notable rebels against Moses and David, with both the ancient and contemporary stories revealing God's protection of his anointed servants (and, not coincidentally, the English nation allegorized as "the Israel of God"). Further, the spiritual meaning of the failure of various traitors and plots was so well understood that Harris could drop familiar names of plotters to support an argument for Elizabeth's divine authority.

---

32 Edward Harris, *A sermon preached at Hitchin in ... 1587. the 17.day of Nouember* (London, 1590), fol. 79, STC (2nd edn) 12804. Available from the database Early English Books Online.
33 For instance, according to the *Dictionary of National Biography*, Somerville's strangulation in his cell was officially explained as suicide, and the fact that Walsingham himself provided the letters-in-the-beer-barrel system for Mary's correspondence with conspirators (and then postponed arrests until Mary had committed herself) gives the outcome a less providential appearance.
34 Harris, *A sermon preached at Hitchin*, fol. 79.

Reading and misreading contemporary history: Essex's rebellion

A noteworthy example of competing scriptural analogies to establish the meaning of recent events is William Barlow's Paul's Cross sermon after the execution of the Earl of Essex.[35] Ostensibly Barlow's text was Matthew 22:21,[36] which he quoted as "*Giue vnto Cæsar the things of Cæsar, and vnto God the things of Gods*," but his exposition of scriptural texts validating the monarchy prefaced an exposition of contemporary history – an interpretation enriched by comparison to sacred and classical history. "*Coriolanus*," for instance, "a gallant young, but a discontented Romane ... might make a fit paralell for the late Earle, if you read his life," suggests Barlow.[37] The sermon continues with an account of the earl's return to England in arms, his refusal to answer the Queen's summons, his abortive assault on the court, and his subsequent confession in the Tower and ultimate execution. Barlow interprets the events he described with comparisons to scripture.

One detail in the story of Essex's downfall illustrates that the practice of drawing parallels between scripture and current events was common beyond the pulpit and could delude as well as enlighten. Barlow quotes such a parallel, "which much mooued me against" Essex. Dr. Thomas Dove, Dean of Norwich,

> asking him why he refused to come to the Lords, being sent for by the appointment of her Maiestie, he answered that, by Scripture, and thus reasoneth, *Dauid* refuseth to come to *Saul* when he sent for him: *Ergo* I might lawfully refuse to come to Queene *Elizabeth*.[38]

This bit of scriptural reasoning, adopting the role of David and casting the Queen as Saul, shows just how deeply ingrained a cultural habit the drawing of analogies between scripture and daily life was late in Elizabeth's reign. (Equally apt as a demonstration of this compelling cultural habit is the familiar but unsubstantiated bit of allegoresis attributed to Elizabeth upon the Shakespearean performance that the earl's party commissioned at the Globe: "I am Richard II. Know you not that?")

---

35 William Barlow, *A sermon preached at Paules Crosse, on the first Sunday in Lent: Martij 1. 1600 With a short discourse of the late Earle of Essex his confession, and penitence, before and at the time of his death* (London, 1601), sig. B3, STC (2nd edn) 1454. Available from the database Early English Books Online.
36 The epigraph mistakenly prints the reference as Matt. 21:22.
37 Ibid., sig. C3ᵛ.
38 Ibid., sigs. C5–5ᵛ.

Allegorical reading in sermon references to history

Essex's allegorical suggestion that God had rejected of Elizabeth in favor of Essex provoked Barlow into an exasperated digression on what constitutes allowable allegoresis: "Heere a diuine cannot be patient, to see Gods worde alleadged in despight of Gods ordinance." Just as Tyndale commended and created allegories when the rhetorical point thus embellished was consistent with a faithful reading of scripture as a whole (see Chapter 1), Barlow insisted that allegoresis must be supported by relevant comparisons:

> For, God be thanked, there is no semblance of this example ... Because *Saule* was rejected by God, but Queene *Elizabeth* is the chosen and the beloued of God, which from heauen by his prouidence ouer her, as in shielding her from many, so from this *Presumptuous* attempt, he hath demonstratiuely shewed. *Dauid* by a Prophet, at Gods appointment was anoynted King, so was not he.[39]

Like Tyndale, Barlow had great contempt for inaccurate allegoresis:

> thus the deuil delt with Christ *Math. 4* in quoting a place of Scripture to iustifie the breaking of his neck. And *Clement* the Frier who killed *Henry* the third the French king, reasoned thus with himselfe to his bloudy murther out of Gods booke, *Ehud* killed king *Eglon*, therefore I may kill *Henry*. *Eglon* was a king, so is *Henry*. What then? *Eglon* signifieth a Calue and *Henry* is a Caluenist, *Ergo* I may kill him by authoritie of Scripture ... Let Papists lay these grounds, and make these proofes, I am sory that any, who carries the name of a Protestant, should argue thus. It is the speach of *Salomon, he that wrings his nose, fetcheth out bloud*, which *Gregory* fitly applies, that he which wresteth the Scripture from the true sence, bringeth foorth either an herisie or a phrensie ... when an interpretation, like a Uiper, eates out the bowels of the text.[40]

Barlow, like Essex, recognized biblical analogies as providing guidance in contemporary situations. They share an exegetical strategy that assumed that biblical figures and Elizabethans were essentially contemporary. Thus, rather than objecting to an identification of Essex with David by citing the incongruities of 2500 years' difference in circumstance, or dismissing as sacrilegious a comparison of an ordinary human to a hero of a sacred text, Barlow seriously examined the terms of comparison. Elizabeth's character makes her impossible to read as Saul. The earl's situation and credentials exclude him as a type of David. Allegorical reading

39 Ibid., sig. C6.
40 Ibid., sigs. C5^v–C6.

of current events in biblical terms was allowable, but Essex proved himself a poor reader.

Indeed, Barlow himself was committed to Essex's method:

> this his offence and treason [is] the compound of all the famous rebellions eyther in Gods booke, or our owne land: (which himselfe in other words scatteringly expressed:) consisting of *Abners* discontment, of *Korahs* enuie, of *Absalons* popularity, of *Shebas* defection, of *Abimelechs* faction, and banding his familie and allyes[,] of *Hamans* pride and ambition: in pretence finall, all one with that of *Henrie* Duke of Lancaster, against *Richard* the second, *remoouing certaine which misled the King.* In pretence originall, that of *Kettes* and *Tylers* for the King, as they in your city cryed in that insurrection *for the Queene, for the Queene.*[41]

Barlow thus read recent history not only in light of the biblical admonition to obey those in authority, but also by comparing it with biblical events and British history, choosing points of reference that were already well understood. As Barlow's evocation of Korah, Absalom, and Haman in the same breath as Henry of Lancaster and Wat Tyler makes clear, English history and biblical history were interchangeable in their value as guides to understanding the present. They were part of the same universal story of God's dealings with men. Both offered a set of characters and situations by which to read, to allegorically interpret, what was unfolding in contemporary London. The events that brought down the earl, events "such daily as styll come to passe," were only the most recent incidents in the unfolding drama of salvation history. Fresh news, secular history, and biblical events were appropriate material for preachers, whose insight and learning qualified them to distill spiritual truth from all three, presumably with more accuracy than the monks or the unfortunate Essex.

In summary, then, typical preachers regarded history as a revelation of God's will, since God was the ultimate controller of the destinies of nations and of men. That revelation, however, required careful analysis and interpretation. Indeed, history records much that, read by the ignorant (or a rebel like Essex), might appear to endorse rebellion or be the result of mere chance, rather than a guiding Providence. Allegoresis might be done correctly or incorrectly. However, tradition had already assigned moral and spiritual value to most biblical as well as many well-known historical figures and events, and when such references were already charged with moral content, the preacher could avail himself of

---

41 Ibid., sigs. D5–5ᵛ.

Allegorical reading in sermon references to history

these as examples to illustrate or even allegorize his immediate points. When recent events demanded exegesis, the preacher proceeded carefully in demonstrating the aptness of a biblical comparison and drawing the appropriate spiritual lesson.

Typology in theory and practice: an Accession Day sermon

Let us return to Holland, quoted at the beginning of the chapter as he defined typology for the large festival audience at England's premier pulpit on the Queen's Day in 1599. His specific interest in typology is dictated by his text, Matthew 12:42, which he gives as "The Queene of the South shall rise in iudgement with this generation, and shall condemne it: for shee came from the vtmost partes of the earth, to heare the wisedome of *Salomon*: and beholde, a greater then *Salomon* is heere."[42] Jesus rebukes his Jewish contemporaries for being backward in appreciating his wisdom and mission, since the non-Jewish queen was so eager to visit Solomon. The preacher reviews the story Jesus invokes and finds much to praise in the Queen's forwardness:

> shee neither careth to parch her beauty in the sun, which many women are so nice to preserve: neither the fiery climate, vnder which shee was to passe: nor the fury of the beastes, the eie of the ravenous crocodile, neither the venimous serpents, wherwith those coasts doe swarme: neither the fell Lyons, which those Climates naturally nourish ... but, all excuses set apart, shee cometh to Ierusalem to see *Salomon*.[43]

But the Queen is not just herself. For Holland as for the Fathers, "the Queene of the south, a figure of the comming of the gentiles vnto Christ," represents the Christian church.[44] Thus her praiseworthy qualities are exemplary for Christians in general, and for Christian rulers in particular.

Because this sermon was preached on Elizabeth's Accession Day, November 17, we might expect him to add: for Queen Elizabeth in especial particular. But to judge by the printed text, Holland had nothing to say in Paul's Church that fall day about Queen Elizabeth. Except by implication, Holland preached a sermon that would be equally applicable on any date, in any service in any Christian church. Not even a prayer for Elizabeth's protection and prosperity is attached. Indeed, whenever

---

42 Holland, Πανηγυρίς *D. Elizabethae*, sig. A1.
43 Ibid., sigs. D1ᵛ–D2.
44 Ibid., sigs. B1–1ᵛ.

Holland has an opportunity to draw a parallel between Elizabeth and the Queen of the South, he refrains, and when he could cite Elizabeth's accomplishments in several statements about women's potential for wisdom, learning, and sanctity, he is silent.

Holland does go farther in his preface. The Queen of the South is "a Mayden Queene[,] ... a woman of great wisdome, a woman endued with rare learning."[45] Elizabeth is all of the above, with "rare wisdome" and internationally recognized "skil of tongues." "Although the comparison heere wil not holde betweene the Queene of the South & the Q of England for vndertaking a iourney &c," Elizabeth's "laborious, perilous, toilesome, [and] chargeable ... regiment of this mighty kingdom" corresponds to the biblical queen's labor, perils, toil, and expense on her journey.[46] Elizabeth is "a mirrour of peace in these troublesome daies," while the Queen of the South was "a daughter of peace" who never would have made her journey if her country had been under threat.[47] The Queen of the South engaged Solomon in religious discussion and embraced true religion, while Elizabeth is "a zealous imbracer of his doctrine whom K. Salomon shaddowed and prefigured."[48] The resemblance is so close that Holland feels the need to add this caution:

> [I]t is a point in al learning obserued, that no comparison, reference, or resemblaunce similitudinary should hold in each part: and for that there are many things appropriate to the person of the Queene of the South, which cannot to any creature else be applied by any apt relation.[49]

This is a very curious sermon. On the one hand, it makes a striking statement upholding the traditional allegorical and typological method of biblical exegesis and provides an expansive demonstration of that method with regard to the text. On the other hand, the sermon ostentatiously fails to exploit the typological possibilities of the text for this occasion and this English queen. Why bury all those flattering parallels in the

---

45 Ibid., sigs. a2^v–a3.
46 Ibid., sig. a3^v.
47 Ibid., sigs. a3^v–4.
48 Ibid., sig. a4.
49 Ibid., sig. b1. Cf. Augustine's similar point, quoted in my first chapter, that "things very different from one another may be called by one and the same name," Augustine, Sermon XXIII [LXXIII Ben.], *Sermons on Selected Lessons of the New Testament*, trans. R. G. MacMullen, in *The Nicene and Post-Nicene Fathers*, ser. 1, vol. 6 (Grand Rapids, MI: Eerdmans, rpt. 1991), 334.

preface in a subsequently printed volume rather than develop them for a large and patriotic audience?

Of course it is possible that the sermon as printed may represent what was left of the spoken version after the parallels with Elizabeth were diverted into the preface. I prefer to advance the argument that the sermon and its preface are analogous to *The Faerie Queene* and the Letter to Raleigh.[50] Spenser usually expects his audience to take the point of comparisons between Elizabeth and his ostensible subject in the body of his work without his explicating them. So did Holland. Hebraic patriotism was so conventional in such settings that drawing an explicit parallel was unnecessary. The Queen of the South functions in this sermon exactly as Una, Belphoebe, Gloriana, or any of the other Spenserian figures for Elizabeth do within the *Faerie Queene*.

Spenser uses "historical allegory" as Holland uses Hebraic patriotism: not as an entertaining puzzle, a daring cognitive experiment, or a psychological stopgap, but as a lens through which to view a widely shared picture of England's national life, a lens that brought its moral and spiritual dimensions into clearer focus. Based on the evidence of occasional liturgies and printed sermons, Holland's auditors were sophisticated consumers of biblical typology applied to Elizabethan contexts; Spenser takes for granted that sophistication in his audience as well, limiting his explicit application of his fictional characters' similarities to Queen Elizabeth mainly to the "Letter of the Authors" and the proems of each book. In its appropriation of biblical rhetoric, the occasional liturgies and typical Elizabethan sermons prepared English churchgoers to penetrate Spenser's "veil" of allegory. The chapters that follow will approach some episodes of the poem with the insights an Elizabethan sermon-goer might have brought to his or her reading of the text.

---

50 "A Letter of the Authors expounding his *whole intention in the course of this worke*," in *Spenser: The Faerie Queene*, 2nd edn by A. C. Hamilton for Longman Annotated English Poets (Harlow and London: Pearson Education, 2001), 714–18.

Part II

The preachers' Bible and Spenser's *Faerie Queene*: alternate allegories

4

"The ground of Storie": genealogy in biblical exegesis and the Legend of Temperance[1]

As we have seen in the three preceding chapters, Elizabethan Bibles, liturgies, and sermons offer evidence that Spenser's contemporaries were very well prepared to approach an allegorical text. Churchgoers routinely encountered rhetoric that required them to make the leap from explicit references to biblical characters and stories to implied references to their country, their queen, and current events at home and on the Continent. This facility with allegory has important implications for what original readers of *The Faerie Queene* would have understood.

The next six chapters consider selected episodes in the cultural context that I have sought to establish: that of a commonly assumed framework of biblical allegoresis. Of course, even when allegory and typology are not in question, Elizabethan religious rhetoric provides an important context for Spenser's poem. This chapter seeks to demonstrate that Elizabethan commentary on biblical genealogies can provide insights for reading the "chronicle histories" of Books II and III.

For we may regard the works that Arthur and Guyon read, "*Briton moniments*" and the "*Antiquitie* of *Faerie* lond," as well as Merlin's prophesied history in III.iii, as genealogies. Spenser, in II.x.1, invokes aid in undertaking a "haughtie enterprise" – to recount "the famous auncestries/ Of my most dreaded Soueraigne." This formulation recurs in III.iii.4, introducing another passage of "chronicle history," Britomart's consultation with Merlin: "Begin, O *Clio*, and recount from hence/ My glorious Soueraines goodly auncestrie," suggesting a list of rulers rather than a more general history. A list of rulers is likewise implicit toward the end of II.x, in Spenser's phrasing of what Arthur has read: "The royall Ofspring of his natiue land" (69). Of course, genealogy and history

---

[1] An earlier version of this chapter appeared in *Spenser Studies* 9 (1991): 61–79, published by AMS Press, Inc.

need not be mutually exclusive: Elizabethans saw in genealogy a useful tool for establishing the meaning of history, whether national or personal. In classical mythology, in Bible stories, and in the sixteenth century, a person's lineage defined not only his physical origins, but also his character and spirit.

The chronicle histories mark moments in *The Faerie Queene* that the characters seem to enjoy more than twentieth- or twenty-first-century readers. For Arthur and Guyon, the high point of the visit to Alma's castle is the visit to Eumnestes's room, and commentators have endeavored to explain its importance to the book. Certainly, to some extent the chronicles illustrate the need for "temperance" or "prudence" in a ruler or on a national level, though one might ask why Spenser, seldom backward in stating his theme, declined to use such words in the passage itself. Much commentary seeks to account for the contrast between the *moniments*' recital of historical defeats as well as victories with the unbroken success and succession of *Antiquitie*. But the narrator and characters do not explore this contrast; nor does Arthur, "quite rauisht with delight" (x.69), share the boredom or perplexity many readers have felt. The comparison with biblical genealogies can illuminate the divergence of these works from each other as well as the delight these chronicles may have offered Spenser's first readers. To establish what insights a genealogical reading of II.x and III.iii might yield, we will look to contemporary biblical commentary to uncover some of the methods and meaning associated with tracing a family tree in the sixteenth century.

No family in England was more conscious of its heritage and history than the Tudors, whose family tree had to validate a claim to the throne. Throughout Elizabeth's reign, those who would flatter her made a point of invoking the memory of her royal predecessors. Beyond political, social, or materialistic concerns, in remembering their ancestors Elizabethans were continuing the practice of biblical heroes and patriarchs. Many chapters of the Bible are given over to genealogies of the Old Testament worthies and of Christ. Thus, two useful parallels to Spenser's "chronicle history" canto, viewed from a genealogical standpoint, are biblical genealogies and sermon references to the Queen's family tree.

Elizabethan discussion of biblical genealogies

The 1560 Genevan commentators asserted the spiritual lessons of genealogy from the earliest pages of Genesis: "[The author] proueth Adams generation by them, which came of Sheth, to shewe which is the true Church, and also what care God had ouer the same from the beginning, in that he continued euer his graces toward it by a continual succession."[2] A generation later, scholars still considered genealogies an important key to the meaning of scripture. Roger Cotton, a draper whose household included the accomplished but irascible Hebrew scholar Hugh Broughton[3] from 1583 to 1589, explains their importance in his *Direction to the waters of lyfe* under the heading "The Genealogies are the ground of Storie":

> And I pray you, what part of the Bible is there, that doth not thereof consist? be not men the grounde and cause of all the matter there? And how can we knowe the matter as we ought, vnlesse we know the men of whom the matter speaketh? As for example, yf the holy Ghost say, *Sheba* and *Seba* shall bring gyftes, or *Nebaioh* and *Kedar* shall come and serue[4]: how can we know rightly what is meant hereby, vnlesse we know the people of whom the holy Ghost doth speake, and also the cause why they were estranged from the Lord, and now shoulde come agayne? Or if the Lorde do tell you, how that he will subdue the *Canaanites*, *Heuites*, *Iebusites*, *Gergesites*, and the rest of those nations, to geue vnto *Israel* their possessions:[5] must you not of necessitie (yf you wyl know the cause cleerely) vnderstande what these people are, and of whom they come, and also vpon what former prophesie and promises these matters do depende? Yes you are bounde to know them ... because without the knowledge of these thinges, you are neyther able to heare or reade the worde of God with vnderstandyng. Therefore in the name of God take heede, that you be not so perswaded by them, to beleeue that the Genealogies in the holy Scriptures be endles, or vnprofitable, or superfluous: for yf you so thinke, then do you nothing els, but take away from the Scripture, and so the curse of God wyll come vpon you, euen to your vtter damnation.[6]

---

2 Note on Genesis 5:6, *The Geneva Bible: A Facsimile of the 1560 Edition* (Madison, WI: University of Wisconsin Press, 1969), fol. 3.
3 Broughton's residence in Cotton's home and employment as his son's tutor, rather than as a professor or within the institutional structure of the church, and his fellow scholars' declining to include him as a translator for the 1611 revision of the English Bible, testify to the bitterness of his professional disagreements and his difficult temperament (G. Lloyd Jones, "Broughton, Hugh [1549–1612]," *Dictionary of National Biography*, 2004; online edn, May 2013).
4 The references are to Psalm 72:10 and Isaiah 60:7.
5 The reference is probably to Joshua 3:10, though several texts have similar lists.
6 Roger Cotton, *A direction to the waters of lyfe Come and beholde, how Christ shineth before the Law, in the Law, and in the Prophetes: and withall the iudgements of God vpon all nations for the neglect of his holy worde* (London, 1590), sig. C1–1^v, STC (2nd edn) 5866. Available from the database Early English Books Online.

Men constitute the matter of scripture; genealogies explain the men by documenting their fathers. With the fathers' names before them, readers should recall the fathers' deeds, and interpret their children's character and fate, for the children embody and experience the results of their forefathers' choices, whether for good or ill. The founder of a nation determines, for Cotton, the national destiny: the Jews were called and blessed through Abraham, and the descendents of Ham were cursed.

The most notable examples of important and useful genealogies are those of Christ, found in Matthew 1 and Luke 3. Of these Broughton writes,

> The holy *Genealogie* of *Iesus Christ* (may not be reckoned in the number of those prophane ones, which *S. Paul* condemneth in I. Tim. 1. 4. for it) doth not consist in a vaine repetition of Names, (as many doe thinke) neither is the knowledge thereof superfluous, (as some doe affirme;) But verily (if it be rightly vnderstood) it is of exceeding great vse and consequence; not onely to prooue *Christ* to be the promised Seede, (which is a weightie poynt;) But also it serueth as a speciall guide, to direct vs in the true vnderstanding of all the *Holy Storie* ... all the *Holy storie* dependeth vpon [our *Lords line of Fathers*].[7]

These gospel genealogies serve two ends: "to prooue *Christ* to be the promised Seede," and "to direct vs in the true vnderstanding" of Christ and his story. And as such important documents, the construction of a properly revealing genealogy is a task requiring careful judgment.

Matthew's and Luke's judgments conflict. Luke traces Jesus's biological heritage all the way back to Adam. Matthew, on the other hand, begins with Abraham. The two gospels agree in the catalog that extends from Abraham to David. Then they follow almost completely different lines from King David to Joseph, the husband of Mary.[8] The two accounts diverge through almost twenty generations, as Matthew follows the line of the kings of Judah, from Solomon to Jehoiachin, and Luke follows the line of Solomon's brother Nathan, from whom, according to the Geneva

---

7   Hugh Broughton, *The holy genealogie of Iesus Christ both his naturall line of fathers, which S. Luke followeth, chap. 3, and his kingly line, which S. Matthew followeth, chap. I, with fit notation of their names* (London, 1612), sig. ¶1, STC (2nd edn) 3867.9. Available from the database Early English Books Online.

8   Augustine's explanation was "that Joseph may have had two fathers, – namely, one by whom he was begotten, and a second by whom he may have been adopted." (Augustine believed the adoptive father's line is recorded by Luke, while the biological line is recorded by Matthew.) "A Statement of the Reason Why Matthew Enumerates One Succession of Ancestors for Christ, and Luke Another," *Harmony of the Gospels Book II*, trans. S. D. F. Salmond, *The Nicene and Post-Nicene Fathers*, ser. 1, vol. 6 (New York, 1888), 103.

Bible (with Broughton following), Christ actually descended.[9] The two branches converge at the point where, during the Babylonian captivity, Jehoiachin died without issue and a son of Nathan's line, Salathiel, succeeded to the throne of Judah (although the exile made the succession an academic rather than political problem). Salathiel's grandson Zerubbabel was ancestor to both Mary and Joseph. Zerubbabel, according to Broughton, had two sons, and Matthew derives Joseph's ancestry from the elder, to whom the theoretical crown should have passed, while Luke follows the younger son's line to Joseph's father-in-law and thus to Mary, Jesus's mother. (Both lists name Joseph rather than Mary, however.) For Broughton, then, the discrepancies between the two accounts result from Matthew's decision to follow Christ's "Kingly" rather than "naturall" line, and his apparent paternal, rather than actual maternal, heritage.[10] Luke, on the other hand, documents Christ's physical forebears rather than his credentials for the kingship of Judah. This confusing circumstance provided Broughton with the occasion to enlarge upon the different purposes and methods of genealogizing.

At least two kinds of genealogies are possible, and one, the kingly line, can "prooue *Christ* to be the promised Seede."[11] Thus, even though Christ was not the biological offspring of the kings in this list, it can still contribute to an understanding of his identity and work, since it endorses him, "holden *Iosephs* sonne, by all Law was borne King of the *Iewes*."[12] While the "Kingly" line can be used to buttress a claim to the throne, so the "naturall" line had its uses as well. This type of genealogy was useful for the analysis of individual characters. Broughton moralizes Luke's bare list of names to show how it enhances an understanding of Christ's character and work. To this end, he supplies the original meaning of each Hebrew name, for "we should not be as Parrets, to regard the bare sond of name, but to know what the notation told".[13] Thus on a

---

9 The Geneva Bible's comment at Luke 3:23 garbles its explanation somewhat: "Matthewe counteth by the legal descent, and Luke by the natural: ... bothe two speaking of the same persones applie vnto them diuers names."
10 Broughton, *The holy genealogie*, sig. ¶3.
11 Ibid., sig. ¶4ᵛ. The Geneva Bible comment on Luke 3:23 explains, "Matthewe extendeth not his rehearsal further then to Abraham, which is for the assurance of the promises for the Iewes."
12 Broughton, *The holy genealogie*, sig. ¶4ᵛ.
13 Hugh Broughton, *Our Lordes Famile and many other poinctes depending upon it* (Amsterdam, 1608), sig. D2ᵛ, STC (2nd edn) 3875. Available from the database Early English Books Online.

one-page 1595 broadsheet, Broughton glosses David "Beloued," Nashon (fifth in descent from Judah the patriarch) "Experimenter. He had experience of the Promise, from Egypt" – that is, he was of the generation of the Exodus. Joash, whose grandmother slaughtered as many of her descendents as she could find in order to have the crown for herself, is glossed "Desperate: and so he had bin, but for Iehoiadah, that saued him from Athalih."[14]

Beyond simply supplying the meaning of each name, however, Broughton reminds his readers of the character and deeds of many of Christ's ancestors, showing how Christ "honoured all his true Fathers [that is, his actual physical forebears] with the gift of fayth."[15] Abraham

> hath no workes to reioice in before God. For his request vnto Sara to hazard her Chastity was a fault ... an egregious trespas, a gross fault, an exceding sin; bred from great mistrust in God; & the cause of Israels sorow & fall in Egypt. So he hath not to reioice before God: Therfore he was not iustified by workes before God ... but by faith he was iustified.[16]

The mention of Abraham's name in the list of Christ's forebears holds a spiritual lesson pointing forward to the need for Christ.

The appearance of Pharez, the son of a Gentile woman, in Christ's genealogy should remind us of two spiritual truths. First, Gentiles can participate in salvation as well as Jews. "God was in disposing counsel how Messias should come of Thamar; of Thamar, a Chananean: of Thamar, Iudas daughter in law: of Thamar, by Iudah."[17] Tamar gave birth to twins, and Pharez shoved past his brother, whose hand had already appeared, to be born first. This eagerness revealed a godly disposition all believers should emulate. "Again Phares striving to be borne before Zara, (who first stredched out his hand) hath his name [glossed "a breach-maker" in *Our Lord his line of Fathers*] of violence, shewing at his byrth that he wold lay strong hand vpon the Kingdome of heauen; & is a patren for all, as Iacob, to striue for the Kingdome from yong yeres."[18] David, the paragon

---

14 Hugh Broughton, *Our Lord his line of fathers from Adam, and his predecessours in the kingdome from Salomon to Iechonias, in whom ended the house: and from Abiud to Ioseph the husband of Marie: with fit notation of their names* (London, 1595), STC (2nd edn) 3874.5. Available from the database Early English Books Online.
15 Broughton, *The holy Genealogie*, ¶ 2.
16 Broughton, *Our Lordes Famile*, C2^v.
17 Ibid., D1.
18 Ibid., D1-1^v. It is interesting to note that the Geneva Bible glosses this portent less approvingly: "Their [Tamar's and Judah's] hainous sinne was signified by this monstruous birth" (Genesis 38:29, margin).

of the kings of Judah, had experiences that not only prefigure Christ's excellences but also typify the need for Christ's forgiveness and grace:

> He, while he was afflicted, was godly; at rest, he fell; in Vriah, & Bathseba; To be an example for all that shall beleue ... And Bathseba the adulteress, rarely Godly in the end, is a grandmother of Christ; celebrated in the psalme of repertance [sic] .51. & [wrote] pro.31 & all prophetes are in the Kingdome of heauen. Lu.13.[19]

A study of Christ's genealogy, according to Broughton, reveals Jesus as the answer to all his ancestors' yearnings and shortcomings, the fulfillment of their expectations. Only by reviewing their faith and their faults can a reader appreciate the significance of his perfections. By looking to the personal history of genealogy, a reader, whether of the Bible or of *The Faerie Queene*, can rightly value and interpret an individual.

Elizabethan biblical exegesis, then, can inform Spenserians that at least two kinds of genealogies are possible and relevant. Spenserians further learn that genealogy does not have to include only blood relatives to provide relevant information: even a genealogy listing men unrelated to Christ can contribute to an understanding of his identity and work. Broughton insists that Christ's natural line of fathers included only men saved by faith: "he honoured all his true Fathers with the gift of fayth, being the roote of goodnes, whom we are to follow in the honouring of our Parents, and can not goe before him."[20] In Christ's family tree, there was thus an identity between his "naturall line" and what we might term his "spiritual line." Many of the kings of Judah, memorialized in Christ's "Kingly line," are "most wicked folke,"[21] and to suggest that such could be Christ's physical ancestors is "*attributing folly vnto the Eternal wisdome of God, to bring the most holy, of the most wicked.*"[22] Indeed, Matthew spares readers some of the embarrassment of this suggestion in the course of recording Christ's "Kingly line" by omitting several of the most notorious. "*Achaziah, Ioaz,* Amaziah.*" appear on Broughton's table with the note, "These badde 3. and worse *Iehoiakim*, which were kild for euill ruling, S. *Matthew* omitteth."[23] Apparently the omission of the least exemplary branches of the family tree did not compromise the value of a genealogy. Indeed, it could testify to the discretion of the chronicler. Including such

---

19 Ibid., D3.
20 Broughton, *The holy Genealogie*, ¶ 2.
21 Ibid.
22 Broughton, *Our Lordes Famile*, sig. E1.
23 Broughton, *The holy Genealogie*, ¶ 2.

names would only suggest avenues of interpretation that must be fruitless, even misleading.

Elizabeth's family tree in printed sermons

The explication of biblical genealogies, however sublime a science, was mostly pursued in learned treatises. Whether too lofty, too occult, or too dull, it found little currency in popular preaching.[24] But the confidence expressed by Cotton and Broughton in the spiritual value of such studies emerged in a different context when preachers treated Queen Elizabeth's forebears. Just as Broughton and Cotton claimed for biblical figures, preachers claimed that knowing the Queen's lineage, her ancestors' qualities and deeds, led to a more accurate appraisal of the Queen herself. Preachers who developed the Queen's genealogy tended to allow themselves as much latitude as the gospel genealogists did: those connections that would be spiritually misleading or simply embarrassing were suppressed, as Matthew omits the more ignominious among the kings of Judah. Thus Mary Tudor, for instance, never appeared in such catalogs of Elizabeth's natural, kingly, or spiritual kin.

Bishop Curteys, in a 1575 sermon, used the biblical types discussed in Chapter 3 as ancestors: to stress the spiritual resemblance between Elizabeth and her father and brother, while he ignored her sister. Henry VIII was God's "noble Moses," who "brought hys people of England out of the Egipt of error, blindnesse, and superstition." Among other benefits, Henry, like Moses, delivered the word of God to the people in their own language ("the reading of the old testament and new"), but he "did not goe ouer Jordayne to it [the Promised Land, "the true Catholike Church of Christ"], but dyed in the Land of Moab." "Josua his sonne," that is, Edward VI, led the people through "the Floud of Jordaine, the labours, troubles, and dissentions in doctrine," into Canaan,

> and with the blast of his worde and the shout of his Ministers, hurled downe the walles of Jericho ... the doctrines and traditions of men: ouerthrewe

---

24 A search in the database Early English Books Online for the word "genealogy" in full-text English-language sermons published in England between 1558 and 1615 yielded (in July 2014) only thirteen publications, including seven translations of continental reformers. Only two of these publications, one a translation of Ludwig Lavater's series on the book of Ruth and the other a collection of Martin Luther's sermons, include sermons whose purpose is to expound biblical genealogy. The other occurrences of the word are off-hand or even metaphorical, as are, for instance, the two in Henry Smith's sermon "The Affinitie of the Faithfull" in his 1593 collection (STC [rev. edn] 22719).

the Giauntes, Masse-mongers and Exorcists of Hebron: discomfited the Sorbonists and Sophisters of Debir: and by the lot of his word possessed his people of England of the truth, his sacraments and Gospell.[25]

The return to Rome under Mary was tactfully blamed on her subjects rather than a member of Elizabeth's family:

> But the Englishe Achans coueted the goodly Babilonian garmentes and the cicles [sic, for "shekels"] of Siluer, and the wedges of Golde: they grew in pride, in ambition, in couetousnesse. The disobedient people dyd not cast out the Jebusites and the Cananites.[26]

With a spiritual heritage defined by Moses and Joshua, biblical types who were themselves not blood relations, Elizabeth was "a gratious Debora, by whome God brought down Jabin, and Cusan, and caused his Churche of Englande to prosper in healthe, wealthe, peace, pollicie, learning, religion, and many good gifts and graces."[27] She recapitulated in her reign the deeds of these worthy forebears, rescuing her people once more out of the slavery of Catholicism and settling them in the promised land of Protestantism. Thus could knowledge of Elizabeth's genealogy enrich an appreciation of her character and achievements, and Spenser evidently considered that the "chronicle history" cantos would similarly enrich his poem.

As queen, the embodiment of the state as well as a private individual, Elizabeth could lay claim not only to Henry and Edward in the Tudor family tree, but to the spiritual bloodlines of the throne of England as well, just as Matthew's genealogy of Christ includes, according to Hugh Broughton, "Kinges that were not fathers to Christ."[28] She could also, according to the culturally current norms of biblical typology discussed in the preceding chapters, count the best of biblical princes as her forebears. Hence, the invocation of her ancestors in the sermons often included biblical figures and her pre-Norman, Norman, and Plantagenet

---

25 Richard Curteys, *A sermon preached before the Queenes Maiesty at Richmond the. 6. of March last past* (London, 1575), sigs. C8^v–D1, STC (2nd edn) 6139. The copy available from the database Early English Books Online is incomplete.
26 Ibid., sig. D1.
27 Ibid., sig. D1^v.
28 The Queen implicitly recognized this as well, citing "our progenitors, sovereigns and kings of ["this Realm"]" in *Queen Elizabeth's Defence of her Proceedings in Church and State: With an Introductory Essay on the Northern Ireland Rebellion* [sic, for "Northern Rebellion"], ed. William E. Collins for Church Historical Society Publications 58 (London, 1899, 1958), 45; Broughton, *Our Lordes Famile*, sig. D3.

antecedents as well as her grandfather, father, and brother. A catalog of this sort from the second Queen's Day sermon by Archbishop Sandys traced the family resemblances that defined and described Elizabeth.

> Israell was well apaide with the good gouernement of Debora, Iudith, and Hester. But they thought themselues twise happie when God gaue them Moses, Samuel, Dauid, Salomon, Iehosaphat, Ezechias, Iosias, to gouerne them. England liked well, and took it for no small blessing of God, when Henrie the first, H. the second, Edward the first, Edward the third, Edward the fourth, H. the fift, H. the sixt, H. the seuenth, H. the eighth, Edward the sixt bare rule ouer it. But did God euer blesse the throne of any man as hee hath doone the royall seate of his annointed at this day? Hath the like euer beene heard of in any nation to that which in ours is seene? Our Debora hath mightily repressed the rebel Iaben: our Iudith hath beheaded Holophernes, the sworne enemie of Christianitie, our Hester hath hanged vp that Haman, which sought to bring both vs and our children into miserable seruitude. And if we may compare with the ancients of Israel Moses was not more milde, nor Samuel more iust, nor Dauid more faithful, nor Salomon more peaceful, nor Iehosaphat more readie to assist his neighbours, nor Ezechias more carefull for Gods cause, nor Iozias more zealous to restore syncere religion: If, ye make the comparison betweene her owne predecessors, neither was Henrie the first better learned, nor Henrie the second more easie to forgiue and put vp iniuries, nor Ed. the first more chast, nor Ed. the third more loth to accept of forrein dominion being offred, nor Ed. the fourth more iust in yeelding all men their owne, nor H. the fift more happie, nor H. the sixt more holie, nor H. the seuenth more prudent, nor H. the eight more valiant in quelling the Pope, nor Ed. the sixt more syncerely affected towardes the Gospell of Christ.[29]

These comparisons approximate to a genealogy in that, in addition to the Queen's legal and physical kin, Sandys selected biblical forebears and invoked their reputations. He seeks to place the Queen not only within a chronological sequence, but also on a spiritual map, showing her as the heir of all these men and women. This genealogy was the ground of Elizabeth's "Storie": the listed characters, qualities, and noble deeds could help auditors to understand and appreciate the Queen – rather as the titular virtues and heroic exploits of *The Faerie Queene* to some extent "shadow" the Queen's virtues and accomplishments.

---

29 Edwin Sandys, "The fourth Sermon. A Sermon preached in the same place, and vpon the same occasion with the former," in *Sermons made by the most reuerende Father in God, Edwin, Archbishop of Yorke* (London, 1585), 68–7 [sic, for 69], STC (2nd edn) 21713. Available from the database Early English Books Online.

Perhaps a rehearsal of some of the parallels that Sandys lists will clarify his method. Deborah (Judges 4–5) was a respected judge in peace and leader in battle; indeed, the general Barak declined to face the forces of the Canaanite Jabin unless Deborah shared his command. Elizabeth's preparations and reliance on God in the face of threatened invasion were considered comparable, and the reference may also glance at the Low Countries' request for Elizabeth's aid against Spain. Another redoubtable woman, Judith used her beauty and resourcefulness to deceive and behead Holophernes, a general of the Babylonian king Nebuchadnezzar, who had subjugated Judah. Elizabeth likewise used both persuasion and force to extirpate Roman Catholicism in England: the comparison highlights the combination of tact and resolution required, as well as the personal risk, to preserve England's religious and political independence during the dangerous early years of her reign.

Elizabeth was the spiritual heir of several great kings of Judah as well. Jehosaphat, for example, the king of Judah in the days of the wicked Ahab and the prophet Elijah, remained true to the Lord and demonstrated his neighborly spirit by accompanying Ahab in a military campaign at Ramoth Gilead. This eagerness to assist neighboring Israel, commendable in itself, met with failure, and Ahab was killed. The quality of Jehosaphat that Sandys praises in Queen Elizabeth led her to aid the Low Countries and the Protestant Scots, although what she represented as aid to her sister queen Mary Stuart brought danger upon herself and her kingdom and eventually (after the date of this sermon) ended in Mary's death, as Jehosaphat's efforts exposed him to danger and could not prevent Ahab's death. Two other kings Elizabeth resembled were Hezekiah and Josiah, both remembered for their restoration of true religion after a period of idolatry.

Sandys carefully stipulated Elizabeth's likeness to her kingly English ancestors. She resembled Henry I, the Norman ruler who was reputed to know Greek, understood Latin, spoke English easily, and had such a remarkable taste for books that he was known as "the clerk."[30] Elizabeth inherited his predilection for learning, even surpassing him as a linguist. Henry II, renowned for his forgiving nature, pardoned his sons for their unsuccessful rebellion against him.[31] With few exceptions,

---

30 C. Warren Hollister, "Henry I (1068/9–1135)," *Oxford Dictionary of National Biography* (Oxford: Oxford University Press, 2004).
31 Thomas K. Keefe, "Henry II (1133–1189)," *Oxford Dictionary of National Biography* (Oxford: Oxford University Press, 2004); online edn, Jan 2008.

Elizabeth handled her rebellious nobles with similar forbearance after the Northern Rebellion, and forgave Mary Stuart several times for her plots and intrigues against her.

Edward I's chastity was celebrated, not because he remained a virgin like his spiritual heir Queen Elizabeth, but because of his deep attachment to his first wife, who bore him at least thirteen children and whom he mourned by erecting the twelve famous Eleanor crosses. Edward I was also celebrated for his faithfulness to his second wife,[32] while the virgin queen lavished her devotion on England. Edward III, when only a teenager, balked at offering the required homage to the French king in return for his French holdings, first obtaining legal opinions that such service did not prejudice his own claims to the French crown. A lover of war, he sought to expand his territory in France and into Scotland.[33] Similarly, Elizabeth began her reign by establishing her independence from Spain; a delicate task when the Spanish king had lately been her brother-in-law and maintained a household in England as its uncrowned king. Though she lacked her progenitor's taste for war, she would eventually execute the Queen of Scotland, bring its council under her influence, and ensure the fulfilment of Edward III's ambition to add Scotland to the dominions of the English crown. Edward IV's ingratiating manners and eagerness to conciliate Lancastrian nobles during and after his chaotic contest with Henry VI led to his building up his political allies with grants of office and land; this policy could be euphemized as justice "in yeelding all men their owne."[34] Perhaps in Elizabeth's case the reference is to her discontinuing Mary Tudor's unpopular efforts to trace and revoke the grants of formerly monastic holdings and wealth. In any case, Elizabeth's nobility felt her to be less demanding an overlord in terms of grants and taxes than many of her predecessors, and noted, if they did not celebrate, her frugality.

While Elizabeth did not resemble Henry V in winning battles in France, she would be fortunate in the outcome of her contest with Spain. Several of her speeches express her solidarity with and commitment to her men-at-arms, thus recalling the sentiments of Henry's battlefield speeches (such as the one before the battle of Agincourt, in which

---

32 Michael Prestwich, "Edward I (1239–1307)," *Oxford Dictionary of National Biography* (Oxford: Oxford University Press, 2004).

33 W. M. Ormrod, "Edward III (1312–1377)," *Oxford Dictionary of National Biography* (Oxford: Oxford University Press, 2004); online ed., Jan 2008.

34 Rosemary Horrox, "Edward IV (1442–1483)," *Oxford Dictionary of National Biography* (Oxford: Oxford University Press, 2004); online edn, Sept 2011.

he assured his troops that his cause was just and England prayed for them).³⁵ Henry VI, considered a martyr and a saint, was remembered for his orthodox piety and foundations of Eton College and King's College, Cambridge.³⁶ Though Queen Elizabeth founded no educational institutions, she was celebrated as narrowly escaping martyrdom in Foxe's *Actes and Monuments*, sermons, and the popular imagination.

Henry VII manifested "prudence" not only in his avarice and cultivation of his personal monarchy at home after the Wars of the Roses, but also in his diplomatic successes abroad – his alliances with Spain and Scotland in particular, the latter of which ultimately led to the union of Scotland and England under James I.³⁷ Elizabeth's prudent handling of the divisive religious issues of the time, marrying Protestant theology with Catholic ritual in her settlement, bore out her resemblance to her grandfather, as did her cautious approach to foreign affairs. Like her father, Henry VIII, she insisted on the English church's independence from the Bishop of Rome, and if she did not, as her brother Edward did, hear ten chapters of the Bible daily, she reissued his prayer book and book of homilies.³⁸ Listeners could recall these or other relevant details of each ruler and trace the spiritual resemblance between Elizabeth and her predecessors to gain a better appreciation of her character in the light of these comparisons. Reference to less exemplary rulers – Edward II, Henry IV, Richard III, Mary Tudor – was avoided.

The form of Sandys's compliment is worth considering. It was patterned after a gospel genealogy in certain particulars. Of Luke's list, Broughton says, "The whole number is disposed in order fit for memorie Ten to the flod: ending the old world; ten to Abraham heyre of the new world."³⁹ Sandys imitates Luke's pattern by listing ten biblical "ancestors" of Queen Elizabeth, all of whom figure in the Old Testament, and ten kingly ancestors, all of the period following the Conquest and well within Britain's Christian era. Such an admirable and varied assortment of qualities and deeds represented by twice ten worthy names helped the auditor

---

35 C. T. Allmand, "Henry V (1386–1422)," *Oxford Dictionary of National Biography* (Oxford: Oxford University Press, 2004); online edn, Sept 2010.
36 R. A. Griffiths, "Henry VI (1421–1471)," *Oxford Dictionary of National Biography* (Oxford: Oxford University Press, 2004); online edn, Sept 2010.
37 S. J. Gunn, "Henry VII (1457–1509)," *Oxford Dictionary of National Biography* (Oxford: Oxford University Press, 2004); online edn, Jan 2008.
38 Dale Hoak, "Edward VI (1537–1553)," *Oxford Dictionary of National Biography* (Oxford: Oxford University Press, 2004); online edn, May 2014.
39 Broughton, *Our Lordes Famile*, sig. A1ᵛ.

to distinguish the Queen's spiritual forebears, and thus to appreciate her own achievements and character.

Briton moniments in the context of Elizabethan biblical genealogy

So how does the text Arthur reads look in light of these roughly contemporary sermons and treatises? As an accurate physical genealogy for Elizabeth, or even for Arthur, *Briton moniments* is disappointing. Arthur cannot trace his "naturall line," to use Broughton's phrase, through all these kings back to Brut, where the chronicle proper begins: Dunwallo's and Coyll's dynasties intervene between the last representatives of Brut's direct line, Ferrex and Porrex, and the second Constantine, founder of Arthur's house. Thus, the greater portion of *Briton moniments* is analogous to the first chapter of Matthew, which traces Christ's ancestry through Solomon, though Solomon was not (according to Elizabethan clerics) his physical ancestor. That is, *Briton moniments* shows Arthur's "Kingly line," the version of the genealogy that validates his (and Queen Elizabeth's) claim to Brut's crown. The wording of II.x.4 seems to emphasize this "kingly" notion of lineage. While Elizabeth derives her name, realm, and race from Prince Arthur, her rule – "that royall mace,/ Which now thou bear'st" – descends to her not only from Arthur, but from other "mightie kings and conquerours in warre," including some who are her "fathers and great Grandfathers" by convention because of their kingly succession, rather than by birth.

The Elizabethan notion of various allowable types of genealogies, among them tracing the kingly and the natural lines, helps resolve one problem posed by the material in II.x: the appearance therein of what Broughton refers to as "most wicked folke." Why should Spenser include them in what we must assume to be a complimentary gesture to the Queen? Hugh Broughton insists that all of Christ's physical forebears had "ye gift of fayth, being the roote of goodnes," and explains the presence of "most wicked folke" in Matthew's table by identifying them as kingly, rather than natural, ancestors of Christ.[40] Similarly, there is nothing to embarrass Queen Elizabeth in the physical ancestors that Spenser provides Tanaquil/Gloriana with as they descend from Constantine II (II.x.62–4) and Artegal (III.iii.26 and following). The unnatural ambition of Ferrex and Porrex, the adultery of Locrine, the usurpation of

---

40 Broughton, *The holy Genealogie*, ¶ 2.

Octavius, do not compromise the value of *Briton moniments* as compliment: because these are not Elizabeth's natural fathers, their moral and political lapses do not reflect on her. Indeed, the contrast of their wickedness throws her humility, chastity, and worthiness in greater relief and shows England's need of her redemptive virtue, just as the wickedness of the kings of Judah and the occasional lapses of David and Abraham are recalled, according to Broughton, to heighten appreciation for Christ's sinlessness, and demonstrate the need for a Savior (and, recalling Niels Hemmingsen and William Tyndale as quoted in Chapter 3, to comfort fallible Christians). The "naturall line," followed from Constantine II to Uther, and then (as traced in Book III, Canto iii) from Artegal to Cadwallader, includes no one who discredits the Queen morally or politically, though some ancestors suffer. For instance, Cadwallin martyrs the Saxon "good king *Oswald*" (III.iii.39) to avenge the "long vassalage" to which the Britons have been subjected (36), and is thus not morally reprehensible. Vortipore, Artegal's grandson, is crossed by "froward fortune" (31); "the good *Cadwallader*" (40) loses his crown to the Saxons. These failures, however, are not those of wicked men, and in Cadwallader's case, are part of a providential design.

The Faery chronicle in the context of Elizabethan biblical typology

Briton moniments in Book II and Merlin's prophecy in Book III provide Elizabeth with a "Kingly line" which extends back to Brut and Aeneas, and a "naturall line" from Constantine II to Cadwallader. Guyon's book, "*Antiquitie* of *Faerie* lond" (II.x.70–6), provides a third genealogy, which further reveals Elizabeth's character and deeds, much as Luke's list of Christ's ancestors complements Matthew's. Matthew's table, directed to a Jewish audience, traces Christ's line from Abraham, founder of the Jewish race, much as *Briton moniments* traces Elizabeth's line from Brut, founder of the British race. Luke begins with Adam, according to many commentators, including the 1560 Geneva Bible, to emphasize Jesus's common origin with all humanity, and the "*Antiquitie* of *Faerie* lond" likewise goes back to a myth of origins. The *Antiquitie* also presents the Queen and her immediate antecedents in much greater detail. While Merlin speaks of her only as "royall virgin" (III.iii.49), Guyon reads of her grandfather, uncle, and father, and is given two names for her, Gloriana and Tanaquill. The myth of origins and the unmistakable portrait of three generations of Tudors are elements that this genealogy shares with the "naturall line" that Luke traces for Christ.

Most critics emphasize the idealized nature of the Faery chronicle, and note its omission of Edward VI's and Mary's "troubled reigns."[41] Fewer note the problematic realism inherent in the inclusion of Henry VII's elder son Arthur:

> After all these *Elficleos* did rayne,
> The wise *Elficleos* in great Maiestie,
> Who mightily that scepter did sustayne,
> And with rich spoiles and famous victorie,
> Did high aduaunce the crowne of *Faery:*
> He left two sonnes, of which faire *Elferon*
> The eldest brother did vntimely dy;
> Whose emptie place the mightie *Oberon*
> Doubly supplide, in spousall, and dominion. (II.x.75)

Oberon had an elder brother – that is, he was not born to rule, as the other Faery emperors inevitably seem to have been. His brother Elferon "did vntimely dy," another shadow on the ideal heritage of Faery. Why introduce, in an ostensibly positive way, the detail of Oberon's marriage to his brother's widow, when the lady allegorized, Katherine of Aragon, was not Elizabeth's mother and Katherine's previous marriage to her husband's older brother was eventually cited as grounds for Elizabeth's father's annulment? But these details, however embarrassing, point to this as the "naturall line" of Elizabeth, and invite readers to see in them a further reflection of the ideal.

Spenser probably includes Elferon, the older brother, because of the historical older brother's name, "by way of salute to the dynastic myth of descent from Arthur," in Cain's words.[42] The detail of Oberon's marriage to his brother's widow emphasizes how completely he filled Elferon's "emptie place," and thus drives home the point that the Arthurian mantle has passed to Henry, and through him, to Queen Elizabeth. Indeed, Spenser's

---

41 See Harry Berger Jr, *The Allegorical Temper: Vision and Reality in Book II of Spenser's Faerie Queene* (New Haven, CT: Yale University Press, 1957), 112–13; Alastair Fowler, *Spenser and the Numbers of Time* (New York, NY: Barnes & Noble, 1964), 180–6; Thomas H. Cain, *Praise in The Faerie Queene* (Lincoln: University of Nebraska Press, 1978), 115; and Michael O'Connell, *Mirror and Veil: The Historical Dimension of Spenser's Faerie Queene* (Chapel Hill: University of North Carolina Press, 1977), 80; The quoted phrase is from David Lee Miller, *The Poem's Two Bodies: The Poetics of the 1590 Faerie Queene* (Princeton, NJ: Princeton University Press, 1988), 207, and also appears in Erik Gray's "Introduction" to *Edmund Spenser: The Faerie Queene, Book Two* (Indianapolis, IN: Hackett, 2006), xxiii.
42 Cain, *Praise in The Faerie Queene*, 115.

formulation was probably constructed to remind readers of a dynastic expedient mandated by Deuteronomy 25:5-6: a brother (or close male relative) was directed to marry a deceased man's childless widow in order to produce an heir who would then inherit the dead brother's title and property. Such an arrangement yielded at least two links in David's, and thus Jesus's, ancestral chain. As recounted in Genesis 38, the patriarch Judah failed to marry his daughter-in-law Tamar to his third son after his older two sons (her first and second husbands) died. Tamar conceived twin boys after seducing her father-in-law, and thus continued Judah's line. Ruth became David's great-grandmother after Boaz, a kinsman of her deceased husband, agreed to redeem his dead kinsman's wife and lands (Ruth 3-4). Tamar and Ruth are two of only three women Matthew mentioned in his list of Christ's forebears (the third is Rahab); except for Fay, the mother of the race, Arthur's and Henry's wife is the only woman the *Antiquity* even alludes to until it arrives at Tanaquill. If Spenser, in this genealogical context, meant to remind his readers of this biblical practice, he intended them to regard Gloriana in some sense as the child not only of Henry/Oberon but also of Arthur/Elferon. Thus, in her Faerie type, Elizabeth is doubly associated with Arthur: as bride as well as daughter. What initially looks like an awkward concession to realism, a jarring reminder of Henry's unlucky first marriage, is transmuted by the genealogical context into compliment.

The Elfin chronicles, like *Briton moniments*, prefixes a different type of genealogy to a "naturall" one. Though two stanzas idealize the Tudors, earlier emperors, Elfin, Elfinan, Elfiline, and the others of stanzas 72 and 73, may not be intended for historical Tudor or British rulers.[43] Spenser's intention is to claim Elizabeth's spiritual descent from the great kings of the earth – a descent that need not have been physical in order to be important, as we saw in the sermon genealogies. In Sandys's sermon, the Queen was likened to each British ruler in a particular quality. Similarly, each pre-Tudor Elfin emperor is distinguished by a great deed, which can be seen as his legacy to Gloriana, and which she as Elizabeth replicated and renewed, thus demonstrating her spiritual heritage. One possible analysis follows.

43 Isabel Rathborne, *The Meaning of Spenser's Fairyland* (New York, NY: Columbia, 1937) proposed identifications for the "historical" figures that Spenser allegorized here. A. C. Hamilton's notes to his edition of *The Faerie Queene* suggest links between figures in the Elfin dynasty and rulers mentioned in *Briton moniments* but suggests that "[t]he identification of the seven named in 72-73 ... remains moot," *Edmund Spenser: The Faerie Qveene* (Harlow, England: Pearson, 2001), note on II.x.70-6 (258-9n.).

Spenser describes Elfin as ruling America and India – an ambition Spenser, a participant in the English imperialist project, would applaud: Elfin's spiritual heir Elizabeth was destined to command an empire of similar extent.[44] Elizabeth does not especially seem to resemble "noble *Elfinan*, who layd/ *Cleopolis* foundation first of all" if we think of literal building, but the heir would only need to restore what the ancestor established – perhaps the honor and independence of the English nation after Mary's troubled reign. This interpretation seems more plausible when we advance to the next line, and observe its concern with defenses: "But *Elfiline* enclosd it with a golden wall." The peace and security in which Elizabeth maintained England's territory was hailed by poets and preachers alike. Elfinell, "who ouercame/ The wicked *Gobbelines* in bloudy field," set Elizabeth the precedent England followed in emerging unscathed from the attempted Spanish invasion in 1588 – a spiritual as well as a military victory, we may infer from the epithet "wicked *Gobbelines*," a moral judgment on a supernatural race.

Elfant's building project, the crystal temple of Panthea, may figure the English church, which Elizabeth was praised for restoring to purity. Elfar killed "two brethren gyants," "The one of which had two heads, th'other three": a heroic personal victory over monstrosities, which Elizabeth duplicated in an astonishing triumph over such obstacles as gender, religious controversy, and international doubts over the legality of her claim to become an effective ruler. Elfinor, a skilled magician, "built by art vpon the glassy See/ A bridge of bras." He passed on to Elizabeth the wisdom to extend her realm's influence across the sea to Ireland, the Netherlands, and the new world.

I do not claim that this reading of the Elfin *Antiquities*, treating it as the same species of selective genealogy that appears in Sandys's sermon, identifies the exact deeds and qualities of Elizabeth that Spenser intended, but it represents an Elizabethan approach to genealogy: analyzing the acts and characters of the fathers in order to place those of the child in perspective; tracing the spiritual as well as physical lineaments of the fathers in the child. Even what Cain calls "the historically murky and morally perplexing British chronicle"[45] makes excellent panegyric

---

44 On Fairyland's connection with India, see Elizabeth Jane Bellamy, "Spenser's Faeryland and 'The Curious Genealogy of India,'" in *Worldmaking Spenser: Explorations in the Early Modern Age*, ed. Patrick Cheney and Lauren Silberman (Lexington: University Press of Kentucky, 2000), 177–92.

45 Cain, *Praise in The Faerie Queene*, 116.

sense when read as "the ground of [Elizabeth's] Storie" – the succession it traces validates her title to the throne, and its "most wicked" characters and actions, like those appearing in Matthew's genealogy of Christ, help readers appreciate their own queen the more. Approaching these passages as genealogies frees a commentator from the burden of distilling a consistent moral and political message from them, while still allowing them to be read as praise.

The Elizabethan interest in genealogy not only manifested itself as the family pride of the nobility but also characterized the contemporary approach to Bible study and accounted for a major strain in contemporary praise of the Queen. The fact that genealogy was thought to offer a key to character and spiritual kinship also explains the prominence Spenser awards the tables of ancestry in *The Faerie Queene*. Biblical commentators and Elizabethan preachers, like Spenser, saw spiritual as well as biological kinship as qualifying criteria for inclusion in such a list, and thus supplied the Queen with a heritage that, for the preachers, embraced biblical elements. Spenser, with his similar concern to capture Elizabeth's essential nature, provided the Queen with spiritually significant ancestors from prehistory and from invention.

5

"Waues of weary wretchednesse": Florimell and the sea[1]

To this point, we have noted the continuities between the ancient and medieval interpretive tradition and that current in England during the sixteenth century. We have considered how a traditional providentialist outlook shared by many biblical exegetes, liturgists, and preachers promoted the use of biblical types when discussing England's history and contemporary concerns. Understanding the allegorical way such biblical names and stories were applied allows us to approach *The Faerie Queene* with a more Elizabethan mindset than we otherwise might. The preceding chapter sought to demonstrate how this mindset might guide a reading of the tables of ancestors Spenser creates for Books II and III. This chapter will consider the image of seafaring and the theme of marriage in contemporary religious rhetoric as a point of entry to Florimell's adventures and a key to the moral meaning of Books III and IV.

Florimell's association with the sea can to some extent be explained by her allegorical identification with Queen Elizabeth. Florimell is destined through her marriage to Marinell to enjoy the plunder of various ill-fated voyages, which we can read as a reference to Elizabeth's share of her privateers' booty. Florimell is courted by a sea god, but his words and gifts fail to win her – perhaps an allusion to Elizabeth's wooers, princes of the various sea powers of her day. Nor did the fisherman's attempted rape (the threatened Spanish invasion on a personal scale) succeed against her. Both in her faithfulness to Marinell and in the sea's protectiveness, Florimell is a compliment to Elizabeth. But beyond conventions honoring Queen Elizabeth as "Cynthia, Lady of the Sea" and celebrating her achievements thereon, at least three separate currents of

---

[1] An earlier version of this chapter appeared in *Spenser Studies* 14 (2000), 133–61, published by AMS Press, Inc.

sea lore might have contributed to an original reader's understanding of the sea that Florimell encounters: the classical material characterizing the sea as a realm not only of danger, but also of opportunity, fertility, and abundance; the Petrarchan image of the lover embarked on the treacherous sea of love;[2] and popular religious rhetoric, particularly sermons.[3] Spenser's first readers were thus familiar with many uses of the figure of the ship at sea. Indeed, it was probably more generally familiar in religious than in erotic and epideictic contexts, since everyone was exposed to religious rhetoric.

The sea in religious rhetoric

The Bible testified that the sea was a dangerous, untrustworthy element. The apostle Paul was helpless in the face of the sea and its perils: "I suffered thrise shipwracke: night & day haue I bene in the depe sea" (2 Cor. 11:25).[4] But the helplessness of man to command the sea served as a foil to the power of Christ, who walked on the water and commanded the storm to cease: "What man is this, that bothe the windes and the sea obey him!" (Matt. 8:27). Where classical lore pictured Neptune sharing authority with such intermediate deities as Nereus, Proteus, and various Nereids, the Christian God withheld control of the sea from the race he appointed to subdue the earth. Noah's flood and Jonah's attempt to escape God's jurisdiction demonstrated the threat the sea posed to humanity and the authority God exercised over it. God's unique power to say to the sea, "Hetherto shalt thou come, but no farther, and here shal it staye thy proude waues" (Job 38:11) constituted part of his reply to Job, and not

---

2 The storm-tossed ship came to both the love lyric and religious discourse with a long-established tradition, traced by Ernst Robert Curtius in the "Nautical Metaphors" section of his *European Literature and the Latin Middle Ages*, trans. Willard R. Trask for the Bollingen Series XXXVI (Princeton, NJ: Princeton University Press, 1953, 1973), 128–30. Puttenham's *Arte* uses the ship metaphor as an example of *Allegoria*. Jerome Dees reviews classical precedents to Spenser's sea images in "The Ship Conceit in *The Faerie Queene*: 'Conspicuous Allusion' and Poetic Structure," *Studies in Philology* 72 (1972) and notes, "There is also the sermon tradition" (210), citing Donne.
3 For Christian traditions of sea iconography, see Don Cameron Allen, *The Legend of Noah: Renaissance Rationalism in Art, Science, and Letters* (Urbana, IL: University of Illinois Press, 1963), and his "Donne and the Ship Metaphor," *Modern Language Notes* 76 (1961), 308–12, and Maurice Evans, "Metaphor and Symbol in the Sixteenth Century," *Essays in Criticism* 3 (1953), 267–84.
4 Except as otherwise noted, biblical quotations in this chapter are from *The Geneva Bible: A Facsimile of the 1560 Edition* (Madison, WI: University of Wisconsin Press, 1969).

even Moses could bid the sea: "The Lord caused the Sea to runne backe" (Exodus 14:21).[5]

Thus beyond human interference, the sea offered a particularly apt arena for God to reveal his power and exercise his goodness: "They that goe downe to the Sea in shippes ... these see the workes of the Lorde, and his wonders in the deepe. For at his word the stormy winde ariseth, and troubleth the waues therof."[6] At the end of time this peril would be removed. When God and man were reconciled in the new heaven and earth, then there would be "no more sea" (Rev. 21:1). But meanwhile, the sea setting offered an especially stark contrast between helpless humanity and omnipotent divinity.

The church's discourse recognized the sea as dangerous. Even before later issues of the prayer book incorporated various prayers specifically for mariners, the 1559 edition classed "all that travel ... by water"[7] with "all women laboring of child, all sick persons and young children," and "all prisoners and captives" as alike vulnerable, needing special intercession in the thrice-weekly use of the litany. The sea's unresponsiveness to human pretensions to authority was proverbial: neither the ship's captain, nor Cyrus, nor King Edgar of the Saxons could command the sea, as we saw in a sermon quoted in Chapter 3: "Dyd the Sea, thinke you tremble at his voice, or was the floodde quailed to heare him speake? no hardelie. For had hee not saued himselfe by flight, the salte foome would haue washed his tynsell Gowne."[8] Moral and spiritual issues came into sharper focus when expounded in terms of seafaring imagery. Human pretensions to autonomy and authority and attempts to escape moral responsibility were most effectively dramatized and rebuked in seafaring imagery.

Here is a typical explication of the image of the sea from an early seventeenth-century sermon by Robert Wilkinson:

> the worlde is like the sea, for so saith S. *Iohn, Before the throne there was a sea of glasse*, Reuel. 4. and that was the world ... tumultuous and

---

5 The Geneva's illustration of this moment and its caption are above, Chapter 1, pages 00–00.
6 Richard Madox quoting Psalm 107:23–4 in *A learned and a godly sermon, to be read of all men, but especially for all marryners, captaynes and passengers, which trauell the seas* (London, 1581), sig. C1, STC (2nd edn) 17180. Available from the database Early English Books Online.
7 John Booty's 1976 edition for the Folger Shakespeare Library (Charlottesville, VA: University of Virginia Press) records the original spelling "travayle" in a note, along with its dual senses of "travel" and "travail" (71).
8 Madox, *A learned and a godly sermon*, sig. A6, quoting Ps. 107.

troublesome like the sea, wherin as the wind raiseth vp the waues, and one waue wallowes in the necke of another, so this troublesome life of ours beginnes in weeping, goes on in sorrow, and the ende of one woe is but the entrance of another. O what time might a man aske to set downe all the miseries of this life![9]

The sea represents "the world," that is, "this troublesome life of ours" whose conditions demand that humans rely on God rather than themselves.

The sea could represent spiritual dangers as well. In his prayer opening a sermon devoted to the story of Christ calming the storm on Galilee, Richard Madox assigned the sea broad meanings: it signified "the rage of this tempestious worlde ... the stormes of the flesh, and ... the wicked spirites which seeke to bring both body and soule vnto shipwracke," that is, the world, the flesh, and the devil – an ambitious equation, since this threesome encapsulates the totality of threat to human blessedness. This triad of world, flesh, and devil, as classic a Christian formula as the Creed or the Ten Commandments, was familiar to every Elizabethan from the regular rehearsal of the litany as well as the catechism and services for baptism and confirmation. Sunday by Sunday priest and churchgoers prayed, "From fornication and all other deadly sin, and from all the deceits of the world, the flesh, and the devil./ Good Lord deliver us."[10] In baptism, through their godparents, they had vowed to "forsake the devil and all his works and pomps, the vanities of the wicked world, and all the sinful lusts of the flesh" – a vow renewed at confirmation.[11]

The infernal triad, like the ocean, was impossible for unaided humanity to withstand; in fact, Christ's miracle in calming the sea was "an outwarde signe ... that in our selues there is no habilitie to resist the stormes and tempestes of this worlde, the rage of the fleshe, and the deuill, without his helpe."[12] Such abject helplessness is the condition Spenser evokes in his use of sea settings.

---

9 Robert Wilkinson, *The merchant royall a sermon preached at White-Hall before the Kings Maiestie, at the nuptials of the right honourable the Lord Hay and his lady, vpon the twelfe day last, being Ianuar. 6, 1607* (London, 1607), 5–6, STC (2nd edn) 25657. Available from the database Early English Books Online.
10 The Litany, *Book of Common Prayer*, ed. Booty, 69.
11 A Catechism, ibid., 283. Compare the services for public and private baptism, 273 and 279. See also Patrick Cullen, *The Infernal Triad: The Flesh, the World, and the Devil in Spenser and Milton* (Princeton, NJ: Princeton University Press, 1974), 18. There is a nice ironic symmetry in Madox's relating this triad to the sea, as the waters of baptism were the Christian's first line of defense against it.
12 Madox, *A learned and a godly sermon*, sig. B5.

The seagoing ship and pilot in sermons

The sea, boat, and pilot might be invoked to explain human psychology. Madox developed the psychological application in impressive detail. Notice how, in his explanation of the image, its tendency to dramatize moral conflict asserts itself:

> More yet I maye saye somewhat, and more particularlie. This body of ours is lyke vnto a Shippe, wherein the reasonable soule, lyke a marriner sayleth: this world is naught else but a sea of wickednesse: and the prouokementes of the fleshe are tempestuous windes, which of our selues wee are not able to asswage: which if they be not in tyme appeased, will bring vs in daunger to be eaten vp of the Sea, and so to make a myserable shipwracke. Let vs therefore be sure, that Christe be in our shippes, yea, let his feare be euer before our eyes ... our God shall make caulme all the vnrulie motions of the fleshe, that striue against the spirite, whether pride or couetousnesse, or lust, or enuie, or whatsoeuer, and shall supple[13] vs with the Oyle of his loue and heauenlie grace.[14]

Thus the mariner, human reason, had to invoke the help of Christ to master the body and its passions in order to navigate the sea of wickedness safely.

Spiritual danger may wreck the soul if the sea, in the form of a cherished sin, is allowed to penetrate:

> Although a Ship bee sound in all parts but one, and leaketh in no place saue onely one, yet it may bee drowned by meanes of that one ... Our soule is as a Ship on the sea, if it haue but one hole where it leaketh, it may make shipwracke of faith and a good conscience.[15]

A single fault may have disastrous spiritual consequences. So fragile is the soul's poise, in fact, that only a seafaring image can suggest adequate peril.

Sophocles, Horace, and Cicero had compared the political fate of a state to a storm-tossed ship. For England as an island nation, this conventional figure was especially pointed: preachers used it to symbolize foreign threats like the Armada, as John Prime did in a 1588 Queen's

---

13 Sic (perhaps) for "supplie." But "supple" is current as a verb during this period, too.
14 Madox, *A learned and a godly sermon*, sigs. C2^v–3. Madox sees the sea as emblematic of the whole triad: "pride" was usually assigned to the devil, "couetousnesse" to the world, "lust" to the flesh, and "enuie" to either the devil or the world. See Cullen, *The Infernal Triad*, xxxiii–xxxiv.
15 William Harrison, *Deaths aduantage little regarded* (London, 1602), 15, STC (2nd edn) 12866. Available from the database Early English Books Online.

Day sermon: "of late time, all the waters of the salt Ocean, and brinish natures [were] ascendinge and leaguinge themselues together to haue ouerwhelmed vs all."[16] Conversely, "the sea about vs" could, if God so willed it, be "a maine defence," as Prime had described it in an earlier sermon.[17] The paradox – the dangerous, threatening ocean revealing itself as a defensive moat – became historical fact in the contest with the Spanish Armada: "And all these waues ... haue swallowed vp many of them, who would haue deuoured vs."[18] Spenser likewise exploits the contradiction between the emotional and spiritual dangers implicit in sea imagery and the literal sea's beneficence under the rule of Providence.

In Prime's sermons, the sea was a literal, physical presence, but in other sermons, sea metaphors elucidate political theory. In this example, again from Madox, the storm at sea represented the temptations of worldly ambition:

> The Shippe maye well be resembled to a Cittie or common wealth: the Windes, be those whisperers that styre up stryfe, and spreade debate betweene man and man: the waues be such ambicious desyres, as doo trouble the peace of the Cittie, and make mennes mindes inordinatelie to swell in pride, in vaineglorie, in emulation, in debate: so wrastling and struglinge togeather, as one byllowe dasheth against an other: which all doo fyll the Cittie with the water of theyr garreboyles,[19] shaking it so sore, tyll it be readie to sincke againe ... Dissention in a Towne is a sore tempest, take heede, vnlesse Christe caulme it with loue, and styll it with agreement, what hope remayneth but a pittifull wracke.[20]

The sea imagery analyzes civics in moral terms, exposing politics as unchristian wrangling which endangers the whole commonwealth. Waves of ambition, "so wrastling and strugling togeather," contrast sharply with the seemly procession of English and Irish rivers to the undersea Hall of Proteus for the Thames–Medway marriage in Book IV

---

16 John Prime, *The consolations of David, breefly applied to Queene Elizabeth in a sermon preached in Oxford the 17. of Nouember* (Oxford, 1588), sig. B3, STC (2nd edn) 20368. Available from the database Early English Books Online.

17 John Prime, *A sermon briefly comparing the estate of King Salomon and his subiectes togither with the condition of Queene Elizabeth and her people preached in Sainct Maries in Oxford the 17. of Nouember* (Oxford, 1585), sig. B4^v, STC (2nd edn) 20371. Available from the database Early English Books Online.

18 Prime, *The consolations*, sig. B3^v.

19 According to the *Oxford English Dictionary*, a garboil is a "confusion, disturbance," "garboil, n," *OED Online*, June 2014.

20 Madox, *A learned and a godly sermon*, sigs. C1^v–C2.

of *The Faerie Queene*: "Yet were they all in order, as befell,/ According their degrees disposed well" (IV.xii.3) – the model of a harmonious and well-governed society.

The most frequent use of sea imagery by Christian writers and preachers from Augustine on was to picture the church as a ship of salvation navigated by Christ through the seas of this world into the harbor of heaven. In this long quotation from Stephen Gosson's 1598 sermon *A Trumpet to Warre*, the failed playwright and romance writer's euphuistic style develops the voyage-of-life metaphor into a full-fledged allegory:

> This world is a very sea of trobles, wherin there be two ships vnder saile, both men of warre. The one is the church, where Christ is the maister, his crosse the maste, his sanctimony the sailes, the tackle is his patience and perseuerance, the caste peeces are the Prophets, Apostles, and preachers whose sound hath been hard ouer all the world, the mariners be the Angels singing their *Celeumata glorie be to God on high*, the fraught is the soules of iust men, woemen, and children, And the rich gifts and deuotions bestowed vpon churches and colledges bound vp in baggs that shall neuer perish. The rudder is charitie, all the motions and actions of the church are wroght in loue, the ancor is hope, the flagge in the top of her is faith, the worde written in it, *Premimur non oprimimur*. We are cast down (saieth the Apostle) *but wee perishe not*. There is another ship at sea which hath this ship in chace, that is the Pyracy of hel, a hot ship and full of wild-fire, where the Diuell is maister, pride the mast, impurity the saile, the wisdome of flesh the Card, the mysterie of iniquity the compasse, *Diagoras* the Atheist, *Iudas* ye traytor, and the whole rabble of hel the Marriners: two tyre of Ordnance planted in her, one mixt of hereticks & schismatiks, another of persecuting heathen princes, that spit smoke & sulphur at the church of God. There belonges no anchor to this vessel, to stay it when the stormes of the wrath of God arise, for it is subiect to despaire. The flag in the top is infidelitie, the word written in it, *Lucrum est pietas. Gaine is godlinesse*.[21]

One senses that Phaedria's gondelay may hove into view at any moment. Though the voyage may be troublesome in either vessel, it is clear which the preacher expect his hearers to prefer.

---

21 Best known as a failed imaginative writer and anti-theatrical polemicist, Stephen Gosson nevertheless conformed to the ritual of the established church and was no Puritan, according to Arthur F. Kinney, "Gosson, Stephen (*bap.* 1554, *d.* 1625)," *Oxford Dictionary of National Biography* (Oxford: Oxford University Press, 2004); online edn, May 2007. His *The trumpet of warre A sermon preached at Paules Crosse the seuenth of Maie 1598* was printed in London in 1598, STC (2nd edn) 12099. Available from the database Early English Books Online. The quote is from sigs. F1–F2.

Christopher Shutte's *A very godlie and necessarie sermon preached bef. the yong countesse of Comberland* offers a similar contrast of the "naughtie arke" with the "ship of god":

> like as a paper arke or ship of leaues had bene a vaine deuise against the water to saue Noe and his familie: so is the whole religion of Antichrist in vaine to saue our soules. What a foolish paradise delight they in, which make their arke or ship, of the rotten boardes of mannes traditions, which can neuer hold together? howe loathsome an ensigne hath that vessell, which caryeth the marke and Image of the beast? How lightlie, how perilously, & howe vainely is he fraughted, that makes the chaff of bulles and pardons, his surest traffique? What loose anchre hold hath he, trow ye, that rests & rides vpon his owne merits and sinfull workes? Howe vncertaine is his course, who directeth his race to saile to heauen by the mediation of saintes? What a cowardly maryner is he, that always is afraid at the paper rockes and painted fyers of purgatorie? ... finally, how can he euer saile in safety, who hath none sitting at the stearne, but only Antichrist, whose purpose is to ouerthrowe the ship? In such a naughtie arke and ship they saile, that row on forward without let, in their owne inuentions and rotten ship of papisme and Idolatrie. but the arke & ship of god, is made of the pyne trees of his word, pitched within & without, with the assured grace of Christ, marked with the spirit of God and faith, fraughted with the weighty merits of Christs passion, casting sure anchor in his promises directed by his mediation to the father, emboldened with his blood against the rocks and gates of death, defended with the ordinance of Christian armour against the force of Sathan, and nourished with the woorde and foode of life. Let vs no more then sayle with them, nor yet retaine any of their abominations."[22]

Shutte's "rotten ship of papisme" is related to Gosson's "Pyracy of hel," not least presentationally. Though the point-by-point explication is unusually detailed, both passages are typical of sermons in exploiting the ship image's overtones of moral and spiritual conflict to underscore the seriousness of life and in insisting on the urgent necessity to choose correctly between alternatives – also Spenser's point in showing that Guyon learns to resist Phaedria during the course of Book II.

---

22 Christopher Shutte, *A verie godlie and necessary sermon preached before the yong countesse of Cumberland in the North, the 14 of Nouember, 1577* (London, 1578), sigs. D1^v–D2^v, STC (2nd edn) 22470. Available from the database Early English Books Online. Margaret Russell, the "yong countesse" of the title page, was seventeen in 1577, the year of this sermon and her marriage to George Clifford, Earl of Cumberland. She became the mother of Lady Anne Clifford.

Stephen Gosson's topic was war and its moral implications, on sea as well as on land; Richard Madox addressed his sermon to the mariners in the port town of Melcombe Regis; Christopher Shutte's text was the story of Noah. Each took the opportunity their material afforded to explore the values and possibilities of sea imagery in unusual detail. But less extended reference to the ocean, boats, and pilots was the rule, and many Elizabethan sermons make brief use of such images. Such brief examples demonstrate how familiar congregations were with the traditional ships of the body, of the state, and of salvation. The sea's associations with physical or spiritual danger were left implicit, as they are in poetry.

John Jewel expected the Queen to interpret such a glancing reference to the ship of the body in a court sermon. Preaching on zeal for God's house, he insisted on reason ruling even the commendable passions. "For, our good meaning maketh not our doinges good," and zeal is dangerous when it is not guided by knowledge, "euen as a shippe for lacke of a Gouernour is euer in daunger of the rockes."[23] Likewise, Edward Dering expected the Queen to recognize herself as the pilot and the ship as the commonwealth in a sea turbulent with doctrinal error: "flee far away from al vnthankfullnes … forget not that God, who was your one-lye Friend in trouble … Now that the Sterne and Helme is in your own hand, guide your Ship so that the waues do not ouer run it."[24] The ocean setting emphasizes the disaster consequent upon misjudgment or neglect of moral responsibility.

Most often the ship of these brief sermon references was not the individual psyche or the commonwealth, but the ship of salvation, the church itself. In an anonymous 1593 court sermon on the resurrection, the preacher promised the godly that "now they are in the tempestuous sea, then shall they be in the quiet hauen,"[25] and in a 1576 court sermon Richard Curteys described in similar terms the present state of the believers: "the Church like a good Shippe is tossed with many waues of the Sea

---

23 John Jewel, "Psalme. 69.9 The seale of thine house hath eaten me," in *Certaine sermons preached before the Queenes Maiestie, and at Paules crosse, by the reuerend father Iohn Iewel late Bishop of Salisburie* (London, 1583), sig. H7, STC (2nd edn) 14596. Available from the database Early English Books Online.

24 Edward Dering, *A sermon preached before the Quenes Maiestie, By Maister Edward Dering, the. 25. day of February. Anno. 1569* (London, 1570), sigs. B2ᵛ–B3, STC (2nd edn) 6700. Available from the database Early English Books Online.

25 L. S., *Resurgendum. A notable sermon concerning the resurrection, preached not long since at the court* (London, 1593), 16, STC (2nd edn) 21508. Available from the database Early English Books Online.

..."²⁶ These references abbreviate Shutte's more explicit treatment: "Thus is the Church of God alwayes in the raging tempestes and byllowes of this worlde afflicted with many tribulations, before she can arriue to the hauen of heauenly happines."²⁷

Britomart's lament

The seas of *The Faerie Queene* teem with properties and figures from romance and the classics: nymphs and gods, treasure, bowers, and dungeons. But Spenser's first readers, including those who were classically educated and followed contemporary poetic developments in Europe, were sermon-goers familiar with the religious significance of such images. Thus the stock sermon uses of sea imagery are relevant as well.

In III.iv, Britomart comes upon the literal ocean, which will shortly dominate the narrative of the poem. This ocean offers a handy metaphor for her emotional and spiritual state, and Britomart extemporizes a lyric that elaborates the psychological version of the preacher's familiar image:

> Huge sea of sorrow, and tempestuous griefe,
>   Wherein my feeble barke is tossed long,
>   Far from the hoped hauen of reliefe,
> Why do thy cruell billowes beat so strong,
> And thy moyst mountaines each on others throng,
>   Threatning to swallow vp my fearefull life? (III.iv.8)

Why? A preacher would answer that Britomart is experiencing the human condition – a sea voyage – with unreliable equipment, a "feeble barke." Her "Huge sea of sorrow, and tempestuous griefe" is dangerous. Like the sermon seas, it is "tumultuous and troublesome,"²⁸ its "moyst mountaines each on others throng," "one waue wallowes in the necke of another."²⁹ She turns to direct address, but an appeal to the "Huge sea of sorrow" to "allay" its "cruell wrath and spightfull wrong" will not be any

---

26 Richard Curteys, *Two sermons preached by the reuerend father in God the Bishop of Chichester the first at Paules Crosse on Sunday beeing the fourth day of March. And the second at Westminster before [the] Queenes maiestie the iij. Sunday in Lent last past* (London, 1576), sig. F5ᵛ, STC (2nd edn) 21508. Available from the database Early English Books Online.
27 Shutte, *A verie godlie and necessary sermon*, sig. E8.
28 Wilkinson, *The merchant royall*, 5.
29 Ibid.

more effective in Britomart's case than in Saxon King Edgar's. No human attempt to assert authority over the sea will prevail.

> For else my feeble vessell crazd, and crackt
>   Through thy strong buffets and outrageous blowes,
>   Cannot endure, but needs it must be wrackt
>   On the rough rocks, or on the sandy shallowes,
>   The whiles that loue it steres, and fortune rowes;
>   Loue my lewd Pilot hath a restlesse mind
>   And fortune Boteswaine no assuraunce knowes,
>   But saile withouten starres gainst tide and wind:
> How can they other do, sith both are bold and blind? (III.iv.9)

Britomart's "feeble vessell crazd, and crackt" is a familiar biblical image for her body:

> Notwithstanding in a great house are not onely vessels of golde & of siluer, but also of wood and of earth, & some for honour, and some vnto dishonour.
> If anie man therefore purge him self from these, he shalbe a vessel vnto honour, sanctified, and mete for the Lord, and prepared vnto euerie good worke. (2 Tim. 2:20–1)

Another biblical text gives the image its conventional association with women's bodies in particular:

> Likewise ye housbands, dwel with them [your wives] as men of knowledge, giuing honour vnto the woman, as vnto the weaker vessel, euen as they which are heires together of the grace of life, that your prayers be not interrupted. (1 Peter 3:7)

The preachers, as we have seen, sometimes interpreted this "vessel" as a ship, a "feeble barke," as Spenser did. "This body of ours is lyke vnto a Shippe, wherein the reasonable soule, lyke a marriner sayleth."[30] But in the case of Britomart's ship, "loue it steres, and fortune rowes" instead of Christ, as Madox urged. Her dependence on restless-minded Love, a "lewd," or bungling, unprincipled, and lascivious pilot (several senses were available in 1590, all of them appropriate), and Fortune, a ship's officer who cannot assure her security, "what hope remayneth but a pittifull wracke"? – unless she receives the relief she prays for.[31]

Her next prayer is better directed:

---

30 Madox, *A learned and a godly sermon*, sig. C2ᵛ.
31 Ibid., sig. C2.

> Thou God of winds, that raignest in the seas,
>   That raignest also in the Continent,
>   At last blow vp some gentle gale of ease,
>   The which may bring my ship, ere it be rent,
>   Vnto the gladsome port of her intent:
>   Then when I shall my selfe in safety see,
>   A table for eternall moniment
>   Of thy great grace, and my great ieopardee,
> Great *Neptune*, I auow to hallow vnto thee. (III.iv.10)

In committing her voyage to the divine guidance of "Thou God of winds," she follows the advice preachers would give: "in our selues there is no habilitie to resist the stormes and tempestes of this worlde, the rage of the fleshe, and the deuill, without his helpe."[32] Though "Thou God of winds" invites identification as Aeolus and seems in line 9 to be Neptune, wind is in John 3 a figure of the Holy Spirit, a member of the Godhead who can in Madox's sermon "make caulme all the vnrulie motions of the fleshe, that striue against the spirite."[33] As for "some gentle gale of ease," according to the *Oxford English Dictionary*, a gale is "in popular literary use, 'a wind not tempestuous, but stronger than a breeze' (Johnson)."[34] This is consistent with the description of the descent of the Holy Spirit on the early Christians in contemporary translations of Acts 2:2: "And suddenly there came a sounde from heauen, as of a rushing and mightie winde" (Geneva Bible), or "the commyng of a mightie wynde" (Bishops' Bible).

The pun on "Continent" encapsulates the moral lesson that preachers found sea imagery so well suited to teach – a rebuke reminiscent of Madox's and Jewel's to the unrestrained passions and the promise of Shutte and of the anonymous court preacher of 1593 of the ultimate arrival at the end of the voyage: "the hauen of heauenly happines."[35] The threats to Britomart's boat are "Loue my lewd Pilot" and "fortune Boteswaine [who] no assuraunce knowes." Madox referred to "the prouokementes of the fleshe … which of our selues wee are not able to asswage,"[36] and the rowing of Spenser's "fortune Boteswaine" sounds like "the labours & sorrowes certaine, the casualties vncertaine" of mortal life.[37] The emotional tone is certainly that of complaint, but Britomart shares her image

---

32 Ibid., sig. B5; "his" = Christ's.
33 Ibid., sig. C3.
34 "gale, n.3," *OED Online*, June 2014.
35 L. S., *Resurgendum*, 16; Shutte, *A verie godlie and necessary sermon*, sig. E8.
36 Madox, *A learned and a godly sermon*, sig. C2v.
37 Wilkinson, *The merchant royall*, 6.

with countless sermons. Further, the complaint's explicit concern with moral issues in its last stanza may remind us more of the sermon than the sonnet tradition. In short, Britomart's conceit introduces the sea of the Marinell–Florimell episodes and establishes its sermonic character, linking the sea of sermon tradition with Book III's theme of romantic love.

Sermon tradition: the sea of lust and the ship of married love

The preachers as a group seem unindebted to the Petrarchans in their romantic exploration of very similar images, though certainly the lusts of the flesh are conspicuous among the perils that preachers dramatize in sea imagery. A sermon Spenser no doubt heard many times, "An Homelie of Whoredome and Unclennesse" from the Book of Homilies, puts the image to arresting use:

> And surely if we would weyghe the greatnes of this synne and consydre it in the right kynde, we shoulde fynde the synne of whoredom to be that most fylthy lake, foule puddle and stynkyng synke, wherinto all kyndes of synnes and evils flow, wher also they have their restynge place and abydinge ... What shal I speake of other incommodities which issue and flowe out of this stinkynge puddell of whoredome![38]

The unruly waters of passions like Britomart's can stagnate and reek to a positively Spenserian extent, becoming a "most fylthy lake, foule puddle and stynkyng synke."

In "The Thirde Part" of the same homily, the author reviews the various biblical punishments meted out to those guilty of sexual impurity, particularly Noah's flood:

> [T]o shewe how greatly he abhorred adultery, whoredome, fornicacion and all unclennes [God] made all the fountaynes of the depe yearth to burste out and the sluces of heaven to be opened so that the rayne came downe upon the yearth by the space of forty dayes and forty nyghtes, and by thys meanes destroyed the whole world and all mankynde ... Manslaughter was committed before, yet was not the worlde destroyed for that, but for whoredome all the worlde, fewe onely excepte, was overflowed with waters and so peryshed: an example worthye to be remembred, that ye maye learne to feare God.[39]

---

38 "An Homelie of Whoredome and Unclennesse," in *Certain Sermons or Homilies (1547) and A Homily aainst Disobedience and Wilful Rebellion (1570): A Critical Edition*, ed. Ronald B. Bond (Toronto: University of Toronto Press, 1987), 174–90. I quote from pages 179 and 180.
39 Ibid., 182.

Madox used the sea as a metaphor for "the stormes and tempestes of this worlde, the rage of the fleshe, and the deuill," that is, all three elements of the infernal triad. Wilkinson used it for the first: "the world ... tumultuous and troublesome like the sea." Thomas Becon, the author of this homily, uses the sea to represent the second element, the lusts of the flesh – and because this sermon was one of a cycle to be used whenever no original sermon was preached, this value for the metaphor was probably reinforced more often than the other two.

Despite the multitude of moral, civic, and ecclesiastical applications preachers found for sea imagery, and despite its aptness to figure illicit sexuality, a reader searches religious rhetoric almost in vain for such metaphors in the context of love, marriage, and virtuous wifehood. Edmund Tilney's *The Flower of Friendship* and the marriage service in the 1559 Book of Common Prayer do without much in the way of rhetorical comparisons.[40] Henry Smith's *A preparatiue to mariage* has a few liquid metaphors, but the closest Smith comes to the sea is to note that "The man & wife are partners like two owers [oars] in a boate." The rest of the sentence is disappointingly landlocked:

> therefore hee must diuide offices, and affaires, & goods with her, causing her to bee feared and reuerenced, and obeied of her children & seruants like himselfe; for she is as an vnder officer in his Common weale, and therefore she must be assisted & borne out, like his deputie, as the Prince standeth with his Magistrates for his owne quiet, because they are the legges which beare him vp.[41]

But if most religious treatments of marriage steer clear of sea imagery, one exception, a marriage sermon by Robert Wilkinson, offers fascinating insight into Florimell's story.[42] Preached at a court wedding eight years after Spenser's death, in January of 1607, this sermon provides evidence

---

40 Edmund Tilney, *The Flower of Friendship*, ed. Valerie Wayne (Ithaca, NY: Cornell University Press, 1992). One could say the same about the other material excerpted by Joan Larsen Klein for her 1992 collection *Daughters Wives & Widows: Writings by Men about Women and Marriage in England, 1500–1640* (Urbana, IL: University of Illinois Press, 1992).
41 Henry Smith's *A preparatiue to mariage, The summe whereof was spoken at a contract, and inlarged after* (London, 1591), 66–7, STC (2nd edn) 22685. Available from the database Early English Books Online.
42 Wilkinson, *The merchant royall*. The marriage of James I's favorite James Hay, first Earl of Carlisle, and Honora Denny, daughter and heir to Edward, future Earl of Norwich, was attended by James and the whole court. The printed version of the sermon was popular: four printings survive from 1607, one each from 1613 and 1615 (Lady Hay died after a miscarriage in 1614), one from 1682, and another from 1708.

for a near-contemporary recognition of both the romantic and the moral potential of sea imagery. Wilkinson took as his text Proverbs 31's chapter-long description of a virtuous woman, quoting verse 14: "Shee is like a Marchants shippe, shee bringeth her food from a farre." With the familiar elements of the sea, boat, and pilot he constructs a figure of married love. Perhaps Wilkinson was influenced by the Petrarchans, perhaps even by Spenser – or perhaps the traditional language that spoke of the church on the one hand as the bride of Christ, and of the church as the ark, the ship with a cargo of souls, on the other, invited him to draw on both images at once. The text, however, is warrant enough: in his sermon, the bride and the sacrament of marriage are ships of safety sailing the treacherous seas of the world.

Wilkinson's sermon shares the familiar assumptions about seafaring with conventional religious discourse: the sea was dangerous; God alone controlled the sea and provided safety for those embarked upon it; sea settings were uniquely appropriate for revelations of moral and spiritual truth. More to the point, this wedding sermon shows how the preacher's sensibility could bring sea imagery to bear on the theme of nuptial love, and how sermon attitudes toward the sea converge with classical lore to restate the old truth that love's magic is the creation of unity out of diversity. Spenser makes a similar statement in the Florimell story, using sea imagery to show the lovers' incompleteness alone and their need for each other and for marriage.

The printed edition is prefaced by an epistle to the newlyweds in which Wilkinson constructs a seafaring metaphor describing both the institution of marriage and the sermon he is about to present to the public: "A ship first built in Paradise and for the pleasure of the land, but since repaired for the Merchants vse against the troubles of the sea: which ... I am enioyned to launch out into the maine."[43] Thus he appropriates the convention to which Spenser often returns: the author as pilot whose work takes him abroad on the open sea.[44]

The ground Wilkinson shares with Spenser hardly ends there. A ship presupposes a sea, and for Wilkinson, as I quoted earlier, the symbolic sea is the world, with its attendant miseries and troubles.

43 Ibid., sig. A3.
44 Dees, "The Ship Conceit in *The Faerie Queene*," discusses the use and importance of nautical metaphors in the poem, as do Angus Fletcher in *The Prophetic Moment: An Essay on Spenser* (Chicago, IL: University of Chicago Press, 1971), 246–7, and Kathleen Williams, "Spenser: Some Uses of the Sea and the Storm-tossed Ship," *RORD* 13–14 (1970–1), 135–42.

against these stormes to saue men from drowning did God ordaine the woman, as a shippe vpon the sea, that as *Noah* made an Arke, and by that Arke escaped the floude, so man by marying with the woman might passe thorough all the labors of this life, vnto which doubtlesse God had respect when he said, *It is not good for man to bee alone, let vs make him a helpe meete for him*: as much as to say, a ship to saue him, therefore hee which hath no wife may seeme to be like *Ionas* in the sea, left in the midst of a miserable worlde to sinke or swim, or shift for himselfe; but then comes a wife like a ship and wafts him home: but yee must stil remember that *Salomon* speaketh here of a good wife ... For otherwise if shee which was made to comfort in euerie storme be stormie and troublesome her selfe, then is shee not like a shippe, but like the sea, and then to bee so shipt, it were better with *Ionas* to be cast into the sea.[45]

The sermon is liveliest when it exploits seafaring imagery to develop the traditional sins, duties, and virtues of women, but at a wedding other points must be made as well, and the spiritual nature of marriage occupied Wilkinson throughout the last section of his sermon. The act of joining husband to wife, man to woman, was no ordinary thing. In his sermon's "Application to the King," the preacher said, "I will not say it is kingly, but diuine and heauenly to vnite into one things of diuided nature: for thus did God."[46] He referred to the apocalyptic marriage between Christ and his church, characterizing the present wedding's festivities as "The cause of this meeting, the ioy of this day, yea the mysterie and little image of this great intended Vnion."[47] Hay's and Denny's marriage was especially symbolic, as it joined noble houses from two countries, Scotland and England: "for simply to marrie ioynes sex and sex, to marrie at home ioynes house and house, but your marriage ioyneth land and land, earth and earth, onely Christ goes beyond it, who ioynes heauen and earth."[48]

Wilkinson closed his sermon with separate charges to the couple. He returned to seafaring imagery in admonishing the bridegroom: "mariage is a sore aduenture, and therefore as mariners vpon the sea in the day time look vp to the Sunne, and in the night to the Pole starre, so looke you vp day and night to God, and God shall giue you good shipping therein."[49] To the predictable advice to the bride to be obedient and complaisant, Wilkinson appended a palliative familiar to Elizabethans and Jacobeans

---

45 Wilkinson, *The merchant royall*, 6–7.
46 Ibid., 23
47 Ibid., 35.
48 Ibid., 36.
49 Ibid., 36.

from the 1563 "Homily of the State of Matrimony" of *The Second Tome of Homilies*: "a good wife by obeying of her husband rules him."[50]

Florimell and the sea of lust

The reader familiar with Britomart's lament is in familiar territory here. In her appropriation of the preachers' seascape for her expression of yearning for marital fulfillment with Artegal, she could be speaking for the bachelor Wilkinson described at the opening of his sermon, "like *Ionas* in the sea, left in the midst of a miserable worlde to sinke or swim, or shift for himselfe." The mythologizing and epideictic readings offer little at this point, for the solution to Britomart's dilemma lies not in diversity returning to unity, or in the sea acknowledging her as mistress. Nor does the Petrarchan context offer a wholly satisfying explanation.[51] Her present "feeble barke" is inadequate; she needs to be a wife. She needs to replace romantic love with wifely submission, and replace "Love [her] lewd Pilott," "bold and blinde," with the husband Wilkinson envisions: one who, hand on the tiller, looks up day and night to God.

Allegorical readings of Florimell's adventures are out of fashion, but typical sermon uses of sea imagery offer evidence of a moral pattern underlying Florimell's sufferings. Comparison with the sermon images shows that they appropriately take place on and around the sea because they dramatize the three perils symbolized by the sea in the sermon tradition – the world, the flesh, and the devil.

Christian tradition interpreted the original world-flesh-devil triad, the triple temptation of Christ in the wilderness, not merely as incitements to sin that Christ had to successfully withstand, but as an initiation. His victory made possible not only a new level of virtue but the very redemption of mankind. Florimell, as a result of her trials, likewise grows beyond the timid, passive figure fleeing imagined peril. When she faces urgent, actual danger, she prays to God for help and actively protects

---

50 Ibid., 38. This homily, which can be found in Klein's *Daughters Wives & Widows* and *The Two Books of Homilies Appointed to be Read in Churches*, ed. John Griffiths (Oxford: Oxford University Press, 1859), probably influenced Wilkinson in ways beyond this quote, which the homilist in his turn probably took from Erasmus (see Griffiths, 504–5).

51 Susanne Lindgren Wofford, "Britomart's Petrarchan Lament: Allegory and Narrative in *The Faerie Queene* III, iv," *Comparative Literature* 39 (1987), 46–7 turns to Psalm 69 to supplement the Petrarchan reading.

her chastity, first through physical struggle with the fisherman, and then through confession of her faithful love in defiance of a supernatural foe.

When we meet her, Florimell, though threatened and pursued, she has not lacked for would-be champions and has felt herself to be in more danger than she actually is: "So fled faire *Florimell* from her vaine feare,/ Long after she from perill was releast" (III.vii.1). But Spenser invites his readers to take Florimell's trials more seriously after she leaves the witch's house. The witch sends after her "An hideous beast, of horrible aspect"; "likest it to an *Hyena* was" (III.vii.22). The witch gives the beast a choice as to what it may do to Florimell: "Ne once to stay to rest, or breath at large,/ Till her he had attaind, and brought in place,/ Or quite deuourd her beauties scornefull grace" (III.vii.23).

This beast is the threat of death, mortality itself, and "feeds on womens flesh, as others feede on gras" (22). This wording echoes the language of Isaiah 40:6: "All flesh is grasse, and all the grace thereof is as the floure of the field." Florimell, the flower whose flesh and grace are about to be devoured like grass, recognizes the hyena-like beast as death: "That it she shund no lesse, then dread to die" (24).

Up to now, Florimell has survived her adventures on land without seeking or acknowledging help. Timias has killed the "griesly Foster" who pursued her (III.i.17), and awe of her beauty has protected her from the witch and the witch's son. But now, as she flees the first of the dangers the sea represents to the preacher – chance and mortality, the uncertainties and dangers and unavoidable death contingent upon existence; "the rage of this tempestious world"[52] – "she gan approch to the sea shore" (III. vii.25). In sermons, sea settings heighten the spiritual stakes, and Spenser is intensifying the threat to Florimell. When Satyrane appears on the scene to subdue the beast, Spenser develops a simile that collapses the identity of the sea and the hyena-like beast. Satyrane struggles to master it, "As he that striues to stop a suddein flood," so overwhelming that it "swell[s] aboue his wonted mood,/ And largely ouerflow[s] the fruitfull plaine,/ That all the countrey seemes to be a Maine" (III.vii.34). The beast and the ocean, representing the same threat – death – have become interchangeable.

Mortality, or "the rage of this tempestious world," does not exhaust the significance of this beast. The Geneva gloss to Ecclesiasticus 13:19 explains the hyena as "a wilde beast that counterfaiteth the voyce of men, and so entiseth them out of their houses and deuoureth them."

52 Madox, *A learned and a godly sermon*, sig. a5.

Hamilton notes that this is "how Florimell rightly regards all men except Marinell,"[53] and Beryl Rowland, citing Spenser's beast in her discussion of the hyena's symbolic value, sees it as "an epitome of lust ... or corrupted flesh and a sign of sin, concupiscence, and a fallen nature."[54] To quote "An Homelie of Whoredome and Unclennesse" once more, "above other vices the outragious seas of adultery, whoredome, fornicacion and unclennesse have not onlye braste in, but also overflowed almoste the whoole worlde."[55] Timias, if he is striving to "stop a suddein flood" of lust threatening to burst in and overflow Florimell, is wrestling the same beast as the homilist.

Florimell and the ship of married love

No less than the homily, Wilkinson's sermon can illuminate the moral dimension of the love story of Florimell and Marinell. Up to the time of her arrival at the sea shore, she is as aimless and helpless as the bachelor in the sermon, "left in the midst of a miserable worlde to sinke or swim, or shift for himselfe." She is in love with Marinell, but her love is unrequited; in Wilkinson's terms we could say that she needs the hand of a husband on the tiller, that she is as directionless and imperiled as a boat without a pilot – or one with Britomart's "lewd Pilot," "bold and blind." So frantic that she is "In minde to leape into the mighty maine," she is spared immediate death only through divine intervention ("high God did so ordaine"): she leaps into a fishing boat. God is master of the sea, and can make even that perilous element an agent of salvation. Spenser emphasizes the paradox: "So safetie found at sea, which she found not at land" (27).

Florimell is safer at sea than she was on land: the sea associated with miracles, magic, and fertility provides the setting for the narrative, while the threatening sea governs the emotional and moral subtext. Seas obedient to God and thus cooperative with humans are, as we have seen, familiar within the sermon tradition. God "did so ordaine" that Florimell's literal ocean is benevolent, as he did in the case of the English defeat of the Armada. When she seeks refuge from the hyena-like beast in the fisherman's boat, the winds consciously cooperate with her:

---

53 In his note to III.vii.22 Florimell seems mistaken to regard Timias, Arthur, and Guyon in this way.
54 *Animals with Human Faces: A Guide to Animal Symbolism* (Knoxville, TN: University of Tennessee Press, 1973), 112.
55 "An Homelie of Whoredome," 174.

> Long so she on the mightie maine did flote,
> And with the tide droue forward careleslie;
> For th'aire was milde, and cleared was the skie,
> And all his windes *Dan Aeolus* did keepe,
> From stirring vp their stormy enmitie,
> As pittying to see her waile and weepe ... (III.viii.21)

Similarly, earlier in the poem when Cymoent heard of her son's mishap with Britomart, her loud grief compelled the compassion of the waves, the sea monsters, and Neptune himself:

> Tho full of bitter griefe and pensiue thought,
> She to her wagon clombe; clombe all the rest,
> And forth together went, with sorrow fraught.
> The waues obedient to their beheast,
> Them yielded readie passage, and their rage surceast.
>
> Great *Neptune* stood amazed at their sight,
>   Whiles on his broad round backe they softly slid
> And eke himselfe mournd at their mournfull plight,
> Yet wist not what their wailing ment, yet did
> For great compassion of their sorrow, bid
> His mightie waters to them buxome bee:
> Eftsoones the roaring billowes still abid,
> And all the griesly Monsters of the See
> Stood gaping at their gate, and wondred them to see. (III.iv.31-2)

Like Neptune's "buxome" waters, even hostile waters like the Red Sea (standing in the Geneva Bible gloss for spiritual threats in the life of the Christian believer) can come from God: "to exercise their faith and pacience [he] continueth their troubles, yea and oftentymes augmenteth them."[56] In just this way, Spenser constructs Florimell's trials as a providential initiation.

While the literal sea is sympathetic, Spenser keeps the danger of the sea in readers' minds as well. In the stanza immediately preceding the description of the sympathetic winds, Spenser describes how cruel Fortune is heaping on Florimell "new waues of weary wretchednesse" (20) – a metaphor that, like "the waters of afflictions" of Shutte's Noah's ark sermon, might have come straight from the pulpit.

---

56 Geneva Bible caption on illustration of the Red Sea; see note 5 above.

Florimell leaps into the first boat she sees, without the deliberation Wilkinson recommended in his marriage sermon ("sound first and saile after").[57] She has not distinguished between the ship of salvation and Gosson's "Pyracy of hel."[58] Deferring to the man aboard in what Wilkinson would consider proper wifely style, she acknowledges his position as pilot:

> But thou good man, sith farre in sea we bee,
> And the great waters gin apace to swell,
> That now no more we can the maine-land see,
> Haue care, I pray, to guide the cock-bote well,
> Least worse on sea then vs on land befell. (III.viii.24)

She needs a professional sailor to take charge, of course. Sermon-goers, familiar with the emphasis that seafaring images place on a competent pilot to navigate the tempestuous seas of life, would share her concern. They would also respond with concern when the old man answers that "his boat the way could wisely tell" (24). According to the logic of standard sermon applications of the sea/boat/pilot image cluster, a pilot abandoning the tiller would correspond to the rational soul relinquishing control to the passions or to the body itself. On the high seas in an open fishing boat, Florimell faces the fisherman's lust, "the stormes of the flesh."

To read the image in Wilkinson's terms, her appeal to the fisherman is a request to adopt the husband/pilot's role, that of commanding the whole ship "by the helme or sterne, a smal peece of wood" just as a good wife ought "to be turned and ruled by a worde of her husband. *Salomon* saith not, she is like a house (as many women be, as good remoue a house, as to disswade or weane them from their wils) but like a ship."[59] The old fisherman embraces the implicit analogy between putting out to sea together and marriage. He also illustrates the loss of control imaged in abandoning the tiller. In the face of attempted rape, Florimell "struggle[s] strongly both with foot and hand,/ To saue her honor from that villaine vild" (27), angrily reproving him and shrieking to heaven for aid. But her resistance doesn't lead her "to leape into the mighty maine" at this juncture, which makes sense metaphorically, since the boat figures marriage and the sea figures "the lusts of the flesh" at this point in the narrative. The combination is almost realized in rape: Proteus appears on the scene

---

57 Wilkinson, *The merchant royall*, 10.
58 Gosson, *A Trumpet to Warre*, sig. F1ᵛ.
59 Wilkinson, *The merchant royall*, 11.

only when the fisherman "did very litle fayle" of "his hoped pray" (III. viii.31). Divine intervention saves her:

> See how the heauens of voluntary grace,
> And soueraine fauour towards chastity,
> Doe succour send to her distressed cace:
> So much high God doth innocence embrace. (III.viii.29)

"[H]igh God," unlike the mere humans represented by Florimell's knightly admirers whom the narrator apostrophizes, is qualified to intervene on the seas.

Initially Proteus looks like a savior. Florimell's plight "smote/ Deepe indignation and compassion frayle/ Into his hart attonce" (31). He tries to reassure her, lifting her out of the fishing boat into his chariot, "And there with many gentle termes her faire besought" (35). Once again, the literal sea and its actual inhabitants are characterized as benevolent and sympathetic. But in the absolutist moral landscape of the preachers' sea, Proteus is merely God's instrument rather than holding sway in his own right. In Spenser's fiction, he resembles Satan in the stories of Job and of Christ in the wilderness: he is an agent of testing and a challenge to growth. Upon Florimell's arrival at his "bowre" "in the bottome of the maine," he begins his efforts at seduction.

> Daily he tempted her with this or that,
> And neuer suffred her to be at rest:
> But euermore she him refused flat,
> And all his fained kindnesse did detest,
> So firmely she had sealed vp her brest. (III.viii.39)

While the mythical interpretation of Proteus as shape-shifter informs us that "Proteus is not committed to any one moral role," and that he "can represent change for the better as well as the worse,"[60] the sermon point of view offers a different perspective. The fisherman, representing the flesh, wanted to enjoy her body; Proteus seeks to corrupt her, heart and soul. Though he is used by God to rescue her from "that old leachour," Florimell meets in Proteus the last of the sea perils. In his sophisticated temptations, especially his power to assume a pleasing shape, Proteus is one of "the wicked spirites which seeke to bring both body and soule vnto shipwracke" – a devil.[61] His final temptation in stanza 40, "Then like

---

60 James Nohrnberg, *The Analogy of The Faerie Queene* (Princeton, NJ: Princeton University Press, 1976), 596.
61 Madox, *A learned and a godly sermon*, sig. a5.

a king he was to her exprest,/ And offred kingdomes vnto her in vew," identical to Satan's offer to Jesus in the wilderness, ensures that his function as devil is uppermost in readers' minds. Florimell's resistance earns her a place in what looks like hell:

> And in the midst thereof did horror dwell,
> And darkenesse dredd, that neuer viewed day,
> Like to the balefull house of lowest hell,
> In which old *Styx* her aged bones alway,
> Old *Styx* the Grandame of the Gods, doth lay. (IV.xi.4)

Certainly the devil would be the most likely candidate to put one in hell, though in Florimell's imprisonment, Spenser may also have intended his audience to remember John Foxe's characterization of Princess Elizabeth, walled by the waters of the Thames in the Tower of London for her spiritual love (her faithful Protestantism). In short, in Proteus Spenser achieves a remarkable synthesis, satisfying the expectations raised both by the sermon tradition of the sea as a metaphor for the infernal triad and by the classical lore of the sea's riches while simultaneously representing a ruler of a naval power who can woo an Elizabeth figure for his Lady, offering her kingdoms which she declines.

Meanwhile, Proteus hosts the river-marriage and the narrator recounts the fruitful sea's "abundant progeny" (IV.xii.1), modulating out of the emotional and moral register of religious rhetoric. But the tormented Florimell continues to inhabit the perilous sea of sermon imagery:

> And lowest hell, to which I lie most neare,
> Cares not what euils hap to wretched wight;
> And greedy seas doe in the spoile of life delight. (IV.xii.6)

One hears an echo of Jonah's prayer, referring to the ocean's depths as "hell": "out of the belly of hel cryed I, and thou heardest my voice."[62] Florimell prays for deliverance:

> Ye Gods of seas, if any Gods at all
> Haue care of right, or ruth of wretches wrong,
> By one or other way me woefull thrall,
> Deliuer hence out of this dungeon strong ... (IV.xii.9)

She also pleads for her love to be reciprocated:

> Then let mee liue, as louers ought to do,
> And of my lifes deare loue beloued be ... (IV.xii.10)

62 Jonah 2:2, Geneva.

Marinell overhears her prayer, pities her when he hears her accusation against him, and longs to carry her away. But in the sermon tradition, God alone is master of the sea, and no human rescue is possible for one in Florimell's situation: "From which vnlesse some heauenly powre her free/ By miracle .../ She lenger yet is like captiu'd to bee" (IV.xi.1).

Here the image of marriage as a ship or a voyage once again becomes important. Though Florimell has passed a series of initiatory trials, and though Proteus's hall has recently witnessed the wedding of the Thames and Medway, she feels herself alone in the midst of a destructive and careless ocean. Marinell, reviewing his options, sees how helpless he is to rescue Florimell:

> And though vnto his will she giuen were,
> Yet without ship or bote her thence to row,
> He wist not how her thence away to bere ... (IV.xii.15)

Even if Proteus and Cymoent both approve, he needs a boat; in metaphorical terms, he needs the title to Florimell that marriage would give him. Carrying her away in a boat would rescue her from literal imprisonment and the spiritual danger of Proteus's seduction, echo and correct Florimell's original mistaken choice of boat and mariner, and satisfy the marriage-directed impulse of the imagery. But the sermonly subtext demands that Marinell establish his interest in Florimell, and the boat he would take her into, as more legitimate than the fisherman's "Pyracy of hel."

Cymoent learns the reason for Marinell's declining health and gives her consent. Rather than confronting Proteus, she appeals to her father Neptune, "the seas sole Soueraine" (IV.xii.30) whom Britomart has identified as "Thou God of winds, that raignest in the seas,/ That raignest also in the Continent" (III.iv.10), noting that Florimell's status as "waift" gives Neptune the sole right to dispose of her. In sermon terms, when Neptune grants Florimell to Cymoent as Marinell's bride, God receives his due as the only effective power over the sea, the only one "able to vndertake the safe landing of all your commodities, and warrant euery voyage that you make,"[63] the one who must bless marriage and "giue you good shipping therein."[64]

The epilogue to Florimell's story is her marriage to Marinell in Book V – an affair celebrated on solid ground "After" (in language echoing sermonly meditations of the trials of life) "long stormes and tempests

---

63 Madox, *A learned and a godly sermon*, sig. a6ᵛ.
64 Wilkinson, *The merchant royall*, 36.

ouerblowne" (V.iii.1). Having resisted by providential grace the perils of the world, the flesh, and the devil, having been "in the raging tempestes and byllowes of this worlde afflicted with many tribulations," and having acknowledged God's sovereignty over the sea and called on him for aid, Florimell has matured – "she can arriue to the hauen of heauenly happines."[65]

Sermon use of seafaring imagery thus clarifies an important aspect of Florimell's history. At a critical moment in Florimell's quest, the setting shifts from land to sea – a shift that would have alerted readers trained by hearing countless sermons to recognize in her torments the spiritual dangers of the world, the flesh, and the devil. Such readers could recognize those trials as initiatory. Further, the sea setting invites the audience to interpret her adventures in moral and spiritual terms: to ask, not whether she will drown or be raped, but whether she will acknowledge her dependence on God or fall into sin. As it dramatizes the moral and spiritual issues and the disaster consequent on the wrong choice, the setting underscores her human helplessness, sharpening the references to divine intervention. Moreover, judging from Wilkinson's uses of sea imagery eleven years after Florimell's adventures were published, not to mention the popularity of his sermon, Elizabethan readers may already have recognized the sea setting as appropriate for a dramatization of the incompleteness of the single life and the impulse that propels men and women toward their destiny of married love. Familiarity with contemporary religious rhetoric can help us see what an original reader would have read throughout *The Faerie Queene* – and certainly here in the Florimell episodes.

---

65 Shutte, *A verie godlie and necessary sermon*, sig. E8.

6

Saracens, Assyrians, and Spaniards: allegories of the Armada

This book contends that recapturing the biblical learning of Spenser's contemporaries can help twenty-first-century readers appreciate the allegorical method at work in *The Faerie Queene*. As Chapters 2 and 3 demonstrate, Elizabethan liturgies and sermons inculcated a collective national experience which was pervasively biblical. Cultural familiarity with typology meant that preachers discussed recent and contemporary figures in biblical terms: Anne Boleyn as Esther, Mary Tudor as Athaliah,[1] Elizabeth as the Queen of Sheba,[2] and the Earl of Essex as Abner, Korah, Absalon, Abimalech, and Haman all rolled into one.[3] In Patrick Collinson's words,

> These people were living, in a sense, in the pages of the Bible. Theirs was a mode of discovering a shared identity which was indirect and is somewhat mysterious to us, but it was as meaningful as those other processes of England's self-discovery which involved chroniclers, antiquarians, topographers, surveyors, and map-makers.[4]

Chapter 4 brought the interpretive strategies Elizabethan churchmen used to read biblical genealogies (and to construct spiritual genealogies

---

1 John Aylmer, *An Harborow for Faithfull and Trewe Subjectes, against the Late Blowne Blaste, Concerning the Government of Women* (Strasburg, 1559), sigs. B4ᵛ, B6, STC (2nd edn) 1005. Available from the database Early English Books Online.
2 Πανηγυρίς *D. Elizabethae Dei gratiâ Angliae Reginae a sermon preached in Pauls Church at London the 17 of November in the yeare of our Lord 1599, the 42 yeare of the most flourishing reigne of Queene Elizabeth* (London, 1601), STC (2nd edn) 13597.
3 William Barlow, Bishop of Lincoln, *A Sermon preached at Paules Crosse, on the first Sunday in Lent; Martii 1. 1600.* [i.e., 1601] *With a short discourse of the late Earle of Essex his confession, and penitence, before and at the time of his death* (London, 1601), STC (2nd edn) 1454, D5–5ᵛ. Available from the database Early English Books Online.
4 Patrick Collinson, *The Birthpangs of Protestant England: Religious and Cultural Change in the Sixteenth and Seventeenth Centuries* (New York, NY: St. Martin's, 1988), 10–11.

for Queen Elizabeth) to the "chronicle history" cantos. Chapter 5 demonstrated how sermon uses of the image of seafaring illuminate the spiritual dimension of Florimell's story. In episodes recognized as historical allegories, Spenser's fictional characters and situations represent real people and recent events in the same way that preachers used Bible characters and stories to represent them. This chapter considers the Souldan episode as a fiction that interprets the defeat of the Spanish Armada – a defeat that, in the view of many observers and participants, reflected God's intervention. After reviewing the sequence of events, we will sample the presentation of the Spanish threat and the Armada's defeat in published prayers, sermons, and other religious discourse. Finally we will return to the actual poem to show how contemporary religious rhetoric confirms the traditional reading of the episode as an allegory of the Armada.

The Armada[5]

By the late sixteenth century, Spain, along with France and the Holy Roman Empire, had long been a dominant European power. Since Elizabeth's accession to the throne, Spanish wealth and influence had only grown: Spanish possessions in the Americas offered a new source of wealth to a population approximately twice the size of England's. Long-standing religious differences, ongoing English assistance to rebels in the Low Countries and attacks on transatlantic Spanish shipping, and ultimately the execution of Mary Stuart in February 1587 provided Philip with incentives to invade England, a plan he had announced in 1585 and which Pope Sixtus V endorsed.

Debate continues over the extent to which the Armada was a religious campaign. Some recent accounts have seen Sixtus as distancing himself from the project, delaying payment of his promised contribution to Philip's effort. They emphasize that Philip had secular reasons enough of

---

5 For the events and historical context of the Armada, see Felipe Fernandez-Armesto, *The Spanish Armada: The Experience of War in 1588* (Oxford: Oxford University Press, 1988), Garrett Mattingly, *The Defeat of the Spanish Armada* (1959 as *The Spanish Armada*; rpt. New York, NY: Mariner, 2005), Roger Whiting, *The Enterprise of England: The Spanish Armada* (Gloucester, UK: Alan Sutton Publishing, 1988), Colin Martin and Geoffrey Parker, *The Spanish Armada*, 2nd edn (Manchester: Manchester University Press, 1999), and James McDermott, *England and the Spanish Armada: The Necessary Quarrel* (New Haven, CT: Yale, 2005).

his own to go ahead without Rome's support.[6] According to one particularly secular analysis,

> much of the nonsense that has been talked grew out of the attempt, not unsuccessfully made, to represent the war as religious; to describe it as a species of crusade instigated by the Pope, in order to bring heretical England once more into the fold of the true Church. In reality nothing can be more inaccurate. It is, indeed, quite certain that religious bitterness was imported into the quarrel; but the war had its origin in ... perfectly clear and wholly mundane causes.[7]

However secular the causes may appear centuries later, contemporary documents show that Philip did consider the campaign a religious duty. Examples citing religious issues abound on all sides. Philip, for instance, thought his campaign assured of success even if it were undertaken in the winter of 1587: "[S]ince it is all for His cause, God will send good weather."[8] Cardinal William Allen's 1588 *Admonition* developed "the whole cause of these present sacred wars" from the Catholic point of view.[9] After the Spanish fleet had disappeared over the horizon, a propaganda pamphlet ostensibly Catholic but generally agreed to be the work of William Cecil, Lord Burghley, pictures the failed invasion as an effort to offer the "succours promised" to "all our countrimen which haue professed obedience to the Church of Rome."[10]

There were many practical arguments against the campaign, including ongoing Anglo-Spanish peace talks and the Council at Corunna's advice to Philip not to pursue the invasion. Nevertheless, the Armada

---

6 See, for example, Martin and Peter Kemp, *The Campaign of the Spanish Armada* (New York, NY: Facts on File, 1988), 131. On the other hand, McDermott's recent interpretation, while giving ample weight to the irritants of English piracy and military interference in the Netherlands, finds the religious difference central.
7 John Knox Laughton, ed., *State Papers Relating to the Defeat of the Spanish Armada*, 2 vols., 2nd edn (London, 1895), xii–xiii.
8 Quoted in Martin and Parker, *The Spanish Armada*, 86.
9 William Allen, *An admonition to the nobility and people of England and Ireland concerninge the present warres made for the execution of his Holines sentence, by the highe and mightie Kinge Catholike of Spaine. By the Cardinal of Englande* (Antwerp, 1588), LIX, STC (2nd edn) 368. Available from the database Early English Books Online.
10 William Cecil, Lord Burghley, *The copie of a letter* (London, 1588), sig. A2, STC (2nd edn) 15413. Available from the database Early English Books Online. Interestingly, *The copie* comments on *The Admonition*: its marginal gloss reads, "Cardinall Allens bookes haue done much hurt to the intended inuasion and conquest. The Cardinals rash & violent writing misliked by the Catholiques" (5).

of about 130 ships carrying 8000 sailors and 18,000 soldiers set sail in July 1588. The plan was to rendezvous off Calais with a Spanish force of about 30,000 commanded by Alessandro Farnese, the Duke of Parma. The Armada was to escort the barges conveying the invasion force across the English Channel.

Poor communications and perhaps a lack of commitment delayed Parma's forces, however, and English forces succeeded in disrupting the Armada's orderly progression, first by skirmishes on July 31 (in which two Spanish ships were lost), August 2, and August 4, and then on August 7 by a nighttime fireship attack on the Armada's close formation in Calais harbor. Spanish captains cut anchor to evade the fireships, and were then at a disadvantage during the battle the following day, August 8, off Gravelines. The Spanish lost five ships, and the plan to join with Parma's army was abandoned. The Armada sailed north, and on August 12, off the Firth of Forth, the pursuing English turned back. Parma's army still seemed a threat, and Elizabeth made her famous visit to encourage her army at Tilbury on August 18. But the Armada rounded the northern tip of Scotland, and the Spanish were heading south on their return to Spain when an Atlantic storm wrecked many vessels on the coast of Ireland.

Thousands of lives were lost, to disease and exposure as well as combat and shipwreck, but Spanish casualties overwhelmingly outnumbered English, and invasion was averted. The Spanish lost sixty-two ships, many more to the storm than in battle, while the English lost only the eight they sacrificed in the fireship attack. Historians point out many weaknesses in Spanish ship design, training, and strategy, but at the time neither nation expected the lopsided Spanish loss, especially in view of Spain's greater power and wealth. Religious differences had energized both sides and provided both with an explanation of the outcome: God's will had been done.

Religious discourse and the Armada

Flavit Deus et dissipati sunt, the motto read on Elizabethan commemorative medals: "God blew, and they were scattered." Modern readers tend to assume that Elizabethans attributed the defeat of the Spanish Armada to divine intervention because they lacked a rational explanation. God and his breath, according to this assumption, filled the gap that we fill today with our fuller knowledge of Spanish strategic shortcomings; ship, armor, and shot design; and meteorology. Here, for example, is John

K. Laughton, who edited the English state papers relating to the campaign for the Naval Records Society a century ago:

> [I]t is not strange that the action of the fleet was for long misunderstood, and that the failure of the Spaniards should have been represented – as it often is even now – as due to a Heaven-sent storm. *Flavit Deus et dissipati sunt* was accepted as at once a true and pious explanation of the whole thing ...
> From the religious point of view such a representation is childish; from the historical it is false.[11]

Fifty years ago, Garrett Mattingly, in his still-standard version of the events of 1588, accounted for the religious explanation in terms of propaganda and psychological necessity:

> It is easy enough to see why the English and Dutch should so ascribe it ... the more the destruction of the enemy could be seen as a direct act of God the clearer it would be that God was Protestant and that the common cause was, as it claimed to be, God's cause ...
> The odd thing is that all these legends are as familiar in Spain as in England ... At first thought, the hardest to understand is why the Spanish should have adopted the myth about the storm. Naturally the English welcomed a material proof that God was with them, but why should the Spanish accept the view that God was against them, that their fleet had contended in vain against the winds and waves of God? ... It is always easier to accept defeat at the hands of God than at the hands of men, and the Judaeo-Christian tradition is rich in resources for explaining apparently irrational behaviour on the part of the Deity.[12]

Lately, however, it has become almost as unfashionable to patronize early modern religious outlooks as it is to seek explanations for military victories in providential design.

Contemporary providentialist views of the Armada's defeat

Historians have begun to study the early modern mental habit of providentialism.[13] These scholars' findings demonstrate that in the case of

11 Laughton, *State Papers*, I.xi–xii.
12 Mattingly, *The Defeat of the Spanish Armada*, 390–1.
13 See Alexandra Walsham, *Providence in Early Modern England* (Oxford: Oxford University Press, 1999), Michael P. Winship, *Seers of God: Puritan Providentialism in the Restoration and Early Enlightenment* (Baltimore, MD: Johns Hopkins University Press, 1996), and David Randall, "Providence, Fortune, and the Experience of Combat: English Printed Battlefield Reports, Circa 1570–1637," *Sixteenth Century Journal* **35** (2004), 1053–77.

the Armada, the English did not seize on explanations of divine intervention by default, after the fact, to fill an explanatory void. God was considered the final arbiter in any combat of arms, even after an English disappointment, as was the case in the unsuccessful 1589 campaign, the so-called "English Armada": "The chaunces of warres bee things most vncertaine: for what people soeuer vndertake them, they are in déede but as chastizements appointed by God for the one side or the other."[14] Nor was this doctrine of providence invoked only by members of the clergy interpreting a war for the reading or sermon-going public: long before his navy sighted the Armada, Admiral Howard was acknowledging God's sovereignty, invoking his name, seeking his assistance, as will witness almost any page of the correspondence he directed to Walsingham.[15] Clergymen were not the only Elizabethans who subscribed to popular providentialism.

Nor were the English alone in this conviction that God was working through the clash of armies and navies, the plans of strategists, and the weather. Thus Philip and Medina-Sidonia could disagree about the meaning of the storm of June 19–20 that had scattered much of the Spanish force, but not its divine origin: "If this were an unjust war," writes Philip in answer to Medina-Sidonia, "one could indeed take this storm as a sign from Our Lord to cease offending Him; but being as just as it is, one cannot believe that He will disband it, but will rather grant it more favour than we could hope."[16] God had sent the storm as his bid in an expectations game, so that the final victory would be even more impressive. Philip later acknowledged God's hand in the disappointing outcome:

> We are bound to give praise to God for all things which He is pleased to do. Now I give thanks to Him for the mercy He has shown. In the storms through which the Armada sailed, it might have suffered a worse fate, and that its ill-fortune was no greater must be credited to the prayers for its good success, so devoutly and continuously offered.[17]

---

14 Anthony Wingfield, *A true coppie of a discourse written by a gentleman, employed in the late voyage of Spaine and Portingale* (London, 1589), 4–5, STC (2nd edn) 6790. Available from the database Early English Books Online.
15 E.g. Laughton, *State Papers*, I.49, 58, 66, 69, 106, 107, and so on. I.198 is one of many passages in which Howard (one senses reflexively) refers the weather to God: "God send us wind."
16 Quoted in Martin and Parker, *The Spanish Armada*, 143.
17 Quoted in Mattingly, *The Defeat of the Spanish Armada*, 390.

London-born Catholic Richard Verstegan's *The copy of a letter* likewise admits "how it hathe of late pleased God, to dispose of mens actions, according to his owne pleasure: which we will rather accepte as a punishment for our sinnes, then take for a discouragement to our cause."[18]

Neither England nor Spain turned to divine providence as an explanation that they would, if they had they possessed more information, have understood in more rational terms. Indeed, English eyewitnesses reporting to the Council routinely ascribed to God the success of maneuvers they had consciously planned and undertaken. Likewise, the author of *A true discourse of the Armie*, one of the earliest accounts offered to the public in 1588, gives God the credit even for the idea of the fireship attack off Calais:

> the lord hath caused the forces of the Spaniards, this their great Armado, to be daunted, and greatly endangered by his great wisedome, putting into the minds of our Captaines and soldiours, to provide six or seauen of the worst of the ships they had at sea, with such necessaries as should serve best to set them on fire withall, which they sent amongst the Spaniards, thereby to remove and scatter them.[19]

Regardless of their degree of familiarity with relevant facts, regardless of national bias, many actors in and reporters of the campaign referred the outcome to divine providence. They would have regardless of the outcome. The providentialist view of history that authorized preachers to make the biblical comparisons noted at the outset of this chapter (among many others) was not universal, but it was ordinary.

Hebraic patriotism in reference to the Spanish threat

The habit of referring to contemporary personages by invoking biblical types was, as we have seen, thoroughly entrenched in religious writing

---

18 Richard Verstegan, *The copy of a letter lately written by a Spanishe gentleman, to his freind in England in refutation of sundry calumnies, there falsly bruited, and spred emonge the people* (Antwerp, 1589), 3–4, STC (2nd edn) 1038. Available from the database Early English Books Online. Verstegan, a resident of Antwerp, published martyrologies of executed English Catholics and worked as an intelligence agent for the superiors of the English mission, William Allen and Robert Persons.

19 Daniel Archdeacon, *A true discourse of the armie which the King of Spaine caused to bee assembled in the hauen of Lisbon, in the kingdome of Portugall, in the yeare 1588. against England* (London, 1588), 14, STC (2nd edn) 22999. Available from the database Early English Books Online.

of the period. Cardinal Pole had referred to Henry VIII as "thee wicked Achab," and was in his turn called "Caiphas" by his translator.[20] By the mid-1580s, many biblical epithets were conventional. John Norden, in his 1586 tract *Mirror for The Multitude*, denounces the Pope as "that fierce *Holophernes* of Rome," calls Catholics "frogges of AEgipte," and refers to "we little Israell of Englande."[21] The biblical stories Norden considered most relevant to English–Spanish relations are the Pope as Pharaoh, from whom Israel/England escapes; the Pope as Sennacherib, whose forces God's angels slaughter; and the Pope as Nebuchadnezzar, king of Babylon. Allegoresis transmutes Bible stories into allegories of current events.

Not officially endorsed but very much in harmony with the occasional liturgies distributed during this period (see Chapter 3) was Christopher Stile's *Psalms of invocation vpon God*, also published in 1588. Stile has reference to several of the Old Testament stories authoritatively invoked in the liturgies:

> We the people of England are thy people O Lord, and thou art our God ... defend vs thy English nation. Turne thy wrath vpon the nations that haue not knowne thee, and that doe not call vpon thy name ... send forth thy angel stil to scatter them, as sometime thou didst in the host of *Senacherib* for *Iudah* and *Hezechiah* in his time. Let the blast of the trumpets blowne by our *Gedeon*, still strike a terror in the harts of the Antechristian Madianites, with their combined powers, and let be hard the sounding of thy host in the aire to the amasing of the Spanish Assyrians, that they and theirs may be a pray for our *Elizabeth*, and our English host? or sinke them in the sea, as thou didst *Pharao* & his host in pursuing thy Israel ...[22]

---

20 Reginald Pole, *The seditious and blasphemous oration of Cardinal Pole both against god [and] his cou[n]try which he directid to themperour in his booke intytuled the defence of the eclesiastical vnitye, mouing the emperour therin to seke the destruction of England and all those whiche had professid the gospele* translated into englysh by Fabyane Wythers (London, 1560), sigs. B1, D4ᵛ, STC (2nd edn) 20087. Available from the database Early English Books Online.

21 John Norden, *A mirror for the multitude, or Glasse Wherein maie be seene, the violence, the error, the weaknesse, and rash consent, of the multitude, and the daungerous resolution of such, as without regard of the truth, endeaour to sinne and ioyne themselues with the multitude: with a necessary conclusion, that it is not the name, or title of a protestant, christian, or catholicke, but the true imitation of Christ, that maketh a Christian*, sigs. *3ᵛ, *7, and p. 17, STC (2nd edn) 18613. Available from the database Early English Books Online.

22 Christopher Stile, *Psalmes of inuocation vpon God to preserue her Maiestie and the people of this lande, from the power of our enemies* (London, 1588), sig. B4-4ᵛ, STC (2nd edn) 23266. Available from the database Early English Books Online.

Since England typologically equals Israel, the English commanding officer becomes "our Gedeon" and the Spaniards are "Madianites" and "Assyrians."

Hebraic patriotism in contemporary celebrations of English victory

Even ostensibly secular works were not exempt from this cultural habit of biblical allegoresis. The list of ships and personnel embarked in the Armada, *A true discourse*, was originally published in many European countries in advance of the campaign as part of the Spanish public relations effort. Daniel Archdeacon's translation was published in London soon after the Spanish defeat. The first indication that this news bulletin will be steeped in biblical language is the verse sharing the title page with a woodcut of a ship: a quote from 2 Kings 19, one of the passages recommended in the officially distributed occasional liturgy. God warns the Assyrians/Spaniards, "Because thou ragest against me, and thy tumult is come vp to mine eares, I will put mine hooke in thy nostrels, and my bridle in thy lippes, and will bring thee backe againe the same way thou camest."[23] The same text is explicitly applied to the Spaniards in the "epistle to the reader" by E. B.:

> And therefore because they had raged against him, and their tumulte was come into his eares, [the Lorde] did put a hooke into their nostrilles and a bridle into their lippes, and brought them backe the same way they came, not suffering them to enter into the land nor to come against it with a shielde, nor to cast a banke about it, but hath deliuered it for his owne sake, and for his servants sake.[24]

The image of the bridle, which suggests the control of horses, is also applied more specifically to the Spanish attempt: "For hence we learne that a horse (and so a ship with men and all meanes els) is but a vayne thing to saue a man ..."[25] (In Spenser's alternate allegory for the same story, the ship becomes a horse again, as we will see.)

One element of the story of the Assyrian assault on Hezekiah's Jerusalem especially apt for the Armada comparison was the accompanying psychological warfare. In the biblical story, the Assyrian general

---

23 Daniel Archdeacon, *A true discourse of the armie which the King of Spaine caused to bee assembled in the hauen of Lisbon, in the kingdome of Portugall, in the yeare 1588. against England* (London, 1588), STC (2nd edn) 22999.
24 Ibid. 12.
25 Ibid. 13.

Rabshakeh addressed the citizens of Jerusalem in Hebrew, over the protests of the government officials, to the effect that God had ordered him to take the city and that Hezekiah could not defend them, promising leniency if they came out of the city peaceably. In his epistle prefacing the English translation, E. B. found a parallel in previous international publication of the list of the ships enlisted in the campaign before the Armada embarked:

> [Philip] hath here as thou mayst beholde, like *Sanacharib* by *Rabschake* by this booke, as by his embassadour, published vnto thee his whole powere.
> Neither yet commeth this embassage either to *Chizkija*, or *Eliakim*, to our gratious prince or her honourable counsayle, that they in his owne tongue might answere him again [as would have been appropriate, given Elizabeth's reputation as a linguist], but he hath published it to all beside our selues, in Italian, Spanishe, Dutch, and French, and yet to them thereby to discourage us: for these he telleth, he hath thus many huge shippes, so many thousandes of armed men, such multitude of munition as no man could deliuer vs out of his hand, or as if hee cried out with *Rabschake*: Let not England deceive you, for it cannot deliver you out of my hand, nor let not *Elizabeth* perswade you to trust in the Lord, saying, doubtlesse the Lorde will deliver vs, and not give over our countrey into the handes of the king of Spaine. But make apointment with me, and come foorth vnto me.[26]

This publication rankled: Burghley's post-Armada propaganda tract *The copie of a letter* singled it out, along with the Pope's bull authorizing the invasion, for purported Spanish regret. As his marginal notes say, "*The vntimely publication of the Popes Bull did hurt to the common cause … The multitude of bookes published to shewe the greatnes of the Spanishe Nauy, did also hurt.*"[27] For the English fraudulently to assert that the Spaniards regretted publication suggests that the English regret was sincere.

Besides the conventional references to Nebuchadnezzar, king of Babylon and Sennacherib, king of Assyria, *A true discourse* develops a comparison between Philip and Nimrod, the "mighty hunter before the Lord" (whom Milton would cast in *Paradise Lost* as the first Tyrant), and between the Pope and the murderous Lamech, who cursed any who should try to avenge his victim:

> Inferiour to none of these [biblical villains] are at this day our Italian *Lamec* and Spanish *Nimrod*, the pope I meane and the Spanishe king: the one whereof trusting to the inventions and practises of his priestly progenie,

---

26 Ibid., 9.
27 Burghley, *The copie*, 4–5.

Allegories of the Armada

to small and great threatneth death without cause, being so much worse then cursed *Lamec*, the other having with *Nimrod*, like beastes hunted men with dogges in *India*, would fayne use the like practise heere in England, and hath by hys ships, made like *Babel* towers, vaunted himselfe to make us afrayd.[28]

The *Discourse*'s use of biblical parallels is especially striking given the fact that it was published as news, not a sermon or religious tract. The review of events, elaborated as it is in biblical language, is followed by an English translation of the much-resented list of ships in the Spanish fleet,[29] names of the "Adventurers which go in the said Army, and their servants that are able to fight"[30] and "those which are entertained and in paie in the said Armie,"[31] and the list of "Provisions," including a description of the "Standarts."[32]

Thus writers with a providentialist understanding of current events appropriated biblical characters and stories as allegorical figurations of their contemporaries. Preachers predictably applied the same range of biblical parallels. In his 1588 Accession Day sermon, John Prime supported his interpretation of recent events with biblical allusions:

> Verily as *Elias* his seruaunt saw a small cloud by little and litle growing to a greater matter: so (good countrimen) the cheefe seruauntes of God in the honorable seruice of the realme and her Maiesty ... haue a long time since ... espied the rising and proceedinge of a cloude to come, sometimes thickning in the North, and sometimes threatning in the West, and of late time, all the waters of the salt Ocean, and brinish natures ascendinge and leaguinge themselues together to haue ouerwhelmed vs all.[33]

The cloud of the Spanish threat, analogous in its initial unimpressiveness to the cloud that answered Elijah's prayers for rain on Mt. Carmel, becomes an ocean full of ships "leaguinge" against England as the Red Sea threatened to overwhelm the Israelites.

> [B]ut ... that onely or cheefe Pole-starre of these home-conspiracies and foraine drifts and troubles euen against her own onely sonne, being taken

---

28 Archdeacon, *A true discourse*, 8.
29 Ibid., 17–36.
30 Ibid., 36–45.
31 Ibid., 46–68.
32 Ibid., 68–70.
33 John Prime, *The consolations of David, breefly applied to Queene Elizabeth in a sermon preached in Oxford the 17. of Nouember* (Oxford, 1588), sig. B3, STC (2nd edn) 20368. Available from the database Early English Books Online.

away, they haue missed theyr aime, *Her will and testament*, mencined in her letters to *Mendoza to giue away the realme, to the King of Spaine*, could not be prooued, nor that *Tragical execution* be executed and performed.[34]

The metaphor of leagued waters gives way to more literal references to Mary Stuart, "taken away" in 1587, whose "will" leaving England and Scotland to Philip of Spain (rather than to her son James) Mendoza as "executor" was never able to effect. In the event, the "leaguinge" waters

> haue swallowed vp many of them, who would haue deuoured vs: and by the prouidence of him that keepeth *Israell*, the strong horse and the proud rider, those tale [sic] ships, and furniture in them lie floting in the waters, and sinke in the sea. for since we desisted to chase and persue them most of this is come to passe, to the ende cheeflie to shew and declare that this was not the worke of man, but the hand of God.[35]

Via an allusion to Exodus 15:21 ("Sing ye vnto the Lord, for he hath triumphed gloriously: the horse and his rider hath he ouerthrowen in the Sea"), Prime reverts to the alternate "First Reading" of the special liturgy: the "leaguinge" waters of the Armada become the Red Sea, England becomes "*Israell*," and Spanish ships become Egyptian horse and riders.

Thus, from its very first sermon treatments, the English victory, interpreted ahead of time in light of the biblical readings for the liturgical services, became an instance of God's providential protection of England. A year later, the Exodus story was still resounding in sermon-goers' ears: "Who can number the *Soules* that perished in the deepe, (as in the daies of *Moses* & *Miriam*) when hee that came riding on the wings of the wind, delt with *Phillip* as he did with *Pharao*?" asked Thomas White in a 1589 Paul's Cross Accession Day sermon.[36] The story of Hezekiah, Rabshakeh, and Sennacherib also appealed to White: "how like hir case was to *Ezechias*, witnes that *Prowde* and *Peereles* Invasion, made by the *Popish Senacherib*, the king of Ashur."[37] As it offered so many parallels, he recounted the story in some detail, underscoring its resemblances to the incidents of the preceding year.

---

34 Ibid., sigs. B3–3ᵛ.
35 Ibid., sig. B3ᵛ.
36 Thomas White, *A sermon preached at Paules Crosse the 17. of November An. 1589. In joyfull remembrance and thanksgiving unto God, for the peaceable yeres of her Majesties most gratious Raigne over us, now 32* (London, 1589), 57, STC (2nd edn) 25407. Available from the database Early English Books Online. As I argue in Chapter 9, Spenser could have known this particular sermon, preached at England's premier pulpit and subsequently printed while Spenser was in London seeing the 1590 *Faerie Queene* through the press.
37 Ibid., 54.

The story begins when Sennacherib's armies first advanced against the walled cities of Judah. Hezekiah, rather than defying the Assyrians or appealing to God, sought an ignoble peace. According to 2 Kings 18.14, "he sent vnto the King ... saying, I haue offended: departe from me, & what thou layest vpon me, I wil beare it. And the king of Asshur appointed vnto Hezekiah ... thre hundreth talents of siluer, and thirty talents of golde."[38] White's sermon suppressed Hezekiah's effort to forestall war with the Assyrians, but offered his congregation an implicit parallel with Queen Elizabeth: "Our *Gracious Soveraigne*, did suffer long, and too long, almost before shee tooke the Sworde in hande, and stoode to her defence in the cause of the *Gospel*, against the *Enimies* thereof."[39] Elizabeth had made several efforts to postpone or avoid war, including negotiating with Parma in the Low Countries up to the moment word arrived that the Armada had been sighted. Indeed, many believed her policy toward Philip had been too conciliatory, and White's mild rebuke suggests that he may have agreed with such critics.

Hezekiah attempted to appease his enemies, but even though he gave the Assyrian king "all the siluer that was founde in the house of the Lord" and "pul[led] of[f] *the plates* [the gold] of the dores of the Temple of the Lord" (2 Kings 18:15–16) as tribute, his strategy failed. Elizabeth's negotiations likewise failed, and in the next episode in the story, the subjects of the legitimate prince (Hezekiah/Elizabeth) suffer harassment while their enemies attempt to undermine their allegiance.

White's account allegorizes his text: "the *Popish Sennacherib* ... openly Pretended the cause of his quarrell to be our Religion."[40] Following E. B.'s preface to *A true discourse*, White equated the biblical horses with Spanish presumption of superior power: the Assyrians "offring ... 2000 horse, if they coulde get but *Riders* for them, Riding, and deriding poore *Israel*, because their *Armie* seemed invincible, as the *Woodden bridge*, or *Spanish Navie* did." "Railing Rabsake," speaking the vernacular to the Jews at large rather than negotiating with their diplomats privately, finds his parallel in the "*Shamelesse* and *Seditious* printed bookes, spread ... over the whole land."[41] Hezekiah first prepares for war, but finding himself helpless in terms of physical power, seeks supernatural intervention.

---

38 *Geneva Bible: A Facsimile of the 1560 Edition* (Madison, WI: University of Wisconsin Press, 1969).
39 White, *A sermon preached at Paules Crosse*, 59.
40 Ibid., 54.
41 Ibid., 55.

"Now whether *Elizabeth* did behave her selfe so or no? If *Men* would denie it, *Angels* wil witnesse it."[42] The outcome is attributed to God's miraculous intervention: the Lord slew 185,000 of Sennacherib's soldiers, just as the providential storm (and here White switches to the Red Sea story, quoted above) scattered and wrecked the Armada.

White's summary statement of the spiritual lessons from the victory over the Armada recurs to types from biblical as well as to secular history in crediting God with the victory:

> But as *Shee* did then prepare her *Arme*, and yet made God her *Strength & Steele*, So let her nowe set vp her rest in *Heauen*, and give no rest to them in earth, that within the compasse of her *Dominions* shal seek the setting vp of *Dagon* againe, either whole, or broken: for why should *Moses* suffer the *Calfe*? or *Ezechias* the *Serpent*? or *Gedeon Ball* [Baal]? or *Elias Bals Priests*? or *Elizabeth Balaam's Prophets*? seing both the *Idol*, and the *Idol maker*, & the *Worshipper* are all accursed of God. And for this cause, the *Pope* is more odious unto vs than *Turke*, or *Iew*, and *Popish Princes*, are as *Sheon*, and *Ogg*, and therefore is it, that wee say of *Philip* of *Spaine*, as the *Lacedemonians* said of *Philip* of *Macedonie*, We would not haue him to come into our Countrie neither a *Friend* nor a *Foe*: for we haue tried his comming both wayes to be naught, though worse to vs in (*Mariage*) than in (*Mart*,) but our God, hath deliuered vs from them both.[43]

Elijah, nemesis of the prophets of Baal, and Trojan resisters of Alexander's father Philip, join Moses, Gideon, and Hezekiah, all familiar from the special invasion liturgies.

In referring to the Armada two decades after the fact, Puritan divine William Perkins asked, "did not God in our late deliuerance, ouerthrow our enemies, not so much by the power of man, as by his owne hand? Did not he fight from heauen? *Did not the starres and the winds in their courses fight against that Sisera of Spaine?*"[44]

A few years later, William Leigh published a Queen's Day sermon, which retold the defeat of the Armada by means of the same Bible story, alluding to Joshua's memorable battle against the five kings as well:

---

42 Ibid., 56.
43 Ibid., 60–1.
44 William Perkins, *A Clovd of Faithfvll Witnesses: Leading to the Heavenly Canaan* (London, 1607), 119, STC (2nd edn) 19677.5. Available from the database Early English Books Online. The reference is to the defeat of Sisera under the leadership of the judge Deborah.

That *Mirabilis annus* of 88. will neuer be forgotten, so long as the sunne, and moone endureth, When the starres fought for our *Deborah*, as the sunne and moone did then for *Iosua*. Nay more, the riuer *Kison* swept them away from *Callis* in *France*, to *Dingle-Cushe* in *Ireland*, Seas, Rockes, and shelues fought for England, shee armed her selfe with praiers to God against that great *Armado*, and preuailed.[45]

Biblical place names ("*Kison*" and "*Cushe*") indicate landmarks of English deliverance (Calais and Dingle), with a reminiscence of Old and New Testament hyperbolic references to trees, ocean waves, and stones acknowledging the power of God.

Spenserian historical allegory as counterpart to biblical typology

While preachers retold the defeat in terms of Old Testament stories, casting Spanish villains as Sennacherib, Pharaoh, and Nimrod, Spenser invents a character, the Souldan, who poses a threat to Mercilla/Elizabeth's throne. When challenged by Mercilla's champion Arthur, the Souldan answers in a high chariot equipped with sinister hardware and drawn by man-eating horses. Arthur, unable to get close enough to land a decisive blow, finally removes the veil from his shield. The Souldan's horses bolt in dismay, overturning the chariot, and the Souldan is "Torne all to rags" and "scattred all about" by its "yron hookes and graples keene" (V.viii.42).

One of the striking features of this allegory is the characterization of the antagonist as the Souldan ("Sultan," a Muslim or Turk). Before sampling the analysis that Spenser's episode has received, then, a review of this figure in contemporary religious rhetoric is in order.

The Turk in Elizabethan religious polemic

"The Turk," a staple of sermon rhetoric from medieval times, developed a new identity in the sixteenth century. The Protestant Reformation posed a new threat to Christendom (at least to its unity), and depending on the affiliation of the polemicist, Luther and his followers, or the Pope and his supporters, became metaphorical Turks. With Mary's death and the Elizabethan settlement of religion, English writers associated Catholics

---

45 William Leigh, *Queene Elizabeth, paraleld in her princely vertues, with Dauid, Iosua, and Hezekia ... In three sermons, as they were preached three seuerall Queenes dayes* (London, 1612), 93, STC (2nd edn) 15426. Available from the database Early English Books Online.

with Turks, and pamphleteers and preachers found various parallels. John Aylmer's 1559 *An harborowe for faithfull and trewe subiectes* refers to "the french Turke."[46] Fabian Withers's 1560 translation of Pole's *De Unitate* included a Protestant and patriotic "glose of Athanasius vpon the oracion of Cardinall Poole." "Athanasius" noted, "This is the general & natural sense of all the popysh secte to count all them which haue professed the gospell for turkes and worse then turkes ..."[47] But the insult can be returned: if violence is a hallmark of the Turks, "haue you not wisely declared herin the pope to play a ryght turkes parte and you yourself to have a turkish mynd or stomak?" Charles is "thee turkish emperour" who "doth much regarde the monkes" rather than "truly worshipp[ing] God and Christ."[48]

The theme flourished in sermons throughout Elizabeth's reign. Thomas Drant, with his characteristic copiousness, multiplies similarities between Catholicism and Islam, both personified as women, to support his contention that Islam is "in" Catholicism:

> The Church of the beloued is fayre, and fayrest of all women. Idolatrous churches are foule, and euill fauored women: and of all foule and euill fauored, I thinke the church of *Rome* to be one of the foulest of women. The evill fauoredness of *Mahomets* woman or church, is in this euill fauored *Romish* woman. That euill fauored *Mahomets* woman or church defendeth many wiues: This *Romish* church defendeth stewes and strumpets, curtizanes, concubines, & boy harlots. *Mahomets* woman, dreameth heauen to be a place of goodly Riuers, pleasaunt Apples, young delycate women, and fayre fruites: The Popes woman dooth say and holde, that S. *Dorathey* made basckettes of Apples that came downe from heauen. *Mahomets* woman defendeth workes: The Popes woman defendeth workes. That woman from the fift chapter of the *Alcaron* [Koran], beleeueth Purgatorie: The Popes woman will needes haue Purgatory.[49]

And so on through another page of comparisons.

There were more scholarly and historical attempts to associate the two religions. According to William Gravet's Paul's Cross sermon of 1587, since "the popes supremacie and Mahumets sect began both about one

---

46 John Aylmer, *An harborowe for faithfull and trewe subiectes* (London, 1559), sig. p8ᵛ, STC (2nd edn) 1005. Available from the database Early English Books Online.
47 Pole, *The seditious and blasphemous oration*, sig. C1.
48 Ibid., sigs. C4, C4ᵛ–C5.
49 Thomas Drant, "A Sermon preached at S. Maryes Spittle," in *Three godly and learned sermons very necessarie to be read and regarded of all men* (London, 1584), sigs. C5ᵛ–C6. STC (2nd edn) 7170. Available from the database Early English Books Online.

time (as is to be seene in the histories) and that was somwhat more than 600 yeeres after Christ ... Mahumetisme may go cheeke by joule with them."[50] Similarly, regarding the veneration of saints' remains and the pilgrimages urged on the Roman Catholic faithful, Meredith Hanmer opined,

> I woulde haue the church of *Rome* to beholde here in the lawe of *Mahomet* her founder in superstition, & shameful enormities ... The flocking to Tombs & sepulchres, the worshipping of dead corpses, bones, & reliques, the visiting *Limina Petri*, diriges, anniuersaries, or yearely seruice ouer the dead, praying for soules, pilgrimages to saintes, and shrines of the dead, sending of money in their absence, the opinion of holinesse and religion therein, we neede not say it is popishe, nay it is *Turkish* and *Mahometicall*.[51]

The two religions being essentially interchangeable, Islam makes an apt allegorical figure for Catholicism.

The identification of Islam with the Roman church was thus comfortably integrated into religious polemic by the time of the Spanish Armada, and that campaign's character as a war of religion made it a suitable context for a crusading vocabulary.[52] The English, for their part, were assured over and over in appropriately biblical language (from Esther to Revelation) that the projected Spanish invasion was undertaken as a war of religion:

> the King of *Spaine*, hath vowed the consummation of halfe his kingdome, but he will winne little Englande to subiection, vnto the vsurped authoritie of the whore of *Babylon* ... to fulfill the most damnable wil of that man of Rome, the red deuouring dragon ... How many haue ther bin martyred in *Spaine*, massacred in *Fraunce*, spoyled in *Portingall*, slaine in *Flaunders*, endangered in *England*, and many other countries & kingdoms ... to please the Popes high holines, to feede his hellish humour, and to fil his belly with the bloud of the Saints of God.[53]

---

50 William Gravet, *A sermon preached at Paules Crosse on the xxv. day of Iune Ann. Dom. 1587 intreating of the holy scriptures, and the vse of the same* (London, 1587), 50–1, STC (2nd edn) 12200. Available from the database Early English Books Online.
51 Meredith Hanmer, *The baptizing of a Turke A sermon preached at the Hospitall of Saint Katherin, adioyning vnto her Maiesties Towre the 2. of October 1586. at the baptizing of one Chinano a Turke, borne at Nigropontus* (London, 1586), sig. C6ᵛ, STC (2nd edn) 12744. Available from the database Early English Books Online.
52 See Christopher Tyerman, *England and the Crusades: 1095–1588* (Chicago, IL: Chicago University Press, 1988).
53 Norden, *A mirror for the multitude*, sig. *7ᵛ.

So John Norden invoked typology in 1586 to identify the Pope as the dragon of Revelation and the Roman Catholic Church as the whore of Babylon.

Catholics, meanwhile, made the same rhetorical move. William Allen's *Admonition* associated English Protestants with Turkish invasions:

> how she hathe by messingers and letters, dealte with the cruel and dreadfull Tirante and enemie of our faithe the *Great Turke* himself, (against whom our noble kinges haue in olde time so valiantly foughten, and vowed themselues to all perriles and peregrinations) for the invasion of sum partes of Christendom, and interception of sum defensible portes and places of the same, as for the disturbance of Christianity and annoiance of the principall defenders of the Catholike religion, she hathe at this day a ledgar in his courte.[54]

For Allen, Elizabeth's trade and diplomacy with Constantinople, breaking ranks with Catholic Europe, was enough to blacken her with the Turkish brush.

The English recognized the projected invasion as a crusade. According to Camden,

> Pope *Sixtus* the Fifth, lest hee should seeme to be wanting, renewes vnto Cardinall *Alane* (an *English* man, sent into the Low-Countries) [*The Declaratory Bulls of* Pius *the Fifth, and* Gregorie *the Thirteenth,*][55] excommunicates the Queene, deposes her from her gouernement, absoules her Subiects from their allegiance, publisheth in print the [*Crusado*] as against Turks and Infidels, whereby out of the Treasury of the Church, hee bestowes vpon all assistants plenarie indulgence.[56]

Though this was to a certain extent an English misunderstanding, the fleet's standard (the Crucifixion, Our Lady, and the motto "Exsurge, Domine, et vindica causam tuam") and the presence of priests on board to celebrate Mass, hear confession, and raise morale, all tended to cast the "Enterprise of England" as a crusade, or at least "a sort of propitiary sacrifice made to God."[57]

---

54 Allen, *Admonition*, XXIIII.
55 These square brackets (and those in the rest of the quoted passage) are in the original.
56 William Camden, *Annales the true and royall history of the famous empresse Elizabeth Queene of England France and Ireland &c. True faith's defendresse of diuine renowne and happy memory. Wherein all such memorable things as happened during hir blessed raigne ... are exactly described* (London, 1625), 255–6, STC (2nd edn) 4497. Available from the database Early English Books Online.
57 According to Fernandez-Armesto, *The Spanish Armada*, 38, 40, Philip did not win a papal indulgence for the participants, but Sixtus did issue a general benediction.

Allegories of the Armada

Not surprisingly, English writers rejected any identification of themselves with Turks, suggesting that Philip had neglected the real enemy:

> He returned with the losse of as many shippes, men, victuals, treasure, and ordinance, as might haue made a good armie by sea: and great pitie it is for Christendome, that both that which is lost, and that which remaineth had not beene vsed by the King Catholik, against the Infidels, and not with ambition to imploy such kinde of forces, to inuade Christian countreys therewith, who if he would liue in peace with them, would be readye to ioine their forces with his, to dilate the fines of Christendome.[58]

The Spanish and English could have joined forces against Muslims to reclaim formerly Christian territory. Rather than making England the object of a crusade, how much better make her a partner in one.

The same point, of England's readiness to unite with other Christians to defend the faith, is made by Anthony Marten in his *Exhortation*, published late in 1588:

> though we be here remoued in a corner from the rest of the world, and may be measured with a span, in comparison of all Christendome besides, yet haue we beene euer as readie, as any other of the mightiest, and richest kingdoms, to trauell ouer sea and land, to spend our liues, lands, and goods, to resist the furie and inuasion of the Turks, & other heathen Nations.[59]

The Spaniards should have directed their hostility in a different direction:

> It had beene farre more for their honor and credite, and for the profite of all Christendome, they hauing such store of men and wealth, if they would haue sought first to enlarge the kingdome of Christ, by compelling Turkes and Infidelles to the faith, rather then to spoyle themselues of their riches, and their Dominions, of Christian souldiers, by making war against a maiden Queene. By the charges and bloud of which vnnaturall war, they might perhaps haue gained many thousand Infidels to the faith of Christ.[60]

---

58 *A packe of Spanish lyes sent abroad in the world: first printed in Spaine in the Spanish tongue, and translated out of the originall. Now ripped vp, vnfolded, and by iust examination condemned, as conteyning false, corrupt, and detestable wares, worthy to be damned and burned* (London, 1588), 10–11, STC (2nd edn) 23011. Available from the database Early English Books Online.

59 Anthony Marten, *An exhortation, to stirre vp the mindes of all her Maiesties faithfull subiects, to defend their countrey in this dangerous time, from the inuasion of enemies* (London, 1588), sigs. B2-2^v, STC (2nd edn) 17489. Available from the database Early English Books Online.

60 Ibid., sigs. B3^v–4.

Similarly, in Lord Burghley's propaganda tract *The copie of a letter*, fraudulently attributed to a Spanish Catholic, the crusade comparison points up the discrepancy between the expectations raised and the Armada's performance:

> And though these armies were in déede excéeding great and mightie, yet they were so amplified beyond all measure in these bookes, as in no preparation of Christendome in former times against the *Sarracins* or *Turks* could be greater.[61]

This ironic thrust is aimed against the understanding that Philip claimed to be, in Marten's words, "enlarg[ing] the kingdom of Christ" and "compelling ... Infidels to the faith" by his enterprise.

A year after the Armada's defeat, English preachers were still comparing the enemy with the Turk – ironically in light of the formula "Turk or Jew," interchangeably with enemies of the Old Testament Israelites. Thomas White, in the Queen's Day sermon already quoted, told his congregation that "the *Pope* is more odious unto us than *Turke*, or *Jew*, and *Popish Princes*, are as *Sheon*, and *Ogg*."[62]

Indeed, even a decade later the comparison of Catholic to Turk had not gone stale. In this quote, anti-theatrical polemicist Stephen Gosson made the same set of associations in explaining the concept of a "just war":

> if either Turke, or Pope, or Idolatrous Princes force the law of *Mahomet* or Idolatrie vpon their peoople [sic], when they are desirous to embrace the Gospel, the Gospel may then bee bronght [sic, for "brought"] in by armes: but if the Turke or Pope, or Idolatrous Princes beguile their people, and their people willingly entertaine a false religion, there is no violence offered, and ... where no violence is offered, defence can take no place. On the contrarie, if the Turk, Pope, or Idolatrous Princes conspire to driue out the Gospel from those Christian kingdomes where it is preached ... The case is not alike: to banish the Gospel is to do an iniurie.[63]

"Idolatry" had long been a reference to Catholicism's veneration of images; here "the law of Mahomet" seems to become a further variant. Going to war without just cause essentially allies a nation with Islam: "whilest by his turbulent spirite christian kingdomes are dashed one against another,

---

[61] Burghley, *The copie*, 6.
[62] White, *A sermon preached at Paules Crosse*, 60.
[63] Stephen Gosson, *The trumpet of warre A sermon preached at Paules Crosse the seuenth of Maie 1598* (London, 1598), sigs. B6^v–B7, STC (2nd edn) 12099. Available from the database Early English Books Online.

the professours of Religion [are] extinguished, Christendome weakened, and the Turke strengthened."[64]

Eventually, the Spanish king's neglect of his true duty – to confront Muslims – came to be understood by some as a reason for the Armada's failure. Thus John Strype quotes a volume he refers to as "The History of the *Expulsion* of the *Moriscoes* out of *Spain*":

> That it was a visible Judgement on the *Spaniard*, for not expelling the *Moors* out of his Country. For God would never make use of the *Spaniard* to reduce Hereticks to the Bosom of the Church, so long as they suffered so many *Mahometans* Apostates to live among them.[65]

(The desired expulsion would finally be completed in 1614, under Philip's son Philip III.)

By 1625, when Bacon published "Of Unity in Religion" in the second augmentation of his collection of essays, it was possible to feel that "to propagate religion by wars," a project Anthony Marten and others had objected to only when the religion propagated was Islam or Catholicism, was to "take up the [forbidden] third sword, which is Mahomet's sword."[66] (The two allowable swords are "the sword of the Spirit, which is the word of God," according to Ephesians 6:17, and the "Temporall.") But the idea of a holy war was certainly alive in Protestant justifications of English intervention in the revolt of the Netherlands,[67] and after reviewing contemporary uses of the language of crusading, it becomes easy to appreciate Spenser's irony in making his figure for Philip a "Souldan." In a neat reversal, Arthur, the figure for English defenders, becomes the crusader, while the "Most Catholic" king becomes a Turk, or (even worse) a "Pagan."

Spenser's Souldan

Over the past few decades, Spenserians have grown tentative in their endorsement of the traditional reading of the Souldan episode. Elizabeth Heale, Humphrey Tonkin, and Russell J. Meyer, in their works for

---

64 Ibid., sig. C6.
65 John Strype, *Annals of the Reformation and establishment of religion, in the Church of England* (London, 1737), vol. 3, p. 525. Available from the database Eighteenth Century Collections Online.
66 Francis Bacon, *The essayes or counsels, ciuill and morall* (London, 1625), 16, STC (2nd edn) 1148. Available from the database Early English Books Online.
67 Tyerman, *England and the Crusades*, 367–8.

first-time readers of *The Faerie Queene*, tend to explain its historical allusions with distancing phrases, such as Heale's "normally taken to refer to," Tonkin's "generally read as," or Meyer's "commonly taken to represent."[68] Likewise Abraham Stoll, editing Book V for undergraduates, annotates the Souldan's first appearance in V.viii.18 this way: "Often read as a figure for King Philip of Spain." Here is his cautious note on the episode as a whole: "Stanzas 28 to 45 are generally read as allegorizing the defeat of the Spanish Armada."[69]

Other critics, as they offer support for or concede the traditional reading of the episode, insist that Spenser's emphasis was actually elsewhere – on the moral, psychological, or theological implications – as though the historical references are less worthy of attention and detachable from the poem's moral, psychology, or theology. For instance, René Graziani's 1964 essay provides persuasive evidence that the Souldan represents Philip II.[70] Graziani's piece is exemplary in its analysis of how moral content inheres in topical reference, but he speaks as if he were separating history from morality, explaining how he hoped "to readjust the emphasis more evenly upon [the] moral implications" of the Souldan episode.[71] Kathleen Williams also privileges moral over historical allegory in her reading of this episode: it "may have topical reference to the Armada ... but chiefly ... [to the] manifestations of a changeless inexorable power which rules events as it will."[72] Darryl Gless, studying *The Faerie Queene*'s theological aspects, suggests that "episodes often treated as expressions of historical allegory focus instead on fundamental doctrines of Reformed theology. And as a consequence, they carry weightier ideological force than more limited,

---

[68] Elizabeth Heale, *"The Faerie Queene": A Reader's Guide* (Cambridge: Cambridge University Press, 1987), 138–9; Humphrey Tonkin, *"The Faerie Queene"* (London: Unwin Hyman, 1989), 165–6; Russell J. Meyer, *The Faerie Queene: Educating the Reader*, Twayne's Masterwork Series 73 (Boston, MA: Twayne, 1991), 104.

[69] Abraham Stoll, ed. and intro. to *Edmund Spenser: The Faerie Queene, Book Five* (Indianapolis, IN: Hackett, 2006), 108n., 110n.

[70] René Graziani, "Philip II's *Impresa* and Spenser's Souldan," *Journal of the Warburg and Courtauld Institute* 27 (1964), 322–4.

[71] Ibid., 322.

[72] Kathleen Williams, *Spenser's World of Glass: A Reading of The Faerie Queene* (Berkeley, CA: University of California Press, 1966), 178. Where I part company with Williams is in my insistence on the analogy with typology: the unity of the moral and historical. For Elizabethans, the "changeless inexorable power which rules events as it will" was on display in the storm that dispersed the Armada. There was no either/or.

partisan sorts of allegory can support" – that is, they can be considered separately from their historical reference.[73]

Though the Armada reading represents the consensus, some critics demur. Humphrey Tonkin, for instance, thinks the Souldan represents "the active intervention of the Catholic powers in the affairs of England during Mary Stuart's captivity on English soil" – and Mary died over a year before the attempted invasion.[74] Other studies have ignored the historical dimension of the allegory. Thomas K. Dunseath's treatment of the episode focuses exclusively on its moral dimension, an approach that is consistent with his view that "a consideration of historical allegory is incidental to an understanding" of *The Faerie Queene*: "[Such episodes] are not dependent for meaning on history."[75] Sean Kane gives single-minded attention to the moral and mythic, rather than the historical, dimensions of the episode, which he sees as fought not in 1588, but (referencing *Works and Days*) "in a kind of Hesiodic age when 'might shall be their right.'"[76] Others subject it to fragmentation: Sheila T. Cavanagh and Thomas Bulger see Spenser as presenting a "bifurcated" view of justice through Artegal, who is human and cannot always succeed, and Arthur, representative of the ideal justice of a supernatural realm. For Bulger, the less satisfactory resolution of Artegal's encounters represents "the vagaries of human history," while "Arthur's overwhelming victories demonstrate the divine influence in British history."[77] This denial of the integral unity of Spenser's moral and historical allegories leads Cavanagh to cite the Souldan episode as an instance when a "distancing from the natural world provides a haven of hope and optimism for men to help offset the devastating chaos that enthralls the real world."[78] But as we have seen from the period Armada discourse, contemporary English observers read the events of 1588 as demonstrating that supernatural power had indeed broken in and reordered the "devastating chaos that enthralls the real world."

---

73 Darryl Gless, *Interpretation and Theology in Spenser* (Cambridge: Cambridge University Press, 1994), 141.
74 Tonkin, "*The Faerie Queene*," 165–6.
75 Thomas K. Dunseath, *Spenser's Allegory of Justice in Book Five of The Faerie Queene* (Princeton, NJ: Princeton University Press, 1968), 192–7, discusses the Souldan episode (the quote is from 59–60).
76 Sean Kane, *Spenser's Moral Allegory* (Toronto: University of Toronto Press, 1991), 149.
77 Thomas Francis Bulger, *The Historical Changes and Exchanges as Depicted by Spenser in The Faerie Queene* (Lewiston, NY: Edwin Mellen Press, 1993), 155.
78 Sheila T. Cavanagh, "Ideal and Practical Justice: Artegall and Arthur in *Faerie Queene* Five," *Renaissance Papers* (1984), 19–28 (the quote is from 27).

It is time to restate what was obvious to Spenser's first readers: the poem purposefully recasts well-known current events as fiction in order to provide them with a moral interpretation. Historical allegory is not disposable topical reference. As Kenneth Borris writes, "The welter of events is not simply represented but recast to manifest some imputed fundamental pattern ... Spenser's allegory conveys a sweeping historical vision ... which interpreted history especially according to the Books of Revelation and Daniel, read as prophecies of the tenets and exigencies of Reformed Christianity."[79]

Although I admire Borris's convincing demonstration that contemporary apocalyptic exegesis provides a key to the last cantos of Book V, I disagree when he claims that Spenser used his biblical material "so differently" from other religious writers. Whenever we try to separate providential from ordinary history, or divorce historical reference from moral message, we read the poem in a fundamentally un-Elizabethan and un-Spenserian way, as the notes of its first readers reveal.[80] Notwithstanding our historical belatedness, we (to quote John Pendergast) "must, to the extent possible, attempt to read *The Faerie Queene* as Elizabethan readers" if we are to get out of it what Spenser put in.[81]

The present chapter, with its contemporary examples of biblical stories pressed into service as moral encodings of current events, proceeds along the trail blazed by John N. King, Richard Mallette, and David Norbrook.[82] I hope my work will, like theirs, demonstrate the unity of the historical, moral, and aesthetic dimensions of the poem – as that unity would have been appreciated by Spenser's original audience. As I noted in earlier chapters, traditional biblical exegesis derives its authority from

---

79 Kenneth Borris, *Spenser's Poetics of Prophecy in "The Faerie Queene" V*, English Literary Studies No. 53 (Victoria, BC: University of Victoria Press, 1991), 9, 33–5.
80 Readers, that is, like John Dixon and the anonymous commentator whose annotations John Manning published in "Notes and Marginalia in Bishop Percy's Copy of Spenser's *Works* (1611)," *Notes and Queries* 229 (1984), 225–7. Bart Van Es, "The Life of John Dixon, *The Faerie Queene*'s First Annotator," *Notes & Queries* 48.3 (2001), 259–61, lists the studies that precede his.
81 John Pendergast, *Religion, Allegory, and Literacy in Early Modern England, 1560–1640: The Control of the Word* (Aldershot, England; Burlington, VT: Ashgate, 2006).
82 John N. King, *Spenser's Poetry and the Reformation Tradition* (Princeton, NJ: Princeton University Press, 1990), 133, 229; David Norbrook, *Poetry and Politics in the English Renaissance*, 2nd edn (1984, Oxford: Oxford University Press, 2002); Richard Mallette, *Spenser and the Discourses of Reformation England* (Lincoln, NE: University of Nebraska Press, 1997).

Allegories of the Armada

an overarching providentialist view of history, which takes in the entire Bible and all of secular history as its material. While co-religionists quibbled over individual details of interpretation and Catholics differed sharply with Protestants on the question of where Providence was leading, Spenser, like every churchgoing Elizabethan, was trained to see England's destiny from a providentialist vantage point.

Spenser's historical allegory as providentialist analysis of history

Biblical typologies of the Armada events were liturgically authorized and "*sermoned at large*." These parallels, treated as allegories by preachers and in printed texts, conditioned Spenser's earliest readers to experience the thwarted invasion as not just politically but spiritually significant and informed Spenser's construction of a fictional allegory to communicate the spiritual meaning of the Armada events. The texts I have sampled show that Spenser and his contemporaries were familiar with (and no doubt many subscribed to) the idea that supernatural intervention determined the outcome, vindicating their queen. Spenser and his original readers had heard the Armada story retold both literally and in biblical terms as a celebration of Elizabeth's reign.

Specific details of the episode suggest that Spenser had in mind some of the Bible stories that English churchgoers heard again and again during 1588, when the special service described in Chapter 3 was in use. The story of the Assyrian attempt on Jerusalem, for example, provides a parallel for Samient, Mercilla's goodwill messenger to the Souldan's wife Adicia. Though Spenser's narrative is tactful, Mercilla's response to the Souldan's "traytrous traines," which, according to stanza V.viii.19, include plots on her own life, is manifestly inadequate. She sends a helpless "Damzell" to the Souldan's "bad wife" (20) (who has been provoking her husband's murderous attempts) "in friendly wise" (21). Samient, lacking Britomart's qualities, soon finds herself in need of Arthur and Artegal's rescue from yet another "traytrous traine" (19) – threatened rape by "two false knights" (23).[83] This conciliatory policy is analogous to Hezekiah's apologetic subservience to Sennacherib, and equally ineffective.

When Arthur challenges him, the Souldan mounts "a charret hye,/ With yron wheeles and hookes arm'd dreadfully,/ And drawne of cruell steeds, which he had fed/ With flesh of men" (V.viii.28). The man-eating horses and

---

[83] Stoll's note on Samient's role misses, I think, Spenser's tone here: "Mercilla's attempt at peaceful relations celebrates E's efforts to avoid open war with Spain" (109n.).

the tall chariot recall passages from the occasional liturgies: the traditional biblical warning, echoed by Rabshakeh, against trusting in "charets and horsemen" (Psalm 20:7, 2 Kings 18:24), the horses contemptuously offered "if thou be able to set riders ypon them" (2 Kings 18:23), as well as the horses and chariots that were swept away by the Red Sea.[84] Likewise the "hookes" with which the Souldan's chariot is equipped, and which ultimately destroy him, recall the hook and bit of the Hezekiah story and the *Discourse* title page: "Because thou ragest against me, and thy tumult is come vp to mine eares, I will put mine hooke in thy nostrels."

The high chariot with its dreadful armaments is also reminiscent of the Spanish ships' towering height and large guns. The English were reluctant to close in on the Armada, and Spenser makes the same point when Arthur "Gaue way vnto his horses speedie flying" to avoid the chariot's "sharpe wheeles" and "fierce horses feet" (V.viii.31–2). After "long they trast, and trauerst to and fro," with Arthur unable to approach close enough to land a blow, "from his victorious shield he drew/ The vaile" (37), and the brilliance of his shield drives the Souldan's horses mad:

> Like lightening flash, that hath the gazer burned,
> So did the sight thereof their sense dismay,
> That backe againe vpon themselues they turned,
> And with their ryder ranne perforce away:
> Ne could the Souldan them from flying stay (V.viii.38)

The unveiling of Arthur's shield, as at I.viii.19 (when the shield's chance uncovering results in the victory over Orgoglio), represents "heauens high decree" (44), the hand of God rather than English might.[85] The scattering of the Armada is represented as providential, just as is the rescue of England from the Pope's clutches when Orgoglio is overthrown, and

---

84 James Nohrnberg, *The Analogy of The Faerie Queene* (Princeton, NJ: Princeton University Press, 1976), 362, 396, and 420–1, and Jane Aptekar, *Icons of Justice: Iconography and Thematic Imagery in Book V of The Faerie Queene* (New York, NY: Columbia University Press, 1969), 218–19, have very useful insights into the classical and contemporary political iconography of the Souldan's chariot. Michael West, "Spenser's Art of War: Chivalric Allegory, Military Technology, and the Elizabethan Mock Heroic Sensibility," *Renaissance Quarterly* 41 (1988), 654–704, has collected and analyzed some arresting contemporary illustrations of such battle wagons (671–9).

85 Upton cites "not only ... the burning of the Spanish fleet, but ... the easiness of the victory over this Invincible Armada" as possible referents for the shield's unveiling. (Upton presumably meant the English fireship attack, which did not succeed in setting fire to any Spanish vessels, but did break the crescent formation.) Quoted in *Variorum* V.228.

the unmanageability of the steeds corresponds to the effect of "Protestant wind" on the ships of the Armada.

Even on the offensive, Arthur still cannot land a blow: "Yet still the Prince pursew'd him close behind,/ Oft making offer him to smite, but found/ No easie meanes" (V.viii.42), just as, once the storm had scattered the Armada, the English defenders pursued from a distance rather than engaging the enemy. The eventual wreck of several ships on the Irish coast is transmuted into the runaway horses' upsetting the chariot and the Souldan's being dismembered:

> At last they haue all ouerthrowne to ground
> Quite topside turuey, and the pagan hound
> Amongst the yron hookes and graples keene,
> Torne all to rags, and rent with many a wound,
> That no whole peece of him was to be seene,
> But scattred all about, and strow'd vpon the greene. (V.viii.43)

With no recognizably human remains to collect, Arthur sets up the Souldan's armor, displayed as "an eternall token" of heaven's just judgment on wrong (44), just as the Armada's ensigns were displayed in churches.

It will be noted that, in this chapter, an exploration of contemporary biblical discourse does not support a new reading but an old one that matches details from Spenser's fiction with those from contemporary events (and Bible stories). My point is that a preoccupation with concrete correspondences does not violate the integrity of the moral allegory. From a providentialist perspective, any historical fact, properly interpreted, had its moral bearing. As we have seen, the fireship attack was credited in the *True Discourse* to the wisdom of God and (since the author does not mention the battle of Gravelines) the English victory.[86]

Nor does the roman-à-clef quality of the episode depart from the poem's other overall aim: praising Elizabeth. A few years later, Camden would attribute the idea of the fireship attack to the Queen herself:

> But the industry of the Queene preuented both [the Duke of Parma's] diligence, and the credulous hope of the *Spaniards* ... For, by her command, the day after the *Spaniards* had cast anchor, in the dead of the night, the Admirall sent eight of his worst Shippes, dawbed on the out-sides with Greeke Pitch and Rosin, & filled full of sulphure, and other materials suddenly combustible ... with a full gale of winde directly vpon the *Spanish Armada*; which, as the *Spaniards* saw approch neerer and neerer to them,

[86] *A true discourse*, 14–15.

(the flame shining ouer all the Sea) thinking those burning ships besides the danger of the fire, to be filled with some deadly Engines; with a howling and fearefull outcry, weyed anchor, cut their Cables, hoysed their sayles, cried out vpon their rowers, and, strooke with a horrible and a pannique feare, with impetuous haste betooke themselues to a confused flight.[87]

The whole episode redounds to the praise of the Queen, while the Spaniards react much as did the Souldan's horses.

A throwaway comment by Michael O'Connell captures the critical attitudes I have been arguing against in this chapter: that the Souldan episode contributes little to the poem thematically, and that the historical and moral allegories are somehow at odds: "one must attribute the victory over the Armada more to seamanship and lucky weather than to Elizabeth's justice."[88] A review of Elizabethan texts, by contrast, reveals the contemporary English view that rewarding a just Elizabeth and safeguarding her peaceful reign were God's motives in favoring English seamen and sending them lucky weather.

For Spenser and his contemporaries, the defeat of the Armada resulted from the same providential design by whose operation the Israelites crossed the Red Sea on dry land, enjoyed victory over Sennacherib's Assyrian army, and returned from Babylonian captivity – and by which Christian warriors should always triumph over the Turk. Thus his contemporaries' treatments of the Armada and its providential destruction demonstrate the links between Spenser's episode and current applications for the language of the crusade, as well as several biblical stories variously involving horses, chariots, hardware, and the sea as agents of God's judgment in ancient Israel as in 1588.

---

87 Camden, *Annales*, 278–80.
88 Michael O'Connell, *Mirror and Veil: The Historical Dimension of Spenser's Faerie Queene* (Chapel Hill, NC: University of North Carolina Press, 1977), 150.

7

"a goodly amiable name for mildness": Mercilla and other Elizabethan types

As we have seen, Elizabethan religious discourse reveals the pervasive biblical culture that Spenser shared with his contemporaries. The last chapter explored how biblical themes and language permeated discussions of the Spanish threat and attempted invasion. To go back in time but forward in Book V of *The Faerie Queene*, another contemporary issue of interest in the poem that preachers discussed in biblical terms was the question of the Scottish queen Mary Stuart. This chapter takes the Mercilla episode as illustrative of Spenser's allegorical method, placing that method in contemporary context by exploring its similarities to the "Hebraic patriotism"[1] or "correlative typology"[2] of sermons preached to Elizabeth about the Northern Rebellion and the threat posed by Mary Stuart.

Sermon types of Elizabeth, Mary, and other threats

The first of the perils associated with Mary Stuart's sojourn in England was the Northern Rebellion. The official "Homelie against Disobedience and Wylfull Rebellion," released in six parts in 1570, used scriptural parallels to clarify the moral issues of very recent and currently unfolding events: the Northern Rebellion of 1569–70 and the papal bull excommunicating Elizabeth in early 1570. The second part is devoted to David, Mary, and Jesus as subjects who declined to disobey even "evyll and unkinde princes."[3]

---

1 Graeme Murdock, "The Importance of Being Josiah: An Image of Calvinist Identity," *Sixteenth Century Studies* 29.4 (Winter 1998), 1043–59.
2 Barbara Lewalski, *Protestant Poetics and the Seventeenth-Century Religious Lyric* (Princeton, NJ: Princeton University Press, 1979), 130.
3 In *Certain Sermons or Homilies (1547) and A Homily against Disobedience and Wilful Rebellion (1570): A Critical Edition*, ed. Ronald B. Bond (Toronto: University of Toronto Press, 1987), 218–24; the phrase quoted is on 219.

In his effort to parallel England's situation with a biblical story, the homily's author creates a dialogue with David. Shall not good men rebel against "a prince hated of God"? "No, saith good and godly David." Shall we not rebel against an unkind king? "No, saith good David." Shall we not rebel against a king who seeks our lives? "No, saith godly David." Shall we not risk our country's "whole estate" with "an armie of such good felowes as we are"? "No, saith godly David." "Are not they … lustie and courageous … valiaunt … and good … that do venture" to rebel against "a naughtie prince"? "They may be as lustie, as couragious as they list, yet, saith godly David, they can be no good nor godly men that so do …"[4]

> If Kyng David woulde make these aunsweres, as by his deedes and wordes recorded in the Holy Scriptures … he doth … what aunswere, thinke you, woulde he make to those that demaunde whether they … may not … depose or destroy [Elizabeth,] their naturall and loving Princes, enemie to none, good to all … the mayntayner of perpetuall peace, quietnesse and securitie …?

David's horror and indignation would be what "no mortall man can expresse with wordes, nor conceave in mynde."[5] The homily, in making David a commentator on current events in England, indicates that the Northern Rebellion carries as clear a spiritual import as biblical stories.

The fourth part of the 1570 homily announces in its opening paragraph that it will "shewe some examples set out in Scriptures" of rebellions and their punishment.[6] After rehearsing the stories of Israel's murmuring against Moses, Absalom's insurrection against David, and the five kings of the plain against their overlord, the homilist suggests that secular history teaches the same lessons:

> Turne over and reade the histories of all nations, looke over the chronicles of our owne countrey, call to mynde so many rebellions of olde tyme, and some yet freshe in memorie, ye shall not finde that God ever prospered any rebellion against their naturall and lawfull prince, but contrarywyse that the rebelles were overthrowen and slaine, and such as were taken prysoners dreadfully executed.[7]

Not that we have to agree: Bond's introduction notes that the Scottish turmoil of the 1560s, which led to Mary Stuart's resigning the crown to her

---

4 Ibid., 221.
5 Ibid., 222.
6 Ibid., 230.
7 Ibid., 233.

infant son and then fleeing Scotland after losing the battle of Langside, illustrates the opposite. The homily itself, however, even in its specific references to the Northern Rebellion, omits any mention of Mary Stuart, in keeping with a prohibition on explicit discussion of her situation.[8]

The homilist draws a biblical parallel between Elizabeth and Solomon to show how unlikely it is that God would choose the leaders of the Northern Rebellion to reform her settlement of religion:

> If peaceable King Salomon was judged of God to be more meete to buylde his temple (wherby the ordering of religion is meant) then his father, King David, though otherwyse a most godly kyng, for that David was a great warrier and had shed much blood, though it were in his warres against the enemies of God, of this may al godly and reasonable subjectes consyder that a peaceable prince, specially our most peaceable and mercyfull Queene, who hath hytherto shed no blood at all, no, not of her most deadly enemies, is more lyke and farre meeter eyther to set up or to mayntayne true religion then are bloddy rebelles, who ... do seeke to shead the blood of Gods freendes, of their owne countreymen, and of their owne most deare freendes and kynsefolke, yea, the destruction of their most gratious prince and naturall countrey.[9]

Analogous stories in the Bible clarify current events: Elizabeth is peaceable King Solomon; the rebels are Absaloms or worse.

The fifth and sixth parts of the homily examine European and English history to show the various bishops of Rome's "spoyling and robbing the Emperours of their townes, cities, dominions and kyngdomes." These "subtil drifts"[10] only succeeded "by ignoraunce of Gods Worde, wherein they kept all men, specially the common people,"[11] and which had blessedly been relieved in England by the religious reforms introduced by Henry, Edward, and Elizabeth. Now, thanks to the English-language Bible and service books, even the common people might know that "God doeth curse the blessinges, and blesse the cursinges of such wicked usurping bishops and tyrauntes" – though "certayne Northen borderers, being men most ignoraunt ... of all people of the realme" did seem malleable to the Pope's evil intention. But "God of his mercy miraculously calmed that raging tempest, not only without any shipwrake of the common wealth, but almost without any shedding of Christian and Englishe

---

8 Ibid., 43.
9 Ibid., 233.
10 Ibid., 239.
11 Ibid., 240.

blood at al,"[12] and the homily itself reflected the Council's purpose that "the vulgar people wold be tought, how this rebellion was pernicious to the Realme, and ageynst the honor of God."[13] As the six-part homily was printed and bound with subsequent reissues of the *Second Tome of Homilies* from 1571 on, no one could be ignorant of rebellion's spiritual meaning in the future.

Always appropriate in sermons, typology was even more useful during the years following the Northern Rebellion given the proscription on making any public reference to Mary. Thomas Drant, preaching in January 1570, after the Northern Rebellion but before the defeat of Leonard Dacre in February, addressed the Queen on the text from Genesis, "They were both naked, and they were not ashamed." Meditating on the sense of "naked" as "without weapon" or "unarmed," Drant notes that, though the rebellion is put down, the rebels are not yet punished. He engages the apparent opposition between "mercy" and "justice":

> But they will tel me, which they tell the prince commonly, that she hath a goodly amiable name for mildnesse, and that now to draw the sword in this sort were the losse of that commendation ... These great merueilers at mildnesse, must remember that mildnes to some is oft times vnmildnes and crueltie to many other ... her maiestie punishing euen to the vttermost Gods enemies, shall neuerthelesse by Gods word reteine the name of a mild, and mercifull prince. She may be iust & seuere, and yet she may be mercifull, and mild.[14]

Drant draws analogies to the idealized reign of David:

> And now to speake of that, that the prince may be iust in punishing, and yet be still called a milde, and a mercifull Prince, it is sayd of *Dauid: Lorde remember Dauid and all his mildenesse.* Yet in the 101. Psal. the sayd *Dauid* doth say: *In the morning I did kill all the sinners of the earth, that I might destroy from the Citie of God all that do euill. Dauid* destroyed all Gods enemies: her Maiestie hath destroyed none of Gods enemies. *Dauid* did it in the morning of his kingdome: it is now farreforth dayes since her Maiestie beganne to raigne, and yet it is vndone. *Dauid* thus doing was a

---

12 Ibid., 244.
13 "Memorial of proceedings to be taken in the North," in *Queen Elizabeth's Defence of her Proceedings in Church and State*, ed. William E. Collins for Church Historical Society Publications 58 (London, 1899, 1958), 30.
14 Thomas Drant, *Two Sermons preached, ... the other at the Court of Windsor the Sonday after twelfth day being the viij of Ianuary, before in the yeare .1569* (London, 1570), sigs. I7^v–8, STC (2nd edn) 7171. Available from the database Early English Books Online.

man according to Gods hart. Let no Prince looke to haue Gods hart, if he do the contrary to *Dauid*.[15]

Even David's musicianship is a rebuke to Elizabeth's lack of severity:

> King *Dauid* him selfe sayth, that his song should be of mercy and iudgement: so that that musicke standeth vpon two stringes, mercy one, and iudgement the other. King *Dauid* touched both the stringes, and stroke them both, and therfore in hys regiment there was a good musicke. Our Prince hath yet but stricken the one string, and played vpon mercy: but if she woulde now strike vpon both the stringes, and let her song be of mercy, and iudgement, then there would be a goodly musicke in her regiment, & all thinges would be in a much better tune then they now are.[16]

Moses's example also admonishes Elizabeth: "It is sayd of *Moses*, that he was the most milde of all men that euer tarried in the earth, yet … when the golden Calfe of Idolatrye was erected," a parallel to the Northern Rebellion's religious dimension, "there was killed three thousand, and *Moses* said they had made holy their handes to God."[17]

The climactic type in this series of mild but severe rulers is Solomon, whose nearest rival, Adonijah, standing in for Thomas Howard, Duke of Norfolk, was eager to marry Abishag, here a type of Mary Stuart. (The handsome, athletic, and eligible kinsman of the Queen had been influenced by other courtiers as well as his retainers, though not by any personal acquaintance with the lady, to project a match with Mary Stuart, who, he persuaded himself, would share the English throne with him after Elizabeth's death.)

> *Salomon* that was so milde in his lawes, and so milde in his sawes, when as an euill hauty harted subiecte named *Adoniah* … being drawen into a great spirit to gape for the crowne, had gotten the kinges owne mother to speake for him to marry the Sunamite, by whom he might make title to the crowne: then milde *Salomon* thus answered his mother: … as the *Lorde liueth*, … *Adoniah* shall dye this daye … *Salomon* can not abide that *Abisag* should be asked to wife for *Adoniah*. For, geue him that wife, and geue him *Salomons* kingdome. *Abisag* is no wife for *Adoniah*, *Abisag* is no wife for *Adoniah*. Thus, *Salomon* was wise, yet *Salomon* coulde punishe.[18]

---

15 Ibid., sig. K1.
16 Ibid., sig. K2. Drant's application recalls the Geneva translation of Psalm 101.1: "I Wil sing mercie and iudgement," and its commentary on v. 8: "Magistrates must immediatly punish vice, lest it growe to farther inconuenience, and if heathen Magistrates are bounde to do this, how muche more thei that haue the charge of the Church of God?"
17 Ibid., sig. K1-1ᵛ.
18 Ibid., sig. K2.

In this case, Elizabeth complied with her councilors' and preachers' advice: Norfolk was executed in 1572, and the suggested marriage came to nothing.

Drant, in contrast to Spenser, delivers his "good discipline" "plainly in way of precepts" (indeed, at his most blunt, he suggests "it must be a clobbe, or it must be an hatchet, or it must be an halter ... or els of a suretie some of their heades will neuer be quiet"[19]), but like Spenser, he uses allegorical versions of Elizabeth to show her what her best self would do.

Edwin Sandys also preached to Elizabeth's court "near the time of either the Northern Rebellion (1569) or the Ridolfi Plot (1571)."[20] Moses is the ideal of mildness and severity he suggested Elizabeth was to imitate:

> Moses was a woorthie magistrate. And his greatest commendation is that he was no lesse sharp and seuere in Gods cause, than milde and gentle in his owne ... Moses so loued the safetie of his people that hee cried, *Lord spare them or wipe me out of the booke of life*. To haue a gouernour like to Moses, milde and mercifull; yet not carelesse to be zealous in Gods cause, nor vnmindefull in iustice to punish great transgressors, is a great & a rare blessing. Which if our God haue bestowed vpon vs (for vnto him wee must acknowledge it, although in this place I passe it ouer, because my desire is not to please but to teache, neither did I euer vse flattering woords as ye know) but if God haue beene mercifull to vs heerein, the Lorde make vs thankefull for it ... he hath wonderfully preserued our Soueraigne his seruant, he hath kept her safe as Moses and Dauid from Pharao, from Dathan and from Amalek; from Goliah, from Saul, from Absolon, from the hands of her open enemies and treasons of her deceitfull friends.[21]

Sandys's clumsy application may make us thankful that Spenser's fiction did not demand such loud stage whispers, but the point is that both Sandys and Spenser enrich their discussion of Elizabeth's behavior by presenting typological parallels. They expect their audience to hold more than one story in mind at a time, and to relate them allegorically: the Bible to current English issues, or Books I and V to recent English events.

---

19 Ibid., sig. K3.
20 Peter E. McCullough, "A Calendar of Sermons Preached at Court During the Reigns of Elizabeth I and James I," a diskette included with *Sermons at Court: Politics and Religion in Elizabethan and Jacobean Preaching*, Cambridge Studies in Early Modern British History (Cambridge: Cambridge University Press, 1998).
21 Edwin Sandys, "The eighth Sermon: A Sermon preached before the Queene," *Sermons made by the most reuerende Father in God, Edwin, Archbishop of Yorke, primate of England and metropolitane* (London, 1585), 123–38 (126-7 and 129 are quoted), STC (2nd edn) 21713. Available from the database Early English Books Online.

Another court sermon, this one by Elizabeth's chaplain Tobias Matthew, is dated by Peter McCullough to 1572, the year of the first Parliamentary appeal for Mary Stuart's execution and the death of the Duke of Norfolk for treasonable aspirations to marry her.[22] Matthew recalls overreachers of the Bible, including Lucifer, Nebuchadnezzar, Nimrod, Korah, Dathan, and Abiram, Adonijah, Absalom, and others, all ultimately punished. Elizabeth should emulate Esther, who ordered Haman's execution:

> Very strange, but certain true ... his traison, or treachery was horrible & heinous, that mought move the mynde of so godly & gracious a woman, so merciful & pitiful a Quene to sue so sharpe & so swift revenge: but she did it. & did she it in defence of a subject, and shall it not be done, for safeguard of a prince? & did she it to revenge another: & shall it not be done to assist your self? And did she worke it being covert barne? Shall not your majestie perform it being all souerain yourself? Did she persuade others thereunto & shall not your highness be persuaded by others?[23]

However harsh Moses, that frequently cited Elizabeth type, appears now, he was commended in the Bible as the meekest man that ever lived. David was a man after God's own heart; Esther was merciful and pitiful. In the face of so much Parliamentary and preacherly persuasion over the course of almost two decades, Elizabeth's delay and reluctance in turning to violence against Mary qualified her as meek and merciful. The preachers conceived these biblical figures as Elizabeth's reference group, much as Spenser would create Una, Mercilla, and other fictional characters for the same purpose. Her biblical counterparts punished their Norfolks and Marys; Elizabeth should, too.[24]

With Mary Stuart in England as a focus for plots, what Spenser and others saw in retrospect as her corrupting influence could touch nobles,

---

22 McCullough, "A Calendar of Sermons." The sermon is available only in manuscript: Tobias Matthew, "Doctor Mathewes first sermon preached before the Quene," Bodl. MS Top.Oxon.e.5, 48–65. I appreciate Dr. McCullough's kind help in deciphering the ms.
23 Matthew, "Doctor Mathewes first sermon," 59–61.
24 Richard McCabe, in his fine article "The Masks of Duessa: Spenser, Mary Queen of Scots, and James VI," *English Literary Renaissance* 17 (1987), 224–42, traces Scottish and English reactions to Mary Stuart to demonstrate the point of many details of Duessa's characterization in both 1590 and 1596 versions. He identifies the Duessa of Book I with Mary and the monster Orgoglio with Norfolk (231–2).

even the first peer of the realm. According to a court sermon by John Whitgift in 1574, flattery is dangerous,

> For it breedeth in them ["ciuill persons" like Norfolk] Ambition, the roote of rebellion and treason. It moueth them, not to be content with their state and calling, but to aspire to greter dignitie, and to take those things in hande which commonly turne to theyr ruine and destruction. And in whome hath not popularitie wrought these effectes? or who euer fell into these inconueniences, but such as first were prouoked thervnto by the flattering of the people?

In whom, indeed? Just as Whitgift sounds ready to give specific examples, he backtracks: "But my meaning was not to speake much of this matter: this only I thought good to note, and to admonishe all ... by the example of Christe, not to giue eare to flatterers."[25] With the Queen among his auditors, Whitgift was wise to draw back from naming those who flattered, or those who fell prey.

More than a decade later, Elizabeth's advisors and preachers would have their way: Mary was tried and convicted; Elizabeth signed her death warrant. Next, the government authorized publication of summaries of the deliberations between Parliament and Elizabeth, including an enumeration of the Commons' reasons for requesting a sentence of death:

> 7 Lastly, your Maiesties most louing & dutifull commons doubt not, but that as your Maiestie is duely exercised in reading the Booke of God, so it will please you to call to your princely remembrance, how fearefull the examples of Gods vengeance bee, that are there to bee founde against King *Saul* for sparing King *Agag*, and against King *Achab* for sauing the life of *Benadad*: both which were by the iust iudgement of God depriued of their kingdoms, for sparing those wicked Princes, whome God had deliuered into their handes, of purpose to be slaine by them, as by the ministers of his eternal and diuine Iustice: Wherein full wisely *Salomon* proceeded to punishment, when hee tooke the life of his owne naturall and elder brother *Adonias*, for the only intention of a marriage, that gaue suspition of treason against him.[26]

---

25 John Whitgift, *A godlie Sermon preched before the Queenes Maiestie at Greenwiche the .26. of March last past* (London, 1574), sigs. B6ᵛ–7, STC (2nd edn) 25431. Available from the database Early English Books Online.

26 Robert Cecil, *The copie of a letter to the Right Honourable the Earle of Leycester* (London, 1586), 10, STC (2nd edn) 6052. Available from the database Early English Books Online.

So deeply did biblical learning permeate the culture that the speaker of the Commons and preachers like Matthew, Sandys, and Drant were working from the same talking points.

After the beheading, Elizabeth famously recoiled. Peter McCullough notes that

> Burghley (like Spenser) actually seized on Elizabeth's postexecution grief and anger as a way to exonerate her, to convince Europe that she had not acted rashly, even that she had not made up her mind before her ministers forced her hand. In her own household chapel, however, Elizabeth's favorite chaplain, Richard Fletcher, rebuked her for precisely this reluctance to take responsibility for the execution.[27]

Fletcher's sermon uses a different typological schema than any other sermon considered here. He preached on Matthew 2:19–20: "The Angell of the Lorde appeared to Ioseph in Egipt in a dreame, saying arise, and take vpp the childe and his mother and returne into the Lande of Israell for they are deade that sought the child[es] Lyfe."[28] The preacher himself is the angel, addressing Elizabeth as Joseph, insisting (in the words of Peter McCullough) that she "look away from the Egypt of the Mary Stuart crisis to the Israel of a secure England."[29]

Soon after Fletcher, in the course of a court sermon during Easter week 1587 (seven weeks after Mary's execution), Peter Wentworth used the familiar type of Solomon to assure the Queen and court that they should not second-guess the severity and zeal of that action:

> I humblie and lowly beseech you (ye honorable Magistrates and Gouernours) perseuere in the course which yee haue taken in hande ... Our plentifull blessings both spirituall and temporall, which wee haue receyued vnder our prudent and learned *SOLOMON*, our gracious Queene, and vnder you her godly and carefull Magistrates, wee do with one mouth confes and acknowledge ... I am onelie (by this texte) to admonishe them which are Magistrates, vnto a godly seueritie, and to shake of their security,

---

27 Peter McCullough, "Out of Egypt: Richard Fletcher's Sermon before Elizabeth I after the Execution of Mary Queen of Scots," in *Dissing Elizabeth: Negative Representations of Gloriana*, ed. Julia M. Walker (Durham, NC: Duke University Press, 1998), 118–49.
28 Richard Fletcher, "A Sermon preached before the Queene immediatly after the execuc[i]on of the Queene of Scotte[s] by the Deane of Peterburghe," St. John's College, Cambridge, MS I.30, fols. 49ᵛ–67ᵛ (49ᵛ is quoted); quoted in McCullough, *Sermons at Court*, 125.
29 McCullough, *Sermons at Court*, 137.

when cause is iustly ministred; for that this seueritie is euer ioined to the feare of the Lord.[30]

The analogy between Solomon's and Elizabeth's severity is not fully developed, but auditors would remember Solomon's execution of Adonijah.

Outside the court as well, preachers used biblical parallels to refer to Mary's unsuccessful plots. William Gravet, preaching that summer in England's premier pulpit, Paul's Cross, compared Elizabeth to David in Psalm 18:

> If euer any Christian prince since the time of our Sauiour, might apply this to himselfe, that through the infinite goodnes of almightie God, may our most gratious soueraigne Queene *Elizabeth* do.
>
> For through many tribulations she was aduanced to hir princely throne, as Dauid was.
>
> Hir first and chiefe care at the entrance of hir kingdome was, to procure the true seruice of the Lord God, as Dauids was.
>
> She hath beene most louing and mercifull to hir peope, ruling with iustice and equitie, moderate seueritie annexed thereunto, after the example of Dauid.
>
> She hath alwaies preferred the glory of God, and the safegard of hir subiects, before the safetie of hir owne roiall person, as did Dauid.
>
> She hath sustained reproches, iniuries, and manifold traitorous attempts both secret and manifest at the hande of hir malitious enemies, as Dauid sustained.
>
> But through the vnspeakable power and goodnes of the almightie Lord God, she hath withstood, dispersed, and vanquished them, euen as Dauid did.
>
> And why? Bicause with Dauid she putteth hir trust in the Lord.[31]

Gravet, like the court preachers, set the series of plots on Elizabeth's life in a biblical context, comparable to Spenser's creation of an historical fiction.

---

30 Peter Wentworth, *A sermon faithfullie and trulie published according as it was preached at the courte, at Greenewiche, the Twesday in Easter weeke, before the Right honourable and diligent Auditory* (London, 1587), 23–4, 28, STC (2nd edn) 25246. Available from the database Early English Books Online. (The "*Parson of Much-Bromelie in Essex, and chaplaine to the Right honorable, the L. Darcy*," this Peter Wentworth is not to be confused with his contemporary, the Parliamentary agitator of the same name.)

31 William Gravet, *A sermon preached at Paules Crosse on the xxv. day of Iune Ann. Dom. 1587 intreating of the holy scriptures, and the vse of the same* (London, 1587), 68–9, STC (2nd edn) 12200. Available from the database Early English Books Online.

Again in 1587, the year of Mary's execution, on Queen's Day, preacher Edward Harris asks his audience, concerning those "carried of the deuill into this sinne of rebellion against the prince," to

> marke the most certaine examples of the holy worde of God. Korah, Dathan and Abiram rebelled against Moses, therefore ... *the earth opened her mouth and swallowed them vp with all that they had, & they went downe quicke into the pit* ... Absolom the goodly though vngodly sonne of righteous Dauid, rebelled against his father the king, and therefore as hee rod vpon his princely mule vnder a great oake, the verie boughs of the tree would not suffer so wicked a wretch to escape vnpunished, but caght hold on his head.[32]

England is "the Israel of God," and rebellion is a crime against him. Mary is Absalom, goodly though ungodly, plotting with her accomplices against righteous Elizabeth/David and ultimately punished.

In an undated sermon published after Mary's execution, former Marian exile and president of Oxford's Magdalen College Laurence Humphrey reminded his listeners that the Jews of Daniel's time were exhorted to pray for Nebuchadnezzar and for Babylon's peace. He contrasts this ideal behavior with Mary's:

> O that our great soiourner [identified in the margin as *Q. of Scots.*] receiued in *England* with fauour, entertained with honour, vsed with al liberal liberty, pardoned many times by mercy, woulde haue sought the peace of the land where shee harboured, or at least had not sought the disquietnes of the state, the disturbaunce of the realme, the hauocke and vndooing of manie Gentleman, the perill of the person of the Prince of the land, so gratiously affected towarde her, beeing but a Queene *quondam*, a Queene withoute a Kingdome, and onely in name.[33]

Mary was a bad guest as well as a rebellious family member. The example of godly biblical exiles put her to shame.

Thomas White, preaching on Accession Day in 1589, compares Mary Tudor, Elizabeth, and Mary Stuart to biblical figures:

> For Dangers, whether shee resemble *Dauid* or no? Consider yee: He afraid of *Saule*, and shee of hir *Sister*. And who was worse beset, he, with *Saul*

---

32 Edward Harris, *A sermon preached at Hitchin in ... 1587. the 17.day of Nouember* (London, 1590), 77–9, STC (2nd edn) 12344. Available from the database Early English Books Online.
33 Laurence Humphrey, "The Second Sermon: The Confvtation of Trayterovs Abishai," in *A view of the Romish hydra and monster, traison, against the Lords annointed: condemned by Dauid, I. Sam. 26. and nowe confuted in seuen sermons to perswade obedience to princes, concord among our selues, and a generall reformation and repentaunce in all states* (Oxford, 1588), 46, STC (2nd edn) 13966. Available from the database Early English Books Online.

before, and *Absolon* behinde; or shee, set betweene two *(Marahs)* the one *Crowned* before hir, the other shrewdlie hastening to hir *Crowne*.[34]

One can talk about David while telling Elizabeth's story, or about Elizabeth while telling David's. Since God is the author of all history and all parts of the narrative teach the same lesson, any number of stories can be read as encoding or typifying Elizabeth's – including, in the case of *The Faerie Queene*, invented allegorical stories.

Mercilla and Duessa as Elizabeth and Mary

Now that we have very briefly placed the execution of Mary Stuart in contemporary sermon context, we may take the Mercilla episode and compare the preachers' treatment with Spenser's. From Book V's initial publication in 1596, James VI of Scotland recognized the Mercilla episode as containing "some dishonorable effects ... against himself and his mother deceassed."[35] Early handwritten annotations show that James was not alone in his interpretation: a copy of Spenser's 1611 *Works* bears marginal notes in an early seventeenth-century hand, which, besides identifying Duessa as Mary, also identify "*Kingdomes care*, with a white siluer hed" with "W^m. Ld Burleigh" and "*Sedition*" with "Dk of Norfolk." Mary's second husband, "Ld Darley," (sic) is "*Murder*," while "E. Bothwel" is "*Incontinence* of lyfe."[36] The following discussion will not insist on figure-by-figure correspondences with this degree of specificity, but supports the standard identification of Mercilla as a type of Elizabeth.

One example of Spenser's tendency to clarify the spiritual lesson at the expense of actual facts is the way he presents the argument made against Duessa. Initially, Duessa's trial deals only with the "vyld treasons,

---

34 Thomas White, *A sermon preached at Paules Crosse the 17. of Nouember An. 1589 Inioyfull remembrance and thanksgiuing vnto God, for the peaceable yeres of her maiesties most gratious raigne ouer vs, now 32* (London, 1589), 53, STC (2nd edn) 25407. Available from the database Early English Books Online.

35 Frederic Ives Carpenter, *A Reference Guide to Edmund Spenser* (Chicago: University of Chicago Press, 1923), 41, and William Wells, ed., *Spenser Allusions in the Sixteenth and Seventeenth Centuries*, Studies in Philology, Texts and Studies, 68–9 (1971), 45, among others, quote English ambassador Robert Bowes's correspondence to the Privy Council.

36 John Manning, "Notes and Marginalia in Bishop Percy's Copy of Spenser's *Works* (1611)," *Notes and Queries* 229 (1984), 225–7. John Dixon also identified the Duessa of the 1590 *Faerie Queene* with Mary Stuart in the 1590s (Graham Hough, "First Commentary on *The Faerie Queene*," *TLS* [April 9, 1964], 294), as did several other early readers.

and outrageous shame,/ Which she against the dred *Mercilla* oft did frame" (V.ix.40). Spenser thus seems to follow the line taken at the historical Mary's trial, which considered only political charges arising out of Mary's behavior since 1585 – not her purported unchastity or undoubted Catholicism.[37] And indeed, Zele follows his charges of treason with a reference to her conspiracy with Blandamour and Paridell to depose Mercilla. But Arthur, "sore empassionate," needs "new accusements" (V.ix.46–7), and eventually Duessa's character, rather than her deeds, is on trial. Though these issues were also held to be irrelevant to the historical case ("not for those she now in question came," V.ix.40), *Incontinence*, *Adulterie*, and *Impietie* are among the witnesses whose testimony finally sways the watching Arthur.

The poem's earlier identification of Duessa with the Roman church and unchastity, claimed to be irrelevant to the trial in stanza 40, correspond with contemporary insistence that the charges against Mary did not include her religion. But Spenser could have invented a new character to embody treason and plotting against Mercilla, rather than reintroduce the established character Duessa as a representative of Mary. Spenser's reintroduction of Duessa in her appealing femininity and duplicity, rather than allegorizing skullduggery and international politics, foregrounds her moral ugliness, both spiritual and carnal, as more important to this episode than the specific charges brought against the historical Mary.[38] This suggests that, to Spenser, the ultimate interpretation of the historical incident would focus more on weighing morals than sifting facts. Certainly the witnesses called against Duessa (*Religion*, *Iustice*, *Kingdomes care*) struck the marginalian of Bishop Percy's copy of the 1611 *Faerie Queene* as historical personages who offer evidence of an attempted coup. But they can also strike us as personifications of the moral forces ranged against Mary and urging Elizabeth to pass judgment against her. Spenser's resolution of the conflicting claims of mercy and justice in the Mercilla episode parallels preacherly treatment of the same themes, as does their use of alternate characters to dramatize it – this time fictional rather than biblical.

---

37 James Emerson Phillips, *Images of a Queen: Mary Stuart in Sixteenth-Century Literature* (Berkeley, CA: University of California Press, 1964), 201–2.
38 Stoll's note to V.ix.40 explains, "Duessa embodies falsehood and doubleness, from the Italian for 'two.' She villainously traps knights with her false appearances throughout *The Faerie Queene*. Here Spenser transforms her into a figure for Mary" (129n.).

Spenser, like the preachers, focuses on Elizabeth's responsibility to her people in executing justice on those who threaten her and themselves. Her judgment heeds "the Peoples cry and Commons sute" as they "Importune care of their owne publicke cause" (V.ix.44). Mercilla pities Duessa, but she must balance this pity with her mercy toward her people. Both Duessa and her people are "the subiect of her skill":

> So much more then is that of powre and art,
> That seekes to saue the subiect of her skill,
> Yet neuer doth from doome of right depart:
> As it is greater prayse to saue, then spill,
> And better to reforme, then to cut off the ill. (V.x.2)

Present-day readers sometimes assume that these lines celebrate an ideal that the episode has not illustrated: Duessa is not reformed, after all, but cut off; spilled rather than saved.[39] But if Elizabeth's Council was at pains in explanations directed to "Nations farre" to emphasize the justice of their queen's action, Elizabeth's subjects (that is, Spenser's first readers), conditioned by sermon publication, Parliamentary proceedings, and almost two decades of alarmist rumors, were presumed by preachers and statesmen alike to see things differently: "But thine owne people do thy mercy prayse much more" (V.x.3). Spenser joins the preachers in assuring the Queen that, by removing Mary and her corrupting influence, she had indeed mercifully saved and reformed her kingdom.

Spenser's focus on Mercilla's mercy to her people in executing justice on Duessa echoes a sermon theme. As Drant's 1570 court sermon had explained, "For some one stroke, at some one time, to some one person, from the princes hand, doth let many thousands of buffets, and blose, which otherwise must be dealt els where."[40] According to the preachers, only a misguided mercy, in its eagerness to forgive one, sacrifices many, and the most natural way to read the episode (according to its early readers) is to see Spenser making the same point: such would be the result if Duessa were preserved to wreak "great care,/ And mickle mischiefe" upon more knights, or succeed in her "vyld treasons" against Mercilla (V.ix.40). Mercilla balances her pity for Duessa with her obligation toward her kingdom. Her tender care of her people, rather than "iust vengeance" (V.ix.50), is the "strong constraint" that "enforce[s]" her judgment against

---

39 McCabe, "The Masks of Duessa," 239, for instance, suggests that V.x.1–3's "insistence upon the claims of mercy against those of justice and their preference for policies of 'reforme' … hardly prepare us for the eventual outcome".

40 Drant, *Two Sermons preached*, sig. I7ᵛ.

Duessa – and her sympathy toward Duessa shows in her tears at the sentencing and the post-execution honors shown to "her wretched corse" (V.x.4). Mercilla has been simultaneously just and merciful by expressing both impulses toward different constituencies (Mary Stuart and the English people) in the act of executing Duessa, just as Moses, David, and Solomon were shown to do in the sermons quoted earlier.

The traditional reading and modern objections

In the last thirty years, critics have found it more difficult to read Mercilla's treatment of Duessa as an idealizing but sincere portrait of Elizabeth's mercy as illustrated in the trial and execution of Mary. Such critics point to discrepancies between Elizabeth's and Mary's actions and Spenser's allegorical representation of them: Mercilla's physical presence as Duessa's case is argued (Elizabeth was absent from Mary's trial) and Duessa's silence throughout the proceedings (the historical Mary challenged the legitimacy of the trial and defended herself with spirit).[41] Also coming in for suspicious critical scrutiny is the equivocal and roundabout way Spenser discloses Duessa's execution, the "unwritten, unwritable proceeding [that] is the guileful heart of Book V."[42] The juxtaposition of the trial scene with the disquieting image of the libelous poet Malfont's punishment has suggested to some that Spenser is alerting readers that, throughout this section, the real subject is power relations between poet and monarch, or the metacritical insight that allegory requires readers to comply with its own vision of meaning and "misrecognize" truths other than the one it communicates.[43] (Spenser's intention is then to

---

41 See Diane Parkin-Speer, "Allegorical Legal Trials in Spenser's *The Faerie Queene*," *Sixteenth Century Journal* 23 (1992), 494–505, particularly 497–8, and McCabe, "The Masks of Duessa," particularly 236–7, for a comparison of the proceedings in Duessa's trial with judicial practice in England (and Mary's actual trial). McCabe's article also shows the point of distinct attitudes to Mary on the part of Arthur (belatedly answering Bishop Leslie's rhetorical question of 1571) and Artegal (as the commissioner Lord Grey).

42 John D. Staines, "Elizabeth, Mercilla, and the Rhetoric of Propaganda in Spenser's *Faerie Queene*," *Journal of Medieval and Early Modern Studies* 31.2 (Spring 2001), 283–312 (quote from 303). Available online at Johns Hopkins University's database Project Muse.

43 For instance, in Jonathan Goldberg, *Endlesse Worke: Spenser and the Structures of Discourse* (Baltimore, MD: Johns Hopkins University Press: 1981), 1–12; Lowell Gallagher, *Medusa's Gaze: Casuistry and Conscience in the Renaissance* (Stanford, CA: Stanford University Press, 1991), 232–54.

"draw attention to the guile of all rhetoric."[44]) Against these sophisticated recent interpretations I want to remind my readers of our distance from Elizabethan concerns.

Unlike its first readers, we have no memory of suspense to draw on as we read *The Faerie Queene*. As far as we are concerned, Elizabeth has always inevitably survived Mary Tudor's reign and ascended the throne in a peaceful transfer of power. If we are aware of her having contracted smallpox, we also know she recovered. We have never worried that she would contract the plague or make a disastrous marriage. We have always known that the St. Bartholomew's Day Massacre was limited to France, that the multiple Spanish attempts at invasion would fail, and that Jesuit missionaries and plotters of regicide would fail to disrupt England's stability. We already know, in short, that Elizabeth's reign was a success, and many of us credit that success in part to the personal qualities and decisions that sometimes infuriated her contemporaries, Spenser apparently among them. But, as the sixteenth-century documents that I have quoted throughout this study make clear, Elizabeth's contemporaries considered England's political and religious stability precarious and temporary. Many of them were insufficiently relaxed to enjoy it, even in moments of strident assertion each November 17.

In 1586 and 1587, several publications rehearsed the legal basis for and the procedures followed in the Queen of Scots' trial.[45] All make the point that Elizabeth was absent and that Mary defended herself – showing that Spenser's departure from these facts in his fiction was, as critics of our day assume, intentional. All likewise make the point that, especially in view of Parliament's calls for Mary's execution in the 1570s, Elizabeth proceeded very slowly and with great reluctance to a determination for Mary's death.

For us, the overriding fact is that Elizabeth executed Mary. Given the distance of more than four centuries, 1570 and 1587 seem essentially

---

44 Staines, "Elizabeth, Mercilla, and the Rhetoric of Propaganda," 291.
45 *A true copie of the proclamation lately published by the Queenes Maiestie, vnder the great seale of England, for the declaring of the sentence, lately giuen against the Queene of Scottes* (London, 1586), STC (2nd edn) 8160; Robert Cecil, *The copie of a letter to the Right Honourable the Earle of Leycester* (London, 1586), STC (2nd edn) 6052; Richard Crompton, *A short declaration of the ende of traytors, ... and wythall, howe necessarie, lawes and execution of iustice are... Wherein are also breefely touched, sundry offences of the S. Queene ... & the manner of the honorable proceding for her conuiction thereof* (London, 1587), STC (2nd edn) 6052. All are available from the database Early English Books Online.

simultaneous. Thus to us the opening of Canto 10 may indeed be "filled with labyrinthine turns," which can seem to rewrite Elizabeth's strategy as "procrastinating [and] self-effacing."[46] But those who lived through those seventeen years in positions of responsibility found them nerve-wracking, and when we read the accounts of those whose position forced them to listen deferentially to Elizabeth's rhetorical hand-wringing (like Sir John Puckering, speaker of the House of Commons, whose speeches Cecil recorded for the absent Leicester, and Sir Thomas Bromley, the Lord Chancellor, who acted as go-between for Elizabeth in her dealings with Parliament), they impress us not as providing plausible deniability in keeping with a recognized cooperative strategy, which required Elizabeth's public reluctance, but as exasperation barely suppressing disrespect. To them, an Elizabeth wondering "whether any other meanes could be thought of, or found out by any of them, how the Scottish Queenes life might be spared, and yet her Maiesties person saued out of perill, and the state preserued in quiet" was a ruler unable to come to grips with the facts.[47]

To the queen's demand that someone find her an alternative, Bromley's answer was, in part,

> he had imparted the same to the Lordes assembled in the vpper house, whome he found by their generall silence much amazed at the propounding thereof, considerring the same had bene before in deliberation amongst them, and resolued vpon, & as appeared by their former petition exhibited to her Highnesse, wherein they had expressed the same resolution. Notwithstanding, for her Maiesties further satisfaction, they had entred into a newe consultation, and for that purpose selected a great number of the choysest persons of that higher house of Parliament, to conferre thereof, either priuately or together with the lower house: which also was done accordingly at seuerall times.[48]

The implication is that if there had been a way to save Mary while safeguarding the Queen, they would have found it.

Of course, there is plenty of room for historians to quarrel with the facts that Puckering, Bromley, and other Parliamentarians thought they knew – the Casket Letters are now recognized as forgeries, freeing Mary of the charge of conspiring in Darnley's murder and Bothwell's abduction and rape of herself. Many scholars now credit Mary with sincerity

46 Gallagher, *Medusa's Gaze*, 239.
47 Cecil, *The copie of a letter*, 21–2.
48 Ibid., 22.

in her protestations that she would not impose her religion on her subjects, whether Scottish or English. But as far as Elizabeth's attitude goes, it seems unlikely that Spenser would be aware of a royal subterfuge that was opaque to her closest councilors. Thus, we may read Mercilla's tears and regret as Spenser's dignified re-imagining of his queen's wistful if self-deluding fancy of herself and Mary "but as two milke maides with pailes vpon our armes" in November 1586 and her guilty rage when Mary was in fact dead in February 1587.[49]

But what of the discrepancies between history and Spenser's fiction? Lowell Gallagher considers a version of the traditional reading that would reflect praise on Elizabeth:

> the silence of Duessa and the presence of Mercilla can be read ... as images that are only apparently false. In them the reader can witness the presumably higher allegorical truth of the represented event that the historical facts alone would not necessarily convey: in Duessa's silence a sign of the ultimate inauthenticity of her position, in Mercilla's presence a sign of the ultimate force of equity in the proceedings.[50]

Thus poetry reconciles inconvenient historical details to the overall moral purpose, the better to teach "good discipline." Gallagher himself, however, finds this reading "patently inadequate" in view of the metacritical training the reader has gained by confronting the Bonfont/Malfont vignette. The real point, for him, is that "allegoresis itself ... must complete the dismembering process of allegory."[51] Gallagher sees *The Faerie Queene*, then, as a species of daring "bottom-drawer literature" analogous to the never-published work of literary dissidents in Communist Eastern Europe – but in this case fortunately published and absentmindedly (and, for its author, even more fortunately) misconstrued by its contemporary readers. But there is no compelling reason to adopt this, or any, reading against the grain.

Biblical uses of improved history

A Sidnean reading, which would give Spenser license to modify history in the interest of making the poem more effective in teaching virtue, is authorized not only by Elizabethan poetic theory but by biblical practice

---

49 Ibid., 14.
50 Gallagher, *Medusa's Gaze*, 239.
51 Ibid.

and Elizabethan hermeneutic. Even conceding that Elizabeth's motives were mixed – that she was to some extent manipulative, disingenuous, and unjustified in sentencing Mary to death – it is not necessarily unfaithful to Truth to omit or to recast negative incidents in the life of a coreligionist held up for praise and emulation. This is just what the New Testament book of Hebrews does for several biblical figures: Samson, for instance, and Sarah.

Best-selling moderate Calvinist Elizabethan divine William Perkins, whose life missed being coterminous with Elizabeth's reign by only one year (born in 1558, he died in 1602), provides a very traditional reading of the material in Hebrews. One remembers that, according to the Bishops' Bible rendering of Genesis 18, during the Lord's appearance at Mamre,

> 10 And he sayde: I wyll certaynely returne vnto thee according to the time of lyfe: and lo, Sara thy wife shall haue a sonne. That heard Sara in the tent doore, which was behynde hym.
>
> 11 Abraham and Sara were both olde, and well stryken in age: and it ceased to be with Sara after the maner as it is with women.
>
> 12 Therefore Sara laughed within her selfe, saying: Nowe I am waxed olde shal I geue my selfe to lust, and my Lorde olde also?
>
> 13 And God said vnto Abraham: wherefore dyd Sara laugh, saying, shall I of a suertie beare a chyle, which am olde?[52]

The author of Hebrews, on the other hand, does not mention Sara's incredulity or laughter: "Through fayth also Sara her selfe receaued strength to conceaue seede, and was delyuered of a chylde when she was past age, because she iudged hym faythfull which had promised."[53]

Perkins reconciles the two accounts:

> *Sarah* that laughed in doubting, yet (withall) *beleeues*. This teacheth vs, that true *faith* is ioyned always with doubting in all Gods children ... heere is one notable thing to be ob[s]erued: the very same word of God, which she *beleeued*, and for beleeuing wherof she is here registred, at the same she also laughed: but behold, her *faith* is recorded, her laughing is not: her faith is commended, her fault silenced. In which holy & merciful practice of God, we learn:

---

52 Genesis 18.10–13, *The. holie. Bible conteynyng the olde Testament and the newe* [Bishops' Bible] (London, 1568), XI, sig. B3, STC (2nd edn) 2099. Available from the database Early English Books Online.
53 Ibid., Hebrews 11.11, CXXXII^v, sig. R4^v.

> First, that God accepteth *true faith*, though it be attended with many infirmities. As a King is content to giue a begger an almes, though hee receiue it with a hand shaking with the palsey: So, God is well pleased with our faith, though diseased with infirmities, and bestoweth grace on a beleeuing soule, though shaken with many temptations ...
>
> Secondly, here we may learne, that God rather obserues and regards good things in his children, then their faults and imperfections: he *writes vp Sarahs faith*, he nameth not her laughing. This is from the goodnesse of his nature, being *goodnesse* it selfe, and therefore most easily apprehendeth, and takes notice of the least goodnesse, where-euer hee findes it.[54]

Perkins gave similar explanations of the discrepancies in the Hebrews 11 accounts of Isaac, Moses's parents, and Rahab: God remembers and records the best of his children's decidedly mixed moral achievements. Hugh Broughton made a similar point (discussed in Chapter 4) with reference to Jesus's progenitors: the ones who were not exemplary were quietly omitted from the gospel genealogies. Following the example of the sacred writers, God's followers (presumably including Spenser), says Perkins, should observe and commend what is praiseworthy in their coreligionists as well.

Duessa's trial illustrates how similar Spenser's attitude toward history was to the preachers'. Spenser gives his fiction the form of the historical Mary Stuart's arraignment and trial, but the substance of the episode, for him, is his understanding of its spiritual import: a contest between spiritual and moral principles, a contest that resulted in and explains Mary's destruction. A reader may claim that the Mercilla episode misrepresents history by idealizing Elizabeth's actual attitude and specific details of the trial, but such an objection misses an important point. For Spenser, as for the preachers, faithfulness to the underlying spiritual principle took precedence over accurate replication of the details of the most recent manifestation in history of that particular spiritual principle.

Put another way, the specific details (Elizabeth's role in Mary's trial and execution, Mary's silence, and the precise proportions of Elizabeth's ambivalence) may have been incidental to the poem's first readers, as

---

54 William Perkins, *A cloud of faithfull witnesses, leading to the heauenly Canaan, or, A commentarie vpon the 11 chapter to the Hebrewes preached in Cambridge by that godly, and iudicious divine, M. William Perkins; long expected and desired, and therefore published at the request of his executours, by Will. Crashawe and Tho. Pierson, preachers of Gods Word, who heard him preach it, and wrote it from his mouth* (London, 1607), 241, 243–4, STC (2nd edn) 19677.5. Available from the database Early English Books Online.

they seem to have been to Elizabeth's preachers. The opposition of spiritual forces, the tension between conflicting moral obligations, interested Spenser and his original readers as much as the poem suggests. Like the preachers quoted in this chapter, those readers may well have considered the spiritual storyline to be the historical incident's true meaning. The topical details that make the episode a recognizable allegory of Mary's trial and execution serve Spenser's patriotic and epideictic purposes, but we can think of them as supplying the form, rather than the substance, of the passage.

8

Court and courtesy: sermon contexts for Spenser's Book VI

The Faerie Queene's Book of Courtesy begins with praise for the court: "Of Court it seemes, men Courtesie doe call,/ For that it there most vseth to abound" (VI.i.1). Spenser assures Elizabeth that "all goodly vertues .../ ... doe adorne your Court, where courtesies excell" (VI.Proem.7). In Book VI itself, however, his knights spend much more time in the countryside, proverbially as far from the court as one could get. The idiom "court and country" (a way of saying "everywhere") gives rise to the narrator's summary of the Blatant Beast's itinerary in VI.ix.3–4: "from court ... to the citties," "from the citties to the townes," "from the townes into the countrie," "from the country back to priuate farmes," and "thence into the open fields".[1] But Queen Elizabeth, "fayre *Elisa*, Queene of shepheardes all" in *The Shepherd's Calendar*, revelled in an image of her court as a pastoral Arcadia where virtue and beauty reigned supreme, where time held no sway – a new golden age. She was its Belphoebe, its Cynthia, its Astraea, ever beautiful, ever young, ideally virtuous; and she presided over a flowering of the arts and a renewal of religion and innocence.

Just as a pastoral court seems paradoxical,[2] Spenser's attitude toward Elizabeth's court and reflections on the ideal of courtesy are complex. He has Meliboe voice a critique of the court in VI.ix.24:

---

1 Among the preachers cited in this chapter, John Baker, Thomas Becon, William Burton, Edwin Sandys, Henry Smith, Edward Topsell, and Thomas White use variations of the idiom "Courtier and countryman" for "everyone," "from the court to the cart" for the whole range of employment possibilities, and "Court and country" or "City, Court, and country" for "everywhere."

2 I like Michael C. Schoenfeldt's formulation that "the entire world of the shepherds [is] a projection of the court in miniature" ("The Poetry of Conduct: Accommodation and Transgression in *TFQ*, Book 6," in *Enclosure Acts: Sexuality, Property, and Culture in Early Modern England*, ed. Richard Burt and John Michael Archer [Ithaca, NY: Cornell University Press, 1994], 151–69), 156.

> The time was once, in my first prime of yeares,
>   When pride of youth forth pricked my desire ...
> And leauing home, to roiall court I sought;
>   Where I did sell my selfe for yearely hire,
>   And in the Princes gardin daily wrought:
> There I beheld such vainenesse, as I neuer thought.

Belphoebe, a type of Queen Elizabeth in her private person, delivers a similar critique in II.iii.40:

> Who so in pompe of proud estate (quoth she)
>   Does swim, and bathes himselfe in courtly blis,
>   Does waste his dayes in darke obscuritee,
>   And in obliuion euer buried is ...
> Abroad in armes, at home in studious kind
> Who seekes with painfull toile, shall honor soonest find.

When Elizabeth herself played at pastoralism, her alter ego Belphoebe may appropriately disdain the compromise of integrity that public life entails. Eventually the courtier Calidore, in comparing the court to the pastoral world, finds that the court is the less attractive:

>   ... I find,
> That all this worlds gay showes, which we admire,
> Be but vaine shadowes to this safe retyre
> Of life ... (VI.ix.27)

In view of these speeches, some critics have concluded that Spenser himself took a cynical attitude toward the court and its "courtesy"[3] – perhaps awkwardly for an aspiring court poet. But this reading fails to account for the complexity of the conventional topos, to say nothing of Spenser's point. Here, too, Elizabethan sermons can offer a valuable context for *The Faerie Queene*: preachers similarly denounced the court, and court preachers did so to the Queen's face. The appearance of these attacks in printed religious discourse indicates the extent to which this material was conventional, officially countenanced, and popularly consumed. It indicates uses to which abuse of the court could be turned. But this is not the whole picture by any means.

---

3 Richard Neuse, "Book VI as Conclusion to The Faerie Queene," *ELH* **35**:3 (1968), 329–53; Thomas H. Cain, *Praise in The Faerie Queene* (Lincoln, NE: University of Nebraska Press, 1978), 155–7; Daniel Javitch, *Poetry and Courtliness in Renaissance England* (Princeton, NJ: Princeton University Press, 1978), 119–62; George E. Rowe, "Privacy, Vision, and Gender in Spenser's Legend of Courtesy," *Modern Language Quarterly* **50**:4 (1989), 309–36.

While there is no shortage of preacherly attacks on courtly vices, many published Elizabethan sermons discuss courtesy in theological terms, while others analyze or celebrate figures like Abraham, an exemplary host in a pastoral setting, and Nehemiah, an exemplary courtier – analogues of figures embodying courtesy in Spenser's poem.[4] Spenserians of the past eighty years have disagreed about whether the courtesy celebrated in Book VI of *The Faerie Queene* is a political strategy, a social grace, a Christian virtue, or all three,[5] but comparing contemporary religious rhetoric with *The Faerie Queene* clarifies the meanings that Spenser's original readers might have gleaned from this part of his poem.

Sermon references to courtiers' vices

Thomas Drant's court sermon of 1570 illustrates how far a preacher could go in anti-court invective while still publishing his sermon immediately afterward.[6] His text, "They were both naked. Adam and Eve, and blushed

---

4 Although the biblical texts I cite are different, this chapter follows up on Michael Tratner's suggestion that "The religious references to courtesy that I have found ... fit Book VI in such detailed ways that they provide straightforward sources – well-known sixteenth-century English texts that discuss 'courtesy' directly as an important religious virtue" (p. 157 in "'The thing S. Paule ment by ... the courteousness that he spake of': Religious Sources for Book VI of *The Faerie Queene*," *Spenser Studies* 8 [1990], ed. Patrick Cullen and Thomas P. Roche, Jr. [New York, NY: AMS, 1990], 147–74).

5 A further sampling of the many contributions to this discussion might include Alexander Corbin Judson, "Spenser's Theory of Courtesy," *PMLA: Publications of the Modern Language Association of America* 47:1 (1932), 122–36; Dorothy Woodward Culp, "Courtesy and Moral Virtue," *SEL: Studies in English Literature, 1500–1900* 11:1 (1971), 37–51; Mark Archer, "The Meaning of 'Grace' and 'Courtesy': Book VI of The Faerie Queene," *SEL: Studies in English Literature, 1500–1900* 27:1 (1987), 17–34; Douglas A. Northrop, "The Uncertainty of Courtesy in Book VI of The Faerie Queene," *Spenser Studies: A Renaissance Poetry Annual* 14 (2000), 215–32; Richard Chamberlain, *Radical Spenser: Pastoral, Politics and the New Aestheticism* (Edinburgh: Edinburgh University Press, 2005), 106–10; and Jane Grogan, *Exemplary Spenser: Visual and Poetic Pedagogy in The Faerie Queene* (Farnham, Surrey: Ashgate, 2009), 138–74.

6 Thomas Drant, *Two sermons preached, the one at S. Maries Spital on Tuesday in Easter weeke 1570 and the other at the court at Windsor for the Sonday after twelfth day, ... 1569* (London, 1570?), sig. I6, STC (2nd edn) 7171. Available from the database Early English Books Online. Drant was a newly minted MA and fellow of St. Johns College, Cambridge, when, courtier-like, he presented the Queen with English, Greek, and Latin verses during her August 1564 visit to the university (R. W. McConchie, "Drant, Thomas [c.1540–1578]," *Oxford Dictionary of National Biography* (Oxford: Oxford University Press, 2004); online edn, Jan. 2008), and Spenser, in his 1579 letter to Gabriel Harvey, notes that they both "make a breache in Maister DRANTS Rules" for English versification.

not," occasioned an anti-court diatribe to flesh out his treatment of the clothed vs. the unclothed state: "The vse of apparell is very lawfull," he summarized after some dozen pages of exposition and application, "and the abuse very vnlawfull.... For what haue I left my selfe to speake of? Agaynst the abuse of apparell in the princes house."[7] After professing hesitancy, he proceeded:

> And they make it doubtful, whether I may speake agaynst that, or no. For all those that be in kinges houses do accompt of them selues as exempt persons from controlement of preachers, and they will seeme to be priuiledged from the xj. chapter of Sainct *Mathew*: where it is sayd: *They that weare soft clothing, are in kinges houses.*[8]

Drant developed the anti-court theme to the length of seven pages, depending on biblical and classical quotations and conventional terms of abuse rather than specific references to Elizabeth's court. Biblical examples of wicked courts abounded: Abimelech's, Pharaoh's, Nebuchadnezzar's, Ahab's. In language that Belphoebe or Melibœ would have approved, courtiers were

> sponges without iuice, clowds without raine, fountaynes without water, trees without fruite, merchauntes of Maiesties bounties, make shifte *Mamonistes*, and meere *Macheualistes*. In kinges houses ... *They sleepe soundly, and drinke profoundly, and goe to the deuyll roundly.*[9]

Since courtiers considered themselves "exempt persons" from preachers' "controlement," Drant compared his situation to that of the poet Martial, whom he quoted: "*My frendes, ye will me to speake the truth, and enbolden me to speake the truth. The truth is this, that you cannot abide to here the truth.*"[10] Drant preached to urge specific military action on the Queen, as discussed in Chapters 6 and 7. His self-endorsement was therefore timely, as was his condemnation of a court he considered less than vigilant and martial.

Drant's accusations against courtiers were traditional and echoed by many of his colleagues. For instance, "gaping Courtiers" ambitious for "the common trash of the world" (that is, "any credit, any worship,

---

7 Ibid., sigs. K4ᵛ-5.
8 Ibid., sig. K5.
9 Thomas Drant, *Three godly and learned sermons very necessarie to be read and regarded of all men* (London, 1584), G7ᵛ, STC (2nd edn) 7170. Available from the database Early English Books Online. (I cite this alternate edition because a page is missing from the 1570 edition, above.)
10 Drant, *Two sermons*, K7ᵛ.

any riches, any offices, any promotions") were condemned by William Burton,[11] while Calvin, in Golding's translation, lamented that the political structure prevailing in much of Europe gave potentially corrupt and biased courtiers influence over appointments:

> Where Princes haue souereigntie, they appoint Iudges at their owne pleasure and liking, and ambition beares all the sway there. In so much that a Courtier which is in credite, shall not onely obtaine offices for himselfe, but also cause them to bee giuen to others at his appointment. Nay there is yet greater and more shameful corruption. For offices are set to sale nowadays aswel as al other kind of marchandize.[12]

Calvin's Swiss colleague Rudolf Gwalther explained court corruption another way, blaming courtiers' pride and greed rather than the structure of monarchy: "for bicause [courtiers] gaped after money, wherby to maintaine their coueted dignitie, it came to passe, that in kinges Courtes, all things went for money."[13] In any case, courtly ambition and corruption went hand in hand.

Another target preachers shared with Belphoebe and Meliboe was courtly luxuries. Thomas White found that "vnmercyfull profusion" in furnishings, tableware, grooming products ("we perfume our selues with the déerest muske"), and culinary variety betrayed "our beastly appetites."[14] William Barlow's translation of Ludwig Lavater agreed that "crushing Courtiers" love their luxuries: "the Court is costly, and will bee gallant: horses, hounds, hauks, harlots, iesters, must be maintained, who wrings for it? the poor subiect, who must rather be vndone, then the Court should want."[15] "The courtier reigns in spending," claimed Henry

---

11 William Burton, *Dauids euidenece [sic], or, The assurance of Gods loue declared in seuen sermons* (London, 1592), 77, STC (2nd edn) 4170. Available from the database Early English Books Online.
12 John Calvin, *The sermons of M. Iohn Caluin vpon the fifth booke of Moses called Deuteronomie ... [t]ranslated out of French by Arthur Golding* (London, 1583), 332, STC (2nd edn) 621. Available from the database Early English Books Online.
13 *An hundred, threescore and fiftene homelyes or sermons, vppon the Actes of the Apostles, written by Saint Luke*, trans. John Bridges (London, 1572), 504, STC (2nd edn) 25013. Available from the database Early English Books Online.
14 Thomas White, *A sermo[n] preached at Pawles Crosse on Sunday the thirde of Nouember 1577. in the time of the plague, by T.W.* (London, 1578), 63–4, STC (2nd edn) 25406. Available from the database Early English Books Online.
15 *Three Christian sermons, made by Lodouike Lauatere, minister of Zuricke in Heluetia, of famine and dearth of victuals* (London, 1596), 24 [sig. C4ᵛ], STC (2nd edn) 15322. Available from the database Early English Books Online.

Smith,[16] but the example of courtly self-indulgence had infected every level of society:

> Once Christ said, that soft clothing is in Kings courts: but now it is crept into euerie house: then the rich glutton ietted in purple euerie day, but now the poore vnthrift iets as braue as the glutton, with so many circumstances about him, that if yee could see how pride would walke herselfe, if she did weare apparell, she would euen goe like manie in the streetes: for she could not goe brauer, nor looke stouter, nor mince finer, nor set on moe laces, nor make larger cuts, nor carrie more trappings about her, then our ruffians and wantons doe at this day. How far are these fashions altered from those leather coates which God made in Paradise? if their bodies did chaunge formes so often as their apparell chaungeth fashions, they should haue more shapes then they haue fingers and toes.[17]

In these particulars as in others, the courtiers' behavior is a contrast not only to country and woodland dwellers like Melibœ and Belphoebe, but also to that of humble Christians, but at least such "light clothes" serve Smith as a metaphor for what Christians should "put on": "Christ the garment."[18]

Biblical prophets, notably Amos and Isaiah, condemned the self-indulgence of the rich in passages that preachers mined for their condemnations of courtly worldliness. Here is William Burton's variation on the theme: "Now do men eat the calues of the stall, and the lambes of the flock, drinke wine out of golden cups, annoint themselues with costly ointment, wallow vpon beds of iuory, and sing to the violl & musical instrument."[19] Here is Drant's:

> In king *Herodes* house, my lady *Herodiada* could commaund halfe a realme, for footing and frisking. *Amos* spake of those in kinges houses in his 6. chapter, when he spake thus: *ye that sleepe in beddes of Iuory, and play the wantons on your conches* [sic]: *ye that warble to the tune of the*

---

16 Henry Smith, *The preachers proclamacion Discoursing the vanity of all earthly things, and proouing that there is no contentation to a Christian minde, but onely in the feare of God* (London, 1591), sig. B6ᵛ, STC (2nd edn) 22684. Available from the database Early English Books Online.
17 Henry Smith, *The sermons of Maister Henrie Smith gathered into one volume. Printed according to his corrected copies in his life time* (London, 1593), 435-6, STC (2nd edn) 22719. Available from the database Early English Books Online.
18 Ibid., 329-30.
19 William Burton, *A sermon preached in the Cathedrall Church in Norwich, the xxi. day of December, 1589* (London, 1590), sigs. I4ᵛ-K, STC (2nd edn) 4178. Available from the database Early English Books Online.

> Viall, and quaffe of wyne by whole goblettes full: ye that supple your ioyntes with the best kinde of oyle.[20]

The Amos passage, or perhaps preacherly paraphrases like those above, clearly informs the details of depraved luxury in Malecasta's Castle Joyous, with its "wals ... apparelled/ With costly clothes of *Arras* and of *Toure*" (III.i.34), "many beds" (39), "sweet Musicke" (40), "sumptuous fare" (51), and wine.

Preachers also decried the connection they saw between courtly luxury and social injustice. Drant's phrase "violent welthy worldlines" has a Spenserian ring.[21] Roger Hacket juxtaposes images of luxury with punishment in urging repentance on those who neglect the plight of religious refugees, whom he allegorizes as the biblical patriarch Joseph:

> [T]ender the affliction of Ioseph, least God in his iust iudgemente visite you vppon youre Ivory beddes, and clothe you with sackloth insteade of silcke, baldnes in steade of beuty, lest hee change your chaines of golde into chaines of iron, strong drinkes and delicate fare into water of trouble and bread of affliction.[22]

One recalls the disturbing glimpses that Redcrosse and his dwarf see of "routs of wretched thralles" as they steal away from the luxurious House of Pride (I.v.51).

Besides their unwarrented consumption, courtiers were known for their idle pursuit of pleasure, or "vainenesse," to use Meliboe's descriptor. Thomas Cooper lamented "lustie Courtiours['] ... gorgeous apparell,...ydle swearing... Dicing, Daunsing, and dalieng."[23] Edward Dering's scathing attack on the Queen's inadequate provision for the church, preached at court in 1570, included an insinuation against her courtiers. Having established that the duty of prince and peers is

---

20 Drant, *Two sermons*, sig. K6ᵛ. White, *A sermo[n] preached at Pawles Crosse*, 63ᵛ–64ᵛ, and Lavater, *Three Christian sermons*, 119, also cite Amos to criticize courtiers.
21 Drant, *Two sermons*, sig. G5.
22 Roger Hacket, *A sermon needfull for theese times wherein is shewed, the insolencies of Naash King of Ammon, against the men of Iabesh Gilead, and the succors of Saule, and his people sent for their reliefe* (London, 1590), sig. A6–6ᵛ, STC (2nd edn) 12589. Available from the database Early English Books Online.
23 Thomas Cooper, *Certaine sermons wherin is contained the defense of the gospell nowe preached against such cauils and false accusations, as are obiected both against the doctrine it selfe, and the preachers and professors thereof, by the friendes and fauourers of the Church of Rome* (London, 1580), 16, STC (2nd edn) 5685. Available from the database Early English Books Online.

to nurture the church, he said, "O if God had called them, for some other purpose, how gladly would they haue executed it? if God had called them to dising and carding, to swearing and lying, to pride & vanitie, the mighty men of our daies, how busely had they done their dutie?" – the clear implication being that these vices characterized life at court.[24]

The vice most closely associated with courtiers was insincerity – that is, flattery. John More, "the apostle of Norwich," cited an idiom familiar to us from Lear's Fool: "flatterie & faire speech is called holy-water of the court."[25] According to William Burton, More's colleague in Norwich, biblical examples of courtiers' flattery and its bad results abound:

> When *Herodes* Courtiers crie, *O vox non hominis, sed dei.* O the voice not of a man but of a God, then must *Herod* come downe with a mischiefe: when the foure hundred false Prophets shall say to *Achab*, goe and prosper, then must *Achab* looke least to thriue, neither shall be return in peace.[26]

Fortunately, evil kings disproportionately suffered flattery's ill effects

Kings need to be on their guard, but according to James Pilkington, common people can be susceptible to the flattery of courtiers as well: "God diliuer vs from such courtiers, for by this meanes he robbed the harts of the people from their natural & leige Prince, and by flatterie wanne the people so to him-selfe, that they rebelled against their King, and set vp *Absalon*."[27] And besides the risk to kings, flattery made relationships

---

24 Edward Dering, *A sermon preached before the Quenes Maiestie, By Maister Edward Dering, the. 25. day of February. Anno. 1569* (London, 1570), sig. C1ᵛ, STC (2nd edn) 6700. Available from the database Early English Books Online. Reprinted more times than any other such work, this sermon better represents such material's popular appeal rather than official tolerance; Dering was not invited back to court.

25 J. M. Blatchly, "More, John (*c.*1542–1592)," *Oxford Dictionary of National Biography* (Oxford: Oxford University Press, 2004). John More, *Three godly and fruitfull sermons declaring first how we may be saved in the day of iudgement, and so come to life everlasting: secondly, how we ought to liue according to Gods will during our life* (Cambridge, 1594), STC (2nd edn) 18074.5. Available from the database Early English Books Online.

26 William Burton, *A sermon preached in the Cathedrall Church in Norwich*, sig. B2ᵛ. Rudolph Gwalther, *An hundred, threescore and fiftene homelyes or sermons*, takes the Herod anecdote as an opportunity to indulge in a political reflection about the dangers of flattering rulers: "For why shoulde God giue them a better Prince, which were not ashamed so to extoll a fylthie and wicked man with godly honor?" (505).

27 James Pilkington, *A godlie exposition vpon certeine chapters of Nehemiah* (London, 1585), 3ᵛ–4. STC (2nd edn) 19929. Available from the database Early English Books Online.

among self-serving courtiers, however superficially amiable, dangerously competitive and unstable.[28]

Even when flattery did not cloak rebellion, it robbed kings of courtiers' honest counsel. Here is Pilkington again:

> [C]ourtyers must needes like and mislike, whatsoeuer the King seemeth to like or mislike, to set vp or pull downe. Courtyers commonly, when the King speaketh, haue lost both sense and witte: for if the King seemeth to fauour any thing, they all, as men without vnderstanding, saie it must needes be so. If the King will not giue eare to heare a matter, they are all deafe and cannot abide to heare speake of it: If the King will not see it, they all crie out, awaie with it. So that it is hard to tell, whither is in more miserable case the king or such dissemblers: for if the King haue no iudgement of him selfe, he shall haue no help of such, and they like witlesse men dare not speake a trueth.[29]

Or conversely, courtiers, according to Calvin, sway well-intentioned but weak-minded rulers in the wrong direction:

> [W]hen euen the greatest kinges and princes are minded to doe right: there needeth but some Courtier to inuegle them, and hee shall so alter their minde as (doe what they can) they must needes yeeld to all naughtinesse ... [T]hey be oftentimes inforced to say, I would faine doe the thing that I knowe to be good, but I dare not for displeasing of such as are about mee, bycause they may stirre mee vp great troubles and vnquietnesse.[30]

The only safeguard rulers had against courtiers' "threatninges, and spitings," according to Arthur Golding's translation of Calvin, is the confidence that "[o]ur God is the keeper of our soules."[31]

William Barlow preached to the Queen in 1602, by which time the court, according to some accounts, was actually declining into cynicism

---

28 See Gwalther, *An hundred, threescore and fiftene homelyes or sermons*, 30, on the risk Nehemiah took in leaving his position at court.
29 Pilkington, *A godlie exposition*, 21ᵛ-22. Interestingly, Pilkington also excused courtiers' care in choosing their words as a matter of respect and courtesy as well as human fear: "This toucheth a man neere when he must needes open the secrets of his heart to a king, whom he cannot tell how he wil take it, or what opinion he hath of him. Many thoughts and suspitions rise in good mens hearts, as wel as ill mens, and cast them into great feare: for euery man is subiect to affection of his owne nature ... The Maiestie of a king wil make anie good nature afraid to speake vnreuerentlie, though they be daylie in company with him and fauour" (14).
30 Calvin, *The sermons*, 1112.
31 Ibid., 331-2.

and vice.³² Barlow seemed to recognize this in what appears to be a singularly tactless piece of imagery, which he borrowed from his text, Luke 17.37: "He said vnto them, *Wheresoeuer the Body is, thether will the Eagles be gathered together.*"³³ Displaying a courtly sprezzatura, he offered various applications for this text. In his first attention-getting possibility, the carrion was the court, with the scavengers as the courtiers. "No bootie so gainefull, no gaine so easie, no office so affected as those of *this place*." But Barlow immediately drew back from this offensive characterization of his setting and audience with a "prayer for a blessing on the Royal Foundresse" of the court, explaining that he speaks "not out of envie of their desire," but "onely to shewe how [the court] doth moralize this *Prouerbe.*"³⁴ The burden of the sermon concerned the godly Christian life and the importance of the established church, a message designed to impress the auditors with the preacher's own importance. Offering the conventional insults to the court thus underscored the preacher's authority. In fact, Barlow discounted the Catholic doctrine of the intercession of the saints by comparing it to the indirections and refinements of courtly behavior:

> Therefore, though [Christ] be placed in the heauens ... yet the *Eagles* (his *Elect*) seize euen *there* vpon him by their *Praiers*, as their *Intercessor*; accompting mediation by Saints (as by fauourites to the *Prince*) ... a courtly reuerence, no celestial courtesie, no canonicall custome; acknowledging *him,* ... to be the ONELY master of requests.³⁵

"[C]elestial courtesie" does not involve mediation by saints. The preacher's authority was greater than either Catholic devotion or courtly protocol.

Those at court did not always show proper respect for religion and its spokespersons; Thomas Drant's concern that courtiers "accompt of them selues as exempt persons from controlement of preachers" was widely shared. Lancelot Andrewes noted that Satan "hath indeed a grace with some vaine youths of the Court, ... to set them a scoffing at the Scripture."³⁶

---

32 Javitch, *Poetry and Courtliness*, 119–21.
33 *The Eagle and the Body described in one sermon preached before Queene Elizabeth of precious memorie, in Lent. Anno 1601* (London, 1509), sig. B1, STC (2nd edn) 1450. Available from the database Early English Books Online.
34 Ibid., sigs. B1ᵛ–2. One notes that this sermon was not published until after Elizabeth's death.
35 Ibid., sig. D1ᵛ.
36 *The wonderfull combate (for Gods glorie and mans saluation) betweene Christ and Satan Opened in seuen most excellent, learned and zealous sermons, vpon the temptations of Christ, in the wildernesse* (London, 1592), 54ᵛ–55, STC (2nd edn) 629. Available from the database Early English Books Online.

Calvin agreed: "the heathen folke thought themseues fine witted and of abilitie, when they despised God … as wee see these courtiers & all the braue laddes of the worlde do nowadays … which skoffe at all religion."[37] Some courtiers even presumed to dictate to preachers what their message should be.[38] Preachers could take comfort in identifying with Elijah, Amos, and Jeremiah, all of whom suffered from courtiers' disrespect.[39] Conversely, a preacher's denunciation of courtiers asserted that they fall within his sphere of judgment. Preacherly anti-court rhetoric is a species of self-advertisement.

Happily, not all courts were sinks of vice. Elizabeth's court was after all preeminently the place one of Elizabeth's oppressed subjects mights come to obtain justice, as illustrated in *The Faerie Queene* (or at least in the Letter to Raleigh) and sermons such as this one by Robert Some (who as one of Leicester's chaplains was in a position to turn his own courtly compliments):

> Our souereigne Ladie *Queene Elizabeth* hath dealt gratiouslie with manie poore suters at the Court, she hath spoken comfortablie to them, and procured restitution accordinglie. If it be no disgrace to this noble Ladie, which sitteth vnder the cloth of estate, to deliuer the oppressed, it is no blot to inferiour magistrates if they doe the like.[40]

Rulers also needed counselors and officials to whom they could delegate some of their many responsibilities. Preachers thus contrasted courtly vice to a courtiers' real obligations, which they sometimes expressed in pastoral terms. As Dering lamented, "But alas, this [dising and carding] is not to feede gods people in *Iacob*, nor his inheritaunce in *Israel*."[41] Many preachers cited godly members of biblical courts. Watch Pilkington make this pivot from negative to positive:

> & although I noted afore the disordred life of some leud courtiers, which make so much of their painted sheath … [t]he court is not ill of it selfe, but a man, if he will, maie serue the Lord vprightlie, and also defend his Church, and profit the common-wealth mightelie, and good men maie liue

---

37 Calvin, *The sermons*, 1112.
38 Thomas Becon, *A new postil conteinyng most godly and learned sermons vpon all the Sonday Gospelles, that be redde in the church thorowout the yeare* (London, 1566), 170, STC (2nd edn) 1736. Available from the database Early English Books Online.
39 For Elijah, see Drant, *Two sermons*, sig. K7ᵛ; for Amos, see Smith, *The Sermons*, 929; for Jeremiah, see Gwalther, *An hundred, threescore and fiftene homelyes or sermons*, 634.
40 Robert Some, *A Treatise against Opression*, printed with Pilkington, *A godlie exposition*, 80ᵛ.
41 Dering, *A sermon*, sig. C1ᵛ.

in it honestlie. It is a dangerous place, I graunt, to liue in, and manie occasions of ill are offred dailie in it: yet not so wicked, but good men liuing in it maie take great occasions to doe much good in it.[42]

Neither the setting nor the office disqualify a courtier from being a godly leader.

Model biblical courtiers: the Ethiopian eunuch, Naaman, and Joseph

A commendable biblical courtier was the Ethiopian eunuch whom Philip baptized. In his eagerness to consult scripture and follow God, "[t]hat noble Eunuch chiefe officer to the Queeene of Ethiopia" is "a woorthie president for Christian Courtiers to behold and followe," according to Edwin Sandys. Rudolf Gwalther joins Sandys in his admiration:

> [I]t plainely appeareth, that he was none of the inferiour Courtyers, but one of the chiefe of the Court. This place teacheth vs that Magistrates and officers ought not for their office sake ... be excluded from the Kingdome of Christ, as the seditious Anabaptistes crie. For *Paule* plainely testifyeth, that such are the Ministers of God."[43]

Certainly criticism of the court's typical vices does not imply that all courtiers are culpable.

At least one other non-Jewish courtier was exemplary as well. In a sermon at court in 1591, Gervase Babington preached on the healing of Naaman, a courtier to the King of Assyria "by [whose] hand the Lord had deliuered the kingdome from great danger."[44] The fact that scripture mentions Naaman's high standing and his service, according to the preacher, teaches "that there is not in this world a more iust cause of honorable regard, and most high accompt to be had and made of a man, not only with people but euen with Prince, then faithful loue and fruteful seruice to king and countrie."[45]

Another biblical courtier whose example was frequently invoked was Joseph. Drant makes the comparison here:

---

42 Pilkington, *A godlie exposition*, 5–6.
43 Sandys, *Sermons*, 132; and Gwalther, *An hundred, threescore and fiftene homelyes or sermons*, 377.
44 *A sermon preached at the Court at Greenewich the XXIIII. Of May 1591* (London, 1591), 2, STC (2nd edn) 1094. Available from the database Early English Books Online.
45 Ibid.

Let vs hartily wishe to her maiesties most honorable Counsaile the spirite of councell and direction, that they may be as *Iosephes* in Egypt, faythfull, and carefull to prouide for the necessities of the realme, specially, that mens soules be not starued with hunger and pine of the worde of God.[46]

Besides his conscientious service, Joseph's virtuous life was examplary. John Bridges singles out his "chaste fidelitie" and "trustie diligence" during his service for Potiphar and within the prison as qualifying him for God's favor and advancement, while Gwalther makes his appointment to high court office a credit to Pharaoh: "Of which example men in authoritie may learne ... howe profitable a thing it is, to put them in office, that worship God truely, bicause the blessing of God followeth suche, and that which is done vnto them, God taketh as done vnto himselfe."[47]

Interestingly, Joseph's example also illustrates how far courtiers might go in subterfuge: "Neither yet are all policies so condemned ... for some are godlie and may bee practised, as wee may see in *Ioseph* with his brethren." While the determining factor for Edward Topsell in the foregoing quote was whether such policy exceeded Joseph's authority (it did not), Joseph's subterfuge protected true religion, since after satisfying himself of his brothers' reformed characters, he provided for their maintenance, thus keeping Abraham's descendants alive.[48] Pilkington stipulated that such subterfuge should never be used toward the ruler. After fasting and prayer, courtiers should emulate Esther or Nehemiah in those communications: "open the sute vnto [the ruler] symply in the feare of God, committing the successe thereof by earnest prayer, to Gods goodwill and pleasure."[49]

On the other hand, not all preachers were impressed with Joseph's piety. The more strenuous John Udall (a controversial figure who died

---

46 Drant, *Two sermons*, sig. B3.
47 John Bridges, *A sermon, preached at Paules Crosse on the Monday in Whitson weeke* (London, 1571), 112, STC (2nd edn) 3736. Available from the database Early English Books Online. Gwalther, *An hundred, threescore and fiftene homelyes or sermons*, 311.
48 Edward Topsell, *Times lamentation: or An exposition on the prophet Ioel, in sundry sermons or meditations* (London, 1599), 444, STC (2nd edn) 24131. Available from the database Early English Books Online. Topsell counts Moses's sending spies into Caanan as a further illustration of the same principle, but Gwalther takes this lesson from the Joseph episode: while we should acknowledge our brothers, "there no cause why their sinnes shoulde not be prerooued and accused" (312).
49 Pilkington, *A godlie exposition*, 12.

Sermon contexts for Spenser's Book VI   191

in prison after being convicted of writing *Demonstration of Discipline*, "a wicked, scandalous libel"[50]) faulted the biblical patriarch for adopting the idiom of his adopted home: "Godlie *Ioseph* dwelling in *Aegypt* amongst the wicked, through custome and long continuance, was brought to break the chiefest point of his religion the worship of God, & to sweare by the life of *Pharaoh*." This failing, like Daniel's use of the conventionally respectful "O king, live forever," illustrated the temptations of life at court.[51]

Most preachers who related Joseph's service as a courtier to his treatment of his brothers did so to commend his acknowledgement of and provision for his poor relations, as John Baker does here: "Ioseph in all his rioltie [sic] and glory, remembred & did acknowledge his poore brethren before Pharao, and all his house."[52] Pilkington likewise cited Joseph (along with Moses, Obadiah [1 Kings 18], David, Daniel, and Mordecai) as an example of his point that godly courtiers can do great good because of their access to power. "*Ioseph*, in Pharaos courte a godlesse king … releeued his father & breethren, then the onely knowne Church of God, in their necessitie."[53] And many sermons cite Joseph's transition from slave to courtier to illustrate God's providence and his lack of regard for rank and status, as well as the necessity for believers to persevere in prayer and faith.[54]

Model biblical courtiers: Moses and David

The biblical ideal for a courtier modeled after the Ethiopian eunuch, Naaman, and Joseph, then, was a God-fearing man, perhaps originally

---

50 Claire Cross, "Udall, John (c.1560–1592/3)," *Oxford Dictionary of National Biography* (Oxford: Oxford University Press, 2004); online edn, May 2008. Cross quotes the phrase from his indictment under the statute of 23 Elizabeth.
51 *Peters fall Two sermons vpon the historie of Peters denying Christ* (London, 1584), sigs. C6^v–7, STC (2nd edn) 24503. Available from the database Early English Books Online.
52 John Baker, *Lectures of I.B. vpon the xii. Articles of our Christian faith briefely set forth for the comfort of the godly, and the better instruction of the simple and ignorant* (London, 1581), sig. I8, STC (2nd edn) 1219. Available from the database Early English Books Online.
53 Pilkington, *A godlie exposition*, 6.
54 For Joseph as a bondservant whom God "exalted," see Smith, *Foure sermons*, sig. D4^v, and James Bisse, *Two sermons preached the one at Paules Crosse the eight of Ianuarie 1580. The other, at Christes Churche in London the same day in the after noone* (London, 1581), sig. C6, STC (2nd edn) 3099. Available from the database Early English Books Online. For Joseph as a believer whose prayers were answered at last, see Becon, *A new postil*, 163; and Babington, *A sermon*, 21 (Babington makes a similar point about Daniel: that his rise to power in the court involved much danger and many prayers).

of low station, divinely ordained to serve ruler and people faithfully, and who might employ policy when required. Moses likewise served God but, as noted by Pilkington, departed from the established model by repudiating the ruler's authority. Notwithstanding, his courtiership in Egypt and subsequent challenge of that kingdom dramatically illustrated God's sovereignty. Gwalther highlights the irony this way: "*Pharao* went about to oppresse and destroye the children of Israell. And yet he brought hym vp in his owne house, and set him on his lap, whome God had appointed to be the delyuerer and reuenger of his people."[55] Indeed, for preachers, the exemplary quality of Moses in his courtier phase was his willingness to walk away from court to serve God and identify with the Israelites rather than the Egyptian elite – rather as Gloriana's knights leave the court envisioned in the Letter to Raleigh to test their mettle and perform their great deeds.[56] Topsell's formulation is typical: "Remember *Moses*, which forsooke the court of all *Pharaohs* disports, to liue among his poore brethren, which daily laboured in making bricke, gathering staw, and bearing many a heauy burthen."[57] Moses forsook "the delycacies of the Court, the pompe of the Realme, the dignities of publike authoritie, the friendship of great-men, riches, ease, and whatsoeuer else like is to be had in the Court," according to Gwalther. "In steade of these," rather like Redcrosse, Guyon, Calidore, and the rest, "he chooseth traueyles, pouertie, shame, and infinite daungers."[58] Pilkington's paraphrase of Hebrews made even the forty-year sojourn in Midian praiseworthy: "*Moses forsooke to liue in pleasure in Pharaos court, & to be called his daughters sonne, & chose to liue in trouble with his Breethren the Iewes, & to keepe Iethros sheepe, so that he might serue the Lord.*"[59] In his abandonment of court, Gwalther sees Moses as a type of Christ:

---

55 Gwalther, *An hundred, threescore and fiftene homelyes or sermons*, 252.
56 That is, they follow the biblical book of Hebrews, which omits the episode of Moses killing the Egyptian overseer and presents his departure from court as a choice, rather than Exodus, where Pharaoh seeks to kill Moses, who flees. Gwalther is exceptional in noting the involuntary nature of Moses's exile: "Thus it behoued, that *Moses* should first be … banished out of the court, or euer he were appoynted to be the reuenger of the people" (*An hundred, threescore and fiftene homelyes or sermons*, 889), but, as quoted below, he also refers several times to Moses's forsaking the delights of courtly life (e.g. 509, 793, 825).
57 Topsell, *Times lamentation*, 158.
58 Gwalther, *An hundred, threescore and fiftene homelyes or sermons*, 320–1.
59 Pilkington, *A godlie exposition*, 25^v.

Moses example comprehendeth in it the mysteries of our redemption, and vpbraydeth vs with our vnkindnesse toward Christ. For as *Moses* forsooke *Pharaos* court, & the riches of *Egypt*, visited his brethren, and tooke vpon him their defence: so Iesus Christ being in the glory of his father, did vouchsafe to humble himselfe, & by his incarnation became our brother, to take vpon him our quarrell & defence.[60]

Certainly all exemplary biblical courtiers made serving the common people a priority, but few took their service to the incarnational extent that Moses did.

Moses's repudiation of the role of courtier to embrace that of shepherd made him a useful figure in the archetypal contrast between the values of the court and the countryside and illustrates the biblical roots of this conventional literary debate. Compared with Moses's, Joseph's and David's examples pointed in the reverse direction: upwardly rather than downwardly mobile. Not only shepherd, but courtier and then king (and poet in all three capacities), David embodied and resolved the debate.

Joseph was first a favored son, then a slave, and then a prisoner. David's status as an outsider likewise underscored the role God played in bringing him to power: "*Dauid* he could haue brought to the kingdome, with halfe the difficultie that he did if he would," commented Babington.[61] "Whom made hee to rule his people after Saule? no Prince, but Dauid a shephearde," noted Bisse.[62] "Remember the example of Dauid, whom the Lord chose and tooke from the Ewes great with young: that hee might feed his people in Iacob, & his inheritance in Israel," echoed Smith.[63] And though, unlike Moses, he never exercised it, preachers noted David's expressed preference in Psalm 84 for less glamorous work in God's cause rather than high position. "[T]his is the case of earnest & zealous men in religion," said Pilkington, "that they can say with *Dauid, I haue chosen rather to bee a dore-keeper in the house of God, then to dwell in the pallaces of sinners.*" "*Dauid*," according to Dering, "*wished rather to be a dore keeper in the house of God, then to dwell in the Pallaces of Princes.*"[64]

---

60 Gwalther, *An hundred, threescore and fiftene homelyes or sermons*, 323.
61 Babington, *A sermon*, 21.
62 Bisse, *Two sermons*, sig. C6–6ᵛ.
63 Smith, *Foure sermons preached by Master Henry Smith. And published by a more perfect copie then heretofore* (London, 1599), sig. D4ᵛ, STC (2nd edn) 22748. Available from the database Early English Books Online.
64 Pilkington, *A godlie exposition*, 21ᵛ; Dering, *A sermon*, sig. C7. These passages and the others quoted in this paragraph are typical in attributing to King David the attitudes expressed in various psalms.

And as king, David insisted on high moral standards among his courtiers: "King Dauid was so carefull of this that hee would not suffer a wicked person, a backebiter, an hawtie hearted man, a subtile deceiuer, a flatterer or a lyer to remaine in his Court," noted Sandys.[65]

In citing biblical examples, preachers admonished courtiers to be virtuous, critiqued their character flaws, and reminded them that they enjoyed high station because of God's favor, not their own efforts or qualities. A David or a Joseph could rise to favor in court, and a Moses could retire or be exiled from court, in obedience to God's will. A court appointment potentially enabled one to do great good, but involved much temptation – not just to self-indulgent pleasure, ambition, and duplicity (hypocrisy and flattery), but also to the grateful or even overawed sense that one must answer expectations and conform to protocol.[66] There were biblical courtiers who stayed at court and those who left, so no hard and fast rule demanded that all Christians abandon its luxuries or opportunities.[67] Indeed, God's people are everywhere, even in sinful courts.[68] Some, however, were better off leaving court, the better to "kill the hearts of many sinnes, and stop the breath of many euils, and auoide the danger of many troubles."[69] God often had his people near the heart of power, but could work his will without their assistance, even through ungodly rulers, as he chose.

The heavenly court

The most exalted among biblical courts was "the Court holden in heauen, before the kings maiesty of the whole earth, and his counsell and assembly of glorious Angels, before my Lord chiefe iustice of the whole earth, and

---

65 Sandys, *Sermons*, 104; compare 233. Later he notes that "Constantius the woorthie christian Emperour" retained only good Christians as his courtiers (230).
66 E.g., Smith, *Foure Sermons*, sig. G4.
67 Theodore de Beze, *Master Bezaes sermons vpon the three chapters of the canticle of canticles wherein are handled the chiefest points of religion controuersed and debated betweene vs and the aduersarie at this day*, trans. John Harmar (Oxford, 1587), 145, STC (2nd edn) 2025. Available from the database Early English Books Online.
68 Gwalther, *An hundred, threescore and fiftene homelyes or sermons*, 252, 509. Hugh Latimer was certain that bishops did not belong among them, however: *27 sermons preached by the ryght Reuerende father in God and constant matir* [sic] *of Iesus Christe, Maister Hugh Latimer* (London, 1562), 17, STC (2nd edn) 15276. Available from the database Early English Books Online. Gwalther (e.g., *An hundred, threescore and fiftene homelyes or sermons*, 651, 656, 842) and Calvin agreed with him.
69 Topsell, *Times lamentation*, 158.

Chauncelour of the whole world, the deare Sonne of God, Iesus Christ the Lord of all."[70] This was the court that Jesus left (as Moses left Pharaoh's) and to which he returned as the foremost of courtiers. Just as the Pharaoh appointed Joseph to hear suits, so God appoints Jesus "who is ordeined of his father to rule and gouerne all thinges in his name."[71] Henry Smith highlighted another aspect of Jesus's courtiership: "Therefore if any affect rich kinsmen or great marriages: heere is a greater then Salomon, marrie thou him. This kinsman of ours is now gone vp into heauen, that we may haue a friend in the Court."[72] Preachers also count as courtiers in this paradigm: "surely if the seruants of *Salomon*, were blessed that hearde his wisedome, and waited in his court, they are much more blessed which waite in the Lords house, and heare and see the secrets of the kingdome of heauen."[73] A courtier should be upright and deserving; how much more a minister.

God's court differs from earthly courts, however. Flattery, for instance, is of no use there. According to John More, "we can make faire weather with men, and with our smooth lookes, sugred wordes, and faire countenances subtilly intrappe our brethren. Alas good brethren this geere will not be good stuffe with our God, when hee calleth vs to answer the matter in his highest court."[74] Conversely, the different protocols of God's court allow more accessibility:

> It was the danger of Esthers life to come before the king vnles shee were called for ... But the scepter of the Lord our God ... is ever held forth to man, woman, childe, bond and free, straunger or citizen, whether they be called or not called, they may safely approch, I name neither outwarde nor inwarde courte, but even to the throne where the King himselfe sitteth ... Surely they doe iniury to his grace, who talke of warders, and porters, and maisters of requestes, Angels and Saintes, to admit vs into presence, and to bring vs to speech with God ... We dreame of outwarde and inwarde courtes, dores and gates, porters and mediatours, impedimentes and stoppes, I graunt, in earthly Courtes. But the Lorde is porter himselfe at these heavenlye gates.[75]

---

70 More, *Three godly and fruitfull sermons*, 36.
71 For Jesus's leaving court, see Gwalther, *An hundred, threescore and fiftene homelyes or sermons*, 320–1, quoted above; Baker, *Lectures of I.B.*, sig. T8.
72 Smith, *The Sermons*, 258.
73 Topsell, *Times lamentation*, 168.
74 More, *Three godly and fruitfull sermons*, 9.
75 John King, *Lectures vpon Ionas deliuered at Yorke in the yeare of our Lorde 1594* (Oxford, 1599), 331–2, STC (2nd edn) 14977. Available from the database Early English Books Online. Barlow (sig. D1ᵛ) made a similar point, quoted above.

"[O]utwarde and inwarde courtes, dores and gates, porters and mediatours" sound as reminiscent of the carefully guarded perimeters of *The Faerie Queene*'s various stately homes as those in the book of Esther. God being well able to look after his own security and dignity, however, none are needed in heaven.

Calidore and Nehemiah

Moses leaving court and turning up among Jethro's sheep may remind us of Calidore's sojourn among the shepherds (though the preachers view Moses's shepherding phase much more favorably than many Spenserians do Calidore's). But another sermon collection, James Pilkington's *A godlie exposition vpon certeine chapters of Nehemiah*, emerges as the most thorough preacherly analysis of a biblical courtier's career in Elizabethan publishing. There is no evidence that Spenser read the volume or heard any sermons reflecting this material, but Pilkington's analysis of the erstwhile cupbearer to the Persian king Artaxerxes insists over and over that Nehemiah is a model for Elizabeth's courtiers: "Let the fine courtier, that had rather be a dainty carpet gentleman, then a labourer at gods building, looke at *Nehemiah*, & learne to be like him."[76] "O worthie, wise, and stout *Nehemiah*, where is one courtier that hath folowed thy footsteps since thou wast borne? God for his mercie raise vp some."[77] Pilkington's treatise is thus a useful context for an analysis of Calidore.

Nehemiah had many excellences as a courtier: "in religion earnest, in great fauour with his Prince, with all vprightnesse of life towards all, in warre skilful, curragious, & painful, and with his penne so learned, that he could so clerkelie put it in writing." Contemporary courtiers among Pilkington's auditors and readers were similarly obligated:

> first to serue the Lord, promote his word and religion earnestlie, minister iustice seuerelie, mainteine peace quietlie, defend the common-wealth stoutlie, releeue the oppressed mightilie, followe learning and studie diligentlie, that so they maie increase in vertue and honestie, as Nehemiah did, and after all these great trauailes refresh themselues with honest pastimes measureablie.[78]

---

76 Pilkington, *A godlie exposition*, 66ᵛ.
77 Ibid., 70. This prayer was answered: according to the *DNB*, Pilkington's younger brother Leonard named his middle son Nehemiah (d. 1602).
78 Ibid., 2ᵛ. Pilkington's analysis in particular is useful as it brings together the discourse of courtesy with morality and martial prowess, paralleling Michael Schoenfeldt's point about Spenser's courtesy "demand[ing] an exercise of martial power" ("The Poetry of Conduct," 52).

Seen in light of this biblical ideal, perhaps rather than begrudge Calidore his interval with the shepherds, readers should remember that it follows efforts to defend the commonwealth and relieve the oppressed. According to the narrator, "So sharply he the Monster did pursew/ That day nor night he suffred him to rest/ Ne rested he himselfe but natures dew" (VI.ix.3). Perhaps some of his time tending Meliboe's flock in Pastorella's company can be explained as his measured self-refreshment with honorable pastimes.

One recalls that, as the biblical book opens, Nehemiah questions travelers about conditions in Judah and Jerusalem. Pilkington celebrated Nehemiah's mobility and accessibility:

> And where *Nehemiah*, walking abroade about the cou[rt]e, beginneth to examin them of the *estate of the Iewes*, how they did, *and of the Citie of Ierusalem*, in what case it was, it declareth the great loue that he had to his people, countrie, and religion. O worthie example for all courtiers to follow, sometimes to walke abroad, to see what suters there be, & learne the state of the countrie from whence they came, & help to further their good causes.[79]

Calidore and other Spenserian courtiers find a model in Nehemiah for having interests outside of Gloriana's court – and certainly Calidore's pursuit of the Blatant Beast as well as his championship of Priscilla and Serena, among others, indicates his willingness to further his people's "good causes."

Nehemiah was emotionally open as well as physically accessible, a creditable character trait in Pilkington's mind as well as Spenser's:

> Nehemiah was in good state to liue, & in great fauour with the King, and needed not to trouble him selfe with the cares of his countrie, if God had not otherwise mooued his mind to pitie, with talking with his countrie men. This good then courtiers, lawiers, and great men may haue by talking with poore suters, that if there be anie sparke of grace in them they wilbe mooued with the lamentable complainte of poore suters. Surely thou that art in authoritie, or hast learning, oughtest to thinke, that the poore suter commeth not to the by chaunce: but the same God, that gaue thee thy authorite and learning, hath sent this poore man to thee to be releiued by thee.[80]

Compassion is a summons to action. And chance, the guise of providence in the comparatively secular Book VI, puts many helpless ladies and even an infant in the way of Calidore and other good knights.

---

79 Pilkington, *A godlie exposition*, 3ᵛ.
80 Ibid., 4ᵛ.

Nehemiah's service led him to abandon the court as "master of the worke" of rebuilding of the walls of Jerusalem: "he ... set euerie man in order, that none loytered, nor wrought otherwyes then he was appointed, and that none troubled his fellowes." The job was exhausting and hardly glamorous: "dayly dabling in the mire, morter, and clay, as long as he might, and yet would not be wearie." Then threats from jealous neighboring peoples forced Nehemiah to assume the mantle of a general. He

> is driuen to put on armour, keepe watch and ward night and daie, and ouersee them him selfe, to sett his people in aray, and appoint them their standing places, giuing them their weapons, and teaching them what they should doe. Such reward shall they haue that forsake the world and will build Gods house and Citie: God and the world cannot be friends: and that maketh so few Courtiers to tread this trodde.

In this sense, Nehemiah reminds Pilkington of Moses:

> *Moses* being brought vp in *Pharaos* house, and might haue bene called as sonne to *Phàraos daughter, refused the Court, and chose to be in trouble with his breethren the Iewes, and serue the Lord, rather then to haue all the dainties in the Court,* liuing in Idolatrie and displeasure of God. I know not many courtiers which might haue liued in the court with such fauour & authoritie, & would not, to set by these two men.[81]

The Faerie Queene features many erstwhile courtiers who might (one assumes) have lived idly, enjoying favor and authority, yet choose to range abroad and defend the right. Calidore, like Nehemiah, is exemplary in choosing the society and practicing the occupation of rural common people – and of course, in the exercise of arms, rescuing Pastorella from a tiger and the brigands.

Courtesy in the sermon tradition

Moving, then, from courtiers and their biblical prototypes to the courtesy they should practice: when the word "courtesy" is used in sermons, it often refers to the appropriate conventional behavior dictated by specific situations, such as the exchange of greetings. "It is a poynt both of curtesie and of humanitie to salute others," according to Pagitt's translation of Ludwig Lavater's sermons on Ruth.[82] "Courtesy" also refers

---

81 Ibid., 63ᵛ.
82 *The book of Ruth expounded in twenty eight sermons*, trans. Ephraim Pagitt (London, 1586), 56ᵛ, STC (2nd edn) 15319. Available from the database Early English Books Online.

to conventional physical gestures. "[C]ap and knee," "cap and curtsey," bowing, giving the hand, and kissing are ways that, as de Beze says, "by … outward gesture a man maketh himselfe inferiour to another to doe him curtesy."[83] These gestures may be consistent with either sincerity or hypocrisy, the latter predictably eliciting more colorful preacherly emphasis, as in John More's denunciation of the citizens of Norwich:

> Such faire lookes, sugred wordes, louing salutations, and courteous embracings as is marveilous, as though there were such perfect loue and friendshippe amongst vs, as could possibly be required, and yet such deepe dissembled hatred and spight in the bottome of our breastes, as we would (if we could) euen pull their hearts out of their bodies, and eate them with garlicke.[84]

But more interesting than these passages are those that explore the moral and theological quality that preachers referred to as courtesy, a quality characteristic of God.

God's courtesy

During Mary's era, the Catholic Roger Edgeworth paraphrased 1 Peter 2 (which itself paraphrases Psalm 34) to read, "you haue tasted (sayth S. Peter) that God is swete, good, & curtise."[85] Other preachers' references to God's courtesy clarify. Calvin saw God's courtesy as an expression of his desire to draw people to himself: "Surely our God could not vse greater curtesie towardes vs, than to allure vs to him by louing of vs, to the intent that wee shoulde loue him againe."[86] And again, later in the same sermon series: "[O]ur Lorde allureth vs to him so gently and with so great courtisie, saying, Go to my children, I desire nothing else but to maintaine you in prosperitie, doe you no more but followe mee."[87] Both passages highlight God's tact in making himself inferior, or at least declining to take advantage of his greater power and higher position. King's comment on God's response to Jonah's outburst draws attention to the same quality: "The manner thereof … is milde,

---

83 de Beze, *Master Bezaes sermons*, 18. The earlier quoted phrases appear in Edgeworth, *Sermons*, xlx (sic; lii is intended) and Smith, *The Sermons*, 445.
84 More, *Three godly and fruitfull sermons*, 91.
85 *Sermons very fruitfull, godly, and learned* (London, 1557), cxlix^v–cl, STC (2nd edn) 7482. Available from the database Early English Books Online.
86 Calvin, *The sermons*, 434.
87 Ibid., 519.

curteous, and peaceable ... I cannot conceiue how he should haue vsed him with so favourable and sparing an increpation, *Doest thou wel to be angry?*"[88] Even in his reproofs God does not assert his superiority to embarrass Jonah, though this tact appears to be squandered on the irritable prophet.

Jesus exemplified courtesy by declining to take credit for his miracles, for instance in his dismissal of the woman whose hemorrhage was cured: "he prayseth the womanne, and speaketh vnto her moste curteously, sayenge: Be of good confort daughter: Thy Faithe hath made thee whole."[89] Humility is allied to courtesy in this comment from Edgeworth: "[Jesus] kept close his mighty power, & euer shewed him selfe curteous, gentle, patient, and as an vnderlinge to euery man."[90] Gwalther characterized Jesus as "courteous and friendly" to Saul on the road to Damascus, and King labeled Jesus's invitation "*Come vnto me all yee that travaile and labour*" as "courteous."[91] As with Calvin's and King's assertions of God's courtesy, these examples suggest that Jesus, the superior, is treating his interlocutor with respect and equality.

Along the same lines, John Baker associates courtesy with the individual of higher status, in this case the Holy Spirit, giving honor to the lowly believer: "euen the holy Ghost, the power of God ... will vouchsafe to abide with you ... giue him thankes for this his so vnspeakeable courtesie and kindenesse."[92]

Courtesy expressed, for these and other preachers, the tactful generosity of God's love and grace, alluring rather than commanding. It followed that on the human level, the higher-ranking individual exercises courtesy by "mak[ing] himselfe inferiour," in de Beze's phrase, that is, in manifesting tact and deference. Courtesy is by nature given freely rather than an obligation: "not of desert or merit."[93] To be "at the courtesy of another" meant being at the mercy of someone who holds the upper

---

88 King, *Lectures vpon Ionas*, 596.
89 Becon, *A new postil*, sig. Zz7 (fol. 183).
90 Edgeworth, *Sermons*, ccciiii.
91 Gwalther, *An hundred, threescore and fiftene homelyes or sermons*, 396; King, *Lectures vpon Ionas*, 514.
92 Baker, *Lectures of I.B.*, sig. D3ᵛ.
93 The distinction is Sandys's, *Sermons*, 173; the second quote comes from Baker, *Lectures of I.B.*, sig. Aa7. Bridges declared that paying ministers was obligatory, "not gift, nor fauour, nor loue, nor curtesy, nor free, nor grace," thus specifying courtesy's lexical field (*A sermon*, 73).

hand, for instance as creditor or landlord;[94] to "make courtesy" meant letting another take the lead.[95] The human level emulating the divine, Christian courtesy contrasted with lordliness, sovereignty, cruelty, and arbitrary exercise of power. For example, God's chosen people Israel courteously asked permission of the Moabites to pass through their land, and when it was denied, skirted their territory.[96] Courtesy, for preachers, characterized the ideal treatment of subordinates and victims: servants, refugees, debtors, and children.

Courtesy also meant offering correction in a tactful and considerate way. For instance, readers should be courteous when they found an error in a book.[97] In the preface to a catechism bound with his sermon, Thomas Wilson appealed to his reader:

> I am to entreat this of thy curtisie, that if thou findest in the foresaid Catechisme any thing eyther vnperfect or vnsound, (for the former it cannot be otherwise as all mens workes are; for the latter I hope it is otherwise, yet we are all men) and wilt certifie me thereof priuately by word or writing, I will thanke thee for thy good will and will trust if God will to giue thee satisfaction.[98]

John King, in a sermon about Jonah, condemned a blameworthy "reprehension" that

> hath no other end, but to reprehende, to fasten a tooth vpon every occasion that is offered; borne of the cursed seed of Cham, delighting in nothinge so much as to vncover the nakednesse of fathers, brethren, all

---

94 Thanks to God's greater power, "wee stande not at the Diuells curtesie," preached Andrewes (*The wonderfull combate*, 98); Jacob "had scarce any corner to liue in, yea, & that was at the curtesie of another," according to Calvin (*The sermons*, 809). When William Burton explained Proverbs' counsel against cosigning for someone else's loan, he offered this reassurance: "we shall not breake the rule of charitie, though we do not commit our selues to the curtesie of all men, without the vse of some honest meanes for our safetie" (*A caueat for suerties two sermons of suertiship* [London, 1593], 35, STC [2nd edn] 4166. Available from the database Early English Books Online.)
95 Pilkington, *A godlie exposition*, 37ᵛ and 77; Sandys, *Sermons*, 106.
96 Calvin, *The sermons*, 798.
97 For an analysis of this familiar appeal and its relevance to the Blatant Beast, see Debra Belt, "Hostile Audiences and the Courteous Reader in *The Faerie Queene*, Book VI," in *Spenser Studies IX*, ed. Patrick Cullen and Thomas P. Roche, Jr. (New York, NY: AMS, 1991), 107–35.
98 *An exposition of the two first verses of the sixt chapter to the Hebrewes in forme of a dialogue. Wherein you have a commendation of catechising, also a declaration of the sixe fundamentall principles wherein the Christians of the Primitiue Apostolicall church were catechized* (London, 1600), 151, STC (2nd edn) 24966. Available from the database Early English Books Online.

sorts;[99] or rather borne of the Devill himselfe ... Hee that prerooveth in this sorte, and he that approveth and fostereth such reproofes, the one hath the Devill in his tongue, the other in his eares ... such are not correctors, but traitors, willing to lay open the offences of other men; not reprovers, but gnawers, because they had rather bite, than amend ought amisse. There is no mercie, nor compassion in this kinde of reprehenders ... The mercie and kindnesse of their lippes, is, as if aspes should vomite ... [T]his is all the treasure and goodnes, that they beare in their tongues; contumelies, slanders, defamations, opprobrious detractions, vncourteous vpbraidings, supercilious, insolent, vncharitable accusations rather to verit [vent] their malice ... then to reforme the defectes of their brethren.[100]

Such a description of misplaced reprehension makes it hard to blame Calidore for protecting Priscilla's reputation in VI.iii,[101] and it would be hard indeed to find a more apt literary context than this sermon for the activities and role of the Blatant Beast, the materialized opposite to courtesy in Book VI. Though Spenser probably never heard or read King's characterization, preached in York in 1594 and published in Oxford in 1599, the scriptural allusions and notions of courtesy were familiar from liturgical readings of King's scripture references and other specimens of religious rhetoric.

Courtesy and humanity

As Spenserians have noted, "kindness," "gentleness," "compassion," and "love" are all words that often appear in proximity to "courtesy" in *The Faerie Queene*. The same proximity exists in sermons. Another word that occurs frequently in sermons as a synonym or an idea associated with courtesy is "humanity."[102] Though this looks contradictory to courtesy's

---

99 The reference is to Ham's mocking Noah's drunken nakedness, which Shem and Japheth courteously covered, walking backward so as not to witness their father's indignity.
100 King, *Lectures vpon Ionas*, 163–4 (page 164 is misnumbered 170).
101 One recalls that, e.g., Castiglione's Lord Gaspard makes lying in such a cause "euerye worthye gentilmans dutye": "for great courtesy and honestie to couer some offence that by mishappe or ouermuch loue a woman is renn into." *The courtyer of Count Baldessar Castilio diuided into foure books ... done into English by Thomas Hoby* (London, 1561), sigs. Ff4ᵛ–Gg, STC (2nd edn) 4778. Available from the database Early English Books Online.
102 Gwalther's "Table" has this entry: "Humanitie or curtesie" (sig. c2ᵛ). In *The Faerie Queene*, the only uses of "humanity" are in Book VI: "No greater shame to man then inhumanitie" at VI.i.26, line 9 (in Calidore's retort to Briana; his appeal to "curtesie" appears in line 8 and again three lines later), and "So milde humanity, and perfect gentle mynd" at VI.v.29, line 9 (of the Salvage Man). Cf. Northrop's distinction between "the courtesy of good manners" and "the courtesy of natural respect for each other as human" ("The Uncertainty of Courtesy," 219–20).

status as a divine attribute, common humanity, the sharing of the same flesh and blood, explains why, like many Christian virtues, courtesy has non-Christian practitioners. As John King explained it, the interaction of the pagan mariners with Jonah offered an apt image of humanity/courtesy in action:

> These men thinke of Ionas (I take it) as of themselues, make it their owne case ... See what a bonde they plotte of reciprocall kindnesse one to the other: Ionas to the marriners in the former verse, willing to forgo his life for preservation of theirs, *Take mee and cast mee into the sea, that it may bee quiet to you*; and these as earnestly labouring with hazard of themselues ... to saue Ionas. It is such an image (me thinketh) of that sociable and mutuall amity, that turning and winding, and retaling of curtesie, which ought to passe betweene man and man ... For what were the life of man, without this harmony and consente of friendshippe? where there is not ... Giuinge and taking, lending and borrowing, gratifying and regratifying, (as it were light for light) changing of offices and good turnes, what were it, but the life of beastes ...? ... the scripture taketh me by the hand, & biddeth me commend humanity once againe.[103]

"[T]he law of nature," then, compelled mariners who knew nothing of the true God "by secret bondes to deale with Ionas, as they wished to be dealt with, themselues." Spenser makes the same point through his various untaught and "Salvage" characters.

Humanity, our shared flesh and blood, also argues for courtesy to override self-interest and overlook differences in rank. Calvin explained Deuteronomy 14's guidelines for feasting this way:

> God meant also to inure his people to humanitie. For we see a number of men that can finde in their hartes to cram themselues til they burst, & in the meane while passe not though others starue ... But our Lordes will is that there should be courtisie among men, that when the maisters haue suffised themselues with meate and drinke, they shold not be nigardly in giuing foode & sustenance to such as take peins in their seruice, but haue a care of them.[104]

Humanity dictates (and courtesy means) that we identify with fellow humans of lower status and treat them as we wish to be treated.

In his comments on Deuteronomy 23:15–16, a passage Calvin found germane to the war-torn European landscape of the sixteenth century (also very relevant to Book VI, where the exemplars of courtesy harbor

---

103 King, *Lectures vpon Ionas*, 201–2.
104 Calvin, *The sermons*, 568.

and protect those under attack), he associated courtesy with accommodating refugees:

> For humanitie perswadeth this of it selfe, that if wee see any poore people which are driuen out of their owne Countries by warres or by any other violent oppressions, it is all one as if God sent vs a message both to receiue them and to entertayne them as curteouslie as wee are able to doe. And so let vs beare in minde, that where there are any poore wretches with vs whome men haue persecuted, and tormented, we are too too vnkind if we deliuer them into their enemies pawes, which seeke nothing else but to vse all violence and all maner of cruelty against them.[105]

Humanity requires courtesy to victims of violence: the oppressed, persecuted, and tormented, and to withhold such courtesy, as Turpine denies Calepine and the injured Serena the hospitality of the Castle of the Ford (VI.iii), is "cursed" and "froward."[106]

Hospitality in court, city, and country

A very important manifestation of courtesy, especially toward the wanderers and victims of *The Faerie Queene*, is hospitality. The perils of Faery Land, however, require that its various stately homes, even ones as ideally welcoming as the House of Holiness, be fortified and guarded:

> Arriued there, the dore they find fast lockt;
> For it was warely watched night and day,
> For feare of many foes: but when they knockt,
> The Porter opened vnto them streight way. (I.x.5)

Besides the Porter Humiltá, Una and Redcrosse encounter a franklin (Zele) and a squire (Reuerence), passing the inspection of each before being admitted to the presence of Dame Caelia, the lady of the house.

Preachers recommend a comparable level of precaution. Gwalther, preaching in Zurich in an era when Switzerland hosted many religious refugees (his preface is dated 1557), strikes a cautiously hospitable note as he applies the lesson of how Jerusalem's Christians recieved the newly converted Saul on Barnabas's introduction:

> For as it is the dutie of Christian charitie to thinke well of all men: so it easily admitteth the honest and credible testimonie, giuen of vnknown

---

105 Ibid., 817.
106 Ibid., 798.

brethren. Let vs therefore vse this moderation at these dayes, seeing the banished for Christes sake wander vp and downe euerywhere, and let vs not yeelde to their sentences, which on both sides being to extreeme, eyther through their ouermuch facilitie [in welcoming potentially hostile strangers] cause all men to laugh at them, or by their to great austeritie, reiect all men without any difference.[107]

Later in the same sermon series, Gwalther reminds his Swiss audience what a "singular prayse with all Nations" their "Predecessours, who by reason of their hospitalitie in *Heluetia*, did purchase themselues," and encourages them to follow in their steps.[108]

Neither Zurich nor the House of Holiness were under seige at the time, so a traveler's knock (or a letter of "honest and credible testimonie") was sufficient to gain entrance. Una's parents' brasen tower, like Alma's Castle, required knightly defense before it admitted guests, but when the dragon lay dead, the brasen gate was opened to the conqueror and the subsequent welcome was hospitable indeed. Thomas Playfere, like Spenser, imagined the reward of the blessed as a courtly reception:

> For euen as a royall King, when one of his nobles returnes home, which hath in a forraine Countrey by chiualry, or feates of armes, or other like excellent parts atchieued great renowne to his realme, presently sendeth for him to the Court, and in open audience giueth him words of grace, and aduanceth him to high preferments and honors: so Christ our most magnificent King, immediatly vpon our arriuall into heauen out of the forraine Countrey of this world, will reach forth vnto vs his holy hand, conducting vs to the eternall tabernacles of rest, and as for … all the … exercises of a Christian life that we haue performed, though neuer so secretly … he will openly reward them, and most gloriouslie crowne them.[109]

Una's father, presenting Redcrosse with "princely gifts of yuorie and gold" and yielding him "thousand thankes … for all his paine," fits perfectly into this picture (I.xii.12).

Sermons abound enjoining hospitality (and courtesy in general) toward preachers, citing biblical examples and complaining that too few

---

107 Gwalther, *An hundred, threescore and fiftene homelyes or sermons*, 412.
108 Ibid., 888.
109 Thomas Playfere, *The pathway to perfection. A sermon preached at Saint Maryes Spittle in London on Wednesday in Easter weeke. 1593* (London, 1597), 117–18, STC (2nd edn) 20021. Available from the database Early English Books Online.

Christians currently follow them.[110] Developing hospitality as a courtesy (and indeed an instance of humanity) incumbent upon Christians is a sermon by Heinrich Bullinger translated by the anonymous "*H.I. student in diuinitie.*" The sermon's focus, according to the title, is "Of the lawfull vse of earthly goods: that is, howe we may rightly possesse and lawfully spende the wealth that is rightly and iustly gotten: Of restitution and almes deedes." Bullinger specifies that one of the ways to "lawfully spende" wealth is to "shew curteise humanitie in one man to an other ... in kéeping hospitalitie for wayfaring strangers, so farre as our substance wil stretch, to mainteyne it." This is not required of the poor, Bullinger explained, but it is the ideal for others: "Let those who are indifferently stoared, and richer menne who haue wealth at wil, be courteous and liberall to enterteyne straungers wyth francke hospitalitie."[111] Lot and Abraham (to the length of two double-columned pages) are his biblical exemplars, with their hospitality offering an interesting context for Calidore's reception by Melibœ.

When Pastorella's foster father summons her home as "the moystie night approach[ed] fast" (VI.ix.13), he sees Calidore "left all alone" and, rather than leaving him to sleep "in the saluage fields," invites him "vnto his simple home" (16). He thus emulates Lot, who, "if it fell out that he mette with a straunger ... did not desire him hoame to his house for fashions sake onely, that is, with fainte or fayned woordes, but hee vsed in earneste all the meanes hée could to compell him perforce to take vp his Inne and lodge with him that night." Likewise Abraham "stayeth not to looke when they should come and request to refreshe themselues wyth him, but starteth vppe and meeteth them."[112] Similarly, the details that Melibœ's wife participated in the welcome ("his aged Beldame .../ ... him besought himselfe to disattyre,/ And rest himselfe, till supper time befell") and that Pastorella "supper readie dight" (17) correspond to Abraham's family's hospitality:

---

110 See, e.g., Becon, *A new postil*, sig. Aaa 7 (fol. 191ᵛ), Drant, *Two sermons*, sig. H2-2ᵛ, Gwalther in several more passages, and John Foxe, *A sermon preached at the christening of a certaine Iew at London* (London, 1578), sigs. A6ᵛ–A7, STC (2nd edn) 11248. Available from the database Early English Books Online.

111 Heinrich Bullinger, *Fiftie godlie and learned sermons diuided into fiue decades, conteyning the chiefe and principall pointes of Christian religion* (London, 1577), 286, STC (2nd edn) 4056. Available from the database Early English Books Online.

112 Ibid. On the following page, Bullinger stresses the rural nature of this salute: "courteously after his countrie manner."

> Neither was hee alone in all his house so francke and liberall, as his wife and familie were readilie giuen and very willing to put that holie excercise in vre and practise. All thinges therefore were readie wyth a trice. In making preparation also no diligence was wantinge, choice was made of all thinges, for riffe raffe and refuse geere was not serued to these straungers, but the best and likelyeste of all that was found ... [H]is countrie fare ... farre doeth excell all costly cates, and princelike dishes.[113]

Abraham's stranger-guest recompenses his and Lot's hospitality by saving Lot's life from Sodom's destruction and by blessing Sarah with the long-awaited pregnancy. Melibœ's humanity and hospitality are likewise rewarded when Calidore rescues Pastorella from the brigands (though he and his wife are slain).

In the literary context of courtier-exiles like Moses and Nehemiah, Calidore's sojourn in the countryside can be seen in a more favorable light as part of a larger narrative plan. Calidore indeed seeks Pastorella's favor rather than the shepherd's life for its own sake, but he adopts the shepherd's life when his "kind courtesies," "queint vsage," and "knightly seruice" fail to win her (VI.ix.34–5). And although Spenser explicitly compares Calidore in his "shepheards weed" to Paris (36), his original readers, conditioned by Bible readings and sermons, would also think of Moses, who also left the court, tended sheep, married his rural host's daughter, and later led a rescue mission.

Sermon references to courtiers and court show that Spenser's treatment of these conventional topoi, far from being subversive or jaded, is very typical. For preachers as well as Spenser, courtiers are characters in God's story, witnesses to God's power, subject to temptations but potential servants and workers of God's will. Courtesy, a virtue with a divine provenance, is properly manifested in court as well as countryside: by noblemen to those in distress and to commoners like shepherds, and conversely by hospitable homeowners like Melibœ to courtly wanderers like Calidore.

---

113 Ibid., 287.

9

"Now lettest thou thy servant depart": scriptural tradition and the close of *The Faerie Queene*[1]

To the devout of Queen Elizabeth's age, few words were more important than last words – the words a family and priest would gather around a deathbed to hear and record for the edification and guidance of the bereft.[2] The Bible provided many models, the most influential being Jesus's words on the cross and Stephen's while being stoned. Indeed, John Foxe makes a point of including the last words of many of the English Protestants who died under Mary, and with few exceptions they quote the Bible: the Lord's Prayer, the last words of Christianity's founder, or those of its first martyr.[3]

Elizabeth's last illness involved an ulcerated throat, so she was unable to participate in this pious tradition. She had, however, on several earlier occasions invoked a related biblical tradition: the pious prayer requesting death should God judge that a lifetime's work is done. This attitude of renunciation is a recurring motif in her speeches to Parliament, as in these excerpts from 1563 referring to her bout of smallpox:

---

1 An earlier version of this chapter appeared in *Christianity and Literature* 42:2 (1993), 205–20, published by Sage Publications Inc. (DOI: 10.1177/014833319304200201).
2 See, for example, George Cavendish's *The Life and Death of Thomas Wolsey* and William Roper's *The Life of Sir Thomas More*. See also Francois Lebrun, "The Two Reformations: Communal Devotion and Personal Piety," in *Passions of the Renaissance*, ed. Roger Chartier and trans. Arthur Goldhammer, History of Private Life, vol. 3 (Cambridge, MA: Harvard University Press, 1988), 85; and Georges Duby, "The Aristocratic Households of Feudal France: Communal Living," *Revelations of the Medieval World*, ed. Georges Duby and trans. Arthur Goldhammer, History of Private Life, vol. 2 (Cambridge, MA: Harvard University Press, 1988), 83–5.
3 According to Foxe, Ridley and Latimer quoted Christ ("Father, into thy hands I commend my spirit" [7:550]) and Cranmer Stephen ("Lord Jesus, receive my spirit" [8:90]). Opening vol. 7 or 8 of *The Acts and Monuments* (8 vols., New York, NY: AMS, 1965) at random will provide other examples.

And though God of late seemed to touch me, rather like one that He chastised than one that He punished, and though death possessed almost every joint of me, so as I wished then that the feeble thread of life, which lasted (methought) all too long, might by Cloe's hand have quietly been cut off; yet desired I not then life (as I have some witnesses here) so much for mine own safety as for yours. For I know that in exchanging of this reign I should have enjoyed a better reign, where residence is perpetual.[4]

But I hope I shall die in quiet with *nunc dimittis*, which cannot be without I see some glimpse of your following surety after my graved bones.[5]

Usually made in response to expressions of concern about the succession or suggestions that Elizabeth marry, several similar statements seem designed to shame or at least silence Parliament.[6]

Elizabeth, then, was ready to die when God judged the moment right. This rhetorical stance had scriptural warrant: Israel's prophets from Elijah to Jonah had begged God to let them die rather than live without validation. Moses had formulated the theme in a gentler key when he offered an angry Jehovah his life in exchange for Israel's survival. The New Testament prophet Simeon, having glimpsed the infant Jesus in the temple, gave this motif its classic Christian formulation: "Now lettest thou thy servant depart in peace, according to thy word, for mine eyes have seen thy salvation." Considering sleep a rehearsal for death, the Benedictines incorporated Luke 2:29–32, the *nunc dimittis*, into the liturgy for the office of Compline, whence by way of the Roman missal it eventually found its way into the 1559 prayer book's service for Evening Prayer.[7] There it followed the lesson from the New Testament.[8] Thus Queen Elizabeth in obedience to her own Act of Uniformity daily gave thanks for spiritual fulfillment and renounced her earthly life.

Some Elizabethans considered their queen's political expropriation and rote liturgical invocation of the *nunc dimittis* inadequate, among them her court preachers (most notably Anthony Rudd) and Spenser

---

4 J. E. Neale, *Elizabeth I and Her Parliaments*, 2 vols. (NewYork: St. Martin's Press, 1958), 1:108.

5 Ibid., 1:127.

6 See also Ibid., 1:149, 367; 2:100, 129, 321, 389, 391.

7 "Nunc dimittis," *New Catholic Encyclopedia* (New York, NY: McGraw, 1967). See also U. Holzmeister, "Canticum *Nunc Dimittis*," *Verbum Dominum* 26 (1948), 363–4, and P. Salmon, *The Breviary through the Centuries*, trans. D. Mary (Collegeville, MN: St. John's, 1962).

8 *Book of Common Prayer 1559: The Elizabethan Prayer Book*, ed. John E. Booty (Charlottesville, VA: University Press of Virginia, 1976), 63.

himself. In this chapter I will consider the *Cantos of Mutabilitie*, in particular the two stanzas of the "unperfite" eighth canto, in the context of court sermon versions of the *nunc dimittis*. I will suggest the last stanzas of the cantos have an important dimension that has been overlooked: a Spenserian *nunc dimittis* meant for Elizabeth's voice. Such a reading, with the Queen central to Spenser's intention throughout, supports a view of the cantos as an integral part of *The Faerie Queene* and their sufficient, though perhaps not necessary, conclusion.[9]

Memento mori: numbering Elizabeth's days in religious discourse

As spiritual counselors, preachers had reminded the Queen of her own mortality from time to time throughout her reign. Mostly, and most safely, they noted the Queen's decline in the context, and as a symbol, of the inevitable human condition. They had a fine line to walk: the conventional *ubi sunt* theme encouraged sermon auditors to meditate on their own deaths, but the Queen memorably resented Parliamentary or preacherly reference to the fact that she could expect to die. The older she grew, the more carefully preachers seem to have tried to avoid insult by making their references as vague and inclusive as possible.

Poet and preacher Thomas Drant, for instance, spoke of her mortality quite bluntly to the thirty-six-year-old queen and the ladies of the court, incorporating the traditional rebuke to women's vanity:

> Yea (madams) thinke it to be as I say. Red earth, blacke earth, and white earth must go *Dauids* way. Yea verely rosiall coulers, and crimson cheekes must goe *Dauids* way, must goe the way of all earthes. Thinke vpon your death, and vpon the next life, for ye must dye, ye must dye, there is no remedie.[10]

The vanity of women's apparel could not forestall the inevitable: bracelets, mufflers, headbands, bonnets, earrings, nose jewels, veils, wimples, and

---

9 J. B. Lethbridge, "Spenser's Last Days: Ireland, Career, Mutability, Allegory," in *Edmund Spenser: New and Renewed Directions*, ed. J. B. Lethbridge (Madison, NJ: Fairleigh Dickinson, 2006), 302–36, provides an overview of the debate over the cantos' relation to the rest of *The Faerie Queene*.

10 Thomas Drant, *Two sermons preached, the one at S. Maries Spital on Tuesday in Easter weeke 1570 and the other at the court at Windsor for the Sonday after twelfth day, … 1569* (London, 1570?), sig. I5ᵛ, STC (2nd edn) 7171. Available from the database Early English Books Online.

crisping pins all availed nothing in the contest against death. Paraphrasing 1 Cor. 6:13, Drant continues,

> God made apparell, and God made the backe, and he will destroy both the one and the other. Yea, those heades that are now to be sene for their tall and bushy plumes, and that other sex that haue fire fresh golden caules so sheene and glosing, geue me but an hundred yeares, nay, halfe an hundred yeares, and the earth will couer all these heads before me, and mine owne to.[11]

However inarguable his conclusion, Drant took care not to be too personal in applying it to the Queen. Aside from addressing her together with all the ladies of the court rather than alone, he stressed earlier in his sermon the universality of death and the contemptible frailty of all human flesh: "Ritch men are ritch dust, wise men wise dust, worshipfull men worshipfull dust, honorable men honourable dust, maiesties dust, excellent maiesties excellente dust."[12] He directed his message to the Queen (the only "excellent maiestie" among his audience) but put her mortality in universal terms.

Richard Curteys, addressing Elizabeth three years later in 1573, used similar indirection. He imagined a proud speaker boasting:

> I am a gentleman, a Noble man, I came in with the conqueror, I can fetche my pedigree long before the Conquest, a King was my father, a Queene was my mother, a King my brother, a Queene my sister: yet muste you say, The graue is my house, darknesse is my bed: yet must you say to rottennesse, you are my father, and to the wormes, you are my mother, you are my sisters.[13]

Obviously the Queen was the only member of Curteys's audience who could truthfully claim kings as father and brother and queens as mother and sister. Nevertheless, by making his imagined speaker "a gentleman, a Noble man," Curteys guarded himself against the charge of impertinence.

Raising the subject of death before an old queen required even greater tact, such as that the preacher "L. S." used in his court sermon. He alluded to advancing years and coming death in very general terms: "As our age

---

11 Ibid., K8ᵛ. A "caul" is a close-fitting netted ladies' cap.
12 Ibid., I2ᵛ.
13 Richard Curteys, *A sermon preached before the Queenes Maiestie, by the reuerende Father in God the Bishop of Chichester, at Grenewiche, the 14. day of Marche. 1573* (London, 1573), sigs. C8ᵛ–D1, STC (2nd edn) 6135. Available from the database Early English Books Online.

and gray haires come on, so let our olde conuersation vanish away, putting on the new man in holinesse of behauiour: the nearer we come to our heauenly countrey, to wish and desire it the more."[14] The queen was growing old, but the speaker includes himself ("our age and gray haires") in the unavoidable aging of humankind.

As the sixteenth century waned, the Queen's anticipated death became something of an obsession within court circles.[15] Councilors and courtiers focused on the problem in terms of the succession, and rumors survive of court sermons, preached at the instigation of Parliament, which exhorted the Queen to name her heir.[16] Even leaving aside its political ramifications, preachers and readers found the inevitability of the Queen's eventual demise quite as fascinating as she found it distasteful. Indeed, toward the end of the century Elizabeth was treated to a few court sermons that came close to suggesting that God should take her soul. Rudd made at least two court sermons of this type, one of which survives only as a morsel of gossip in John Manningham's diary:

> Dr. Rud made a sermon before the Queene upon the text, "I sayd yee are Gods, but you shall all dy like men;" wherein he made such a discourse of death that hir Majestie, when his sermon was ended, said unto him, "Mr. Dr. you have made me a good funerall sermon, I may dye when I will."[17]

This was in or shortly before February 1602, when the Queen was sixty-eight.

Rudd's temerity in preaching such a sermon was the more remarkable given his earlier experience. In 1596, when the Queen was almost sixty-three (in numerology her "grand climacteric," the product of the

---

14 L. S., *Resurgendum. A notable sermon concerning the resurrection, preached not long since at the court* (London, 1593), 9, STC (2nd edn) 21508. Available from the database Early English Books Online.
15 According to John N. King, *Spenser's Poetry and the Reformation Tradition* (Princeton, NJ: Princeton University Press, 1990), "As the queen's life drew toward its close, the political anxieties that her mythology was designed to neutralize became increasingly difficult to stifle. Nevertheless, Spenser's acknowledgement of her mortality takes place on a cosmic scale that identifies her mutability with 'the order of the entire universe'" (146–7). See also David Norbrook, *Poetry and Politics in the English Renaissance* (London: Routledge, 1984), 151–4, whom King quotes in the final phrase above.
16 John Harington, *A Briefe View of the State of the Church of England* (London, 1653), 186–91, tells an amusing anecdote of one such sermon, preached by Matthew Hutton: Wing H770. Available from the database Early English Books Online.
17 *The Diary of John Manningham of the Middle Temple 1602–1603*, ed. Robert Parker Sorlien (Hanover, NH: University Press of New England, 1976), 194.

mystically significant numbers seven and nine), he had preached at court on Psalm 90:12, "Teach us so to number our dayes, that we may applie our hearts unto wisedome."[18] Rudd develops his exposition predictably, recommending to each generation the religious duties proper to its age, but the sermon's most remarkable feature is an extended "*soliloquia*" for the Queen which comprises a personal *nunc dimittis*. "Let me now come," says Rudd at the climax of his numbering of days, "to the most reuerend age of my most deare and dread Soueraign, who hath (I doubt not) learned to number her yeares, that she may apply her hart vnto wisdome. And therefore I conceiue in mind, that in her *soliloquia* or priuate meditations, she frameth her speech in this wise:"[19]

> O Lord, I am now entred a good way into the Climactericall yeare of mine age, which mine enemies wish & hope to be fatall vnto me ... I haue now put foote within the doores of that age, in the which the Almond tree flourisheth: wherein men begin to cary a Calender in their bones, the senses begin to faile, the strength to diminish, yea all the powers of the body daily to decay ... I haue out-liued almost all the Nobles of this Realme whom I found possessed of Dukedome, Marquisats, Earledoms & Barronries at mine entring into the Kingdome: and likewise all the Iudges of the land, and all the Bishops set vp by me after my comming to the Crowne.[20]

This public reckoning of her years no doubt sounded harsh within a court accustomed to celebrating its queen as Venus, Diana, and Astraea, immortal and beautiful. But Rudd elaborated. He filled this *soliloquia* with Elizabeth's recognition of her sinfulness, a prayer for cleansing "lest the Zion and Ierusalem, that is, the Church and Commonwealth of England, should be in daunger of thy wrath, through my former sinnes,"[21] a confession of God's miraculous protection of England, and a petition that, while the outward man perishes, the inner man be renewed day by day. She has lived, Rudd has her say, "in respect of my self long inough" and can "say with *Elias*: It is inough, ô Lord, take my soule, for I am no better than my fathers; and with *Paul*: I desire to be loosed, and to be

---

18 Anthony Rudd, *A sermon preached at Richmond before Queene Elizabeth of famous memorie, vpon the 28. of March, 1596* (London, 1603), STC (2nd edn) 21432. Available from the database Early English Books Online.
19 Ibid., 49–50.
20 Ibid., 51–4.
21 Ibid., 50.

with Christ."[22] Nevertheless, Rudd has her pray not to die "vntil I haue met with dangers present, or imminent, and established the state for the time to come ... that after my departure out of this life, they may in the future age, liue in peace and plentie in euery quarter and corner of the Realme."[23] He puts in her mouth a hope to live so uprightly "That so at length I may go to the sepulchers of my fathers in a good time, as a ricke of corne that is ripe caried into the barne; yeelding the spirite like *Dauid* in a good age full of dayes, riches and honour."[24]

Rudd's offer to the Queen of a *nunc dimittis* can be read as disrespectfully condescending. After all, had he really believed the Queen to be so meditating, there would have been no point in doing so on her behalf – to the length of seven pages. In any case, notwithstanding the *soliloquia*'s prayer that she live as long as would serve England's security, Elizabeth read his sermon as an invitation to "depart in peace." Remarking after Rudd's sermon that "he should have kept his Arithmetick for himself, but I see ... the greatest Clerks are not the wisest men," she held the preacher under house arrest "for a time" and ordered his sermon suppressed.[25] Though the sermon duly languished in obscurity until the event it predicted took place, it surfaced – and was published – shortly after Elizabeth's death in 1603 with a preface that suggests the scandal it occasioned:

> THIS Sermon bred much speech long ago, and the sight of it was greatly desired by many. But it had bene concealed these seuen yeares and more, by him that had the copy therof. Howbeit, now at the last it is published, vpon hope that it may with as good meaning be construed by the Reader, as it was formerly vttered by the Author.[26]

A thankless job, constructing a *nunc dimittis* for Elizabeth, but many of her religious mentors regarded it as their duty nevertheless, and their efforts put the close of *The Faerie Queene* in its cultural context.

---

22 Ibid., 54–5.
23 Ibid., 55.
24 Ibid., 56–7.
25 John Harington, *A briefe view of the state of the Church of England as it stood in Q. Elizabeths and King James his reigne, to the yeere 1608* (London, 1653), 162–3, Wing H770. Available from the database Early English Books Online.
26 Rudd, *A sermon*, sig. A2.

The Cantos of Mutabilitie as an allegory of Elizabeth facing mortality

Though no one since Mary K. Woodworth in 1944 has suggested the *Cantos of Mutabilitie* were suppressed,[27] they likewise appeared after the event they foreshadowed and sound a similar note of valediction. Many readers of *The Faerie Queene* find the cantos a thematically satisfying completion of the epic, and commentators increasingly judge them a formal success as well. Certainly the poem as a whole reflects an obsession with mutability: the fleeting nature of human happiness, the inevitability of decay and death. The sentiment that "bliss cannot abide in state of mortal men" appears at intervals throughout the poem,[28] and the cantos are the poem's final exploration of the meaning of mutability. Spenser invites us to seek that meaning in an allegory in which Elizabeth finds her life and rule threatened by a personification of mutability. Mutabilitie, having subdued the earth, aspires to rule the heavens as well. Her first celestial attack is directed against Cynthia, goddess of the moon:

> Thence, to the Circle of the Moone she clambe,
> Where *Cynthia* raignes in euerlasting glory ...
> Ne staide till she the highest stage had scand,
> Where *Cynthia* did sit, that neuer still did stand. (VII.vi.8)

Several details of the Cynthia episode make it clear that Spenser intends us to identify Cynthia as Elizabeth. For instance, Cynthia's name associates her with Elizabeth, even more than does the name Belphoebe, credited to Raleigh in "A Letter of the Authors": "fashioning her name according to your owne excellent conceipt of Cynthia."[29] This goddess reigns in "the Circle of the moone," and the moon, at least during the tenure of a virgin queen, was England's national orb. Furthermore, Spenser twice uses the word "glory" to characterize Cynthia's reign, here and in stanza 10: "Shee gan to burne in her ambitious spright,/ And t'envie her that in such glorie raigned." "Glory," like "glorious" and the name Gloriana, is a word associated with Elizabeth (and occasionally with her antitheses, such as Lucifera).

---

27 Mary K. Woodworth, "The Mutabilitie Cantos and the Succession," *PMLA* 59 (1944), 985–1002. In referring to "*Mutabilitie*'s being ... unpublishable in Elizabeth's [lifetime]," Gordon Teskey comes close. "Mutability, Genealogy, and the Authority of Forms," *Representations* 41 (1993), 112.
28 For instance, in I.vii.44.9, II.ii.2.8, II.xi.30.3, III.iv.28.6, III.vii.39.8, VI.iii.5.2, and VII. viii.1.6.
29 "A Letter of the Authors," in Hamilton, *Spenser: The Faerie Queene*, 716.

Another touch that associates Cynthia with Elizabeth is the black and white color of her horses, the Queen's favorites. Finally, Spenser describes Cynthia's resistance to Mutabilitie in terms that recall the storm that scattered the Armada in 1588 and incorporating Elizabeth's sense of personal insult regarding threats to her realm – notably toward Philip in the speech attributed to her at Tilbury ("I have the heart and Stomach of a King, and a King of *England*, too; and I think foul scorn that *Parma* or *Spain*, or any prince of Europe, should dare to invade the borders of my Realm"[30]):

> But shee that had to her that soueraigne seat
> By highest *Ioue* assign'd, ...
>   ... regarded not her threat, ...
> But with sterne countenaunce and disdainfull cheare ...
> And boldly blaming her for comming there,
> Bade her attonce from heauens coast to pack,
> Or at her perill bide the wrathfull Thunders wrack. (VII.vi.12)

The "wrathfull Thunder" recalls the storm that climaxed the English victory, and "wrack" summarizes the results.

The episode's implications for Elizabeth are negative, however. Successful as she was against Philip, the Queen meets in Mutabilitie a more formidable opponent.[31] Cynthia is not equal to the intruder's

---

30 Taken down by Lionel Sharp (chaplain to the Earl of Essex and later to the Queen herself) and printed in *Cabala, mysteries of state, in letters of the great ministers of K. James and K. Charles* (London, 1653), 260, Wing (2nd edn, 1994) C183. Available from the database Early English Books Online.

31 For the most comprehensive characterization, see Thomas Greene, "Mutability and the Theme of Process," in *Edmund Spenser*, ed. Harold Bloom (New York, NY: Chelsea, 1986), 70, repr. from *The Descent from Heaven: A Study in Epic Continuity* (New Haven, CT: Yale, 1963), "Mutabilitie is partly the Titaness daughter of Earth, partly Mary Stuart challenging Cynthia/Elizabeth, partly the Christian Satan who introduced original sin, partly a natural principle, partly a philosophic doctrine." (One notes that Elizabethan preachers, with their easy recourse to biblical types, prepared Spenser's readers to accommodate to this order of representational flexibility.) With regard to the mythological character, Blissett, "Spenser's Mutabilitie," in *Essays in English Literature from the Renaissance to the Victorian Age, Presented to A.S.P. Woodhouse*, ed. M. MacLure and F. W. Watt (Toronto: University of Toronto Press, 1964), 31, and Lewis J. Owen, "Mutable in Eternity: Spenser's Despair and the Multiple Forms of Mutabilitie," *Journal of Medieval and Renaissance Studies* 2 (1972), 64, note the identity of Diana, Hecate, and Cynthia; Owen adds that Hecate is Mutabilitie's sister Titanness, suggesting a degree of affinity between this character and Elizabeth. At least, as Blissett puts it, Mutabilitie and Gloriana "are of comparable stature and allegorical weight." John N. King, *Spenser's Poetry and the Reformation Tradition* (Princeton, NJ: Princeton University Press, 1990) refers to "Mutabilitie's standing as a dark double of the aging queen" (146).

force: "the lower World ... was darkned quite," and all feared "least *Chaos* broken had his chaine,/ And brought againe on them eternall night" (14). Apparently the Queen is not proof against mutability and must submit herself to divine judgment – a point that the preachers had already made.

The Ovidian tale that follows, presenting the site where Nature will appear to judge Mutabilitie's case against Cynthia, also seems to bode ill for Cynthia notwithstanding all its charming detail and imagery. In this digression the wood god Faunus corrupts Molanna, one of the goddess's favored nymphs, for the sake of a glimpse of Cynthia/Diana's naked beauty. (Both names for Elizabeth's mythological stand-in are used in the episode.) The goddess's realm is violated by the intruder, and the goddess is "abashed" (47.1); she deserts her Irish haunt, which is laid waste and made a prey to "Wolues and Thieues" (55.8). Eternal darkness, wolves and thieves – this, in hyperbolic terms, was what Elizabeth's councilors feared for England and Ireland should she die without designating her successor.

Robin Headlam Wells and Thomas H. Cain, two commentators who have analyzed the contribution of the Mutability cantos to the encomiastic design of *The Faerie Queene*, disagree sharply as to whether the cantos reflect praise or blame upon Elizabeth, whether the poet envisions her as *semper eadem*, always the same, as Wells heads his chapter, or satirizes her as a fickle, decaying old woman.[32] But the focus appears to shift as the case is brought before Dame Nature.[33] By the time Mutabilitie is arguing that she is already the *de facto* ruler of things earthly and heavenly, her challenge to Cynthia is clearly a fraction of the cantos' larger design. Neither the Arlo Hill episode nor the trial itself clarifies Elizabeth's personal fate. Nature's solution ignores Mutabilitie's local assault on Cynthia. Though Jove is "confirm'd in his imperiall see" (VII.vii.59), Nature does not decree Cynthia's restoration to hers. Likewise, the river Molanna is left in disgrace and "whelm'd with stones" (VII.vi.53), and the goddess does not return to Arlo Hill. Though the allegorical transposition cannot be so simply factored, one infers that Elizabeth is indeed eclipsed, at least as an individual, and that her pleasant haunts must see her no more. Spenser does, however, provide a resolution to the problem that Mutabilitie's usurpation of Cynthia's throne creates. Like the court

---

32 Robin Headlam Wells, *Spenser's Faerie Queene and the Cult of Elizabeth* (Totowa, NJ: Barnes), 1983, 146–57; Thomas H. Cain, *Praise in The Faerie Queene* (Lincoln, NE: University of Nebraska Press), 1978, 180–5.
33 A. Bartlett Giamatti, "A Prince and Her Poet," *Yale Review* 73 (1984), 321–37, views Dame Nature as Spenser's "last version of Elizabeth," Spenser's admission that "he cannot encompass her" (335).

preacher Rudd, Spenser through Dame Nature offers the Queen a personal immortality as well as a literary one, and this personal redemption participates in the redemption of the universal order.

Dame Nature formulates this redemption in two ways – first in philosophical, then in spiritual terms. Thus,

> ... all things stedfastnes doe hate
> And changed be: yet being rightly wayd
> They are not changed from their first estate;
> But by their change their being doe dilate:
> And turning to themselues at length againe,
> Doe worke their owne perfection so by fate:
> Then ouer them Change doth not rule and raigne;
> But they raigne ouer change, and doe their states maintaine. (VII.vii.58)

Angus Fletcher usefully defines dilation as "the continuing fulfilment of the idea of a thing."[34] England and its monarchy would continue to "dilate" and define their natures after Elizabeth's death and another's succession; as James Nohrnberg observed, "Elizabeth Tudor, as a 'mortal moon,' can be eclipsed, but the throne of England, like its planetary guardian the moon, survives changes of house."[35] Mutability, according to Dame Nature, reveals the essential character of things, which is to be immutable or, as the Queen's motto had it, *semper eadem*. Mutability's allegorical stand-in has the power to corrupt only the surface of things, not their essence. According to this formulation, the Queen's death would confirm, rather than cancel, her place in history. Once dead, Elizabeth's demoralizing mental and physical decline would be arrested; her court's impatience, most dangerously evident in Essex's rebellion, would be resolved in nostalgia; and an assessment of her reign could be made. She would be immortal and therefore changeless.

The second solution, which Spenser, like Rudd, finds in religious faith, depends on an identification of Mutabilitie with the fallen state:

> She ... made them all accurst
> That God had blest ...
> O pittious worke of *MVTABILITIE!*
> By which, we all are subiect to that curse,
> And death in stead of life haue sucked from our Nurse. (VII.vi.5–6)

---

34 Angus Fletcher, *The Prophetic Moment: An Essay on Spenser* (Chicago, IL: University of Chicago Press, 1971), 222.
35 James Nohrnberg, *The Analogy of The Faerie Queene* (Princeton, NJ: Princeton University Press, 1976), 769.

According to Christian eschatology, however, God would someday restore the earth to its original Edenic state and abolish death and change. Dame Nature, just before her disappearance, reminds the assembly of this ultimate change: "But time shall come that all shall changed bee,/ And from thenceforth, none no more change shall see" (VII.vii.59). Thus mutability will become obsolete: after the final change, the apocalypse, no longer will change be necessary to "dilate" the nature of things.

Neither Nature's philosophical nor her spiritual solution mentions Cynthia. Nor does the narrator's response.[36] Reacting to Mutabilitie and Dame Nature in separate stanzas, the narrator first acknowledges the strength of the Titaness's case, then turns with what critics have variously perceived as weariness, anxiety, or the appropriate decorum to "the final vision of a transcendent stability and repose."[37] Where does this leave Queen Elizabeth?

As most critics have become wary of overly specific historical allegory, so they have declined to see any direct application in the cantos' conclusion to Spenser's queen. Harry Berger, Jr. argues that the final stanzas form the delineation of the contemporary Renaissance "phase of experience" in the Mutability cantos. This claim would seem to invite inspection of these lines for topical allusions, but Berger characterizes them as Renaissance in their attitude or mood of "lyric... anxiety" rather than with reference to events or persons.[38] Humphrey Tonkin observes that the cantos "make no allusion to the poem or to the person of the Faerie Queene," and judges that they are "not so much a continuation of *The Faerie Queene* as a translation of the argument to a new plane. They move beyond the chivalric, beyond the focus of a particular

---

[36] Several commentators have seen the narrator (for some of them in these last two stanzas, Spenser himself) as dissatisfied with Nature's verdict. Among them are Arnold F. Davidson, "Dame Nature's Shifting Logic in Spenser's 'Cantos of Mutabilitie,'" *Neuphilologische Mitteilungen* **83** (1982), 451–56; Greene, "Mutability and the Theme of Process," 65; Graham Goulden Hough, *A Preface to The Faerie Queene* (New York, NY: Norton, 1962), 216; William Nelson, *The Poetry of Edmund Spenser* (New York, NY: Columbia University Press, 1963), 313; Michael Holahan, "*Iamque opus exegi*: Ovid's Changes and Spenser's Brief Epic of Mutability," *English Literary Renaissance* 6 (1976), 268; and Harry Jr. Berger, "The Mutabilitie Cantos: Archaism and Evolution in Retrospect," in *Spenser: A Collection of Critical Essays*, ed. Harry Berger, Jr. (Englewood Cliffs, NJ: Prentice Hall, 1968), 148.

[37] Sherman Hawkins, "Mutabilitie and the Cycle of the Months," in *Form and Convention in the Poetry of Edmund Spenser*, ed. William Nelson (NewYork, NY: Columbia University Press, 1961), 100.

[38] Berger, "The Mutabilitie Cantos," 148.

queen and a particular realm, to take in the very universe itself ... We are concerned here not with Elizabeth and England but with universal patterns."[39]

But from what we see of Spenser's habit of thought in *The Faerie Queene*, including in Mutability's sixth-canto Ovidian digression,[40] it seems difficult for him to stop thinking about Elizabeth, whatever larger implications he may intend. Indeed, the convergence of the numerological felicities that Alastair Fowler and A. Bartlett Giamatti describe, reflections on eternity, and a reference to the Queen would bring the epic to an eminently Spenserian close. And such a convergence is just what we find. Far from losing sight of her in his meditation on the cosmic implications of change, Spenser, like Elizabeth's less risky court preachers, has constructed a wide backdrop, the universal context in which his *nunc dimittis* will be theologically correct and personally palatable. Though Nature does not explicitly restore Cynthia to her throne or return Diana to her erstwhile favorite haunt in Ireland, and though Spenser does not invoke her prototype by her English name, in the final stanza of *The Faerie Queene* Spenser makes another reference to scripture, a Hebrew pun on "Elizabeth," which serves to focus the poem once more on its dedicatee:

> Then gin I thinke on that which Nature sayd,
>   Of that same time when no more *Change* shall be,
> But stedfast rest of all things firmely stayd
>   Vpon the pillours of Eternity,
> That is contrayr to *Mutabilitie*:
> For, all that moueth, doth in *Change* delight:
> But thence-forth all shall rest eternally
> With Him that is the God of Sabbaoth hight:
> O that great Sabbaoth God, graunt me that Sabaoths sight. (VII.viii.2)

Nohrnberg has already observed that Elizabeth's name in Hebrew can mean "God of rest" or "Sabbath God."[41] The closing cadences of a Queen's Day sermon offer further possibilities for this play on words:

---

39 Humphrey Tonkin, *The Faerie Queene* (London: Unwin Hyman, 1989), 197, 202–3.
40 Tonkin says that "the [Arlo Hill episode] swings round to become both local and cosmic myth simultaneously" (ibid., 199).
41 Nohrnberg, *The Analogy of The Faerie Queene*, 83. See also A. C. Hamilton, "Our New Poet: Spenser, 'Well of English Undefyld,'" in *Essential Articles for the Study of Edmund Spenser* (Hamden, CT: Archon, 1972), 496–7. William Camden, *Remains Concerning Britain*, ed. R. D. Dunn (Toronto: University of Toronto Press, 1984) defines the name Elizabeth as "Peace of the Lord, or Quiet Rest of the Lord; the which England hath found ver[i]fied in the most honoured name of our late Soveraigne" (83). Regarding

> Let vs euerie *Moone* solemnelie, by *Sacrament,* remember him to whom we owe euerie *Moment* of our life, but euery *Twelue-Moneth*; let vs in *Thankesgiuing* remember *Hir,* to whom (*Vnder God*) we owe al our seruice vpon Earth. And let *Hir Posie* bee from henceforth for euer (*Eloi-Sabaoth; Elizabeth, Alleluia*). And he shall be hir God of *Saboth*; of Rest, and Peace, who hath beene *Hir God* of *Sabaoth,* of Force, and Armes.[42]

Spenser probably knew this sermon – may indeed have heard it preached at Paul's Cross, England's premier public pulpit, when he was in London in November of 1589. It was published within months. Assuming Spenser heard or read this sermon, it suggests that his use of "Sabbaoth" and "Sabaoth" was not a confusion of two Hebrew words. Beyond its contemporary parallel for Spenser's pun, this sermon suggests a third dimension to the play on words: an invocation of Elizabeth and of her God on her behalf. With this "posie" offered by Thomas White to Elizabeth as a cue, we can recognize in these two stanzas Spenser's invitation to his queen to see his universal solution as specifically her own. Like Anthony Rudd, the court preacher in the suppressed 1596 sermon, Spenser does not promise his queen continued life in the lunar sphere or in the British Isles, but a personal immortality nevertheless – the eternal joy in the presence of God, which follows her yielding the spirit in a good age, full of days, riches, and honor. To quote Rudd: "And so the dust of this body returning to the earth as it was, my spirit may returne to thee that gaue it: to enioy alwaies thy presence, in the which there is fulnesse of ioy, and to be alwayes at thy right hand, where be pleasures for euer more."[43]

If the poet's allegorical treatment of Cynthia's eclipse was as effective as Rudd's sermon, Elizabeth would have been newly aware of her own mortality. Here Spenser, like the preacher, provides her with an

---

the more familiar orthographical puzzle in the last two lines, Don Cameron Allen's article, "On the Closing Lines of *The Faerie Queene*," *Modern Language Notes* 64 (1949), 93–4, seems to be the most recent argument for taking both "Sabbaoth" and "Sabaoth" as meaning "of hosts" rather than "Sabaoths sight" including the meaning "Sabbath's sight." L. S. Friedland, "Spenser's Sabaoth's Rest," *Modern Language Quarterly* 17 (1956), 199–203, cites Francis J. Child as arguing that Spenser meant "Sabbath" for both spellings. Since Friedland, no one seems to have dissented from the prevailing orthodoxy that Spenser was making a play on the two words, intending both meanings.

42 Thomas White, *A Sermon Preached at Paules Crosse the 17. of Nouember An. 1589. In ioyfull remembrance and thank.sgiuing vnto God, for the peaceable yeres of her Majesties most gratious Raigne ouer vs, now 32* (London, 1589), 64 (misnumbered 63), STC (2nd edn) 25407. Available from the database Early English Books Online.

43 Rudd, *A sermon,* 56–7.

appropriate response to the issues he has raised. Not that it is irrelevant to himself: Spenser's readers (among them his most important reader, the Queen) are drawn into identifying with the narrator speaking these last words. Rather like Curteys ("a king was my father, a Queene was my mother") and Rudd ("so at length I may go to the sepulchers of my fathers"), Spenser joins the Queen in acknowledging mortality. In addition to the poet's yearning farewell,[44] these final two stanzas, like the unappreciated soliloquia of Rudd's sermon, are probably meant to be understood as Elizabeth's invocation in her own voice of "hir God of *Saboth*; of Rest, and Peace, who hath beene *Hir God* of *Sabaoth*, of Force, and Armes." Spenser offers them to her as a *nunc dimittis* suitable to any hopeful Christian. More particularly, they can function as her response to Mutabilitie's challenge and Nature's vindication of her: the Faery Queen's imagined farewell to a challenging and unexpectedly successful life as a Christian and as England's queen.

---

44 For the cantos as a revelation of Spenser's personal mood, see Lethbridge, "Spenser's Last Days"; Berger, "The Mutabilitie Cantos"; Cain, *Praise in The Faerie Queene*, 183; Marion Campbell, "Spenser's Mutability Cantos and the End of *The Faerie Queene*," *Southern Review: Literary and Interdisciplinary Essays* 15.1 (1982), 52; Friedland, "Spenser's Sabaoth's Rest," 199; Isabel G. MacCaffrey, *Spenser's Allegory: The Anatomy of Imagination* (Princeton, NJ: Princeton University Press, 1976), 432; Owen, "Mutable in Eternity," 49; and Judah K. Stampfer, "The Cantos of Mutabilitie: Spenser's Last Testament of Faith," *University of Toronto Quarterly* 21 (1952), 140–56. For objections to this reading, see Hawkins, "Mutabilitie and the Cycle of the Months," 100.

Conclusion

After a summer spent reading Elizabethan sermons for dissertation research in the 1980s, I joked to a fellow Spenserian that I not only understood *The Faerie Queen*, I was planning to finish it. I remain convinced that contemporary sermons are one important avenue (among many) into the poem. Beyond returning the poem to its cultural context, the sermons' easy turn to allegoresis and routine use of an array of biblical types suggest that Spenser's first readers were eminently equipped to penetrate its allegorical veil. Early modern marginal comments bear this out. Indeed, Austen Saunders's recent discovery that John Dixon, *The Fairie Queene*'s earliest marginalian, transcribed some of his most apparently "personal and complex allegorical response[s]" directly from the apparatus of the Geneva Bible makes my point almost too perfectly.[1]

On the other hand, when Spenserians talk or write about allegory nowadays, they often identify the psychological or cognitive work the mode does for its practitioner (whether reader or writer). Here is Kenneth Gross:

> allegories feed our fantasies that ideas have a fate distinct from their existence as verbal ciphers ...; that they can be possessed; that they can be built upon, produce offspring, or turn a person to stone. One additional desire fulfilled by allegory may be that ideas can work without our having to understand them.[2]

Gordon Teskey, whose theory of allegory as a poetics of capture and insistence on the violence of allegorical representation have influenced

---

[1] Austen Saunders, "New Light on a Puzzling Annotation to Spenser's *Faerie Queene*," *Notes & Queries* 57.3 (2010), 356–7.
[2] Kenneth Gross, "The Postures of Allegory," in *Edmund Spenser: Essays on Culture and Allegory*, ed. Jennifer Klein Morrisson and Matthew Greenfield (Burlington, VT: Ashgate, 2000), 167–79 (175).

many, explains that allegory appeals to us (and appealed to Spenser) as "the sensation of thinking, a process of making connections between a self and things external to it."[3]

Sermons and their allegoresis invite us into Spenser's mind in a different way: they help us come to terms with Spenser's didacticism. Certainly there are tensions between the allegory's portrayal and historical reality – for instance, between the knightly successes on behalf of Eirena and Belge that Book V narrates and the actual failure of English efforts in Ireland and the Low Countries. And certainly the ambitious Spenser expressed his disappointments and disenchantments in other works. In making a case for the traditional readings of several passages, I acknowledge that Spenser's original readers found the poem less disturbed and less disturbing than we do, four centuries later. Am I saying that Spenser was more simpleminded and less capable of intellectual complexity and ambiguity than, say, Sidney or Shakespeare?

Not at all. Spenser wrote to Raleigh that *The Faerie Queen* had a particular purpose: to praise the Queen and deliver good discipline. Self-consciously iconic and canonical, it is not "bottom-drawer literature" or *samizdat* directed to an underground audience during an oppressive regime. Sermons, similarly aspiring to orthodoxy, offer a way to look at the contradictions between *The Faerie Queene*'s fictions and Elizabethan fact. As Perkins preached in his application of Hebrews 11, "God rather obserues and regards good things in his children, then their faults and imperfections ... Thus should wee deale one with another: what good thing we see in any man, we should obserue & commend it: his faults we should not see, but couer and omit them."[4] A biblical perspective sees the complexity of the person, the sinful individual who is at the same moment a member of the elect and destined to be glorified, and focuses on commendation.

Spenser had "glory" as his "generall intention" in the Faery Queene, and Spenser saw God working out his glorious purpose in England through Elizabeth just as Foxe did – Foxe, whose establishment blockbuster *Actes and Monuments* celebrated Elizabeth while some of his many

---

3 Gordon Teskey, "Thinking Moments in *The Faerie Queene*," *Spenser Studies* 22 (2007), 103–25. Teskey's influential writings on allegory include his article "Allegory" for the *Spenser Encyclopedia* (Toronto: University of Toronto Press, 1990, 1992) and *Allegory and Violence* (Ithaca, NY: Cornell University Press, 1996).

4 William Perkins, *A cloud of faithfull witnesses, leading to the heauenly Canaan* (London, 1607), 241, 243–4, STC (2nd edn) 19677.5. Available from the database Early English Books Online.

other projects show he differed markedly with aspects of that establishment. Elizabeth did not have to be perfect to be God's instrument, or even to be "most excellent and glorious," because God was going to be successful in any case. Contradiction, ambiguity, and irony are set aside in certain literary and religious contexts.

We have seen that preachers and churchgoers, producers and consumers of liturgies, homilies, and sermons – that is, Elizabethans – related biblical types to Elizabethan persons and events with little obscurity, irony, or nuance. The preachers omitted many details to simplify and clarify their moral: the David of the sermons I have quoted is not usually identified as an adulterer or murderer. Moses's lapses and Solomon's building temples for the gods of his non-Jewish wives go unmentioned. Their Joash never apostatized; their Hezekiah did not beg for his life and receive fifteen more years during which his pride and naïveté would open Jerusalem once more to invasion. These details were not suppressed; they were still available to readers of the Bible. But preachers did not expect their listeners to find a relevance for them that subverted the sermon type's evident application. The comparison between preachers, who constructed biblical allegories for English events, and Spenser, who invented fictional versions to represent contemporary issues and events, suggests that we latter-day readers sometimes respond to Spenser's allegory in a fundamentally un-Elizabethan way.

I make this point because, after immersing myself in documents representing Spenser's religious culture, I think some critical approaches over-read and overcomplicate Spenser's allegory.[5] Some ambiguities – those contingent on word order and multiple word meanings – are perhaps best understood as metrically enforced rather than slyly undermining the official line. Comparison to contemporary sermons, one of Spenser's benchmarks for *The Faerie Queene*, we should recall, entitles us to read ostensible praise as laudatory and ostensible condemnation as blame.

---

5 I exempt individual stanzas like II.ix.22, with its self-consciously esoteric code numbers, which are analogous to John's portentously mysterious "number of a man" in Revelation, or Matthew's cryptic but also uncharacteristic "abomination of desolation."

Works cited

Primary sources

Allen, William. *An admonition to the nobility and people of England and Ireland concerninge the present warres made for the execution of his Holines sentence, by the highe and mightie Kinge Catholike of Spaine. By the Cardinal of Englande.* Antwerp, 1588. Retrieved from the ProQuest database Early English Books Online. Copy from the British Library.

Ambrose. *Two Books Concerning Repentance*, trans. H. De Romestin. *The Nicene and Post-Nicene Fathers*, ser. 2, vol. 10. Grand Rapids, MI: Eerdmans, 1955.

Andreas, Hyperius. *The Practise of preaching, otherwise called the Pathway to the Pulpet*, trans. John Ludham. London, 1577. Retrieved from the ProQuest database Early English Books Online. Copy from the Henry E. Huntington Library and Art Gallery.

Andrewes, Lancelot. *The wonderfull combate (for Gods glorie and mans saluation) betweene Christ and Satan Opened in seuen most excellent, learned and zealous sermons, vpon the temptations of Christ, in the wilderness.* London, 1592. Retrieved from the ProQuest database Early English Books Online. Copy from the Bodleian Library.

Archdeacon, Daniel. *A true discourse of the armie which the King of Spaine caused to bee assembled in the hauen of Lisbon, in the kingdome of Portugall, in the yeare 1588 against England.* London, 1588. Retrieved from the ProQuest database Early English Books Online. Copy from the Henry E. Huntington Library and Art Gallery.

Athanasius of Alexandria. "Letter X. Easter, 338," trans. John Cardinal Newman, ed. Archibald Robertson. *The Nicene and Post-Nicene Fathers*, ser. 2, vol. 4. Grand Rapids, MI: Eerdmans, 1953.

Augustine. *Sermons on Selected Lessons of the New Testament*, trans. R. G. MacMullen. *The Nicene and Post-Nicene Fathers*, ser. 1, vol. 6. Grand Rapids, MI: Eerdmans, 1991.

—— "A Statement of the Reason Why Matthew Enumerates One Succession of Ancestors for Christ, and Luke Another," in *Harmony of the Gospels Book II*, trans. S. D. F. Salmond. *The Nicene and Post-Nicene Fathers*, ser. 1, vol. 6. New York, 1888.

Aylmer, John. *An harborowe for faithfull and trewe subiectes.* Strasburg, 1559. Retrieved from the ProQuest database Early English Books Online. Copy from the Henry E. Huntington Library and Art Gallery.

—— *The order of prayer, and other exercises, vpon Wednesdays and Frydayes, to auert and turne Gods wrath from vs, threatned by the late terrible earthquake: to be vsed in all parish churches and housholdes throughout the realme.* London, 1580. Retrieved from the ProQuest database Early English Books Online. Copy from the Folger Shakespeare Library.

—— *The order of prayer vpon Wednesdayes and Frydayes, to auert and turne Gods wrath from vs, threatned by the late terrible earthquake to be vsed in al parish churches.* London, 1580. Retrieved from the ProQuest database Early English Books Online. Copy from the Henry E. Huntington Library and Art Gallery.

Babington, Gervase. *A sermon preached at the Court at Greenewich the XXIIII. Of May 1591.* London, 1591. Retrieved from the ProQuest database Early English Books Online. Copy from the British Library.

Bacon, Francis. *The essayes or counsels, ciuill and morall.* London, 1625. Retrieved from the ProQuest database Early English Books Online. Copy from the Cambridge University Library.

Baker, John. *Lectures of I.B. vpon the xii. Articles of our Christian faith briefely set forth for the comfort of the godly, and the better instruction of the simple and ignorant.* London, 1581. Retrieved from the ProQuest database Early English Books Online. Copy from the British Library.

Barlow, William. *The Eagle and the Body described in one sermon preached before Queene Elizabeth of precious memorie, in Lent. Anno 1601.* London, 1609. Retrieved from the ProQuest database Early English Books Online. Copy from the Folger Shakespeare Library.

—— *A sermon preached at Paules Crosse, on the first Sunday in Lent: Martij 1. 1600 With a short discourse of the late Earle of Essex his confession, and penitence, before and at the time of his death.* London, 1601. Retrieved from the ProQuest database Early English Books Online. Copy from the Cambridge University Library.

Becon, Thomas. *A new postil conteinyng most godly and learned sermons vpon all the Sonday Gospelles, that be redde in the church thorowout the yeare.* London, 1566. Retrieved from the ProQuest database Early English Books Online. Copy from the University of Chicago Library.

Beze, Theodore de. *Master Bezaes sermons vpon the three chapters of the canticle of canticles wherein are handled the chiefest points of religion controversed and debated betweene vs and the aduersarie at this day,* trans. John Harmar. Oxford, 1587. Retrieved from the ProQuest database Early English Books Online. Copy from the Henry E. Huntington Library and Art Gallery.

Biblia latina cum glossa ordinaria: a facsimile reprint of the editio princeps. Adolph Rusch of Strassburg 1480/81, vol. 4. Brepols: Turnhout, 1992.

The Bishops' Bible (1568). Retrieved from the Chadwyck-Healey database The Bible in English.

The holie Bible conteynyng the olde Testament and the newe [Bishops' Bible]. London, 1568. Retrieved from the ProQuest database Early English Books Online. Copy from the Henry E. Huntington Library and Art Gallery.

Bisse, James. *Two sermons preached the one at Paules Crosse the eight of Ianuarie 1580. The other, at Christes Churche in London the same day in the after no one.* London, 1581. Retrieved from the ProQuest database Early English Books Online. Copy from the British Library.

The Book of Common Prayer 1559: The Elizabethan Prayer Book, ed. John E. Booty. Charlottesville, VA: University Press of Virginia for the Folger Shakespeare Library, 1976.

Bridges, John. *A sermon, preached at Paules Crosse on the Monday in Whitson weeke*. London, 1571. Retrieved from the ProQuest database Early English Books Online. Copy from the Yale University Library.

Broughton, Hugh. *The holy genealogie of Iesus Christ both his naturall line of fathers, which S. Luke followeth, chap. 3, and his kingly line, which S. Matthew followeth, chap. I, with fit notation of their names.* London, 1612. Retrieved from the ProQuest database Early English Books Online. Copy from the Bodleian Library.

—— *Our Lord his line of fathers from Adam, and his predecessours in the kingdome from Salomon to Iechonias, in whom ended the house: and from Abiud to Ioseph the husband of Marie: with fit notation of their names.* London, 1595. Retrieved from the ProQuest database Early English Books Online. Copy from the Bodleian Library.

—— *Our Lordes Famile and many other poinctes depending upon it.* Amsterdam, 1608. Retrieved from the ProQuest database Early English Books Online. Copy from the British Library.

Bullinger, Heinrich. *Fiftie godlie and learned sermons diuided into fiue decades, conteyning the chiefe and principall pointes of Christian religion.* London, 1577. Retrieved from the ProQuest database Early English Books Online. Copy from the Henry E. Huntington Library and Art Gallery.

Bunny, Edmund. *Certaine prayers and other godly exercises, for the seuenteenth of Nouember: Wherein we solemnize the blessed reigne of our gracious Soueraigne Lady Elizabeth.* London, 1585. Retrieved from the ProQuest database Early English Books Online. Copy from the British Library.

Burton, William. *A caueat for suerties two sermons of suertiship*. London, 1593. Retrieved from the ProQuest database Early English Books Online. Copy from the Bodleian Library.

—— *Dauids euidenece* [sic]*, or, The assurance of Gods loue declared in seuen sermons.* London, 1592. Retrieved from the ProQuest database Early English Books Online. Copy from the Folger Shakespeare Library.

—— *A sermon preached in the Cathedrall Church in Norwich, the xxi. day of December, 1589.* London, 1590. Retrieved from the ProQuest database Early English Books Online. Copy from the British Library.

The Byble in Englyshe [Great Bible]. London, 1539. Retrieved from the ProQuest database Early English Books Online. Copy from the British Library.

Cabala, mysteries of state, in letters of the great ministers of K. James and K. Charles. London, 1653. Retrieved from the ProQuest database Early English Books Online. Copy from the British Library.

Calvin, John. *The sermons of M. Iohn Caluin vpon the fifth booke of Moses called Deuteronomie ... [t]ranslated out of French by Arthur Golding.* London, 1583. Retrieved from the ProQuest database Early English Books Online. Copy from the Henry E. Huntington Library and Art Gallery.

Camden, William. *Annales the true and royall history of the famous empresse Elizabeth Queene of England France and Ireland &c. True faith's defendresse of diuine renowne and happy memory. Wherein all such memorable things as happened during hir blessed raigne ... are exactly described.* London, 1625. Retrieved from the ProQuest database Early English Books Online. Copy from the Henry E. Huntington Library and Art Gallery.

——*Remains Concerning Britain*, ed. R. D. Dunn. Toronto: University of Toronto Press, 1984.

Castiglione, Baldassarre. *The courtyer of Count Baldessar Castilio diuided into foure books ... done into English by Thomas Hoby.* London, 1561. Retrieved from the ProQuest database Early English Books Online. Copy from the Henry E. Huntington Library and Art Gallery.

Cavendish, George. *The negotiations of Thomas Woolsey, the great Cardinall of England containing his life and death.* London, 1641. Retrieved from the ProQuest database Early English Books Online. Copy from the British Library.

Cecil, Robert. *The copie of a letter to the Right Honourable the Earle of Leycester.* London, 1586. Retrieved from the ProQuest database Early English Books Online. Copy from the Henry E. Huntington Library and Art Gallery.

Cecil, William, Lord Burghley. *The copie of a letter sent out of England to Don Bernardin Mendoza ambassadour in France for the King of Spaine.* London, 1588. Retrieved from the ProQuest database Early English Books Online. Copy from the Henry E. Huntington Library and Art Gallery.

Certain Sermons or Homilies (1547) and A Homily against Disobedience and Wilful Rebellion (1570): A Critical Edition, ed. Ronald B. Bond. Toronto: University of Toronto Press, 1987.

Certaine praiers collected out of a fourme of godly meditations, set foorth by her Maiesties authoritie in the great mortalitie, in the fift yeere of her Highnesse raigne. London, 1593. Retrieved from the ProQuest database Early English Books Online. Copy from the Henry E. Huntington Library and Art Gallery.

Clay, William Keatinge, ed. *Liturgical Services of the Reign of Queen Elizabeth.* Parker Society. London, 1840.

Clement of Alexandria. *The Stromata, or Miscellanies*, ed. A. Cleveland Cox. *The Ante-Nicene Fathers*, 2. Grand Rapids, MI: Eerdmans, 1951.

Clement of Rome. *The First Epistle of Clement to the Corinthians*, trans. Alexander Roberts and James Donaldson. *The Ante-Nicene Fathers*, 1. Grand Rapids, MI: Eerdmans, 1953.

Cooper, Thomas. *Certaine sermons wherin is contained the defense of the gospell nowe preached against such cauils and false accusations, as are obiected both against the doctrine it selfe, and the preachers and professors thereof, by the friendes and fauourers of the Church of Rome.* London, 1580. Retrieved from the ProQuest database Early English Books Online. Copy from the Folger Shakespeare Library.

—— *An order of praier and thankes-giving, for the preseruation of the Queenes Maiesties life and salfetie.* London, 1585. Retrieved from the ProQuest database Early English Books Online. Copy from Henry E. Huntington Library and Art Gallery.

Cotton, Roger. *A direction to the waters of lyfe Come and beholde, how Christ shineth before the Law, in the Law, and in the Prophetes: and withall the iudgements of God vpon all nations for the neglect of his holy worde.* London, 1590. Retrieved from the ProQuest database Early English Books Online. Copy from the British Library.

Crompton, Richard. *A short declaration of the ende of traytors, ... and wythall, howe necessarie, lawes and execution of iustice are... Wherein are also breefely touched, sundry offences of the S. Queene ... & the manner of the honorable proceding for her conuiction thereof.* London, 1587. Retrieved from the ProQuest database Early English Books Online. Copy from Henry E. Huntington Library and Art Gallery.

Curteys, Richard. *A sermon preached before the Queenes Maiestie, by the reuerende Father in God the Bishop of Chichester, at Grenewiche, the 14. day of Marche. 1573.* London, 1573. Retrieved from the ProQuest database Early English Books Online. Copy from the British Library.

—— *A sermon preached before the Queenes Maiesty at Richmond the. 6. of March last past.* London, 1575. Retrieved from the ProQuest database Early English Books Online. Copy from the Bodleian Library.

—— *Two sermons preached by the reuerend father in God the Bishop of Chichester the first at Paules Crosse on Sunday beeing the fourth day of March. And the second at Westminster before [the] Queenes maiestie the iij. Sunday in Lent last past.* London, 1576. Retrieved from the ProQuest database Early English Books Online. Copy from the British Library.

Dering, Edward. *A sermon preached before the Quenes Maiestie, By Maister Edward Dering, the. 25. day of February. Anno. 1569.* London, 1570. Retrieved from the ProQuest database Early English Books Online. Copy from the British Library.

Drant, Thomas. *Three godly and learned sermons very necessarie to be read and regarded of all men.* London, 1584. Retrieved from the ProQuest database Early English Books Online. Copy from the British Library.

—— *Two Sermons preached, the one at S. Maries Spittle on Tuesday in Easter weeke. 1570. and the other at the Court of Windsor the Sonday after twelfth day being the viij of Ianuary, before in the yeare 1569.* London, 1570. Retrieved from the ProQuest database Early English Books Online. Copy from the Boston Public Library.

Edgeworth, Roger. *Sermons very fruitfull, godly, and learned.* London, 1557. Retrieved from the ProQuest database Early English Books Online. Copy from the Bodleian Library.

Erasmus, Desiderius. *The first tome or volume of the Paraphrase of Erasmus vpon the Newe Testamente,* trans. Nicholas Udall. London, 1548. Retrieved from the ProQuest database Early English Books Online. Copy from the Harvard University Library.

Fisher, John. *A sermon had at Paulis by the commaundment of the most reuerend father in god my lorde legate.* London, 1526. Retrieved from the ProQuest database Early English Books Online. Copy from the British Library.

Fletcher, Richard. "A Sermon preached before the Queene immediatly after the execuc[i]on of the Queene of Scotte[s] by the Deane of Peterburghe." St. John's College, Cambridge, MS I.30, fols. 49^v–67^v.

A fourme of common prayer to be vsed, and so commaunded by auctoritie of the Queenes Maiestie, and necessarie for the present tyme and state 1572. London, 1572. Retrieved from the ProQuest database Early English Books Online. Copy from the Henry E. Huntington Library and Art Gallery.

A fourme of prayer, necessary for the present time and state. London, 1588. Retrieved from the ProQuest database Early English Books Online. Copy from the Henry E. Huntington Library and Art Gallery.

A fourme of prayer, with thankes geuyng, to be vsed euery yeere, the .17. of Nouember, beyng the day of the Queenes Maiesties entrie to her raigne. London, 1576. Retrieved from the ProQuest database Early English Books Online. Copy from the British Library.

A forme to be vsed in Common praier euery Wednesdaie and Fridaie …, to excite all godlie people to praie vnto God for the deliuerie of those Christians, that are now inuaded by the Turke. London, 1565. Retrieved from the ProQuest database Early English Books Online. Copy from the Lambeth Palace Library.

A fourme to be vsed in common prayer, euery Sunday, Wednesday, and Fryday, through the whole realme. London, 1566. Retrieved from the ProQuest database Early English Books Online. Copy from the British Library.

A Fourme to be vsed in Common prayer twyse a weke, and also an order of publique fast, to be vsed euery Wednesday in the weeke. London, 1563. Retrieved from the ProQuest database Early English Books Online. Copy from the Folger Shakespeare Library.

Foxe, John. *The Acts and Monuments.* 8 vols. New York, NY: AMS, 1965.

—— *A sermon preached at the christening of a certaine Iew at London.* London, 1578. Retrieved from the ProQuest database Early English Books Online. Copy from the Harvard University Library.

The Geneva Bible: A Facsimile of the 1560 edition. Madison, WI: University of Wisconsin Press, 1969.

The Geneva Bible. Geneva, 1560. Retrieved from the ProQuest database Early English Books Online. Copy from the Henry E. Huntington Library and Art Gallery.

Golding, Arthur. *A discourse vpon the earthquake that hapned throughe this realme of Englande, and other places of Christendom, the first of Aprill. 1580. betwene the houres of fiue and six in the euening*. London, 1580. Retrieved from the ProQuest database Early English Books Online. Copy from the British Library.

Gosson, Stephen. *The trumpet of warre A sermon preached at Paules Crosse the seuenth of Maie 1598*. London, 1598. Retrieved from the ProQuest database Early English Books Online. Copy from the Bodleian Library.

Gravet, William. *A sermon preached at Paules Crosse on the xxv. day of Iune Ann. Dom. 1587 intreating of the holy scriptures, and the vse of the same*. London, 1587. Retrieved from the ProQuest database Early English Books Online. Copy from the Cambridge University Library.

Gregory the Great. *Morals on the Book of Job*, trans. John Henry Parker. London, 1844.

—— *Register of the Epistles of Saint Gregory the Great*, Book I, trans. James Barmby. *The Nicene and Post-Nicene Fathers*, ser. 2, vol. 12. Grand Rapids, MI: Eerdmans, 1989.

Gregory Nazianzen. "Oration XXVII, The First Theological Oration: A Preliminary Discourse against the Eunomians," trans. Charles Gordon Browne and James Edward Swallow. *The Nicene and Post-Nicene Fathers*, ser. 2, vol. 7. Grand Rapids, MI: Eerdmans, 1955.

Grindal, Edmund. *Remains of Edmund Grindal, D.D*, ed. William Nicholson. Parker Society. Cambridge, 1843.

Gwalther, Rudolf. *An hundred, threescore and fiftene homelyes or sermons, vppon the Actes of the Apostles, written by Saint Luke*, trans. John Bridges. London, 1572. Retrieved from the ProQuest database Early English Books Online. Copy from the Henry E. Huntington Library and Art Gallery.

Hacket, Roger. *A sermon needfull for theese* [sic] *times wherein is shewed, the insolencies of Naash King of Ammon, against the men of Iabesh Gilead, and the succors of Saule, and his people sent for their reliefe*. London, 1590. Retrieved from the ProQuest database Early English Books Online. Copy from the Folger Shakespeare Library.

Hanmer, Meredith. *The baptizing of a Turke A sermon preached at the Hospitall of Saint Katherin, adioyning vnto her Maiesties Towre the 2. of October 1586. at the baptizing of one Chinano a Turke, borne at Nigropontus*. London, 1586. Retrieved from the ProQuest database Early English Books Online. Copy from the Bodleian Library.

Harington, John. *A Briefe View of the State of the Church of England*. London, 1653. Retrieved from the ProQuest database Early English Books Online. Copy from the Union Theological Seminary Library, New York.

Harris, Edward. *A sermon preached at Hitchin in … 1587. the 17.day of Nouember*. London, 1590. Retrieved from the ProQuest database Early English Books Online. Copy from the Bodleian Library.

Harrison, William. *Deaths aduantage little regarded.* London, 1602. Retrieved from the ProQuest database Early English Books Online. Copy from the British Library.

Hemmingsen, Niels. *The preacher, or Methode of preaching.* London, 1574. Retrieved from the ProQuest database Early English Books Online. Copy from the Bodleian Library.

Holland, Thomas. Πανηγυρίς *D. Elizabethae, Dei gratia Angliae, Franciae, & Hiberniae Reginae. A sermon preached at Pauls in London the 17. of November Ann. Dom. 1599. the one and fortieth yeare of her Maiesties raigne, and augmented in those places wherein, for the shortness of the time, it could not there be delivered.* Oxford, 1601. Retrieved from the ProQuest database Early English Books Online. Copy from the Bodleian Library.

Humphrey, Laurence. *A view of the Romish hydra and monster, traison, against the Lords annointed: condemned by Dauid, I. Sam. 26. and nowe confuted in seuen sermons to perswade obedience to princes, concord among our selues, and a generall reformation and repentaunce in all states.* Oxford, 1588. Retrieved from the ProQuest database Early English Books Online. Copy from the Bodleian Library.

Jerome. *Against Jovinianus,* trans. and intro. W. H. Fremantle. *The Nicene and Post-Nicene Fathers,* ser. 2, vol. 6. Grand Rapids, MI: Eerdmans, 1954.

Jewel, John. *Certaine sermons preached before the Queenes Maiestie, and at Paules crosse, by the reuerend father Iohn Iewel late Bishop of Salisburie.* London, 1583. Retrieved from the ProQuest database Early English Books Online. Copy from the Henry E. Huntington Library and Art Gallery.

John Chrysostom. *Homilies on I Corinthians,* trans. H. K. Cornish and John Medley. *The Nicene and Post-Nicene Fathers,* ser. 1, vol. 12. Grand Rapids, MI: Eerdmans.

John Chrysostom. *Homilies on Matthew,* trans. George Prevost. *The Nicene and Post-Nicene Fathers,* ser. 1, vol. 10. Grand Rapids, MI: Eerdmans, 1989.

Justin Martyr. *Dialogue with Trypho,* ed. Alexander Roberts and James Donaldson, rev. A. Cleveland Coxe. *The Ante-Nicene Fathers,* ser. 2, vol. 1. Grand Rapids, MI: Eerdmans, 1981.

King, John. *Lectures vpon Ionas deliuered at Yorke in the yeare of our Lorde 1594.* Oxford, 1599. Retrieved from the ProQuest database Early English Books Online. Copy from the Henry E. Huntington Library and Art Gallery.

L. S. *Resurgendum. A notable sermon concerning the resurrection, preached not long since at the court.* London, 1593. Retrieved from the ProQuest database Early English Books Online. Copy from Cambridge University Library.

Latimer, Hugh. *27 sermons preached by ... Maister Hugh Latimer.* London, 1562. Retrieved from the ProQuest database Early English Books Online. Copy from the Henry E. Huntington Library and Art Gallery.

Lavater, Ludwig. *The book of Ruth expounded in twenty eight sermons,* trans. Ephraim Pagitt. London, 1586. Retrieved from the ProQuest database Early

English Books Online. Copy from the Henry E. Huntington Library and Art Gallery.
—— *Three Christian sermons, made by Lodouike Lauatere, minister of Zuricke in Heluetia, of famine and dearth of victuals*, trans. William Barlow. London, 1596. Retrieved from the ProQuest database Early English Books Online. Copy from the Bodleian Library.

Leigh, William. *Queene Elizabeth, paraleld in her princely vertues, with Dauid, Iosua, and Hezekia … In three sermons, as they were preached three seuerall Queenes dayes*. London, 1612. Retrieved from the ProQuest database Early English Books Online. Copy from the British Library.

Madox, Richard. *A learned and a godly sermon, to be read of all men, but especially for all marryners, captaynes and passengers, which trauell the seas*. London, 1581. Retrieved from the ProQuest database Early English Books Online. Copy from the Bodleian Library.

Manningham, John. *The Diary of John Manningham of the Middle Temple 1602–1603*, ed. Robert Parker Sorlien. Hanover, NH: University Press of New England, 1976.

Marten, Anthony. *An exhortation, to stirre vp the mindes of all her Maiesties faithfull subiects, to defend their countrey in this dangerous time, from the inuasion of enemies*. London, 1588. Retrieved from the ProQuest database Early English Books Online. Copy from the Folger Shakespeare Library.

Matthew, Tobias. "Doctor Mathewes first sermon preached before the Quene." Bodl. MS Top.Oxon.e.5, 48–65.

More, John. *Three godly and fruitfull sermons declaring first how we may be saved in the day of iudgement, and so come to life everlasting: secondly, how we ought to liue according to Gods will during our life*. Cambridge, 1594. Retrieved from the ProQuest database Early English Books Online. Copy from the Peterborough Cathedral Library.

A most necessary and godly prayer, for the preseruation of the right honourable the Earle of Leicester. London, 1585. Retrieved from the ProQuest database Early English Books Online. Copy from the Emmanuel College (University of Cambridge) Library.

Nicholas of Lyra. "de commendatione sacrae Scripturae in generali," *Patrologia Latina* 113:28c; "*In moralitates Bibliorum*" 33c. Retrieved from from the ProQuest Patrologia Latina Database.

Norden, John. *A mirror for the multitude, or Glasse Wherein maie be seene, the violence, the error, the weaknesse, and rash consent, of the multitude, and the daungerous resolution of such, as without regard of the truth, endeaour to sinne and ioyne themselues with the multitude: with a necessary conclusion, that it is not the name, or title of a protestant, christian, or catholicke, but the true imitation of Christ, that maketh a Christian*. London, 1586. Retrieved from the ProQuest database Early English Books Online. Copy from the University of Cambridge Library.

An order of prayer and thankesgiuing, for the preseruation of her Maiestie and the realme, from the traiterous and bloodie practises of the Pope, and his adherents.

London, 1586. Retrieved from the ProQuest database Early English Books Online. Copy from the Henry E. Huntington Library and Art Gallery.

Origen. *Commentary on the Gospel of John*, Book I, trans. Allan Menzies. *The Ante-Nicene Fathers*, 10. Grand Rapids, MI: Eerdmans, 1951.

—— *Contra Celsus*, trans. Frederick Crombie. *The Ante-Nicene Fathers*, 4. Grand Rapids, MI: Eerdmans, 1951.

A packe of Spanish lyes sent abroad in the vvorld: first printed in Spaine in the Spanish tongue, and translated out of the originall. Now ripped vp, vnfolded, and by iust examination condemned, as conteyning false, corrupt, and detestable wares, worthy to be damned and burned. London, 1588. Retrieved from the ProQuest database Early English Books Online. Copy from the Henry E. Huntington Library and Art Gallery.

Parkhurst, John. *A prayer to be sayd in the end of the mornyng prayer daily (through the dioeces of Norwich)*. Norwich, 1571. Retrieved from the ProQuest database Early English Books Online. Copy from the Jesus College (University of Cambridge) Library.

Perkins, William. *A Clovd of Faithfvll Witnesses: Leading to the Heavenly Canaan*. London, 1607. Retrieved from the ProQuest database Early English Books Online. Copy from the Pembroke College (University of Cambridge) Library.

Pilkington, James. *A godlie exposition vpon certeine chapters of Nehemiah*. Cambridge, 1585. Retrieved from the ProQuest database Early English Books Online. Copy from the University of Cambridge Library.

Playfere, Thomas. *The pathway to perfection A sermon preached at Saint Maryes Spittle in London on Wednesday in Easter weeke. 1593*. London, 1597. Retrieved from the ProQuest database Early English Books Online. Copy from the British Library.

Pole, Reginald. *The seditious and blasphemous oration of Cardinal Pole both against god [and] his cou[n]try which he directid to themperour in his booke intytuled the defence of the eclesiastical vnitye, moulng the emperour therin to seke the destruction of England and all those whiche had professid the gospele translated into englysh by Fabyane Wythers*. London, 1560. Retrieved from the ProQuest database Early English Books Online. Copy from the Henry E. Huntington Library and Art Gallery.

A prayer and thanksgiuing fit for this present: and to be vsed in the time of common prayer. London, 1587. Retrieved from the ProQuest database Early English Books Online. Copy from the Folger Shakespeare Library.

Prime, John. *The consolations of David, breefly applied to Queene Elizabeth in a sermon preached in Oxford the 17. of Nouember*. Oxford, 1588. Retrieved from the ProQuest database Early English Books Online. Copy from the British Library.

—— *A sermon briefly comparing the estate of King Salomon and his subiectes togither with the condition of Queene Elizabeth and her people preached in Sainct Maries in Oxford the 17. of Nouember*. Oxford, 1585. Retrieved from the ProQuest database Early English Books Online. Copy from the British Library.

Puttenham, George. *The arte of English poesie Contriued into three bookes: the first of poets and poesie, the second of proportion, the third of ornament.* London, 1589. Retrieved from the ProQuest database Early English Books Online. Copy from the Henry E. Huntington Library and Art Gallery.

Queen Elizabeth's Defence of her Proceedings in Church and State, ed. William E. Collins. Church Historical Society Publications 58. London, 1899, rpt. 1958.

Roper, William. *The mirrour of vertue in worldly greatnes. Or The life of Syr Thomas More Knight, sometime Lo. Chancellour of England.* Paris, 1626. Retrieved from the ProQuest database Early English Books Online. Copy from the Harvard University Library.

Rudd, Anthony. *A sermon preached at Richmond before Queene Elizabeth of famous memorie, vpon the 28. of March, 1596.* London, 1603. Retrieved from the ProQuest database Early English Books Online. Copy from the British Library.

Sandys, Edwin. *Sermons made by the most reuerende Father in God, Edwin, Archbishop of Yorke.* London, 1585. Retrieved from the ProQuest database Early English Books Online. Copy from Cambridge University Library.

A short forme of thankesgeuing to God for the delyuerie of the Isle of Malta from the inuasion and long siege therof by the great armie of the Turkes both by sea and lande, and for sundry other victories lately obteined by the Christians against the saide Turkes. London, 1565. Retrieved from the ProQuest database Early English Books Online. Copy from the British Library.

Shutte, Christopher. *A verie godlie and necessary sermon preached before the yong countesse of Cumberland in the North, the 14 of Nouember, 1577.* London, 1578. Retrieved from the ProQuest database Early English Books Online. Copy from the British Library.

Sidney, Philip. *Miscellaneous Prose of Sir Philip Sidney*, ed. Jan Van Dorsten. Oxford: Clarendon, 1973.

Smith, Henry. *Foure sermons preached by Master Henry Smith. And published by a more perfect copie then heretofore.* London, 1599. Retrieved from the ProQuest database Early English Books Online. Copy from the Henry E. Huntington Library and Art Gallery.

—— *The preachers proclamacion Discoursing the vanity of all earthly things, and proouing that there is no contentation to a Christian minde, but onely in the feare of God.* London, 1591. Retrieved from the ProQuest database Early English Books Online. Copy from the British Library.

—— *A preparatiue to mariage, The summe whereof was spoken at a contract, and inlarged after.* London, 1591. Retrieved from the ProQuest database Early English Books Online. Copy from the Bodleian Library.

—— *The sermons of Maister Henrie Smith gathered into one volume. Printed according to his corrected copies in his life time.* London, 1593. Retrieved from the ProQuest database Early English Books Online. Copy from the Henry E. Huntington Library and Art Gallery.

Some, Robert. *A Treatise against Opression.* Printed with Pilkington, James. *A godlie exposition vpon certeine chapters of Nehemiah.* Cambridge, 1585. Retrieved from the ProQuest database Early English Books Online. Copy from the University of Cambridge Library.

Spenser, Edmund. *The Faerie Queene*, 2nd edn, ed. A. C. Hamilton, Hiroshi Yamashita, and Toshiyuki Suzuki. London: Longman, 2001.

—— *The works of Edmund Spenser: A Variorum Edition*, ed. Edwin Greenlaw et al., 11 vols. Baltimore, MD: Johns Hopkins University Press, 1932–45.

Stile, Christopher. *Psalmes of inuocation vpon God to preserue her Maiestie and the people of this lande, from the power of our enemies.* London, 1588. Retrieved from the ProQuest database Early English Books Online. Copy from the Folger Shakespeare Library.

Strype, John. *Annals of the Reformation and establishment of religion, in the Church of England*, 3 vols. London, 1737. Retrieved from the Gale Cengage Learning database Eighteenth Century Collections Online. Copy from the British Library.

Tertullian. *An Answer to the Jews*, trans. Sydney Thelwall. *The Ante-Nicene Fathers*, 3. Grand Rapids, MI: Eerdmans, 1951.

—— *On the Resurrection of the Flesh*, trans. Peter Holmes. *The Ante-Nicene Fathers*, 3. Grand Rapids, MI: Eerdmans, 1951.

Tilney, Edmund. *The Flower of Friendship*, ed. Valerie Wayne. Ithaca, NY: Cornell University Press, 1992.

Topsell, Edward. *Times lamentation: or An exposition on the prophet Ioel, in sundry sermons or meditations.* London, 1599. Retrieved from the ProQuest database Early English Books Online. Copy from the Henry E. Huntington Library and Art Gallery.

A true copie of the proclamation lately published by the Queenes Maiestie, vnder the great seale of England, for the declaring of the sentence, lately giuen against the Queene of Scottes. London, 1586. Retrieved from the ProQuest database Early English Books Online. Copy from the Bodleian Library.

The Two Books of Homilies Appointed to be Read in Churches, ed. John Griffiths. Oxford: Oxford University Press, 1859.

Tyndale, William. *The Obedience of a Christen Man (Antwerp), 1528*, facsimile edn. Norwood, NJ: Walter J. Johnson, Inc., 1977.

—— *Tyndale's New Testament*, ed. and intro. David Daniell. New Haven, CT: Yale University Press, 1989.

—— *Tyndale's Old Testament: Being the Pentateuch of 1530, Joshua to 2 Chronicles of 1537, and Jonah*, ed. and intro. David Daniell. New Haven, CT: Yale University Press, 1992.

Udall, John. *Peters fall Two sermons vpon the historie of Peters denying Christ.* London, 1584. Retrieved from the ProQuest database Early English Books Online. Copy from the Folger Shakespeare Library.

Vermigli, Peter Martyr. *The common places of the most famous and renowmed diuine Doctor Peter Martyr diuided into foure principall parts: with a large* addition of manie theologicall and necessarie discourses, some neuer extant before. Translated and partlie gathered by Anthonie Marten. London, 1583. Retrieved from the ProQuest database Early English Books Online. Copy from the Henry E. Huntington Library and Art Gallery.

Verstegan, Richard. *The copy of a letter lately written by a Spanishe gentleman, to his freind in England in refutation of sundry calumnies, there falsly bruited, and spred emonge the people.* Antwerp, 1589. Retrieved from the ProQuest database Early English Books Online. Copy from the British Library.

Wentworth, Peter. *A sermon faithfullie and trulie published according as it was preached at the courte, at Greenewiche, the Tuesday in Easter weeke.* London, 1587. Retrieved from the ProQuest database Early English Books Online. Copy from the Bodleian Library.

White, Thomas. *A sermon preached at Paules Crosse the 17. of November An. 1589. In joyfull remembrance and thanksgiving unto God, for the peaceable yeres of her Majesties most gratious Raigne over us, now 32.* London, 1589. Retrieved from the ProQuest database Early English Books Online. Copy from the British Library.

—— *A sermo[n] preached at Pawles Crosse on Sunday the thirde of Nouember 1577 in the time of the plague, by T.W.* London, 1578. Retrieved from the ProQuest database Early English Books Online. Copy from the Henry E. Huntington Library and Art Gallery.

Whitgift, John. *A godlie Sermon preched before the Queenes Maiestie at Greneniche the .26. of March last past.* London, 1574. Retrieved from the ProQuest database Early English Books Online. Copy from the All Souls College (University of Oxford) Library.

—— *An order for publike Prayers to be vsed on Wednesdayes and Fridayes in euery parish church within the Province of Canterburie, conuenient for this present time set forth by authoritie.* London, 1586. Retrieved from the ProQuest database Early English Books Online. Copy from the Henry E. Huntington Library and Art Gallery.

Wilkinson, Robert. *The merchant royall a sermon preached at White-Hall before the Kings Maiestie, at the nuptials of the right honourable the Lord Hay and his lady, vpon the twelfe day last, being Ianuar. 6, 1607.* London, 1607. Retrieved from the ProQuest database Early English Books Online. Copy from the British Library.

Wilson, Thomas. *An exposition of the two first verses of the sixt chapter to the Hebrewes in forme of a dialogue. Wherein you have a commendation of catechising, also a declaration of the sixe fundamentall principles wherein the Christians of the Primitiue Apostolicall church were catechized.* London, 1600. Retrieved from the ProQuest database Early English Books Online. Copy from the British Library.

Wingfield, Anthony. *A true coppie of a discourse written by a gentleman, employed in the late voyage of Spaine and Portingale.* London, 1589. Retrieved from the ProQuest database Early English Books Online. Copy from the Henry E. Huntington Library and Art Gallery.

Young, John. *A sermon preached before the Queenes Maiestie, the second of March. An. 1575*. London, 1576. Retrieved from the ProQuest database Early English Books Online. Copy from the Cambridge University Library.

Secondary sources

Allen, Don Cameron. "Donne and the Ship Metaphor," *Modern Language Notes* 76 (1961), 308–12.

—— *The Legend of Noah: Renaissance Rationalism in Art, Science, and Letters*. Urbana, IL: University of Illinois Press, 1963.

—— "On the Closing Lines of *The Faerie Queene*," *Modern Language Notes* 64 (1949), 93–4.

Anon. "MS Notes to Spenser's *Faerie Queene*," *Notes & Queries* 4 (1957), 509–15.

Aptekar, Jane. *Icons of Justice: Iconography and Thematic Imagery in Book V of The Faerie Queene*. New York, NY: Columbia University Press, 1969.

Archer, Mark. "The Meaning of 'Grace' and 'Courtesy': Book VI of *The Faerie Queene*," *SEL: Studies in English Literature, 1500–1900* 27:1 (1987), 17–34. Retrieved from the Chadwyck-Healey database Literature Online.

Auerbach, Erich. "Figura," in *Scenes from the Drama of European Literature*. Minneapolis, MN: University of Minnesota Press, 1984, 9–76.

Bellamy, Elizabeth Jane. "Spenser's Faeryland and 'The Curious Genealogy of India,'" in *Worldmaking Spenser: Explorations in the Early Modern Age*, ed. Patrick Cheney and Lauren Silberman. Lexington, KY: University Press of Kentucky, 2000, 177–92.

Belt, Debra. "Hostile Audiences and the Courteous Reader in *The Faerie Queene*, Book VI," in *Spenser Studies IX*, ed. Patrick Cullen and Thomas P. Roche, Jr. New York, NY: AMS, 1991, 107–35.

Berger, Harry Jr. *The Allegorical Temper: Vision and Reality in Book II of Spenser's Faerie Queene*. New Haven, CT: Yale University Press, 1957.

—— Jr. "The Mutabilitie Cantos: Archaism and Evolution in Retrospect," in *Spenser: A Collection of Critical Essays*, ed. Harry Berger, Jr. Englewood Cliffs, NJ: Prentice Hall, 1968, 146–76.

Blissett, William. "Spenser's Mutabilitie," in *Essays in English Literature from the Renaissance to the Victorian Age, Presented to A.S.P. Woodhouse*, ed. M. MacLure and F. W. Watt. Toronto: University of Toronto Press, 1964, 26–42.

Borris, Kenneth. *Spenser's Poetics of Prophecy in The Faerie Queene V*. English Literary Studies No. 53. Victoria, BC: University of Victoria Press, 1991.

Bulger, Thomas Francis. *The Historical Changes and Exchanges as Depicted by Spenser in The Faerie Queene*. Lewiston, NY: Edwin Mellen Press, 1993.

Burke, Kenneth. *The Rhetoric of Religion: Studies in Logology*. Berkeley, CA: University of California Press, 1961.

Cain, Thomas H. *Praise in The Faerie Queene*. Lincoln, NE: University of Nebraska Press, 1978.
Campbell, Marion. "Spenser's Mutability Cantos and the End of *The Faerie Queene*," *Southern Review: Literary and Interdisciplinary Essays* 15:1 (1982), 46–59.
Carpenter, Frederic Ives. *A Reference Guide to Edmund Spenser*. Chicago, IL: University of Chicago Press, 1923.
Cavanagh, Sheila T. "Ideal and Practical Justice: Artegall and Arthur in *Faerie Queene* Five," *Renaissance Papers* (1984), 19–28.
Chamberlain, Richard. *Radical Spenser: Pastoral, Politics and the New Aestheticism*. Edinburgh University Press, 2005.
Charity, A. C. *Events and Their Afterlife: The Dialectics of Christian Typology in the Bible and Dante*. Cambridge: Cambridge University Press, 1966.
Collinson, Patrick. *The Birthpangs of Protestant England: Religious and Cultural Change in the Sixteenth and Seventeenth Centuries*. New York, NY: St. Martin's Press, 1988.
Cullen, Patrick. *The Infernal Triad: The Flesh, the World, and the Devil in Spenser and Milton*. Princeton, NJ: Princeton University Press, 1974.
Culp, Dorothy Woodward. "Courtesy and Moral Virtue," *SEL: Studies in English Literature, 1500-1900* 11:1 (1971), 37–51. Retrieved from the Chadwyck-Healey database Literature Online.
Curtius, Ernst Robert. *European Literature and the Latin Middle Ages*, trans. Willard R. Trask. Bollingen Series 36. Princeton, NJ: Princeton University Press, 1953, repr. 1973.
Danielou, Jean. *From Shadows to Reality: Studies in the Biblical Typology of the Fathers*, trans. Dom Wulstan Hibberd. London: Burns & Oates, 1960.
Davidson, Arnold F. "Dame Nature's Shifting Logic in Spenser's 'Cantos of Mutabilitie,'" *Neuphilologische Mitteilungen* 83 (1982), 451–6.
Dees, Jerome. "The Ship Conceit in *The Faerie Queene*: 'Conspicuous Allusion' and Poetic Structure," *Studies in Philology* 72 (1972), 208–25.
Dictionary of National Biography. Oxford: Oxford University Press, 2004. Online edition, 2008–14.
Duby, Georges. "The Aristocratic Households of Feudal France: Communal Living," in *Revelations of the Medieval World*, ed. Georges Duby and trans. Arthur Goldhammer, History of Private Life, vol. 2. Cambridge, MA: Harvard University Press, 1988, 35–85.
Dunseath, Thomas K. *Spenser's Allegory of Justice in Book Five of The Faerie Queene*. Princeton, NJ: Princeton University Press, 1968.
Evans, Maurice. "Metaphor and Symbol in the Sixteenth Century," *Essays in Criticism* 3 (1953), 267–84.
Farmer, Alan B. and Zachary Lesser. "What is Print Popularity? A Map of the Elizabethan Book Trade," in *The Elizabethan Top Ten: Defining Print Popularity in Early Modern England*, ed. Andy Kesson and Emma Smith. Burlington, VT: Ashgate, 2013, 19–54.

Felch, Susan. "'Halff a Scrypture Woman': Heteroglossia and Female Authorial Agency in Prayers by Lady Elizabeth Tyrwhit, Anne Lock, and Anne Wheathill," in *English Women, Religion, and Textual Production, 1500–1625*, ed. Micheline White. Burlington, VT: Ashgate, 2011, 147–66.

Fernandez-Armesto, Felipe. *The Spanish Armada: The Experience of War in 1588*. Oxford: Oxford University Press, 1988.

Fishbane, Michael. *Biblical Interpretation in Ancient Israel*. Oxford: Clarendon, 1985.

Fleck, Andrew. "Early Modern Marginalia in Spenser's *Faerie Queene* at the Folger," *Notes & Queries* 55:2 (2008), 165–70.

Fletcher, Angus. *The Prophetic Moment: An Essay on Spenser*. Chicago, IL: University of Chicago Press, 1971.

Fowler, Alastair. "Oxford and London Marginalia to *The Faerie Queene*," *Notes & Queries* 8 (1961), 416–19.

—— *Spenser and the Numbers of Time*. New York, NY: Barnes & Noble, 1964.

Friedland, L. S. "Spenser's Sabaoth's Rest," *Modern Language Quarterly* 17 (1956), 199–203.

Froehlich, Karlfried. *Biblical Interpretation from the Church Fathers to the Reformation*. Burlington, VT: Ashgate, 2010.

Frye, Northrop. *The Great Code: The Bible and Literature*. New York, NY: Harcourt, 1982.

Gallagher, Lowell. *Medusa's Gaze: Casuistry and Conscience in the Renaissance*. Stanford, CA: Stanford University Press, 1991.

Giamatti, A. Bartlett. "A Prince and Her Poet," *Yale Review* 73 (1984), 321–37.

Gless, Darryl. *Interpretation and Theology in Spenser*. Cambridge: Cambridge University Press, 1994.

Goldberg, Jonathan. *Endlesse Worke: Spenser and the Structures of Discourse*. Baltimore, MD: Johns Hopkins University Press, 1981.

Goppelt, Leonhard. *Typos: The Typological Interpretation of the Old Testament in the New*, trans. Donald H. Madvig. Grand Rapids, MI: Eerdmans, 1982.

Gray, Erik, ed. and intro. *Edmund Spenser: The Faerie Queene, Book Two*. Indianapolis, IN: Hackett, 2006.

Graziani, René. "Philip II's *Impresa* and Spenser's Souldan," *Journal of the Warburg and Courtauld Institute* 27 (1964), 322–4.

Greene, Thomas. "Mutability and the Theme of Process," in *Edmund Spenser*, ed. Harold Bloom. New York, NY: Chelsea, 1986, 57–71.

Grogan, Jane. *Exemplary Spenser: Visual and Poetic Pedagogy in The Faerie Queene*. Burlington, VT: Ashgate, 2009.

Gross, Kenneth. "The Postures of Allegory," in *Edmund Spenser: Essays on Culture and Allegory*, ed. Jennifer Klein Morrisson and Matthew Greenfield. Burlington, VT: Ashgate, 2000, 167–79.

Hamilton, A. C. "Our New Poet: Spenser, 'Well of English Undefyld,'" in *Essential Articles for the Study of Edmund Spenser*. Hamden, CT: Archon, 1972, 488–506.

Hawkins, Sherman. "Mutabilitie and the Cycle of the Months," in *Form and Convention in the Poetry of Edmund Spenser*, ed. William Nelson. NewYork, NY: Columbia, 1961, 76-102.

Heale, Elizabeth. *'The Faerie Queene': A Reader's Guide*. Cambridge: Cambridge University Press, 1987.

Herr, A. F. *The Elizabethan Sermon: A Survey and Bibliography*. Philadelphia, PA: University of Pennsylvania Press, 1940.

Hobbs, R. Gerald. "BIBLE: Biblical Hermeneutics and Exegesis," in *The Oxford Encyclopedia of the Reformation*, 4 vols. Oxford: Oxford University Press, 1996, 1.152-71.

Holahan, Michael. "*Iamque opus exegi*: Ovid's Changes and Spenser's Brief Epic of Mutability," *English Literary Renaissance* 6 (1976), 244-70.

Holzmeister, U. "Canticum *Nunc Dimittis*," *Verbum Dominum* 26 (1948), 363-4.

Hough, Graham. "First Commentary on *The Faerie Queene*: Annotations in Lord Bessborough's Copy of the First Edition of *The Faerie Queene*," *TLS* (April 9, 1964), 294.

—— *A Preface to The Faerie Queene*. New York, NY: Norton, 1962.

Javitch, Daniel. *Poetry and Courtliness in Renaissance England*. Princeton, NJ: Princeton University Press, 1978.

Jeffrey, David Lyle. "Houses of the Interpreter: Spiritual Exegesis and the Retrieval of Authority," *Books and Culture* 8:3 (May/June 2002), 31, 35-8.

Judson, Alexander Corbin. "Spenser's Theory of Courtesy," *PMLA: Publications of the Modern Language Association of America* 47:1 (1932), 122-36.

Kane, Sean. *Spenser's Moral Allegory*. Toronto: University of Toronto Press, 1991.

Kaske, Carol V. "Bible," *Spenser Encyclopedia*, ed. A.C. Hamilton. Toronto: University of Toronto Press, 1990. 87-90.

—— *Spenser and Biblical Poetics*. Ithaca, NY: Cornell University Press, 1999.

Kemp, Martin and Peter. *The Campaign of the Spanish Armada*. New York, NY: Facts on File, 1988.

King, John N. *Spenser's Poetry and the Reformation Tradition*. Princeton, NJ: Princeton University Press, 1990.

—— *Tudor Royal Iconography: Literature and Art in an Age of Religious Crisis*. Princeton, NJ: Princeton University Press, 1989.

Klein, Joan Larsen, ed. *Daughters Wives & Widows: Writings by Men about Women and Marriage in England, 1500-1640*. Urbana, IL: University of Illinois Press, 1992.

Laughton, John Knox, ed. *State Papers Relating to the Defeat of the Spanish Armada*, 2 vols., 2nd edition. London, 1895.

Lebrun, Francois. "The Two Reformations: Communal Devotion and Personal Piety," in *Passions of the Renaissance*, ed. Roger Chartier and trans. Arthur Goldhammer, History of Private Life, vol. 3. Cambridge, MA: Harvard University Press, 1988, 69-109.

Lethbridge, J. B. "Spenser's Last Days: Ireland, Career, Mutability, Allegory," in *Edmund Spenser: New and Renewed Directions*, ed. J. B. Lethbridge. Madison, NJ: Fairleigh Dickinson, 2006, 302–36.

Lewalski, Barbara. *Protestant Poetics and the Seventeenth-Century Religious Lyric*. Princeton, NJ: Princeton University Press, 1979.

Lewis, C. S. *The Discarded Image: An Introduction to Medieval and Renaissance Literature*. Cambridge: Cambridge University Press, 1964.

Lubac, Henri de. *Medieval Exegesis: The Four Senses of Scripture*. 1959, trans. E. M. Macierowski. Grand Rapids, MI: Eerdmans, 2000.

Luxon, Thomas H. *Literal Figures: Puritan Allegory and the Reformation Crisis in Representation*. Chicago, IL and London: University of Chicago Press, 1995.

MacCaffrey, Isabel G. *Spenser's Allegory: The Anatomy of Imagination*. Princeton, NJ: Princeton University Press, 1976.

MacLure, Millar. *Register of Sermons Preached at Paul's Cross, 1534–1642*. Centre for Renaissance and Reformation Studies, Victoria College, University of Toronto, 1958. Rev. and expanded by Peter Pauls and Jackson Campbell Boswell. Ottawa: Dovehouse Editions, Inc., 1989.

Mallette, Richard. *Spenser and the Discourses of Reformation England*. Lincoln, NE: University of Nebraska Press, 1997.

Manning, John. "Notes and Marginalia in Bishop Percy's Copy of Spenser's Works (1611)," *Notes & Queries* 31 (1984), 225–7.

Martin, Colin and Geoffrey Parker. *The Spanish Armada*, 2nd edn. Manchester: Manchester University Press, 1999.

Mattingly, Garrett. *The Armada*. 1959. Rpt. New York, NY: Mariner, 2005.

McCabe, Richard. "The Masks of Duessa: Spenser, Mary Queen of Scots, and James VI," *English Literary Renaissance* 17 (1987), 224–42.

McCullough, Peter. "A Calendar of Sermons Preached at Court during the Reigns of Elizabeth I and James I," diskette included with *Sermons at Court: Politics and Religion in Elizabethan and Jacobean Preaching*. Cambridge: Cambridge University Press, 1998.

—— "Out of Egypt: Richard Fletcher's Sermon before Elizabeth I after the Execution of Mary Queen of Scots," in *Dissing Elizabeth: Negative Representations of Gloriana*, ed. Julia M. Walker. Durham, NC: Duke University Press, 1998, 118–49.

—— *Sermons at Court: Politics and Religion in Elizabeth and Jacobean Preaching*, Cambridge Studies in Early Modern British History. Cambridge: Cambridge University Press, 1998.

McCullough, Peter, Hugh Adlington, and Emma Rhatigan, eds. *The Oxford Handbook of the Early Modern Sermon*. Oxford: Oxford University Press, 2011.

McCullough, Peter and Lori Anne Ferrell, eds. *The English Sermon Revised: Religion, Literature and History 1600–1750*. Manchester: Manchester University Press, 2000.

McDermott, James. *England and the Spanish Armada: The Necessary Quarrel.* New Haven, CT: Yale University Press, 2005.

Meyer, Russell J. *The Faerie Queene: Educating the Reader*, Twayne's Masterwork Series, 73. Boston, MA: Twayne, 1991.

Miller, David Lee. *The Poem's Two Bodies: The Poetics of the 1590 Faerie Queene.* Princeton, NJ: Princeton University Press, 1988.

Murdock, Graeme. "The Importance of Being Josiah: An Image of Calvinist Identity," *Sixteenth Century Studies* 29:4 (Winter 1998), 1043–59.

Neale, J. E. *Elizabeth I and Her Parliaments*, 2 vols. New York, NY: St. Martin's, 1958.

Nelson, William. *The Poetry of Edmund Spenser.* New York, NY: Columbia University Press, 1963.

Neuse, Richard. "Book VI as Conclusion to *The Faerie Queene*," *ELH* 35:3 (1968), 329–53. Retrieved from the Chadwyck-Healey database Literature Online.

Nohrnberg, James. *The Analogy of The Faerie Queene.* Princeton, NJ: Princeton University Press, 1976.

Norbrook, David. *Poetry and Politics in the English Renaissance*, 2nd edn. Oxford: Oxford University Press, 2002.

Northrop, Douglas A. "The Uncertainty of Courtesy in Book VI of *The Faerie Queene*," *Spenser Studies: A Renaissance Poetry Annual* 14 (2000), 215–32. Retrieved from the Chadwyck-Healey database Literature Online.

"Nunc dimittis," *New Catholic Encyclopedia.* New York, NY: McGraw, 1967.

Oakeshott, Walter. "Carew Ralegh's Copy of Spenser," *The Library*, n.s. 26 (1971), 1–21.

O'Connell, Michael. *Mirror and Veil: The Historical Dimension of Spenser's Faerie Queene.* Chapel Hill, NC: University of North Carolina Press, 1977.

OED Online. Oxford: Oxford University Press, December 2014.

Owen, Lewis J. "Mutable in Eternity: Spenser's Despair and the Multiple Forms of Mutabilitie," *Journal of Medieval and Renaissance Studies* 2 (1972), 49–68.

Paffenroth, Kim. "Allegorizations of the Active and Contemplative Lives in Philo, Origen, Augustine, and Gregory," 1999. The Ecole Initiative, ecole.evansville.edu/articles/allegory.html.

Parkin-Speer, Diane. "Allegorical Legal Trials in Spenser's *The Faerie Queene*," *Sixteenth Century Journal* 23 (1992), 494–505.

Patrides, C. A. *The Grand Design of God: The Literary form of the Christian View of History.* London: Routledge, 1972.

Pendergast, John. *Religion, Allegory, and Literacy in Early Modern England, 1560–1640: The Control of the Word.* Burlington, VT: Ashgate, 2006.

Phillips, James Emerson. *Images of a Queen: Mary Stuart in Sixteenth-Century Literature.* Berkeley, CA: University California Press, 1964.

Prescott, Anne Lake. "Two Copies of the 1596 *Faerie Queene*: Annotations and an Unpublished Poem on Spenser," *Spenser Studies* 23 (2008), 261–73.

Randall, David. "Providence, Fortune, and the Experience of Combat: English Printed Battlefield Reports, circa 1570–1637," *Sixteenth Century Journal* 35 (2004), 1053–77.

Rathborne, Isabel. *The Meaning of Spenser's Fairyland*. New York, NY: Columbia University Press, 1937.
Riddell, James A., and Stanley Stewart. *Jonson's Spenser: Evidence and Historical Criticism*. Pittsburgh, PA: Duquesne University Press, 1995.
Rowe, George E. "Privacy, Vision, and Gender in Spenser's Legend of Courtesy," *Modern Language Quarterly* 50.4 (1989), 309–36. Retrieved from the Chadwyck-Healey database Literature Online.
Rowland, Beryl. *Animals with Human Faces: A Guide to Animal Symbolism*. Knoxville, TN: University of Tennessee Press, 1973.
Salmon, P. *The Breviary through the Centuries*, trans. D. Mary. Collegeville, MN: St. John's Press, 1962.
Saunders, Austen. "New Light on a Puzzling Annotation to Spenser's *Faerie Queen*," *Notes & Queries* 57.3 (2010), 356–57.
Schoenfeldt, Michael C. "The Poetry of Conduct: Accommodation and Transgression in *TFQ*, Book 6," in *Enclosure Acts: Sexuality, Property, and Culture in Early Modern England*, ed. Richard Burt and John Michael Archer. Ithaca, NY: Cornell University Press, 1994.
Staines, John D. "Elizabeth, Mercilla, and the Rhetoric of Propaganda in Spenser's *Faerie Queene*," *Journal of Medieval and Early Modern Studies* 31:2 (Spring 2001), 283–312. Retrieved from the Johns Hopkins University database Project Muse.
Stampfer, Judah K. "The Cantos of Mutabilitie: Spenser's Last Testament of Faith," *University of Toronto Quarterly* 21 (1952), 140–56.
Stoll, Abraham, ed. and intro. *Edmund Spenser: The Faerie Queene, Book Five*. Indianapolis, IN: Hackett, 2006.
Strong, Roy. "The Popular Celebration of the Accession Day of Queen Elizabeth I," *Journal of the Warburg and Courtauld Institutes* 21 (1958), 86–103.
Teskey, Gordon. "Allegory," *Spenser Encyclopedia*. Toronto: University of Toronto Press, 1990, 16–22.
—— "Allegory, Materialism, Violence," in *The Production of English Renaissance Culture*, ed. David Lee Miller, Sharon O'Dair, and Harold Weber. Ithaca, NY: Cornell University Press, 1994.
—— *Allegory and Violence*. Ithaca, NY: Cornell University Press, 1996.
—— "Mutability, Genealogy, and the Authority of Forms," *Representations* 41 (1993), 104–22.
—— "Thinking Moments in *The Faerie Queene*," *Spenser Studies: A Renaissance Poetry Annual* 22 (2007), 103–25.
Tonkin, Humphrey. '*The Faerie Queene*.' London: Unwin Hyman, 1989.
Tratner, Michael. "'The thing S. Paule ment by … the courteousness that he spake of': Religious Sources for Book VI of *The Faerie Queene*," *Spenser Studies* 8 (1990), ed. Patrick Cullen and Thomas P. Roche, Jr. New York, NY: AMS, 1990, 147–74.
Tyerman, Christopher. *England and the Crusades: 1095–1588*. Chicago, IL: Chicago University Press, 1988.

Van Es, Bart. "The Life of John Dixon, *The Faerie Queene*'s First Annotator," *Notes & Queries* 48:3 (2001), 259–61.
Walsham, Alexandra. *Providence in Early Modern England*. Oxford: Oxford University Press, 1999.
Wells, Robin Headlam. *Spenser's Faerie Queene and the Cult of Elizabeth*. Totowa, NJ: Barnes, 1983.
Wells, William, ed. *Spenser Allusions in the Sixteenth and Seventeenth Centuries, Studies in Philology*, Texts and Studies, 68–9 (1971–2).
West, Michael. "Spenser's Art of War: Chivalric Allegory, Military Technology, and the Elizabethan Mock Heroic Sensibility," *Renaissance Quarterly* 41 (1988), 654–704.
Whiting, Roger. *The Enterprise of England: The Spanish Armada*. Gloucester: Sutton, 1988.
Whitman, Jon, ed. *Interpretation and Allegory: Antiquity to the Modern Period*. Leiden: Brill, 2000.
Willen, Diane. "The Case of Thomas Gataker: Confronting Superstition in Seventeenth-Century England," *Sixteenth Century Journal* 43 (2012), 727–49.
Williams, Kathleen. "Spenser: Some Uses of the Sea and the Storm-Tossed Ship," *RORD* 13–14 (1970–1), 135–42.
—— *Spenser's World of Glass: A Reading of The Faerie Queene*. Berkeley, CA: University of California Press, 1966.
Winship, Michael P. *Seers of God: Puritan Providentialism in the Restoration and Early Enlightenment*. Baltimore, MD: Johns Hopkins University Press, 1996.
Wofford, Susanne Lindgren. "Britomart's Petrarchan Lament: Allegory and Narrative in *The Faerie Queene* III, iv," *Comparative Literature* 39 (1987), 28–57.
Woodworth, Mary K. "*The Mutabilitie Cantos* and the Succession," *PMLA* 59 (1944), 985–1002.
Zerba, Michelle. *Doubt and Skepticism in Antiquity and the Renaissance*. Cambridge, MA: Cambridge University Press, 2012.

Index

Bold numbers indicate biblical references (chapter and verse).

Accession Day *see* Elizabeth I of England, accession
see also liturgy, Accession Day; sermons, Accession Day
Adlington, Hugh 3
allegoresis 3–5, 11–34, and *passim*
Allen, Don Cameron 105, 220–1
Allen, William (1532–1594) 146
   An admonition to the nobility and people of England and Ireland 131, 135, 146
Ambrose (337–397)
   Two Books Concerning Repentance 13, 20
Andreas Hyperius (1511–1564)
   The Practise of preaching 69
Andrewes, Lancelot (1555–1626)
   The wonderfull combate 187, 201
Aptekar, Jane 154
Archdeacon, Daniel (fl. 1588)
   A true discourse of the armie 135, 137–9
Archer, Mark 178, 180
Arthur, Prince of Wales (1486–1502) 100–1
Athanasius of Alexandria (296–373) 15–16
Auerbach, Erich 1, 12
Augustine (354–430) 19, 64, 110
   Harmony of the Gospels 88
   Sermons on Selected Lessons 18–20, 22–3, 25–6, 66, 80
Aylmer, John (c.1520–1594)
   An harborowe 48, 73, 129, 144
   The order of prayer 46
   The order of prayer, and other exercises 47–8

Babington, Anthony (1561–1586) 54, 75
Babington, Gervase (c.1549–1610)
   A sermon preached at the Court 189, 191, 193
Bacon, Francis (1561–1626)
   The essayes 149
Baker, John (fl. 1581) 178, 191, 195, 200
   Lectures of I.B. 178, 191, 195, 200
Barlow, William (d. 1613) 5
   The Eagle and the Body 186–7, 195
   Lavater's Three Christian sermons 182
   A sermon preached at Paules Crosse 76–8, 129
Becon, Thomas
   "An Homelie of Whoredome and Unclennesse" 116–17
   A new Postil 178, 188, 191, 200, 206
Bellamy, Elizabeth Jane 102
Belt, Debra 201
Berger, Harry Jr. 100, 219, 222
Beze, Theodore de (1519–1605)
   Master Bezaes sermons 194, 199, 200

Bible
　Acts 35; **2:2** 115; **2:22–47** 38; **7** 55;
　　8 189; **9** 45; **12** 43, 51–2, 185;
　　16:25–6 47
　　see also biblical figures, Paul
　　　(formerly Saul); Peter; Stephen
　Amos **6** 183–4
　2 Chronicles **20** 42, 51; **34** 37
　　see also biblical figures,
　　　Jehosaphat, Josiah
　1 Corinthians **10** 13, 69
　Daniel 152
　　see also biblical figures, Daniel;
　　　Nebuchadnezzar
　Deuteronomy **14:22–7** 203;
　　23:15–16 203–4; **25:5–6** 101;
　　28 37–8, 43–5
　Ecclesiasticus **13:19** 121; **36** 56–7
　Ephesians **4–5** 38; **5** 45; **6:17** 149
　Esther 55, 73, 145, 196; **4** 195; **6** 55;
　　7 55, 163; **8** 55; **9** 55
　　see also biblical figures,
　　　Ahasuerus; Esther; Haman;
　　　Mordecai
　Exodus **2** 192; **14** 31–2, 42, 51,
　　140, 154; **14:21** 105–6; **15** 42,
　　51, 55, 140; **15:21** 140; **17** 42;
　　17:8–16 51; **32** 142, 161
　　see also biblical figures, Miriam;
　　　Moses; Pharaoh
　Ezekiel **17** 49; **18** 37; **19** 37
　Galatians **4:22–31** 12; **5** 38
　Genesis **2:25** 160; **5:6** 86–7; **14** 50;
　　18 206–7; **18:10–13** 175–6;
　　19 206–7; **21:9–14** 12; **22:8**
　　12–13; **38** 101; **38:29** 90
　　see also biblical figures,
　　　Abraham; Adam and Eve;
　　　Joseph the patriarch; Judah;
　　　Lamech; Lot; Nimrod; Noah;
　　　Rachel and Leah; Sarah; Tamar
　Hebrews 27; **11** 175–6, 192, 224
　Hosea **11:1** 25

　Isaiah 35; **1** 37; **5** 49; **11:1** 32; **40:6**
　　121; **58** 46, 49; **59** 49; **60:7**
　　87; **65** 49
　Jeremiah **1:10** 31; **18** 37; **22** 37
　Job 20, 24–5; **38:11** 105
　Joel **1** 46, 49; **2** 37, 46, 49
　John **1:29** 12; **3:8** 115; **9** 57; **11** 20;
　　12:24 14; **20** 55
　　see also biblical figures, Caiaphas;
　　　Jesus; Thomas
　1 John **3** 49
　Jonah **1:12–13** 203; **2–3** 37; **4:4**
　　199–200
　　see also biblical figures, Jonah
　Joshua **3:10** 87; **6** 50; **10** 43, 50–1,
　　142–3, 158; **10:12–13** 143–4
　　see also biblical figures, Achan;
　　　Joshua; Rahab
　Judges **4–5** 95, 142–3; **5** 55; **6–7**
　　142; **7** 42, 51; **15** 50
　　see also biblical figures, Abimelech;
　　　Barak; Deborah; Gideon
　Judith **8–16** 54
　　see also biblical figures,
　　　Holophernes; Judith
　1 Kings **2:13–25** 161–6; **10** 79–81;
　　18 142, 185, 191; **20** 164
　　see also biblical figures, Adonijah,
　　　Ahab, Elijah, Queen of Sheba,
　　　Solomon
　2 Kings **7** 42, 51; **18–19** 137–8,
　　140–2, 153–4; **18:4** 142;
　　18:14–16 141; **18:23–4** 154; **19**
　　42, 51, 137; **24** 41
　　see also biblical figures, Athaliah;
　　　Hezekiah; Josiah; Naaman;
　　　Rabshakeh; Sennacherib
　Leviticus **26** 28, 37–8
　Luke **2:29–32** 209–10, 213–14,
　　221–2; **3** 5, 88–91, 97, 99, **8:48**
　　200; **10:38–42** 19–22; **13** 38;
　　15 45; **16** 49; **17** 45; **17:37** 187;
　　18 45; **21** 45, 49

see also biblical figures, Jesus;
  Mary and Martha; Mary,
  mother of Jesus
Mark **5:34** 200
  see also biblical figures, Jesus
Matthew **1** 5, 88–93, 98–9, 101, 103;
  2:14–15 25; **2:19–20** 165; **3** 38,
  45; **5–7** 45; **6** 38, 42; **7** 38; **9:22**
  200; **10** 45; **12:42** 79; **13:3–23**
  13–19, 22; **16** 45; **22:21** 76; **24**
  38, 42, 45; **24:15** 225; **25** 38,
  45, 49
  see also biblical figures, Caiaphas;
  Jesus; Joseph, husband of
  Mary; sower, the
Nehemiah **1** 197; **3–4** 198
  see also biblical figures, Nehemiah
Numbers **12:3** 161–3; **14:13–19**
  29–30; **16** 78, 167; **22** 142
  see also biblical figures, Aaron,
  Balaam; Korah, Dathan, and
  Abiram; Miriam; Moses
1 Peter **2** 199
Proverbs 201; **31:14** 118–20
Psalms **18** 166; **20:7** 154; **21** 53, 56,
  57, 60; **22** 47; **30** 46; **33:12** 51;
  34:7 51; **34:8** 199; **44:5** 34; **46**
  46; **51** 91; **69** 120; **69:9** 112;
  72:10 87; **81** 57; **84** 193; **85**
  56, 60, **86** 56; **87** 56; **88** 56;
  90:12 70, 213–14; **91** 46; **95** 60;
  101:1 161; **102:14** 31; **107** 57;
  107:23–4 106; **124** 56, 60
Revelation 152; **12–13** 145–6; **13:18**
  225; **17** 144–6
Romans **2** 38, 45; **6** 38; **12** 38, 45;
  13 38, 57
Ruth 92, 198; **3–4** 101
  see also biblical figures, Ruth
1 Samuel **4–6** 40–1; **15** 164; **17** 51;
  23 42, 51; **26** 157–8
  see also biblical figures, David;
  Samuel; Saul, king of Israel

2 Samuel **15–18** 74, 78, 158–9, 163,
  167, 185; **24** 37, 41
  see also biblical figures, David;
  Absalom
Song of Songs **1:1** 30; **1:4** 31; **1:8,
  5:9, 6:1** 144
1 Thessalonians **2** 45; **5** 45
1 Timothy **2** 38, 45; **2:1–3** 56, 60
2 Timothy **3:16** 25
Zechariah **7** 49
biblical figures
  Aaron 40
  Abimelech 78, 181
  Abraham 12, 50–1, 88–90, 97, 99,
    175, 180, 190, 206–7
  Absalom 74, 78, 158–9, 163, 167
  Achan 93
  Adam and Eve 64, 86, 88, 90,
    99, 180–1
  Adonijah 161–6
  Ahab 95, 136, 164, 181, 185
  Ahasuerus 73
  Amos 183, 188
  Athaliah 74, 129
  Caiaphas 136
  Daniel 37, 40, 167, 191
  David 6, 12, 37, 53–4, 61, 74–7, 88,
    90–1, 94, 99, 101, 157–61, 163,
    166–8, 171, 191, 193–4, 225
  Deborah 54–5, 93–5, 142–3
  Elijah 95, 139, 142, 188, 209, 213
  Esther 37, 55, 73, 94, 129, 145, 163,
    190, 195–6
  Ethiopian eunuch 189, 191
  Ezra 12
  Gideon 42, 52, 136–7, 142
  Hagar 12, 39
  Haman 55, 73, 78, 94, 129, 163
  Hezekiah 37, 39, 42, 57–9, 64–5,
    94–5, 136–8, 140–3, 154, 225
  Holophernes 95
  Ishmael 39
  James 43

Index

biblical figures (*cont.*)
- Jehosaphat 37, 42, 57–9, 94–5
- Jeremiah 31, 188
- Jesus 12–14, 17, 19–20, 22–5, 27, 31, 33, 38, 45, 55, 57, 62, 64, 77, 79, 88–91, 98–9, 101, 105, 107–9, 119–20, 125–6, 157, 164, 176, 183, 192–5, 200, 205, 208–9
- Job 24–5, 39–40, 105, 125
- John the Baptist 12, 38
- Jonah 39–40, 49, 105, 119–20, 126, 199–200, 203, 209
- Joseph, husband of Mary 88–90, 165
- Joseph the patriarch 7, 184, 189–91, 193–5
- Joshua 12, 50–1, 92–3, 142–3
- Josiah 37, 50, 57–9, 64–5, 92, 94–5, 157
- Judah 90, 101
- Judith 37, 54, 94–5
- Korah, Dathan and Abiram 74, 78, 129, 163, 167
- Lamech 138
- Lot 206–7
- Mary and Martha 11, 19–22, 26
- Mary, mother of Jesus 89, 157
- Miriam 54, 140
- Mordecai 73, 191
- Moses 6, 50, 55, 74–5, 92–4, 140, 142, 158, 161, 162–3, 167, 171, 176, 190–6, 198, 207, 209, 225
- Naaman 189, 191
- Nebuchadnezzar 73, 95, 136, 138, 163, 167, 181
- Nehemiah 7, 180, 186, 190, 196–8, 207
- Nimrod 138–9, 143, 163
- Noah 27–8, 112, 201–2
- Obadiah 191
- Og, king of Bashan 47, 142, 148
- Paul (formerly Saul) 12–13, 18, 47, 68–9, 88, 105, 189, 200, 204, 213–14
- Peter 27–8, 38, 43, 199
- Pharaoh 52, 54, 58, 136, 140, 143, 162, 181, 190–3, 195, 198
- Philip 189
- Queen of Sheba 79–81, 129
- Rabshakeh 137–8, 140–1, 154
- Rachel and Leah 21, 28
- Rahab 101, 176
- Ruth 92, 101, 198
- Samuel 94
- Sarah 12, 90, 175–6, 207
- Saul, king of Israel 42, 51, 74, 76–7, 162, 164, 167–8, 193
- Sennacherib 42, 52, 136, 138, 140–3, 153, 156
- Sihon, king of the Amorites 142, 148
- Solomon 61, 77, 79–80, 94, 119, 124, 159, 161, 164, 166, 195
- sower, the 11, 13–19, 22, 25–6
- Stephen 55, 58, 208
- Tamar 90, 101
- Thomas 55, 58

biblical marginal commentary 2, 29–33, 60, 90
see also biblical translations, Geneva Bible *and* Glossa Ordinaria; liturgy, composite psalms; Tyndale, William

biblical translations
- Bishops' Bible (1568) 12, 13, 25, 41, 57, 69, 115, 175
- Geneva Bible (1560) 2, 6, 11, 12, 30–4, 41, 44, 57, 86–7, 88–9, 90, 99, 105–6, 115, 121, 123, 126, 161, 223
- Glossa Ordinaria (*Biblia latina cum glossa ordinaria*) 16, 21
- Great Bible (1539) 37, 41

Index

biblical types 6, 11–13, 20–5, 30–3, 36–63, 65–81, 85, 92–3, 99, 101, 104, 129–43, 145–6, 150, 157–68, 192, 216, 223, 225
  see also biblical figures; Elizabeth I, biblical types for
Bishops' Bible see biblical translations, Bishops' Bible
Bisse, James (fl. 1580)
  Two sermons 191, 193
Blissett, William 216
Book of Common Prayer see Liturgy, Book of Common Prayer
Borris, Kenneth 7, 152
Bridges, Brook (1733–1791) 53
Bridges, John (c.1535–1618)
  A sermon, preached at Paules Crosse 190, 200
Bromley, Thomas (c.1530–1587) 173
Broughton, Hugh (1549–1612) 87, 99, 176
  The holy genealogie 88–92, 98
  Our Lord his line of fathers 89–90
  Our Lordes Familie 89–91, 93, 97
Bulger, Thomas Francis 151
Bullinger, Heinrich (1504–75)
  Fiftie godlie and learned sermons 206
Bunny, Edmund (1540–1618)
  Certaine prayers 59–63
Burke, Kenneth 13
Burghley see Cecil, William
Burton, William (c.1545–1616) 7, 178
  A caueat for suerties 201
  Dauids euidenece [sic] 181–2
  A sermon preached in the Cathedrall Church in Norwich 183, 185

Cabala, mysteries of state (1653) 216
Cade, Jack (d. 1450) 74
Cain, Thomas H. 100, 102, 179, 217, 222
Calvin, John (1509–1564) 7
  The sermons 182, 186, 188, 194, 199, 201, 203–4

Camden, William (1551–1623)
  Annales 146, 155–6
  Remains Concerning Britain 220
Campbell, Marion 222
Carpenter, Frederic Ives 168
Castiglione, Baldassarre (1478–1529)
  The courtyer 202
Cavanagh, Sheila T. 151
Cavendish, George (1494–c.1562)
  The negotiations of Thomas Woolsey 208
Cecil, Robert (1563–1612)
  The copie of a letter to ... the Earle of Leycester 164, 172–3
Cecil, William (c.1520–1598), Lord Burghley 40, 165, 168
  The copie of a letter sent out of England 131, 138, 148
Certain Sermons or Homilies see homilies, *Certain Sermons or Homilies*
Chamberlain, Richard 180
Charity, A. C. 11, 65
Clay, William Keatinge (1797–1867) 42, 46, 50, 51, 54, 56, 57
Clement of Alexandria (c.150–c.215) 14–15, 25, 26
Clement of Rome (d. 99) 13–14, 26
Collinson, Patrick 129
Cooper, Thomas (c.1517–1594)
  Certaine sermons 184
  An order of praier 53
Cotton, Roger (1557–1602)
  A direction to the waters of lyfe 87–8, 92
court 178, 181–9
  biblical courtiers 189–98
  Elizabeth I's 76, 146, 178–9, 186–8, 213, 218
  heaven 194–6, 205
  see also *Faerie Queene*, courts; sermons, court

courtesy 198–202
  see also hospitality; humanity
Crompton, Richard (c.1529–c.1599)
  A short declaration of the ende of traytors 172
Cullen, Patrick 107–8
Culp, Dorothy Woodward 180
Curteys, Richard (c.1532–1582) 5, 7
  A sermon ... at Grenewiche 71–4, 211, 222
  A sermon ... at Richmond 92–3
  Two sermons ... at Westminster 112–13
Curtius, Ernst Robert 105

Danielou, Jean 13
Davidson, Arnold F. 219
Dees, Jerome 105, 118
Dering, Edward (c.1540–1576)
  A sermon ... before the Quenes Maiestie 112, 184, 185, 188, 193
Devereux, Robert, second earl of Essex (1565–1601) 74, 76–8, 129, 216, 218
Dictionary of National Biography 75, 87, 95–7, 110, 180, 185, 191
Dixon, John (fl. 1597) 2, 62, 69, 152, 168, 223
Dove, Thomas (1555–1630) 76
Drant, Thomas (c.1540–1578) 6–7, 165, 168, 180
  Three godly and learned sermons 144, 181
  Two sermons ... at S. Maries Spital and Windsor 160–2, 170, 180–1, 183–4, 187, 188, 189–90, 206, 210–11
Duby, Georges 208
Dudley, Robert, earl of Leicester (c.1532–1588) 49–51, 173, 188
Dunseath, Thomas K. 151

Edgeworth, Roger (c.1488–c.1559) 199, 200
Edward I (1239–1307) 94, 96
Edward II (1284–1327) 97
Edward III (1312–1377) 94, 96
Edward IV (1442–1483) 71–2, 78, 94, 96
Edward VI (1537–1553) 36–7, 50, 73, 92–4, 97, 100, 159
Elizabeth I (1533–1603) 75–6, 79–80, 104, 126, 132, 138, 141–2, 146, 155–6, 157, 159, 162–5, 170–4, 178, 188, 208–16, 221
  accession (1558) 54, 55
    see also liturgy, Accession Day; sermons, Accession Day
  biblical types for 65–6, 92–5
    see also biblical figures, David; Deborah; Esther; Hezekiah; Jehosaphat; Joseph, husband of Mary; Josiah; Judith; Moses; Queen of Sheba; Saul, king of Israel; Solomon
  genealogy and royal predecessors 5, 92–8, 99–103
  plots against 53, 75, 96, 162–3, 166–7, 172
    see also liturgy, plots
  praise of 5, 62–3, 102–3, 155–6, 174–7
    see also Elizabeth I, biblical types for
  relation to *The Faerie Queene* 33, 63, 81, 103, 155, 171–7, 214–15
    see also *Faerie Queene, The*, characters, Belphoebe; Cynthia; Florimell; Gloriana; Mercilla; Una
  and sermons see sermons, court
Erasmus, Desiderius 25, 120
  The first tome or volume of the paraphrase 19, 21–2
Essex, Earl of see Devereux, Robert
Evans, Maurice 105

Faerie Queene, The **I.** 32; **I.v.** 184; **I.vii.** 215; **I.x.** 39, 204; **I.xii.** 205; **II. ii.** 215; **II.iii.** 179; **II.ix.** 225; **II.x.** 85–6, 98–103; **II.xi.** 215; **III.i.** 121, 184; **III.iii.** 85–6, 98–9; **III.iv.** 113–16, 123, 127, 215; **III.vii.** 121–2, 215; **III.viii.** 122–6; **III.ix.** 126–7; **IV.xi.** 126–7; **IV.xii.** 110, 126–7; **V.iii.** 127–8; **V.viii.** 130, 143–56; **V.ix–x.** 168–77; **VI. Proem** 178; **VI.i.** 178, 202; **VI.iii.** 202, 204, 215; **VI.v.** 202; **VI.ix.** 178–9, 197, 206–7; **VII.vi.** 215–20; **VII.vii.** 215, 219–22

characters
  Artegal 53, 98–9, 120, 151, 153, 171
  Arthur 6, 53, 85–6, 122, 143, 149, 151, 153–5, 169–71
  Belphoebe 81, 178–9, 181–3, 215
  Blatant Beast 178, 197, 201–2
  Britomart 6, 85, 113–6, 120, 122–3, 127, 153
  Calepine 204
  Calidore 53, 179, 192, 196–8, 202, 206–7
  Cynthia 7, 178, 215–21
  Duessa 53, 163, 168–71, 174, 176
  Florimell 6, 104–5, 116–18, 120–8
  Gloriana 62, 81, 98–9, 101, 192, 197, 215–16
  Guyon 6, 85–6, 99, 111, 122, 192
  Marinell 53, 104, 116, 122, 127
  Meliboe 178, 181–4, 197, 206–7
  Mercilla 6, 53, 143, 153, 157, 163, 168–74, 176
  Mutabilitie 7, 215–22
  Nature 7, 217–22
  Neptune 115, 123, 127
  Pastorella 197–8, 206–7
  Priscilla 197, 202
  Proteus 105, 109–10, 124–7
  Redcrosse 39, 62, 184, 192, 204–5
  Satyrane 121
  Serena 197, 204
  Souldan 6, 143, 149–56
  Timias 53, 121–2
  Turpine 204
  Una 54, 62, 81, 163, 204–5
courts 179, 204
marginal commentary 2, 30, 41, 50, 53, 62, 69, 152, 168–9, 223

Farmer, Alan B. 3
Felch, Susan 33
Fernandez-Armesto, Felipe 130, 146
Ferrell, Lori Anne 3
Fishbane, Michael 12, 66
Fisher, John (1469–1535)
  A sermon had at Paulis 17
Fleck, Andrew 53
Fletcher, Angus 118, 218
Fletcher, Richard (c.1544–1596) 6, 165
  "A Sermon preached before the Queene" 165
Fowler, Alastair 50, 100, 220
Foxe, John (c.1516–1587) 126, 224–5
  Actes and Monuments 97, 208
  A sermon preached at the christening of a certain Iew 206
Friedland, L. S. 221–2
Froehlich, Karlfried 13
Frye, Northrop 12

Gallagher, Lowell 171, 174
genealogy, biblical 86–92, 93, 98–9, 103
genealogy, Elizabeth's *see* Elizabeth I, genealogy and royal predecessors
Geneva Bible *see* biblical translations, Geneva Bible
Giamatti, A. Bartlett 217, 220
Gless, Darryl 150–1

Glossa Ordinaria *see* biblical
    translations, *Biblia latina cum
    glossa ordinaria*
Goldberg, Jonathan 171
Golding, Arthur (c.1535–1606)
    *A discourse vpon the
        earthquake* 47–8
    The sermons of M. Iohn Caluin
        182, 186
Goppelt, Leonhard 12
Gosson, Stephen (c.1554–1625) 6, 110
    The trumpet of warre: A sermon 71,
        110–12, 124, 148
Gravet, William (d. 1599) 6
    A sermon preached at Paules Crosse
        144–5, 166
Gray, Erik 100
Graziani, René 150
Great Bible *see* biblical translations,
    Great Bible
Greene, Thomas 216, 219
Gregory the Great (c.540–604) 71, 77
    Morals on the book of Job
        20–1, 24–5
    Register of the Epistles 21, 26, 28
Gregory Nanzianzen
        (c.325–389) 18, 25
Grindal, Edmund (c.1517–1583) 59
    A Fourme to be vsed 36–40
    Remains 40–1
Grogan, Jane 180
Gross, Kenneth 223
Gwalther, Rudolf (1519–1586) 7
    *An hundred, threescore, and fifteen
        homelyes* 182, 185, 186,
        188, 189–90, 192–4, 200,
        202, 204–6

Hacket, Roger (1559–1621)
    *A sermon needful for theese
        times* 184
Hamilton, A. C. 101, 122, 220
Hanmer, Meredith (1543–1604) 6
    The baptizing of a Turke 145

Harington, John (1560–1612)
    *A Briefe View of the State of the
        Church of England* 212
Harris, Edward (fl. 1587) 6
    A sermon preached at Hitchin
        74–5, 167
Harrison, William (d. 1625)
    Deaths aduantage little regarded 108
Hawkins, Sherman 219, 222
Heale, Elizabeth 149–50
Hebraic patriotism *see* biblical types
Hemmingsen, Niels (1513–1600)
    The preacher, or Methode 68–9, 99
Henry I (1068–1135) 94–5
Henry II (1133–1189) 94–5
Henry III of France (1551–1589) 77
Henry IV, formerly Duke of Lancaster
        (1367–1413) 78, 97
Henry V (1387–1422) 94, 96–7
Henry VI (1421–1471) 71–2, 94, 96–7
Henry VII (1457–1509) 94, 97, 100
Henry VIII (1491–1547) 26, 36, 50,
        73, 92–4, 97, 100–1, 136, 159
Herr, A. F. 3
Hobbs, R. Gerald 24
Holahan, Michael 219
Holland, Thomas (d. 1612) 5
    Πανηγυρίς D. Elizabethae 55–6,
        66, 79–81
Holzmeister, U. 209
homilies
    Certain Sermons or Homilies
        (issued 1547, reissued 1559)
        38, 97, 116
        "Of the Declinyng from God" 38
        "An Exhortacion against the
            Feare of Deathe" 38
        "A Fruitfull exhortacion to
            the Readyng of Holye
            Scripture" 24
        "An Homelie of Whoredome and
            Unclennesse" 116–17, 122
        "A godlie Admonition for the time
            present" (issued 1580) 47–8

A Homily of Disobedience and Wilful Rebellion (issued 1570) 156–60
"An Homyly, concerning the Justice of God" (issued 1563) 38–40
Second Tome of Homilies (issued 1563) 38, 51, 120
  "Of Almes dedes" 38, 51
  "Of good Works … Fastyng" 38, 51
  "Homily of the State of Matrimony" 120
  "An Homylye of Prayer" 38
  "Of Repentaunce" 38, 46–7, 51
hospitality 204–7
Hough, Graham 50, 62, 69, 168, 219
Howard, Thomas, duke of Norfolk (1538–1572) 161–4, 168
humanity 202–7
Hume, Anthea 7
Humphrey, Laurence (c.1525–1589)
  A view of the Romish hydra 167

Islam 6
  see also Turk

James VI and I (1566–1625) 97, 117, 140, 168
Javitch, Daniel 179, 186–7
Jeffrey, David Lyle 33
Jerome (347–420)
  Against Jovinianus 16, 26, 64
Jewel, John (1522– 1571)
  Certaine sermons 112, 115
John Chrysostom (c.349–407)
  Homilies on I Corinthians 16, 18, 22
Judson, Alexander Corbin 180
Justin Martyr (100–165)
  Dialogue with Trypho 17, 25

Kane, Sean 7, 151
Kaske, Carol V. 7, 11, 23
Kemp, Martin and Peter 131
Kett, Robert (d. 1549) 78

King, John (d. 1621) 7
  Lectures vpon Ionas 195, 201–3
King, John N. 7–8, 50, 152, 212, 216
Klein, Joan Larsen 117, 120

L. S. (fl. 1593) 7
  Resurgendum 112, 115, 211–12
Latimer, Hugh (1487–1555) 208
  27 Sermons 18, 194
Laughton, John Knox 131, 133–4
Lavater, Ludwig (1527–1586) 7
  The book of Ruth 92, 198
  Three Christian sermons 182, 184
Lebrun, Francois 208
Leicester, Earl of *see* Dudley, Robert
Leigh, William (1550–1639)
  Queene Elizabeth, paraleld 142–3
Lesser, Zachary 3
Lethbridge, J. B. 8, 210, 222
Lewalski, Barbara 11, 65–7, 157
Lewis, C. S. 64
liturgy
  Accession Day (17 November)
    Bunny's *Certaine prayers and other godly exercises* (1585) 59–63
    A fourme of prayer, with thankes geuyng (1576) 55–60
  Book of Common Prayer 35, 41, 49, 58, 60, 62, 97, 105, 106, 117, 209
  composite psalms (psalm collages) 33, 36, 43, 54, 57, 59, 60–1, 136
  London earthquake (6 April 1580)
    The order of prayer (London) 46–7
    The order of prayer (national) 47–8
  Massacre of St. Bartholomew's Day
    A fourme of common prayer 45–6
  plague
    Certaine praiers (1593) 41–2
    A Fourme to be vsed (1563) 36–41

liturgy (*cont.*)
  plots against Elizabeth
    An order of praier (1585) 53–4
    An order of prayer (1586) 54–5
    "A Prayer of Thanksgiving" (1585) 54
  Queen's Day *see* Accession Day
  Spanish invasion
    A fourme of prayer (1588) 52–3
    A most necessary and godly prayer (1585) 49–51
    An order for publike Prayers (1586) 48–9
    A prayer and thanksgiuing (1587) 51–2
  Turkish invasions
    A Fourme to bee vsed (1565) 42
    A fourme to be vsed (1566) 42–3
    A short forme of thankesgeuing (1565) 42
  weather
    A prayer to be sayd 43–5
  see also Clay, William Keatinge
Lubac, Henri de 13
lust 19, 107–8, 116–24, 175
Luxon, Thomas H. 67

McCabe, Richard 163, 170–1
MacCaffrey, Isabel G. 222
McCullough, Peter 3, 8, 162–3, 165
McDermott, James 130–1
MacLure, Millar 3
Madox, Richard (1546–1583) 6
  A learned and a godly sermon 72, 106–9, 112, 115, 117, 121, 125, 127
Mallette, Richard 7
Manning, John 2, 30, 152, 168
Manningham, John (c.1575–1622)
  The Diary 212
marriage 16, 117–20, 124, 127, 172, 195
  of Elizabeth I 172
  of Florimell to Marinell 104, 127
  of Jacob to Rachel and Leah 21
  of Oberon to Elferon's widow 100–1
  of the Thames and the Medway 109, 126–7
  of Thomas Howard, Duke of Norfolk, to Mary, Queen of Scots 162–4
  of Una to Redcrosse 62
  sermons
    "Homily of the State of Matrimony" 120
  see also Smith, Henry; Wilkinson, Robert
Marten, Anthony (c.1542–97) 65
  An exhortation 147–9
Martin, Colin 130–1, 134
Mary Stuart, Queen of Scots (1542–1587) 6, 75, 95–6, 130, 140, 151, 157–77, 161, 216
Mary I of England (1516–1558) 36, 39–41, 74, 92–3, 96–7, 100, 129, 167, 172, 208
Matthew, Tobias (c.1544–1628) 6, 165
  "Doctor Matthewes first sermon" 163
Mattingly, Garrett 130, 133–4
Mendoza, Bernardino de (c.1540–1604) 140
Meyer, Russell J. 149–50
Miller, David Lee 100
More, John (c.1542–1592) 7
  Three godly ... sermons 185, 194–5, 199
Murdock, Graeme 46, 157
Mutabilitie see Faerie Queene, The **VII.vi, VII.vii**

Neale, J. E. 4
Nelson, William 219
Neptune 105
  see also Faerie Queene, The, characters, Neptune
Neuse, Richard 179

Nicholas of Lyra (c.1270–1349) 4, 25
Nohrnberg, James 125, 154, 218, 220
Norbrook, David 7, 152, 212
Norden, John (c.1547–1625)
   A mirror for the multitude 136, 145–6
Norfolk *see* Howard, Thomas
Northern Rebellion 6, 93, 96, 157–62
Northrop, Douglas A. 180, 202
nunc dimittis 208–14, 221

Oakeshott, Walter 2, 53
O'Connell, Michael 100, 156
Origen (c.184–c.253) 13, 23–4
   Commentary on ... John 14, 19, 24
   Contra Celsus 17
Owen, Lewis J. 216, 222
Oxford English Dictionary 1, 109, 115

A packe of Spanish lyes (1588) 147
Paffenroth, Kim 19
Parker, Geoffrey 130–1, 134
Parkhurst, John (c.1511–1575)
   A prayer to be sayd 43–5
Parkin-Speer, Diane 171
Patrides, C. A. 64
Peasants' Revolt (1381) 74, 78
Pendergast, John 152
Perkins, William (1558–1602)
   A clovd of Faithfvll Witnesses 142, 175–6, 224
Philip of Macedon (382–436 BC) 142
Philip II of Spain (1527–1598) 49, 53, 130–1, 134, 138–42, 145–50, 216
Phillips, James Emerson 169
Pilkington, James (1520–1576) 7, 196
   A godlie exposition vpon ... Nehemiah 185–6, 188–93, 196–8, 201
plague liturgies *see* liturgy, plague
Playfere, Thomas (c.1562–1609)
   The pathway to perfection 205
Pole, Reginald (1500–1558) 41, 74

The seditious and blasphemous oration [*De Unitate*] 136, 144
Pope, the 144, 146, 148, 154
Pope Gregory XIII (1502–1585) 45, 47, 144
Pope Pius V (1504–1572) 146
Pope Sixtus V (1521–1590) 54, 130–1, 136, 138, 142, 146, 148, 159
Prescott, Anne Lake 2
Prime, John (c.1549–1596) 6
   The consolations of David 108–9, 139–40
   A sermon briefly comparing ... 109
providentialism 4, 36, 44, 47, 65–7, 71, 73, 75, 78, 99, 109, 122–3, 128, 132–5, 139–40, 142, 152–6, 191, 197
psalm collages *see* liturgy, composite psalms
Puttenham, George (1529–c.1590)
   The arte of English poesie 105

Queen Elizabeth's Defence 93, 160

Raleigh, Walter 2, 53
   see also Spenser, Edmund, "A Letter"
Randall, David 133
Rathborne, Isabel 101
Rhatigan, Emma 3
Richard II (1367–1400) 76, 78
Richard III (1452–1485) 97
Riddell, James A. 2
Roman Catholicism 6, 36, 42, 45–6, 48, 74–5, 93–7, 131, 135–6, 143–53, 169, 187
Roper, William (c.1498–1578)
   The mirror of vertue 208
Rowe, George E. 179
Rowland, Beryl 122
Rudd, Anthony (c.1548–1615) 7, 209, 218
   A sermon preached at Richmond 69–70, 212–14, 221–2

Salmon, P. 209
Sandys, Edwin (c.1519–1588) 5–6, 59, 162, 165, 178
  Sermons 94–7, 101–2, 162, 189, 194, 200–1
Saunders, Austen 2, 223
Schoenfeldt, Michael C. 178, 196
sea imagery 13, 102, 104–28
  King Edgar 72, 106, 114
  Noah's flood 105, 116, 119
  Red Sea 31–2, 42, 51–2, 55, 136, 139–40, 142, 154, 156
  see also biblical figures, Jonah; Noah
sermons
  Accession Day 5, 55–6, 62, 66, 74–5, 79–81, 94–8, 139–43, 148–9, 167–8, 220–1
  court 3, 70, 71–2, 112–13, 115, 160–2, 163–6, 170, 179–81, 184–5, 186–7, 188, 189–90, 193–4, 210–14
  marriage
    "Homily of the State of Matrimony" 120
    see also Smith, Henry; Wilkinson, Robert
  Paul's Cross 3, 5, 17, 56, 66, 71, 76–9, 79–81, 110, 112, 129, 140–2, 144–5, 148, 166, 167–8, 190, 191, 220–1
Shaheen, Naseeb 7
Shuger, Debora 7
Shutte, Christopher (d. 1626)
  A verie godlie … sermon 111–13, 115, 123, 128
Sharp, Lionel (c.1560–1631) 216
Sidney, Philip (1554–1586) 68–9, 224
Smith, Henry (c.1560–1628) 7, 178
  Foure sermons 191, 193–4
  The preachers proclamation 182–3
  A preparatiue to marriage 117
  The sermons 92, 183, 188, 195, 199
Some, Robert (1542–1609)
  A Treatise against Oppression 188
Somerville, John (1560–1583) 75
Spanish Armada 6, 33, 108–9, 122, 130–56, 216
Spenser, Edmund (c.1552–1599) 1–2, 81, 140, 172, 202, 221
  "A Letter of the Authors" 1, 24, 28, 33–4, 62, 81, 188, 192, 215
  Spenser–Harvey correspondence 180
Staines, John D. 171–2
Stampfer, Judah K. 222
Stewart, Stanley 2
Stile, Christopher (fl. 1588)
  Psalmes of invocation vpon God 136
Stoll, Abraham 150, 153, 169
Strong, Roy 62
Strype, John (1643–1737) 149

Tertullian (c.155–c.240) 13
  An Answer to the Jews 15
  On the Resurrection of the Flesh 22
Teskey, Gordon 23, 67, 215, 223–4
Throckmorton, Francis (1554–1584) 75
Tilney, Edmund (c.1535–1610)
  The Flower of Friendship 117
Tonkin, Humphrey 149–51, 219–20
Topsell, Edward (c.1572–1625) 178
  Times lamentation 190, 192, 194–5
Tratner, Michael 180
A true copie of the proclamation … against the Queene of Scottes (1586) 172
Turk 42–3, 45–6, 51, 142–9, 156
Tyerman, Christopher 145, 149
Tyler, Walter [Wat] (d. 1381) 74, 78
Tyndale, William (c.1494–1536) 4, 11, 26–30, 33, 77, 99
  New Testament 27
  The Obedience of a Christen Man 26–8, 30
  Old Testament 27, 29–30, 68–9

Index

typology *see* biblical types

Udall, John (c.1560–c.1592) 190–1
   Peters fall: Two sermons 191

Van Es, Bart 2, 152
Vermigli, Peter Martyr (1499–1562)
   The common places 65
Verstegan, Richard (c.1549–1640)
   The copy of a letter 135

Walsham, Alexandra 36, 133
Weatherby, Harold 7
Wells, Robin Headlam 217
Wells, William 168
Wentworth, Peter (d. 1599) 6, 166
   A sermon 71, 165–6
West, Michael 154
White, Thomas (c.1550–1624) 6
   A sermon ... at Pawles Crosse (1577) 178, 182, 184
   A sermon ... at Paules Crosse (1589) 140–2, 148, 167–8, 220–1
Whitgift, John (c.1530–1604) 6, 59
   A godlie Sermon 164

An order for publike Prayers (1586) 48–9
An order of prayer and thankesgiuing (1586) 54
Whiting, Roger 130
Whitman, Jon 12
Wilkinson, Robert (fl. 1607, d. 1617?) 6
   The merchant royall: a sermon 106–7, 113, 115, 117–20, 122, 124, 127–8
Willen, Diane 4
Williams, Kathleen 118, 150
Wilson, Thomas (c.1562–1622)
   An exposition of ... Hebrewes 201
Wingfield, Anthony (fl. 1589)
   A true coppie of a discourse 134
Winship, Michael P. 133
Wofford, Susanne 120
Woodworth, Mary K. 215

Young, John (c. 1532–1605)
   A sermon preached before the Queenes Maiestie 70, 74

Zerba, Michelle 4

EU authorised representative for GPSR:
Easy Access System Europe, Mustamäe tee 50,
10621 Tallinn, Estonia
gpsr.requests@easproject.com

www.ingramcontent.com/pod-product-compliance
Lightning Source LLC
Chambersburg PA
CBHW070236240426
43673CB00044B/1815